FORMS OF VALUE AND VALUATION

Theory and Applications

Rem B. Edwards
The University of Tennessee

John W. Davis
The University of Tennessee

WIPF & STOCK · Eugene, Oregon

Wipf and Stock Publishers
199 W 8th Ave, Suite 3
Eugene, OR 97401

Forms of Value and Valuation
Theory and Application
By Edwards, Rem B. and Davis, John W.
Copyright©1991 Robert S. Hartman Institute
ISBN 13: 978-1-62564-847-1
Publication date 4/16/2014
Previously published by University Press of America, 1991

To the memory of

Robert S. Hartman

TABLE OF CONTENTS

Page

Preface..

PART I. AXIOLOGICAL THEORY

I. What Led to Formal Value Theory?..1
   Rita Hartman

II. The Nature of Valuation 9
    Robert S. Hartman

III. Systemic Value and Valuation 37
     Rem B. Edwards

IV. Extrinsic Value and Valuation 59
    John W. Davis

V. Universals, Individuals and Intrinsic Good 81
   Rem B. Edwards

VI. The Norm of Intrinsic Valuation 105
    Robert E. Carter

VII. Value Combinations 125
     Frank G. Forrest

VIII. Hartman's Value Theory: Formal Models 171
      Mark A. Moore

PART II. APPLICATIONS OF AXIOLOGY

IX. Applications of the Science of Axiology 193
    Robert S. Hartman

X. Uses of Axiology in Business 211
   Vera Mefford

XI. Uses of Axiology in Stock Selection and Portfolio Management 229
    Kurt Kaltreider

Table of Contents

XII. The Hartman Value Profile 243
   John J. Austin

XIII. Psychology and Value Theory 291
   Leon Pomeroy and Arthur R. Ellis

XIV. Behavioral Axiology: Cross Cultural Study of Values 315
   Leon Pomeroy and Richard Bishop

XV. Self Knowledge and Self Development 329
   David Mefford

XVI. Why Good People Do Bad Things...345
   Wayne Carpenter

XVII. A New Education for the Integral Development of
   Man's Personality..379
   Alfonso Lozano

XVIII. Axiology and Education 387
   Robert E. Carter

XIX. The Theological Implications of the Axiological Formulations
   of Robert S. Hartman..403
   C. Stephen Byrum

BIBLIOGRAPHY

A Bibliography of the Writings of Robert S. Hartman 427

A Selected Bibliography of Secondary Discussions 439

CONTRIBUTORS 447

INDEX 459

Preface

Since the untimely death of Robert S. Hartman in 1973, many of his friends, colleagues, and former students have worked diligently on his formal theory of value and have made important advances in developing both the theory itself and practical applications of it. Those who are familiar with his work are convinced that he made extremely significant advances in theoretical and applied axiology. **Bob Hartman saw the form of the good.** He laid the foundations for a science of values. This book is written to acquaint others better with his achievements and to forge ahead where he left many problems unresolved.

Each of the two parts of the book contains a previously unpublished essay by Robert S. Hartman himself. The first, titled "The Nature of Valuation," is an excellent short introduction to this theory. The editors thank Robert E. Carter for calling this article to our attention. The second, titled "Applications of the Science of Axiology," explains how the theory illuminates value issues in economics, politics and interpersonal relations. It was the fifth in a series of lectures titled "The Science of Value: Five Lectures on Formal Axiology" which Hartman presented at the University of Guadalajara not too long before his death. If any readers find his writings to be difficult, they should read the other explanatory articles first and then come back to Hartman himself.

The book begins with an essay by Rita Hartman in which she tells how events in his life contributed to her husband's thinking, his writing, and the development of the Hartman Value Profile test. It further includes seven theoretical essays on his formal axiology and eleven essays dealing with applications of his theory in the areas of business, psychology, education, cross cultural studies, and theology. Readers acquainted with Hartman's work will find that many of these essays contribute significantly to the development of formal axiology as both a theoretical and an applied science. The papers in this volume were commissioned by the editors, and most of them were presented at the Fall 1990 meeting of the R. S. Hartman Institute for Formal and Applied Axiology at The University of Tennessee, Knoxville, TN. Each paper has been extensively revised.

About half of our authors are non-academicians. They are professionals in clinical psychology, business, investment and management consulting, etc., who are practitioners of Hartman's formal axiology. Some of our authors have developed successful business enterprises that market applied axiology, especially through the use of the Hartman Value Profile.

Table of Contents

Their essays reflect the variety of their professional activities and their success in applying this new and revolutionary value science.

Obviously, formal axiology still has many unsolved problems, and a discerning reader will discover that there are some fundamental philosophical differences of opinion among the contributors to this volume. Yet, all have been deeply influenced in one way or another by Robert S. Hartman.

The editors wish to extend special thanks to the contributors on whom we have made great demands, to Rita Hartman for her permission to quote from the published and unpublished works of Robert S. Hartman, and to the Southern Illinois University Press for their permission to quote extensively from Hartman's <u>The Structure of Value: Foundations of Scientific Axiology</u> which they published in 1967. The "Bibliography of the Writings of Robert S. Hartman" on pages 413-424 is an updated version of the bibliography which John W. Davis published in his <u>Value and Valuation: Axiological Studies in Honor of Robert S. Hartman</u>, pp. 323-330. We thank The University of Tennessee Press, Knoxville, for permission to include this. John Austin of Research Concepts, the publisher of <u>The Hartman Value Profile (HVP): Manual of Interpretation</u>, has given his permission to use material quoted from this work (much of which appears in his own article). The article by Frank Forrest has been copyrighted previously for his <u>Valuemetrics: The Science of Personal and Professional Ethics</u>, 1988; and we thank him for allowing us to republish it in hopes that others will come to know and appreciate his insightful work on the formal (mathematical) logic of axiology.

We wish to express our appreciation to our Department Head, Dr. George Brenkert, for the encouragement and support which he has given to this project. Special thanks are extended also to the Secretaries, Ann Beardsley and Marie Horton, in the Department of Philosophy at the University of Tennessee for their assistance in putting several of these articles onto computer disks, particularly to Ann who worked for weeks on Frank Forrest's very difficult to type essay. Thanks also to Glenn Graber, Richard Aquila, and Roy Cebik for assistance with computer problems.

Chapter I

WHAT LED TO FORMAL VALUE THEORY?

Rita Hartman

It was the year 1933, the year Hitler "broke out", as I like to say, (as the Nazi years were a scourge, a disease and an abomination). The brown masses spread over Europe like a plague. Their philosophy was infectious, and their perversities and death-dealing rampages lamed people of good will all over the territories they invaded.

Robert Schirokauer (Hartman) was 23 years old then, a card carrying member of the Social Democratic party of Germany and a fierce opponent of the brutes that had proclaimed the Third Reich for a thousand years. He had been born in Berlin in 1910. Four years later the first world war broke out; and his father, a writer, became a war correspondent. In the meantime another boy had been born, and his children were shipped off to Bavaria with the expectation that there would be more food in that State of the German Reich. So it came to be that Bob was schooled in Munich, and his class mates were all these misbehaving brats that later became the heads of all sorts of Nazi party section, battalions, "Gauleiter" and leaders of youth groups spreading the philosophy of the superiority of the Arian Race, the inferiority of Jews, Communists and other nationalities and all those that opposed the Nazi party. They spread hate and taught that killing those that did not think as they did was good. They looked at their victims as lice, vermin to be exterminated where ever they could be found.

As Bob saw all this developing under his eyes, he kept thinking: "What makes these persons evil? Why did they think that this philosophy was good?

Why was it impossible for them not to see the difference between good and evil? Why would they so readily kill their fellow men?"

After the First World War, when the boys father came back from the front, the family settled in Munich. By this time, Bob was ready to enter the Gymnasium (high school) where he saw more of what he had experienced in grade school. He joined the Social Democratic Party, as had his father, and soon became one of their more outspoken members, giving speeches and demonstrating. Often he was beaten up when the Nazis would attack their gatherings. He wrote and published articles which were printed in "Das Freie Wort" and similar publications.

After having taken his Abitur, he became a student at the Berlin University in Charlottenburg and studied Law in the belief that he would find the answer to the question "What makes people good or evil?" But all he found was the Law. He discovered that the law is The Law--nothing else. No wonder that when ever Justice is depicted it is blindfolded. He had time to take his doctorate and became an assistant judge at the court of Charlottenburg in Berlin.

Shortly after he had been at the court, elections took place; and Hitler became Reichschancellor. As Bob had been elected by his party to become a representative or delegate of his party, the Social Democrats, in the Reichstag, the Nazis immediately came to his house to arrest him; but he eluded them by getting out the back door while they were at the front door. He went to his party's headquarters to get a false passport, as he did not dare to use his own. They gave him a passport with the name of Hartman. From then on he was Hartman. He left for France with a camera and ten marks in his pocket, and from then on he had to earn a living just to keep the hunger away. He took news pictures and sold them--a meager enough occupation; but he somehow survived until he decided to go to England via Holland where his step-mother and sister had gone. He visited them and then crossed the channel to England. He tried to get some kind of a job, but it was difficult. He knew quite a number of people, as he had attended both the Sorbonne in Paris and the London School of Economics. Yet, just as in Paris, there was nothing for him in London. He became a publicity agent for all sorts of things, for a man by the name of Zucker, among others, who had come from Germany with a rocket he had invented and which he exhibited in a technical exhibition which Bob dropped in on. This rocket was to deliver mail to remote habitations, such as the Scilly Islands. Robert was fascinated. It was decided that he should become Zucker's publicity agent and try to get permission to fly the thing in a demonstration, so the government would become interested in it and ultimately would finance its manufacture and use for postal service.

Bob, through his various former school connections, got Parliament to debate the feasibility to try out this new invention in order to use it for the postal services. Parliament granted them permission; and these two young men scouted London for the right mixture of the fuel with which those things were sent aloft. The day of the trial came. All went to the field to witness the shooting of the rocket. It went aloft, but it exploded in midair. Apparently the fuel was not the correct mixture. Zucker, who was only in England on a visitor's visa, was sent back to Germany by the British. He was immediately apprehended by the Nazis, then put into a concentration camp; and he was either killed or he died. The rocket research center at Peenemünde was the result. The English felt the impact during the Second World War; but Zucker was and is forgotten.

Bob again had to find something to keep him in food and lodging. Seeing a Walt Disney movie of Mickey Mouse, which enchanted him, he had the bright idea that these wonderfully entertaining films could be made into books for children. With that idea he went to the Walt Disney representative, who just had come to England, to interest him in the idea. He was informed that Disney already had produced books of his films. Bob, who was fascinated with this new industry, saw Mr. Kamen, the representative of Walt Disney, now and then--just visiting. He noticed how the business thrived. One day Mr. Kamen remarked that business was so good that they were going to open offices here and there on the continent and also in Scandinavia. When he said that, Bob remarked, "I'll go to Scandinavia for you." And he did.

He became a businessman, but he never forgot his goal--to find what Good and Evil actually are, to define the concept of good and evil. Where did the thinking of humankind go wrong? What was it that compelled persons to make the wrong choices?

On the day of Munich, Bob called me from his office and said for me to pack; we are going to the United States. He saw the war coming, and he did not want to be on the wrong side of the Atlantic. In Hollywood, Disney could not believe that there was a war coming; but he sent Bob to Mexico as his representative. Bob again started studying Mathematics, Logic and Philosophy at the National University of Mexico. Three years later we wanted to visit Bob's brother, who by this time had come to the United States and settled. We went to the U.S. Embassy in Mexico City to apply for a visa. We had become stateless in the meantime and travelled on a Swedish Foreigner's Passport. The Consul, who gave out visas, said to us: "Why don't you emigrate? I still have three quota numbers. At the end of May everything goes back to Washington, but these three numbers are still available." We asked for 24 hours of time to think about this. All we actually wanted was a tourist visa, and this was a momentous decision to make. It simply boiled down to what we wanted to do with our lives. If we stayed in Mexico we would live in splendor and beautiful weather, but then Bob would never go back to what he originally set out to do. Or we could leave everything here and start all over again, not knowing if Bob would get a job, <u>etc</u>. We left and went to New York where Bob's brother was, and we started all over again.

The first job he got, after many false tries, was a teaching job at Lake Forest Academy, replacing a man who had been drafted into the army. While we were there, Bob enrolled at Northwestern University to study for his doctorate in Philosophy. His thesis was titled "Can Field Theory be applied to Ethics?" He graduated and obtained a job at Wooster College in Ohio, and it was there that he submerged himself into the research necessary for his task. We had discussions, debates, and tentative theories until one day he wrote a paper he intended to read to the meeting of the Western Division of the American Philosophical Association. It was the first time he aired the basic outline of his theory. It was for us--I was along--an historical occasion. The audience was fascinated; you could have heard a pin drop. He started with Moore's statement: "Good is good and that is the end of the matter." He developed it, as we know it today, in the pattern which he then formulated in <u>The Structure of Value</u>. Pandemonium broke out. The professors were excited, incredulous, and did everything in order to refute and disprove what Bob had said; but in order to do so, they had to use Bob's reasoning. He told the professors so, which brought gales of laughter, and a sense of relief, actually.

Then came the Council of Profit Sharing Industries--Ethics in Business. Some Wooster businessmen came to Bob to ask him to teach them ethics-- actually value theory, for they had asked themselves what they were doing when they installed Profit Sharing in their enterprises. From his lecturing came the idea to form an association (The R. S. Hartman Institute for Formal and Applied Axiology) which exists today, not only in the U.S. but also here in Mexico and in Germany and Sweden. He was called to Germany after the war to help them start up their industries with the right philosophy toward labor. Out of this came the "Mitbestimmungsrecht" (the right of the worker to have a voice in the management of the enterprise).

After we returned from Germany, he really set to work on his <u>The Structure of Value</u>. He had been working on it off and on, but now he buckled down. It was quite a job, but a fascinating one. I enjoyed being the hands that typed and the sounding board and discussion partner on whom he often tried out his ideas. He also taught what he was writing, and his students were enthralled.

The fifteen years Bob spent at the National University of Mexico were very prolific ones. He initiated a book program which was quite successful. He translated books in Philosophy by different philosophers who were not Mexican that were needed here. He was a popular lecturer and knew how to instill his pupils with the "passion of philosophy," as he liked to say.

When the invitation to teach at The University of Tennessee came, he was delighted, if not to say happy. Unfortunately he was a professor there only three short years, but they were happy ones for him (and, incidentally, for me too). His dynamism was appreciated, his theories were accepted, and his scholarship was appreciated. A man cannot ask for more. I can only say that he showed his esteem for The University of Tennessee by willing his papers, research notes and unpublished manuscripts to the University Library, where they now reside. This year I will give them the papers that I have been finding while moving, after thirty years in the same house.

The Structure of Value was published in 1967. It was ecstasy for us, as its birth indeed had been difficult. The negotiations with the publisher were lengthy and complicated. Then came the proof reading and the index making, which were sheer agony. I had never been exposed to the birth of a book, and the patience and diligence one has to have is something fearful.

One day Bob came home from the University of Mexico to tell me that there was a test in his book. The Value Chart on pp. 272 and 273 made one of his students explain: "Why sir, you have a test here." There was no holding him. He sat down to make the test. The phrases had to be strictly formal according to the value theory. Each word was weighed for Extrinsic, Intrinsic and Systemic value meanings. On our trips to the States he dictated to me a million of his famous small notes, sentences, words, thoughts and phrases (all at the University of Tennessee Library now), which we took home and spread out on tables, chairs and the floor to order them so that they could be incorporated or discarded depending on their suitability or correctness to Value Theory. The phrases, ordered into 18 categories, were tried out on our friends who were willing and eager to do the test. They were fascinated. I remember one particular dinner party to which we had been invited. As usual, the conversation got around to Value Theory. Bob mentioned that he was working on a value test which could determine the value pattern of the individual person. This incited the curiosity of all, of course. One of the guests, the wife of the then German Ambassador, a lovely person who to this day is one of my best friends, who I regularly visit when I am in Europe, insisted that she wanted to take this test. Bob had his little notes with the phrases we had worked out with him, and this lovely person sat down on the floor and started ordering the little notes that Bob had. It took some time, of course; but when it was all done, Bob retired to calculate and figure. After a while, he came back and told this lovely lady the results--what her value pattern was. She was speechless. It was, as she said, completely accurate. After that, everyone wanted to be in on this, and I think we didn't get out of there until very late that night.

Of course, the test is only one small result of the theory. The theory is a wonderful tool. It has helped me not only to make decisions but also to recognize the value pattern of the people with whom I come into contact. It helps to understand people's often very peculiar attitudes and opinions. One becomes tolerant of their peculiarities, and it definitely helps me to make decision in certain situations.

I have Bob's copy of <u>The Structure of Value</u> and the notes and comments he made on his own work. These are copious and interesting, which is making an understatement. He himself told me many times, "each paragraph has the making of a book." It is so compact and concise that it would be well if someone could sit down to work on it. In my opinion (which doesn't really count, since I am not a trained philosopher or thinker) but in our son's opinion as well, value theory needs to be researched much more and in greater detail. The world is clamoring for values. People want to know what they are doing when they value. One reads time and time again in newspapers, magazines, pamphlets and treatises that "We need values." I also hear this in political speeches both at home and abroad.

People want to have more exact guidelines; politicians need to have deeper knowledge; and ordinary human beings are hungering for some knowledge of what to do when they are in some kind of quandary.

Bob had projected a Calculus of Value. If I were a trained logician or philosopher I would try to put this into a book. I would use the notes with which Bob embellished <u>The Structure of Value</u> and try and decipher what more he wanted to say and didn't have time to say. He had too many interests, perhaps. He was deeply involved in the Peace Movement. He assembled a book--<u>Peace Fund of the Non-Nuclear Nations</u>. We assembled it and had it bound and delivered it to every mission of the United Nations. In the book he strongly emphasized that it was necessary to have nuclear power exclusively in the hands of the United Nations. If it were not thus controlled, each nation, big or small, would try and obtain it and would manufacture nuclear power in order to threaten whom they considered their enemy. Of course this wasn't done, and the proliferation of nuclear power is menacing, frightening us today as never before. Bob was nominated and accepted by the Nobel Committee for the Nobel Peace Prize in 1973. He received the message two days before he died, which made him very happy. He planned what he would say if he were the recipient of the Prize, and we thought of the trip to Sweden and of being with the family under such circumstances. It was not to be.

I think it is essential that the theory of value should be popularized, spread, explained, propagandized and taught whenever and wherever there are people who are capable of doing just that. Bob wanted the world to become a peaceful place where people could live without fear of bombs, threats of annihilation, bloodshed and force. The value theory was meant to help people to choose the right, the good, the beneficial for them and their communities. Look where we are now. There is threat on the horizon. Men of ill will and selfish aggrandizement are again willing to risk all--no matter what. We again are gathering troops to be sent off (to Saudi Arabia and Kuwait) to die in a war they don't believe in and which will not solve anything. The world's politicians don't think of people as living, breathing human individuals. They think of empty grandiose phrases with which to send their young men to die--for what?

Bob wrote a foreword for The Revolution Against War which is entitled "I was born to die for Germany." He never could understand why he should have been born to die for Germany. Is one not born to live? Unless we know, realize and act according to the highest value there is, Life, we will always be born to die for something totally irrelevant. We have to go out and teach people values, life, how to live fully and in total consciousness of our good fortune to be on this beautiful planet Earth.

The first book Bob wrote, On God's Side, never saw the light of day. I have the manuscript. Although I think it would need a lot of editing, it makes fascinating reading. He was an ardent writer. Some of his German stories make compelling reading, and the few poems he left are touching and very sensitive. His zest for life was contagious, and his sense of humor and wit enhanced his lectures and made his classes an experience to attend.

To write about Bob's life would take several volumes. He had really many lives--the life of the boy; the young man seeing the deterioration of Germany; the immigration years, where he had to try his hands at many things in order to make a living; his marriage, fatherhood, and the life of a professor. He had to live in various countries, to learn their customs, languages and social outlook. He thought and wrote about all this. Since he was six years old he kept journals and wrote into them every day, never missing a one. There one could see the life that went too fast, the thoughts that were put down, and the feelings he so deeply felt. His interests and involvements were wide ranging, and his convictions were passionate and keenly observed. He was multifaceted and brilliant, a fierce debater, and merciless in his logic when he was convinced that he was right.

His immediate contribution to our age is his Formal Theory of Value, which needs to be popularized, researched, amplified and explained. Today, wherever men are confronted with problems that involve the well being of men, we hear: "What we need is values" or "the understanding of values." Every decision that is made which affects humankind, be it in Africa, Asia, America, Europe or all other parts of our earth, involves values. Humanity, now regarding more their color than their humanness, has to learn to be tolerant, not because the law says so, but because each person is a sovereign human being, a fellow human being, who loves, cries, worries and feels like him or her.

Bob was dreaming of a world of peace. Hitler's horrendous crimes colored his whole thinking, and he hoped to be influential in seeing to it that such a nightmare would never happen again. His Theory of Value was his answer to the challenge of a horror which only ended with the victory of the allies over Germany. Hopefully the Theory of Value contributes to the aim that it could never happen again.

Chapter II

THE NATURE OF VALUATION[1]

Robert S. Hartman

The Nature of Axiology

The task of creating an instrument of precise thinking is more difficult in the realm of value than in that of fact. In the realm of fact, the objects of thought, namely, the facts of experience are accessible to the senses. In the value realm the very same facts of experience constitute the objects of value thought, but this time not in their aspect as facts but in their aspect as values. As long as it is unknown what this aspect is, the fact aspect and the value aspect of things must be confused, and the fact aspect, because of its obvious availability to the senses, must prevail. Thus, while scientific thinking could empirically proceed by the investigation of facts, value thinking in its attempt to proceed empirically - as it has done from Plato to the English philosopher, G. E. Moore, in 1903 - has not gotten anywhere. G. E. Moore showed that empirical thinking on value could not lead anywhere. But after the publication of his book, <u>Principia Ethica</u>, value theory went on defining value in empirical terms - as pleasure, self-realization, sympathy, loyalty, reason, the fitting, growth and so on - and no advance was made. Only recently a small school of philosophers has taken up G. E. Moore's challenge and produced

---

[1] This is an edited (shortened) version of the first two thirds of Robert S. Hartman's previously unpublished essay by this title. The editors have deleted diagrams and some quoted material. Transitional words and phrases, shown in brackets, have been added to bridge some gaps.

a formal system of value. This formal system is called Axiology. The concept of axiology as a formal science is a new one. In order to understand our definition of value, and the definitions of value experience arising from it, we must discuss the nature of axiology and its place in modern thought.

In one sentence, it may be said that axiology has the same position in moral philosophy that mathematics has in natural philosophy. Until about a hundred years ago neither the natural nor the social sciences existed as such; both were a part of philosophy. Natural philosophy has since developed into the natural sciences, and moral philosophy into the so-called social sciences. Only ethics, aesthetics, logic, and metaphysics have remained with the field of philosophy proper.

Whereas the development of the natural sciences has led to control of natural phenomena, the development of the social sciences has not led to a corresponding control of social phenomena. On the contrary, the extended scientific tools have brought the danger of destroying society itself. What is needed, therefore, is a scientific development of moral philosophy as effective as that of natural philosophy.

The Philosophers who, starting in the Renaissance, designed the natural sciences did so in two ways: (a) by developing a powerful tool which served as the method of the sciences, namely, the pure science of mathematics, and (b) by designing frames of reference for each realm of phenomena and confining their inquiry to the particular frame of reference in question. These philosophers saw that the book of nature was written in the symbols of mathematics - only that in their time mathematics did not exist and they had to design the tool as they went along. Gradually pure and applied mathematics separated. The pure mathematicians further elaborated mathematics, and, on the simple foundation of a few basic axioms, built the imposing structure of modern mathematics.

Mathematics became a pattern of all kinds of possible frames of reference. Applied scientists borrowed from it freely, fitting their observations into appropriate mathematical frames. Thus, astronomy used the calculus, differential and integral equations, and later non-euclidean spaces; electrical theory used the science of complex numbers; quantum theory borrowed the matrix calculus; thermodynamics, the calculus of probability. This meant, and this was the second important fact in the development of the natural sciences, that each frame of reference had its own laws and significance. Natural philosophy split up into physics, chemistry, biology, astronomy, and so on, but all the sciences, different as they were from one another, partook in the pure super structure of mathematics.

Axiology is the pure science which is to the social sciences as mathematics is to the natural sciences. It is formal and universal, built on simple axioms, and contains all possible frames of reference for the social sciences as value sciences. It is the logic of value as mathematics is the logic of fact.

Let us now discuss the role of axiology for the future of moral philosophy. Let us suppose that it exists as a system of rules and norms which is to the social sciences as mathematics is to the natural sciences and that it is (a) formal, (b) contains the possible frames of references for the social sciences, and (c) dispenses with metaphysics and theology.

(a) The formalism of axiology implies its universality. Axiology is as valid as is logic, for anyone thinking in the realm of social phenomena, whether he be Russian or Chinese, American or Australian, French or Turkish, no matter what his rank, race, religion or social roots - just as "2 + 2 = 4" is valid for everyone. Axiology, in other words, is indeed the logic of values (Greek axiai). We can never escape logic in judgments, no matter how true or false these judgments are; even the insane man is still logical, only, his premises or procedures are false or nonsensical. It is logic - taken in a wider sense of the word - that allows us to detect the nonsense. Similarly we can never escape axiology in value judgments, no matter how true or false our value judgments may be.

(b) The formalism of axiology, secondly, supplies the frames of reference for the social and humanistic sciences. This implies that the propositions of axiology, in order to be materially meaningful, have to be applied, just as the propositions of mathematics. The proposition "2 + 2 = 4" has no practical meaning until and unless it is applied to actual events or things which appear in couples. The sum total of all the systematic applications of the mathematical rules to concrete material constitutes the body of the natural sciences. Similarly the norms of axiology have to be applied, and these applications of axiology are the social and humanistic sciences.

Axiological value is, as we shall see, either extrinsic or intrinsic. The application of axiological rules to phenomena produces the social and humanistic sciences in the following way: The application of extrinsic rules to things produces economics; to persons, psychology and individual sociology; to groups, group sociology; to thoughts, logic. The application of intrinsic rules to things produces aesthetics and symbolism; to persons, ethics; to groups, political science and religion; to thoughts, metaphysics and theology. Anthropology, education, and similar social disciplines result as intermediary sciences of those mentioned above. The application of axiology to cooperation and competition means an intrinsic application of the principle of community on the one hand, and of the extrinsic application of the principle of collectivity, on the other hand, to group organization.

(c) Axiology not only dispenses with metaphysics and theology as frames of reference for the social and humanistic sciences but supplies itself the frames of reference for metaphysics and theology. Instead of the present practice of applying vague and undefined concepts of metaphysics and theology to equally vague and undefined concepts, as for example of ethics, and thus compounding confusion by confusion, axiology clarifies and differentiates by its clear and distinct norms both metaphysics and ethics. Thus at one stroke it secularizes ethics, by emancipating it from theology, clarifies ethics by applying to it the rules of value logic, and at the same time by the same process clarifies and elaborates metaphysics and theology.

The secularization of ethics does not mean the irreligiousness of ethicists or of morality, as little as the secularization of natural philosophy meant the irreligiousness of scientists or of scientific subject matter. On the contrary, if ethics is to be a science and teach people to live "good" lives, then the aims of religion will be served by replacing the metaphysical vagueness of ethics by definite norms of behavior just as the metaphysical vagueness in chemistry was replaced by the detailed rules of the periodic table or the metaphysical vagueness in astronomy by Newton's and Laplace's laws. This is acknowledged today by at least the Protestant denominations who in a recent conference, convened by the Federal Council of Churches of Christ of America, on February 16 - 19, 1950, in Detroit, inserted the following statement in the Conference document The Responsibility of Christians in an Interdependent Economic World: "Christian principles must be translated into concrete measures expressive of the Christian idea. This is a task for stewards whose engineering genius, executive ability, and research skills are regarded as a sacred trust. Scientific means must be discovered with which to realize moral ends." On the other hand, the present metaphysical and theological content of ethics does not mean that ethicists are particularly religious; it only means that they are still ignorant of the scientific presuppositions of their field.

This is only another implication of the fact that axiology keeps the frames of reference apart and in this way clarifies thinking on value, being not only a science of values, but also a science of axioms (Greek - axiomata).

The function of axiology in secularizing the social and humanistic sciences changes the character of normativity in these sciences, and particularly in the science of ethics. When we speak of axiological norms, we mean that the rules of axiology have within them a certain obligation, but this obligation is nothing mystical - we do not have to follow them because they are the laws of God or because we would have to go to Hell otherwise, but we have to follow them for the same reason that we have to follow the norms of, say, mathematics or physics. Everybody is free to say that $2+2=5$, but he would get into considerable difficulty applying this proposition. Anybody is free to disregard the law of gravitation and try to walk out of his window. However, he would break his neck. It is equally disastrous, though equally easy, to try to break the laws of axiology. This is particularly obvious in the field of ethics; although God's mills grind slowly they grind exceedingly fine. It is less obvious in the other social sciences. Here false thinking can be exposed as violation of the rules of axiology and the penalty made to be seen logically in prevention of its being felt empirically.

The norms of axiology are not <u>ethical</u> norms. Axiology is not ethics, but it sets the norms for ethics as it does for all the other social and humanistic sciences. When we speak of ethical norms, therefore, we mean the norms of ethics, namely, of axiology as applied to ethics. We may, however, use the term "moral norms" for axiological norms in the sense that moral philosophy was distinguished from natural philosophy and the word "moral" referred to all the disciplines which today are the social and humanistic sciences.

The role of axiology as corresponding in moral philosophy to the position of mathematics in natural philosophy implies, finally, that social or humanistic scientists in the future will have to learn axiology, just as today physicists and chemists have to learn mathematics...

To understand the relationship between axiology and logic we must now discuss the fundamental definition of value in axiology.

The Formal Principles of Value

If value is to be defined purely formally it must be defined in terms of a formal system. There are at present two such systems - logic and mathematics. We shall define value in terms of logic. We shall not do so in logically strict language but in a language sufficiently precise for the present purpose.

Let us define anything as good (or valuable) if it is <u>what</u> or <u>as</u> it is supposed to be.

Extrinsic Value

This gives us two cases of goodness (or value), those signified by the word "what" and those signified by the word "as." Beginning with the first case, we say that "anything is good if it is <u>what</u> it is supposed to be." If something is supposed to be a plate then it is a "good plate" if (a) it is a plate and (b) it has all the attributes a plate is supposed to have. If someone is supposed to be a teacher, then he is a "good teacher" if (a) he is a teacher and (b) he has all the attributes a teacher is supposed to have. Generally speaking, anything is good if it is a member of a class - "plate," "teacher," - and has all the attributes of the class, which means all the attributes the class is supposed to have, or all the attributes which the class name or concept connotes. Here "anything" - let us call it "x" - is not supposed to be good in itself but in its function as a good so-and-so, namely, a good member of a certain class, say the class C. We shall call this kind of goodness <u>extensional</u> goodness, because x belongs to the extension of a certain concept; or <u>functional</u> goodness, because it refers to a function of x rather than to x itself. We may also call this kind of goodness <u>extrinsic</u> goodness because it refers to something which is outside of x, namely, the relation between x and the class C of which x is a member or the concept "C" of which x is an instance. Thus, in asking what x is supposed to be we really ask what kind of thing x is supposed to be or to what class x is supposed to belong or what concept it is to exemplify. And in predicating goodness of the fact that x is what x is supposed to be we predicate goodness of the fact that x belongs to a certain class or exemplifies a certain concept, and has all the attributes of that class or concept. When goodness is thus predicated of a class membership we say that the member of the class is a good member of the class, or in terms of x's exemplification of the concept, that x is "a good C." Thus, the first case of our definition, "anything is good if it is what it is supposed to be," means "anything is a good member of a class if it is a member of the class and has all the attributes which members of the class are supposed to have." Or, "x is a good C if x is a member of the class C and has all the attributes of C." This presupposes, among other things, that a thing may be a member of a class without possessing all the attributes of the class. Thus, if man is, among other things, a rational biped, even a one-legged moron may be a man.

Intrinsic Value

When we come to the second case, "anything is good if it is <u>as</u> it is supposed to be," we are not thinking of a class to which x belongs but we think of x itself: "x is good if x is as x is supposed to be." The goodness here is not predicated of x's membership in a class but of x itself. We are not concerned with the question whether x is a good so-and-so but whether x is concerned with the question whether x is a good so-and-so but whether x is good. The latter may be interpreted as "x is a good X," where "X" signifies a class, the class whose only member is x, or the unit class of x. This kind of goodness we shall call <u>intensional</u> goodness, because what is good is the totality of all the attributes of X, or the intension of the concept X; or <u>individual</u> goodness because there is no other individual x exactly like this x with all these attributes; or we may call it <u>intrinsic</u> goodness, because the goodness inheres in x itself and not in x's membership in a class other than X. In this case "good" is predicated of x, and our definition "x is good if x is as x is supposed to be" means "x is good if x has all the attributes of X," where "X" stands for "x as x is supposed to be." If x is a person, then "x as x is supposed to be," or "X," may be interpreted as x's "self;" it depends on x, for it is up to x to be what x is supposed to be, as well as to suppose what X is to be. This self-reflective and self-directive part of a person is usually called the person's conscience. In the case of a person our definition may thus be formulated "x is a good person if x is as x's conscience demands" or "x is good if x follows his conscience," or in some similar fashion. If x is not a person the supposing is done by the person who defines the meaning of "x."

Relation of Extrinsic and Intrinsic Value

We thus have two kinds of goodness or value, extrinsic value and intrinsic value. Both are defined roughly by "anything is what and as it is supposed to be." For extrinsic value this means "x is a good C if x is a member of the class C and has all the attributes of C," and for intrinsic value it means "x is good if x has all the attributes of X," which latter, in the case of persons, means "x is a good person if x follows his conscience." (Extrinsic value refers to a function of x, intrinsic value refers to x itself, or x's self, i.e., the integral totality of all of x's attributes.) In the case of persons this integral totality is called "integrity," "character," or "personality." Intrinsic value for persons may thus be defined as the value of personality. The extrinsic value of a person, on the other hand, is his function, of which a person has an infinite number, such as teacher, commuter, Rotarian, father, customer, advertiser, etc. Indeed, every situation finds the person in a different function. All these functions are expressions, elaborations, and differentiations of the personality, whose functional value is evinced by the skill[1] in meeting and adjusting to the situation.

Intrinsic value thus precedes extrinsic value. A person in order to function must first be, namely, a person. His being a person and his functioning are not the same. A man may be a good person and a bad function, e.g., a good person and a bad lawyer, or a bad person and a good lawyer; he can be extrinsically good and intrinsically bad or extrinsically bad and intrinsically good or both extrinsically and intrinsically good or bad. The norm for the extrinsic value is a practical science - a person to be a good lawyer must know the law, to be a good chemist must know chemistry, to be a good baker must know baking. The norm for the intrinsic value is the person's conscience; to be a "good himself" he must first know himself, be a co-knower with himself of himself. Since conscience is the norm of intrinsic value and science is the norm of extrinsic value, and intrinsic value precedes extrinsic value, conscience precedes science.[2]

Conscience is a particular case of intrinsic value, the relation, so to speak, between the second and the third "x" in the definition of intrinsic value in cases where x is a person: "x is good if x is as x is supposed to be." The second "x" stands for x as x actually is, whereas the third "x" stands for x as x is supposed to be, that is, X. The former is the actual, the latter the ideal or potential x. The first "x" combines the second and third, for x is good if the actual x, "x", is as the ideal or potential x, "X." The relation between the actual and the ideal x is conscience. The actual x is a member of the unit class of x, that is, "X", for "x is good" is equivalent to "x is a good x," or the concept of x. This concept has the totality of all the attributes which any actual x may posses. The totality of all of these attributes is a unique configuration. Uniqueness, we may say, is the intension of a unit class: a thing which is intrinsically valuable is "in a class by itself."

All intrinsic value, according to our formula, exhibits the dialectic between the actuality and the ideality of the thing valued, x, which in spite and because of this antinomy is one and unique. Where this dialectic is disregarded x appears as merely actual and momentary and nothing intrinsically valuable can be said of it except in so far as actual momentariness is in itself valuable; but such attribution of value seems impossible since making momentary actuality valuable presupposes at least one other frame of reference than momentary actuality. But if such a frame of reference were supplied, momentary actuality would not be any more momentary actuality. Hence momentary actuality, as such, cannot be valuable. It is axiologically vacuous. Such vacuous actuality is sometimes applied to persons. Their actual-ideal constitution is disregarded and the drive for momentary "satisfaction" is regarded as their essential "ethical" feature. The ethical view of persons thus flattened out into shadows is the hedonism proclaimed by Thrasymachus in Plato's Republic and by Nietzsche. A more important use of it is in the science of economics. The "economic man" is nothing but a mechanism of satisfactions and dissatisfactions.

Badness

Both extrinsic and intrinsic value presuppose correct attribution of class attributes to a thing, or correct subsumption of a particular under a universal. I can judge whether x is a good lawyer only if I know both the particular function of x and the class attributes connoted by the term "lawyer". I can judge whether x is good only if I know the present properties of x and the potentialities of x as the set of those properties of which the present properties of x are special cases, namely, actualities. Correct subsumption or attribution is itself a value, namely, an extrinsic value, i.e., the exercise of a function of judgement, to be exact, a value judgment. A value judgment is the correct subsumption of a fact under the logic of value. We can apply our definition of extrinsic value to the act of value subsumption, or <u>valuation</u>, and say that an act of value subsumption is good if (a) it is a value subsumption, i.e., it sees an event in a value-logical context, and (b) it has all the attributes of a subsumption, i.e., the axiological frame of reference is appropriate to the event. When several subsumptions are possible, say, an extrinsic and an intrinsic valuation, then the intrinsic valuation takes precedence over the extrinsic.

Since extrinsic value is the correspondence in a specific case of actual attributes with class attributes, extrinsic disvalue or "bad" is the non-correspondence of actual attributes and class attributes. For example, Jones is not a good lawyer if either (a) he is not a lawyer, or (b) he does not have the attributes of a lawyer, or (c) he neither is a lawyer nor has the attributes of a lawyer. Let us say that being a lawyer means taking the bar examination and that having all the attributes of a lawyer means to know the law. Then, if Jones has not taken the bar examination but knows the law, he is not a good <u>lawyer</u>, and if he has taken the bar examination but does not know the law, he is not a <u>good</u> lawyer. In neither case is he a <u>good</u> <u>lawyer</u>. Neither, of course, is he a good lawyer if he has neither taken the bar examination nor knows the law. In all these cases we have a non-correspondence of actual attributes and class attributes. In the first case, (a) Jones does not belong to the class of lawyers but he has the attributes of the class; in the second case, (b) he has the attributes of the class but does not belong to it; and in the third case, (c) he neither belongs to the class nor has its attributes.

In all these cases we have a wrong coordination of class and class-member. Jones fails in being a lawyer; he may, for that matter, be a good baker or candlestick maker. The badness of Jones is a badness-as-lawyer; the wrong concept has been applied to him. Thus, badness in all cases is a transposition of concepts or of frames of reference. A bad C may always be a good D; a bad house may be a good ruin and a bad chair a good stool. The art of valuation is, therefore, to classify things under correct frames of reference. Persons, axiologically, must be classified as persons, that is, intrinsically, and not under extrinsic concepts, such as color of skin, social status, and the like.

In order to understand better these distinctions of valuation we must now discuss more in detail the relationship of axiology and logic.

Axiology and Logic: Principles of Organization

The relationship of axiology to logic is important because it gives rise to a third kind of value besides extrinsic and intrinsic value - which may be called the axiological values proper - namely, <u>logical</u> or <u>systemic</u> value. The relationships between the three kinds of values are at the level of axiology.

Logical "Valuation"

Since valuation is a matter of thinking it is important to see what kind of valuation regular logical thinking represents. In logical thought we subsume a phenomenon or event under a concept but we do not analyze the concept itself. If a thing is logically subsumed under a class C then the thing either is a C or is not a C. It cannot be a good or a bad C but only all of a C or no C. This is obvious in theoretical or exact science. If, for example, a certain figure is subsumed under the geometrical concept "circle" then the figure either is a circle or is not a circle. It cannot be a bad circle, for in that case it simply is not a circle, nor a good circle, for in that case it simply is a circle. There are only circles and not circles, but not better or worse circles. In theoretical science, in other words, there is no room for valuation or rather, valuation is very primitive: The thing either is perfect or no good...

[Consider the] concept, say, "circle," which has a certain number of attributes called the definition or the intension of the concept; and [consider the] class of circles or the extension of the concept. The definition of "circle," as we can see in any dictionary, is "a closed plane curve consisting of all points equidistant from a point within it, called the center." All members of the class of circles must have all these attributes; otherwise they are not members of the logical class of circles. No actual circle drawn in space-time is such a circle, for the curve when drawn has a thickness and thus innumerable points which are at different distances from the center. But the circle as a construct of the human mind has no thickness, and its ideal form is contained in every actual circle. As such, each circle is a legitimate member of the logical class of circles. What is true of the circle is true of all constructs of the human mind, whether in the natural or the social sciences. In the natural sciences electrons, spaces, waves, and the like are constructs, but also horses, flowers, and all empirical things insofar as they are elements of zoological, botanical, etc. systems. As such they are referred to by Latin names. Lilac, for example, is botanically "Syringa vulgaris." <u>Syringa vulgaris</u> has the minimum attributes which any lilac must have to belong to the botanical class. But a lilac has many attributes which <u>Syringa vulgaris</u> does not have, all the fragrance and beauty which the poets - but not the botanists - extol. "Lilac" determines not a logical but an empirical or axiological class. "When lilacs last in the door-yard bloom'd" is full of everyday meaning. "When <u>syringa vulgaris</u> last in the door-yard bloom'd" sounds, in comparison, like a joke, and <u>is</u> a joke, for a joke is a transposition of frames of reference. Actually, the transposition means that what the line says is not so or nonsense, and it is; for <u>syringa vulgaris</u> cannot "bloom". <u>Syringa vulgaris</u> belongs in the botany books and exists only there; and in botany books plants do not "bloom"; they pullulate. "Pullulate" connotes the minimum-and exact-set of attributes which is to "bloom" as <u>Syringa vulgaris</u> is to lilac - and <u>homo sapiens</u> is to man, and <u>homo economicus</u> is to man in a certain setting. All these are the minimum sets of attributes within an everyday concept which make that concept a logical rather than an axiological one, and the thing referred to a member of a logical rather than an axiological class. Such a minimum set of attributes is called a <u>Schema</u>. Logical classes consist of schemata. The schemata of a particular class are all alike. For if any of them should deviate from the conceptual norm it would not be a member of the class. The members of empirical or axiological classes, on the other hand, may all be different.

What is true of constructs in the natural sciences is also true of constructs in the social sciences. "Homo economicus" is a social science construct. Especially in the law human situations are schemata, constructs. These constructs must not be confused with the empirical or <u>experiential facts</u>. The former are members of logical classes, the latter of empirical or axiological classes. Thus, marriage, legally, belongs to the class of "contracts made in due process of law by which a man and woman reciprocally agree to live with each other during their joint lives, and to discharge towards each other the duties imposed by law on the relation of husband and wife." This is the legal definition of marriage. It must not be confused with the empirical marriage which is a physical, spiritual, and intellectual relationship between two persons. There is no "love" in the legal marriage; only legal relations. Similarly, any empirical thing, event, or situation may be a member of a scientific or logical frame of reference, but this membership must not be confused with the axiological or empirical membership. If it is confused, very significant <u>transpositions of frames of reference</u> result, namely, transpositions of the logical and the axiological framework. This produces badness in human relations. Thus, if the law is applied strictly without any "human" or axiological considerations, inhumanity and injustice may result; persons are then regarded not as persons but as instances of legal norms; and moral crimes may legally be performed, as is illustrated in Menotti's opera "The Consul." In order to soften this legal strictness of the law moral rules have been introduced into the law and made into legal rules in the form of equity.

Any bureaucratic procedure that sees not humans but instances of a rule, any authoritarian person that tries to impose his will by using the rules of a system, any procedure that imposes conformity is guilty of this evil of transposition of the logical and the axiological. It is the use of a system which gives evil the power to extend its range and, at the same time, to assume the resemblance of good. All great evil is systemic evil.[3]

The reason is that systemic valuation denies all degrees of value and sees things in either black or white; the thing either is or is not a member of its class, it either is <u>perfect</u> or <u>no good</u>. In a systemic organization you either belong or you don't belong. Shades and differences of opinion and character are not tolerated. The one value is conformity and the one disvalue non-conformity - which leads to expulsion or "liquidation." All members of a system must be the same or else be no members.

Where there are no differences and distinctions between things, there can be no order. Things that are all the same are indistinguishable of one another and interchangeable. Order, however, presupposes distinction and variety among things. Systemic things, therefore, cannot be in order. Rather, one such thing being like the next, the only "order" prevailing is the system itself. But this, as far as the elements of the system are concerned, constitutes disorder; all the elements are on the lowest common denominator, namely, as elements of the system, and all their intrinsic or extrinsic differences are erased; they are, as individuals, unavailable. There is nothing but a mass of interchangeable, formless elements: Chaos numbered and indexed. The culmination of such systemic organization was Nazi Germany.

Every dictatorship is of this kind. It always arises in answer to a real or imaginary emergency. To overcome chaos by systemization is always the first impulse of humanity. Thus, the age-old prescription for tyrants is first to manufacture emergencies and then appear as savior. Actually, the system only replaces one chaos by another;[4] it even intensifies chaos by card-indexing it. The culmination of this kind of chaos were the German concentration camps. But any secret police falls into this pattern, when it imposes uniformity. Its order is merely a formal one. Material order consists of the variety of elements rather than their uniformity. It exists in extrinsic and, in even higher degree, in intrinsic organization; in axiological rather than logical valuation.

Order, thus, is between the dynamic disorder of chaos and the static disorder of a system.

Axiological Valuation

Extrinsic Valuation

Let us now, in the light of what has been said of systemic or logical valuation, return to axiological valuation. All things of human experience, that is, all things in space and time - all things that are not scientific constructs - must be valued axiologically. This means that the concept which determines the class of which the thing is a member is analyzed and not unanalyzed. In other words, when we subsume an empirical thing under a concept we cannot strictly use the properties of the definition of the concept but must admit into the class things that possess, or do not possess, these attributes in higher or lower degrees. Thus, when we say "A is a chair," we do not mean that A either is or is not a chair, as we do in scientific or in logical discourse. What we mean is that A belongs to the class of actual empirical things called chairs and that A is more or less a chair but not that A is exactly like any other chair. There are all kinds of chairs, of all degrees of greater or less "chairhood"; and it is these degrees that non-scientific or axiological thought values.

The axiological concept has many more attributes than the logical concept.[5] The members of the class have these attributes in different degrees. Empirical definition can never be as precise as logical or nominal definition, for the reason that the thing defined exists in nature - and is not a construct of the mind - and the attributes of it have to be abstracted from nature. By abstraction is meant the synoptic view of attributes possessed by a number of things in common. The greater the number of things the fewer the number of attributes they have in common, and the smaller the number of things the larger the number of attributes they have in common. The minimum number of common attributes is that of the attributes of all the chairs, that is of the logical class of chairs, and this set may be called the definition of "chair"; while the maximum number of common attributes would be the set which only two things have in common. Unless there are at least two things there are, of course, no common attributes and hence no abstraction. Any two chairs have many more properties in common than have all chairs. All chairs have only a minimum of properties in common such as, for example, a knee-high seat with a back, three properties in all. This minimum definition corresponds to the schema of the chair and looks like this: h . Any two chairs, on the other hand, or any specific number of chairs, for that matter, will have many more properties in common, such as a round back or wooden seat or a certain number of legs, or arm rests, and so on. The set of these properties is called the Exposition rather than the Definition of "chair." While every chair must have the definition, or the minimum properties if it is to be a chair, no actual chair must have all the expositional properties. In the degree in which an actual chair possesses these expositional properties lies its value, its goodness or badness as a chair. The more such properties the actual chair has the better a chair it is, and the fewer such properties it has, the worse a chair it is. Thus, if an actual chair has a broken seat or a broken back or one leg missing it is still a chair since it is being thought under the schema of chair, but it is not a very good chair. If one chair has, say, seven expositional attributes and another chair has only, say, three expositional attributes, then the first chair is a better chair than the latter. But both must have the three definitional attributes if they are to be a chair.

Any object which is bad under one concept, say "chair," may be good as we have seen, under another concept. Thus, a bad chair may be a good stool, if it has no back. By the same token one has to say that a good chair is a bad stool, a good house a bad ruin, a bad house a good ruin, a good jalopy a bad car, a good car a bad jalopy, a good nag a bad horse, a good horse a bad nag, and so on. Since goodness and badness of a thing depend on the concept which is applied to it, any bad situation can be changed into a good one by giving it a different name. This is one of the ways by which evil can be overcome by good. Simply subsume the bad thing under the concept which corresponds to the bad state and make it good. If I expect a chair and I get a stool, instead of being unhappy about having a bad chair, I may be happy about having a good stool. This is the secret of Pollyanna; but it works only with extrinsic value.

Intrinsic Valuation

In intrinsic valuation, the class in question consists of only one member. Thus, to take a chair again, ...the concept is "This chair" and the member is this chair. Obviously, if we only deal with one thing of its own kind we cannot abstract any properties from it. Rather, the "definition" or "exposition" of the unique thing contains all the properties the thing has; the thing is good because it is as it is. I love a person because he is the way he is; not because he is better than some other persons. Since in intrinsic valuation I deal with only one thing, I cannot compare this thing with any other thing; there is no standard of comparison, as in the case of extrinsic valuation. The number of properties of this one thing is infinite, they cannot be counted, since there is no abstraction. Rather there is pure experience between me and the one thing; at best, I experience the thing in its whole fullness without any thought of anything else, at worst, I am indifferent. Being indifferent to the uniqueness of a thing means not being interested in or neglecting its intrinsic value. Such indifference is <u>intrinsic badness</u>. In this sense we must understand Stephen Crane's words: "Philosophy should always know that indifference is a militant thing. It batters down the walls of cities and murders the women and children amid flames and the purloining of altar vessels. When it goes away it leaves smoking ruins where lie citizens bayonetted through the throat. It is not a children's pastime like mere highway robbery." Indifference being intrinsic evil, intrinsic good is love or sympathy; it is <u>agape</u>, loving concern, translated often by "charity."

In axiological terms it means that since I do not abstract in intrinsic valuation, I concentrate on the thing as it is, I am fully concentrated on this one thing. For this reason, intrinsic valuation when applied to things brings about aesthetic valuation: the artist is fully concentrated on the thing he creates. He and the thing are empathically related; they form one unit. Applied to persons this valuation is ethical; it is complete involvement of one person with another, complete concentration of one person on another; the persons are sympathetically related and form one unit. We may call this relationship between persons <u>Community</u>. The application of extrinsic valuation to persons, on the other hand, is functional; both are regarded intellectually as members of the same class and compared as such. Such an extrinsic relationship between persons we shall call <u>Collectivity</u>. When two persons are intrinsically related, they are related each as a class by himself. In their mutual self-involvement they produce a new class of which their own classes are intrinsic parts. Here we have the phenomenon of <u>Cooperation</u>. Both are in the same situation, that is, both form part of one organic unit, and there is no opposition between them since they are both intrinsically good, being good by being the way they are...

[When a person intrinsically valuates himself,] the class is the person's concept of himself, "I" or "MY self" and the member of the class I now, every moment of the person, every actual I...

[In a community, two persons intrinsically value themselves and one another.] In community persons are experiences to one another, they are not functions serving a concept that is above them; they serve each other, forming one organic unity which cannot be dissolved unless one stops being as he is. On the other hand, a collectivity is what we showed above in extrinsic valuation. Here individuals are instances of the same concept in different degrees. They may change without changing the collectivity for they are only functionally related. Whenever the concept changes, the collectivity changes. If the concept is "customer" the members are customers, if the concept is "seller" the members are sellers, when the concept is "buyer" the members are buyers. There is an affinity of functions, both under the same concept and under different concepts... Here we have two persons related with reference to a common concept, but not with reference to their own selves... The intrinsic unity [of each person] is cut up in segments. The segments are the functions, which never reach the inner core of the persons. The persons are connected by one function, as customers, but this leaves the core of their personality untouched.

The difference between extrinsic collectivity and intrinsic community then is that community is a unit of intrinsic values, each unique in its kind and all achieving unity <u>only</u> by the play of their full powers and capacities. Collectivity is an aggregate of functions, a class of properties common but not intrinsic to persons. Any violation of the individual as such weakens the community, but it leaves the collectivity untouched unless the section of the person that is violated is that by which it is a member of the collectivity. For this reason, in a collectivity people do not bother if another person is harmed; it "does not concern them." In a community, any man's violation is my own. Thus, if I am a member of a community and try to weaken another member I weaken myself. In a collectivity, on the other hand, it may well be that the better I am, that is, the more I fulfill the concept which determines the collectivity, the worse I show off my competitor; therefore, in a collectivity it may help <u>me</u> if I make the other look worse. <u>Competition is a matter of extrinsic valuation in collectivity while cooperation is a matter of intrinsic valuation in community.</u> In cooperation I consider the other like myself as a human being in his whole unique value, in competition I regard him and myself as functions and part of a supervening concept.

Both, competition and cooperation, must be opposed to conformity, the inter-relationship of elements in systemic valuation. Here, one concept is enforced equally on all the members of the group, making them appear all alike. In this case, individuals are not regarded either as persons or as functions, but as elements of a system. The virtue in an intrinsic organization is personality in cooperation, in an extrinsic organization skill in competition, and in a systemic organization obedience in conformity.

There are, thus, three kinds of organizational principles, the cooperative (intrinsic or moral), the competitive (extrinsic or social), and the conformative (systemic or authoritarian).

Interrelationships Between the Three Kinds of Organizations

In order to understand more fully the interrelationship between the three kinds of organizational principles we shall now discuss some of their characteristics.

The Subjects of Valuation

The subjects of <u>logical or systemic</u> valuation are things in a minimum relationship: as elements of a system or as schemata. A schema is less real than any empirical thing. When human beings are valued systemically they are less real than, say, a piece of paper. In a bureaucratic procedure a person does not exist unless he has a birth certificate. At a border he does not exist unless he has a passport. If, by accident, he crosses a border without a paper, a complicated bureaucratic procedure must be instituted to legalize the situation. When a French tourist in the U.S.A. recently by accident crossed into Canada a formal order of expulsion from Canada had to be issued so that

(a) Canada would have proof that he entered illegally,
(b) The United States would have proof that he had been in Canada,
(c) The United States would have reason to let him back in.

Not always are there such ingenious solutions. In Europe and Asia, where systems are stronger and less flexible than in this country, people without papers have for weeks and months oscillated between borders, living on ships, unable to get off at any port. On the other hand, the more impressive the paper, the more important the person. A German refugee travelled for years with a Swedish alien's passport which somewhat resembled a diplomatic passport. He often got preferential treatment at borders, especially in Latin America.

What counts in a system is the system and its procedures and nothing else. This goes not only for the system's victims but also for its agents. They act as elements of the system and as nothing else. The system, as a body of legal rules, lends their actions both justification and sanction. Therefore, the love of the uniform in Europe, Asia and South America which cancels individuality and gives anonymity and prestige in uniformity. Therefore also the self-righteousness of the professional bureaucrat. The world of systemic value is the haven of those who lack Self, that is, fully differentiated intrinsic value, and it is hell for those who are alive consciously their own inner Self.

Hence the tragedies when the two dimensions of value collide, from Antigone to Dr. Jhivago.

The subjects of <u>extrinsic</u> valuation are everyday empirical things and persons, things and persons in space and time. As we have seen, extrinsic valuation presupposes at least two things in every class; this, in turn, presupposes space and time, for two things must either occupy space or follow in time. These empirical things are valued in the degree that they have the fullness of their class attributes. They are better when they have more such attributes and worse when they have less. Due to this gradation, things in extrinsic valuation exist in great variety. They are not all alike as are systemic things. Their order is a material, not a formal order, a quantitative order of qualities, in which mathematical relations <u>may</u> play a role, as they do in economics, sociology, psychology, and so on.

The subjects of <u>intrinsic</u> valuation are non-empirical things, or rather, empirical things in their non-empirical aspects. They are, as such, neither in time nor in space. Each thing here is regarded as unique; all there is is this thing. Since time and space are defined as succession and interrelationship of things, where there is only one thing there is no time and no space in this sense. The thing itself is, so to speak, the universe. Extrinsically seen, a picture for example, is one of many in a class of pictures. As such it is comparable with other pictures and may have a price. But intrinsically seen, the picture is unique, there is none other like it; it is priceless. Extrinsically seen, a child is one of many in the class of children. As such it is comparable, weighing so and so much, and may even have a price as it had in the England of Karl Marx, when children were sold and bought as chimney sweeping instruments, or in the America of slavery days. Intrinsically seen, a child is unique, there is no other like it and it is priceless. Extrinsically seen, a clerk or executive is one of many in the class of clerks and executives, he is better or worse than others and paid accordingly. Intrinsically seen, he is a person and incomparable. Extrinsically seen, a woman is one among many, being of such and such a shape, features, and "build." Intrinsically seen, a woman is "the only one in the world," "the one and only," "there is nothing like her," "she is Woman."...

The Three Kinds of Knowledge

Knowledge of <u>systems</u> is purely intellectual and abstract. A person, as Galileo has said, may be an excellent logician, yet incapable of judging correctly a situation. The pure specialist as such only knows systems; as a specialist he looks at the world itself as a system. In doing so, the world becomes distorted. In relation to the world the specialist becomes, as Ortega y Gasset says, a learned ignoramus. Specialization thus becomes a curse of the modern world. The modern scientist, says the Spanish philosopher in the Revolt of the Masses, New York, 1932, (Ch. XII), becomes the prototype of the systemic man, the undifferentiated mass-man... Thus, our very (scientifically) specialized civilization brings us continuously into the danger of systemic valuation.

A system is never connected with the space-time reality of things which is the realm of extrinsic common-sense valuation. For this reason the specialist's system may easily lose all touch with reality and become an unreality. In such cases, as a writer on Ethics, William H. Roberts, has written in The Problem of Choice, Boston, 1971, (p. 84): "The most disastrous policies are frequently the results deduced by flawless logic from mistaken premises. In such cases the very excellence of the reasoning increases the havoc wrought. It checks any suspicion that there may have been a mistake. It discourages any impulse to re-examine original data or underlying assumptions. It can blind naturally kind individuals and peoples to monstrous wrongs and cruelties." From this distortion of reality there is only one step to technical insanity. In the words of another philosopher, Immanuel Kant, in his Anthropology (Par. 42) "Dementia is that disturbance of the mind where everything which the instance tells does accord with the formal laws of thought. But, through a pervertedly active imagination, invented ideas are regarded as facts. This is the kind of people who believe to be surrounded by enemies; who interpret expressions, words, and other indifferent acts as directed against them and as traps to ensnare them. They are, in their unfortunate madness, often so acute in interpreting what others do in all innocence, as directed against them, that their argument would do all honor to their intellect, if only the data were true." The curse of our time thus, is the combination of specialists and psychotics. Its acme - or nadir - is the psychotic specialist, as we had him in Germany. But even in this country, it is well to remember that 70% of all public hospital beds are occupied by mental patients.

The whole development of our time thus conspires to bring about systemic valuation. Against this, the men of common sense - who value extrinsically - and those of spiritual insight - who value intrinsically must stand together. Their means of fighting must be the articulation of sanity: the rational understanding of valuation.

The knowledge relevant to extrinsic valuation is the knowledge of the world of things, of the order and classification of things which correspond to their actual variety. This is the valuation of common sense, of sound situational understanding. Here we have the capacity of comparison, of judging the present in terms of the future, that is, of anticipation, and the solid open-mindedness that used to distinguish the American mind. Its philosophical elaboration is found in the work of John Dewey. Unfortunately, Dewey's most important contribution, that to American education, has been misunderstood and his - justified - horror of systems has led to intellectual license and lack of discipline. Also he never knew intrinsic value, and this has led to a worship of "success," materialism, and lack of human valuation. There are serious flaws in the value picture of the American scene. On the other hand, there still prevails in America the soundness of common sense and the capacity so to order one's life circumstances that success is wrought out of the chaos of events. Dewey's America is strong in extrinsic valuation, but weak in systemic and intrinsic valuation. This may also be expressed by saying that America is strong in the trivialities of existence but weak in the things that really matter.

The kind of knowledge relevant to <u>intrinsic</u> valuation is exceedingly rare. It is the capacity of complete concentration on a thing or person, the personal involvement of the artist, the inventor, the teacher: the capacity of empathy and sympathy. It is the kind of knowledge possessed in the highest degree by the creative genius. It is possible only in a person who is himself fully integrated and has all his powers available for outgoing and meeting persons or things. This is not the "outgoing" of the extrovert or the back-slapper, who meets persons extrinsically. (It is the projecting of the whole person into others.) In philosophy the meeting of things and persons has been described by Phenomenology and some existential writers. This kind of knowledge is direct, immediate, "intuitional;" it is that of the complete person encompassing the world. It is not a matter of the intellect but of character. A strong character with a mediocre intellect is a more creative person than a mediocre character with a strong intellect. True genius is strong character with strong intellect. The world abounds with strong intellects of mediocre character - the professional intellectuals who have to find their security in systems; also, it has many strong characters of mediocre intellect, from business tycoons to politicians - but it lacks the combination of intellect and character - of strong minds that are, at the same time, receptive to value. This sensitivity to value arises out of sensitivity for the value of self, of self-respect. Only where there is self-respect there is respect for the essential, both in men, things, situations, and problems. "Philosophy," says Kierkegaard, "has answered every question, but no adequate consideration has been given the question concerning what sphere it is in which each question finds its answer." Philosophers, in other words, have not discriminated among questions. They have not been persons enough to distinguish problems as to their value; they have been intellectuals who discussed every problem no matter how trivial, with equal fervor; or pedants who, according to Sartre, hide from themselves by their very lack of discrimination, treasuring every scrap written by another author and collecting facts to find their security in them and fill up their own Nothingness. And so in every field. Genius is at a premium because there are so few personalities able and willing to concentrate their whole lives on one problem; and where there are no distinct personalities willing to do this there is no distinction of problems that are worth while from those that are not...

Intrinsic valuation means dedication of the whole person and all its capacities. It means fully living persons. Where there is no such full dedication and full life thought withers - and the nation perishes. For it is half dead already.

Three Kinds of Truth

Systemic truth is consistency. That is true which fits the system. Facts as they actually are of no relevance for systemic truth; for it is not facts that fit into the system but schemata of facts, and sometimes even schemata produced by the imagination. The mind does not have to go outside itself and its processes to determine systemic truth.

Extrinsic truth is correspondence between empirical things and the concepts used to refer to them. The proposition "This is an apple" is true if this thing is what is usually called "apple." The mind, in order to determine extrinsic truth, must go outside itself into the world of space-time things and compare these things with the concepts that it uses to refer to them. Thus facts - the actual things, relations, properties, found in the outside world - are relevant to extrinsic truth. The more integrated a psyche - the more senses and mind work together - the more the individual in question will be able to determine extrinsic truth.

Intrinsic truth is reality itself. That is true which is and because it is as it is. In intrinsic valuation the subject and object of knowledge form an inseparable unit, and the subject, in the process of knowing, completely interpenetrates the nature of the object. Knower and known form an organic unity, a comm-unity; the object known is part of the knowing subject, and the knowing subject is one with the object known. Knowing and being fuse into one... [This occurs in Kierkegaard's "subjective knowledge" of God.][6] This is the concept of existential truth. It is the sense of "truth" used by Jesus: "I am the way, the truth, and the life." Truth is equivalent to life and to intrinsic value - the way to the Kingdom of God.

The Three Kinds of Language

Systemic language is technical and precise; extrinsic language is empirical and descriptive; intrinsic language is metaphorical. <u>Systemic</u> language is technical language, designed to bring out the minimum properties of the thing in question and make it available for scientific handling. <u>Extrinsic</u> language is everyday language, full of valuational comparison, unprecise, but in continuous touch with fact. Here concepts are used to refer to things and to describe them enough for identification, but not exactly enough for precision. <u>Intrinsic</u> language deals with objects not as members of classes but as unique beings. Hence concepts must be used in unique senses and not in the sense of referring to classes. Such a use of concepts, as uniquely characterizing rather than as extensively classifying, is the metaphor. When I say of my wife that she is a peach I do not mean to say that she belongs to the class of peaches. Rather, I mean that the word "peach" connotes something which uniquely reminds me of my wife - and not of a peach or of any other thing or person in the world. Metaphors, thus, have no class reference nor do they have - for that same reason - any definite connotation. When I call my wife a peach, I mean a different peach than when I call my uncle "a peach of a man."

Systemic and extrinsic language present few problems; they are used constantly, understood by all and taught in school and college. Intrinsic language is not so well known; although it is taught in some courses in English, under Poetry, its logical an axiological structure is still unknown. We shall discuss it in greater detail in the next Section, when we apply the axiological categories.

The Three Kinds of Process

Things in the three kinds of valuation are subject to three kinds of processes. Systemic process is logical deduction; extrinsic process is causality; intrinsic process is spontaneous creativity. The systemic whole consists of elements, the extrinsic whole consists of causes and effects linked in and parts of a spatio-temporal process. The intrinsic whole is Gestalt or pattern, consisting of interdependent parts and wholes, where the part is as large as the whole, independent of space and time, and continuously creative. In community, each part is as important as the whole, as can be seen, for example, in the democratic rule of majority where one vote can decide the destiny of the whole community, or in the voting rules of a cooperative as against those of a corporation, where each has a vote, no matter how much or how little capital he holds. Intrinsic values are not <u>caused</u> as are extrinsic values, which arise in space and time by exterior relations. Causal process is, for example, the pushing of billiard balls; non-causal creativity the generation of life itself. According to Berdyaev, a personality, unlike an individuality, has no parents in the physiological sense; it is love and arises out of love in the intrinsic sense; "it makes its appearance from another world." A painter is not the cause of beauty, that is, the intrinsic value, of his picture; but he is the cause of the picture, as a constellation of colors on a canvas. The latter - the colored canvas - was produced by the painter as the cause with his brush, by moving the brush over the canvas. In this way he brought about a picture among pictures, an extrinsic value. But the beauty or intrinsic value of the picture arises not from the mechanics of putting color on canvas but from the artist's putting his life and soul into the picture. This comes about by the artist's capacity to concentrate his whole personality in every hair of the brush, so that every stroke of the brush contains the artist's whole being. Thus, while in the extrinsic view the artist is the cause, the brush an effect and in turn a cause of which the picture is an effect; in the intrinsic view the brush is part of the painter, an extension of his personality; brush and painter form one organic unit. This unity, fully present in each stroke of the brush, brings forth the beauty of the picture, its organic unity, its uniqueness, its intrinsic value. The picture becomes part of the organic unity of painter and brush; and the new whole contains three rather than two parts: it has generated a new part out of itself. This is the process of the creation of intrinsic value. Instead of cause and effect we have a self-generating whole. We find this process wherever there is intrinsic value. Father and mother are physiological causes of the physiological child. This is the extrinsic process. But they are also an intrinsic unity, and this produces out of itself a third part; now the family forms a larger unit. The mother can love each child - no matter how many - with all her heart -she is part of each of them and the family as a whole, and so are the children a part of her and the family as a whole. Finite arithmetic has no place in this relationship.

The personality itself is an ever creative intrinsic whole. "Personality," says Berdyaev, "must construct itself, enrich itself, fill itself with universal content, achieve unity in wholeness in the whole extent of its life. But for this, it must already exist. There must originally exist that subject which is called upon to construct itself..."

Application of the Axiological Categories: Examples

The categories of axiology can be applied to anything. Anything whatever, from the lowest to the highest, can be valued in all three processes, systemically, extrinsically, intrinsically. Let us take some examples, say, a thing, a person, and a concept. Take a button. A button can be valued purely systemically, when, for example, we see that one is missing on our coat.

Even though we never use this particular button we shall want it to be sewed on, because the gap disturbs the symmetry of the pattern. The pattern of buttons on the coat is a system. The button either is or is not there; and for this reason we cannot stand it when it is half there and half not, hanging on one thread. The button can also be valued extrinsically, as a thing of its kind, possessing certain properties and being compared with others of its kind. This is the case when we go and buy buttons. Finally, the button can be valued intrinsically, as a being in itself. Of course, since intrinsic valuation means progressive self-involvement, and at the height of intrinsic valuation the thing valued is the whole universe, a button is an unlikely object of intrinsic valuation. A person who values a button intrinsically transposes frames of reference; hence, a complete intrinsic valuation of a button is bad. It is fetishism. I knew a fetishist of this kind who had a button sewed to his navel and this was the dearest thing he had. Any kind of valuation, when it leads to transposition of frames of reference, is bad. Transposition of frames of reference is the universal definition of bad.

Now let us turn to the valuation of a person, say, a woman, in all three forms. To value a woman systemically would be the case in the WACS, for example, or in a prison, and even in a hospital, where she is a "case." Some writers have deplored this universal systematization of so much of our social life. Ralph Borsodi, in his <u>This Ugly Civilization</u>, regards it as the extension of the factory system over all of society; whereas the factory system, as well as these other systematizations are actually expressions of our systemic pattern of valuation.

> In a civilization reflecting at every point the conquering factory system it is fitting to find that we have applied the factory system to the business of being born, of being sick, and in the end of dying and being buried. We now have maternity hospitals, nurseries, and nursery schools, sanitariums and even funeral churches, all of them efficient - and hard.
>
> The modern mother is merely maternity case number 8, 434; her infant after being finger and foot printed, becomes infant number 8,003.
>
> By virtue of the same mania for system, a modern corpse becomes number 2,332; while a modern funeral becomes one of a series scheduled for parlor 43 for a certain day at a certain hour, with preacher number fourteen, singer number 87, rendering music number 174, and flowers and decoration class B.

The Nature of Valuation 33

Thus the factory system begins and finishes the citizen of the factory-dominated world.

It introduces him to his world in a systematized hospital, furnishes him a standardized education, supports him in a scientifically managed factory, and finishes him off with a final factory flourish, by giving him a perfectly efficient funeral and a perfectly scientific entrance into the regions of eternal bliss.[7]

This, of course, is a powerful condemnation of systemic valuation, even though its value character as such is not recognized but it is regarded as the extension of the factory system. In any case, it is recognized as a transposition of frames of reference. On the other hand, not all systemic valuation is evil. It is evil only when it is a transposition - when applied to situations where it is inappropriate. Many things in our individual and social life must be valued systemically. Scientific constructs must be valued in this way, and the rigorous discipline of systemic valuation in general is necessary for modern society and is precisely what...American education [is] lacking, as against European education. There are even life situations where systemic valuation is necessary: all situations where no play is allowed and it is a matter of either being or not being. Thus, when meeting a deadline, when making a train, when stopping at a red light or before a railroad crossing - you either do or you don't - and when you don't you miss, and sometimes [lose] your life. The saying that a miss is as good as a mile expresses systemic valuation. Systemic valuation is necessary in all situations that demand discipline. In this sense Kierkegaard said that the heart of ethics is energy, and that he knew as a boy he had to hand in his school work, and if not the world would come to an end. It is necessary in all situations of emergency. Discipline may, in this sense, be defined as voluntary emergency. Until a child develops this kind of self-emergency education must provide it, and it can only do so by force - this is the very nature of emergency. It is here where progressive education is axiologically deficient.

In most life situations, however, systemic valuation is out of place, as in the situation of a funeral, as Borsodi shows, and as a glance at <u>Mortuary Management</u>, "The most readable magazine in funeral service," will make hideously clear. We have here a transposition of the economic and the sublime of horrendous proportions. On the other hand, not all of Borsodi's examples are evil. Only those are that transpose frames of reference. If a woman would be valued systemically not merely in a maternity ward but by being put into a concentration camp, then she would be reduced to a figure and evil would be committed. But where numerical order is important, as in tagging the right baby of the right mother, there is no badness in the systemic valuation. A woman can be extrinsically valued, as we have seen, when she is compared with other women, and this again is quite in order as long as one is not engaged or married to her. Marriage introduces intrinsic valuation: the woman is the one and only with whom one is to share his life. But in marriage, too, the three kinds of valuation continuously recur. At some high moments there is intrinsic valuation, at many others there is extrinsic valuation, and at again others there is systemic valuation, for example when the wife is regarded as the force that makes the household machine run. Thus, when something is missing or not running smoothly, the husband gets "cross" - transposition of frames of reference! - and scolds her - systemically.

Finally, let us evaluate a concept in all three forms, say, God. The systemic valuation of God is the theological one. Here God is regarded as a "being" which is perfect and unless it is perfect it is not God. God is, actually, defined as the perfect being. This means, he is the prototype of all systemic things. This very thought has been systematically elaborated by Spinoza, who showed the whole world to be the system that is God. When God is extrinsically valued he is valued as one among many, and compared with others of his kind. This, of course, is polytheism. Significantly, since extrinsic valuation deals with the things of the world, polytheistic gods are conceived in terms of mortals. Between extrinsic and systemic valuation is that which makes a perfect God become a man, and hence sees this man in two aspects, as the Second of the Trinity and as prototype of the class of men, namely, Man, the Son of Man, the Saviour of Mankind. Finally, there is intrinsic valuation of God, where the human person is fully involved in God as a being personally approachable. Here we have true religiosity, mysticism, and religious existentialism, such as Kierkegaard's. Here Jesus is neither the Son of God nor the Son of Man, he is my own Self, the Friend and Companion who suffers for me and in whom I suffer. He carries my sins and I live in his salvation.

NOTES

1. The word "skill" etymologically means "difference." Cf. Swedish "skillnad" (difference), "skilja" (to separate), "skilsmassa" (divorce), etc. The word "person" on the other hand, meant originally function or role in a particular situation ("mask") and later one's cosmic role or one's role in the world at large, in the totality of individual skills and situations.

2. This is true particularly for the science of the lawyer, the law. This particular precedence of intrinsic over extrinsic value is guaranteed the protection of the state in the First Amendment of the American Constitution, as well as the laws concerning conscientious objectors and similar statutes. Where such guarantees do not exist they ought to be legally established. Whenever the claims of conscience and science conflict, as, for example, in the making of atomic bombs, it is conscience which ought to be free to follow its own course. Here is the significance of the Oppenheimer case.

3. This is particularly true of war. They are between systems, not between people. It is people who die for those systems. See Jacques Maritain, Men and the State, London, 1954, p. 47: "Ce sont toujours les memes qui se font tuer."

4. See the article on Venizuela in Time, 2/28/55.

5. What we call "the axiological concept" Collingwood calls "the philosophical concept." R. G. Collingwood, An Essay on Philosophical Method, London, 1933.

6. Søren Kierkegaard, Concluding Unscientific Postscript, Princeton, 1944, pp. 178 ff.

7. Ralph Borsodi, This Ugly Civilization, New York, 1929, p. 199.

Chapter III

SYSTEMIC VALUE AND VALUATION

Rem B. Edwards

Robert S. Hartman identified a form of value which no one had recognized before. He called it "systemic value." He wrote that systemic value is "rarely recognized,"[1] indeed that "The whole realm of what we call <u>systemic value</u> is new to value theory."[2] Although systemic values are implicitly present in human experience, only a creative genius like Hartman could discover them and make explicit our awareness of them. What did Hartman mean by "systemic value" and its counterpart form of involvement "systemic valuation"?

Systemic Objects and Values

According to Hartman, in the most general sense of the term, value is the correspondence between the properties of an object and the predicates contained in the intension or meaning of the concept of that object.[3] This is the axiom or first principle of formal axiology. The concept of an object (or logical subject) consists in a set of predicates or attributes, and this set functions as a norm or standard by which things of that kind can be measured. Things have value to the extent that they fulfill their norms or standards.

However, there are many different kinds of objects, and there are many different kinds of concepts or standards by which to measure their correspondence. If we take an inventory of the universe, we will find that it consists fundamentally of individuals, the general properties that belong to individuals, and many entities which are pure creatures of thought and imagination that exist only in thought and imagination. Many purely mental entities belong to the domain of art and are the stuff of fiction and poetry, but many also belong to science and logic and are the stuff of the formal systems of science which give us immense power of prediction and control over the processes of nature. There are many things in the intellect which were not first in the senses. All the basic laws of logic and the fundamental axioms and concepts of all branches of mathematics are intellectual constructs. They are created by our minds, not abstracted from experience. Of course, we believe that numbers and formulas somehow express deep truths about reality as well, that an established harmony exists between intellect and reality.

Many basic and extremely useful notions of the physical sciences are also intellectual constructs, such as the concepts of points which have position without magnitude, lines which have length without breadth, bodies which are absolutely at rest, objects that travel faster than the speed of light, etc. Creations of the mind are among the most important and powerful concepts available to us in our attempts to know and control the world and its processes. We are interested in intellectual constructs partly because they are inherently fascinating and partly because they are extremely useful, but we definitely are interested in them. They are themselves important and distinctive human values. This was Hartman's brilliant insight when he first identified them and called them systemic values.

Just as all values involve the correspondence of objects with properties inherent in their concepts, so to do systemic values. However, systemic objects and concepts are quite peculiar. We cannot acquaint ourselves with systemic objects by sensory observation or introspective self-awareness, for they are not empirical objects. They are not perceived or experienced parts of the furniture of nature, though approximations to them may exist in nature. They exist only in our minds, but they order the furniture of nature for us in remarkable ways. We cannot perceive oneness, twoness, or threeness, but we can apply numbers to things and determine just how rich or poor we are. All purely systemic objects are like numbers in that they exist only as elements of, or terms within, mentally created or constructed systems. We create such systems to bring order out of chaos, but they exist only in our minds and only because we have created them. Their objects are mental constructs, not abstractions from experience.[4]

Not only are systemic <u>objects</u> mental constructs, but the <u>concepts</u> by which we measure them are mental constructs also. In fact, their objects <u>are identical</u> with the concepts which we have of them. In this respect also they are very different from other kinds of objects and concepts. Persons and pains and are not identical with our concepts of persons and pains, and

Socrates is not identical with our concept of Socrates. Yet, oneness is identical with our concept of oneness, and contradiction and identity are identical with our notions of contradiction and identity. All systemic intensional objects are identical with our concepts of them.

How can pure constructs ever be values that involve the correspondence of object and concept when they are objects that are their concepts? Can there be such things as systemic values? Yes. Hartman defined systemic value as "the fulfillment by an object of the schematic intension of its concept."[5] However, unlike other values, systemic values can never fail. Cars and trucks can fail to be good cars and trucks by not fulfilling the standards which we set for those kinds of things, but geometrical circles and triangles can never fail to be good circles or triangles as long as they are truly circles or triangles. Since systemic objects consist simply of their defining characteristics and of nothing more, they always have them. They always fulfill their concepts. Thus they are always valuable and cannot fail to be so as long as they are what they are. Hartman wrote that "In systemic value, the thing in question, by virtue of being, is as it ought to be...When it is not as it ought to be it is not."[6]

For this reason, Hartman believed that only two value predicates could ever apply to systemic objects, those of perfection on the one hand and nonperfection (or nonvalue) on the other.[7] A systemic object either perfectly fulfills its concept or it is just not that systemic object. According to Hartman, "A geometric circle that lacks a single one of the properties of the concept 'circle' - which is 'a plane closed curve equidistant from a center' - is not a circle. Hence, there are, geometrically, only perfect circles or noncircles."[8]

Just how finite, definite, and non-empirical are such formal geometrical concepts as "circle," "point," "line," etc. may be seen from examining the concept of a "circle," which is:

    a. a figure (shape) that is
    b. plane (flat, two dimensional),
    c. involving a line (a continuous connection between two points having no breadth or thickness),
    d. that is closed (turns back upon itself),
    e. curved (bent without angles),
    f. with points (positions in space having no size or magnitude)
    g. all along the line
    h. and in the center,
    i. with each point along the line at exactly an equal distance from the point in the center.

Obviously, no one has ever seen a geometrical circle, for they are composed of absolutely imperceptible lines without breadth and points without magnitude in exact relations. They exist only in thought.

Mental constructs such as those of logical systems, numbers, geometrical forms, points, lines, etc., have one great asset that other kinds of concepts do not have. Their meaning is absolutely precise, and they do not suffer from the indefiniteness of empirical concepts. This is so partly because they exist only as <u>terms</u> in a formal system and take their meaning from the precise position which they have in that system.[9] The number "one" takes its meaning from all its very precise relations with all other numbers. Indeed, any systemic concept is a constructed synthetic concept "in the sense of being part of a synthetic system."[10] Also, the elements of meaning, the intensional sets, incorporated into constructed concepts are always <u>definite and finite</u> in number and can be represented mathematically by the letter "n".[11] Almost any formal concept can be precisely and exhaustively described in one good sentence, but volumes would be required to describe exhaustively a chair, an automobile, a mountain, or an individual person. Hartman explained the precision of synthetic concepts and the systems which generate them in these words:

> The synthetic concepts...are constructed by the human mind, as for example, the concept "circle." The precision of any concept consists in the complete determination of its meaning in a minimum of terms...Only with constructive concepts can one be absolutely certain they contain all that their object does, for these constructs come about together with, and actually are, their object. They possess <u>complete</u> precision, for they are the creations of the human mind itself rather than abstractions.[12]

Systemic and Pseudo Systemic Values

Hartman realized that as we ordinarily use the word "system," there are several varieties of systems, i.e. of abstract patterns of interrelated elements; and this raises the possibility that there might be more than one kind of systemic value. Paradigmatic systems are those synthetic systems in which all components are precise formal systemic terms that have been created mentally and that exist only mentally. But in the natural sciences as we know them, in addition to such formal systems, we find many non-formal or pseudo-formal systems. These systems are composed of conceptual elements, but at least some of the concepts have an empirical reference.

For example, Latin words that have empirical reference are incorporated into our modern system of biological classification and nomenclature. The empirical meaning is never quite the same as that of everyday discourse, however. In biological nomenclature, our human species is "homo sapiens," meaning "man the knower." The beautiful flower which we call the "lilac" has the name "Syringa vulgaris," which means "common pipe." Hartman called these non-formal scientific definitional concepts "schemata," and he suggested that we can easily see the difference between a lilac and a Syringa vulgaris by substituting the latter for the former in a poem, or by trying to smell its fragrance.[13]

Hartman extended the scope of the concept of "systemic object" beyond purely formal constructs to include any finite and definite conceptual sets. Thus, the purely definitional intensions of all concepts, empirical or technical as well as formal, are systemic objects. Definitions are "schemata" for all concepts.[14] Their content is as definite as we can make it. As intensional systemic objects, they are also finite systemic values.

As organized bodies of knowledge, the natural and social sciences also make an important place for organized or systematic interrelations of purely empirical concepts, but these intermeshed concepts (which are systemic values) should not be confused with the phenomenal objects to which they refer (which are extrinsic values). The empirical parts of a living body, for example, are organized into such systems as the skeletal system, the respiratory system, the digestive system, the nervous system, the reproductive system, the muscular system, the excretory system, the circulatory system, the endocrine system, etc. The human body is a veritable system of systems! Societies, sub-groups, and societies of societies are organized into social systems, political systems, legal systems, caste systems, family systems, economic systems, ecosystems, solar systems, etc. Furthermore, in our attempt to know these empirical systems, we create the interpretative systems of psychology, sociology, history, political science, economics, ecology, astronomy, etc. Purely conceptual theories about empirical objects are systemic values; the phenomena themselves are extrinsic values.

Hartman did not think highly of systems of knowledge constructed entirely out of empirical concepts. He called them "analytic systems" because they are "nothing but chains of implications of more or less abstract concepts,"[15] i.e. of concepts which have been abstracted from our sensory experience of the world. He also called them "pseudo-systems,"[16] and he was convinced that they make little or no advance beyond ordinary language and common sense. In an unpublished paper titled "System and Pseudo-System in the Social Sciences," Hartman wrote:

The difference between a pseudo-system and a system proper is in the difference of language used in each. <u>A pseudo-system is any account of a set of phenomena in everyday language</u>. Nobody would call a newspaper editorial a system; but a work in philosophy is often called a system, though its logic is essentially the same as that of an editorial: its concepts are abstracted from sense reality, albeit to a very great height, and the procedure is by implication and analogy. <u>A system proper is an account of a set of phenomena in technical language, in particular in the formulae of mathematics</u>. In this sense Kant said rightly that there is only so much science in any account of reality as there is mathematics in it. A scientific or systematic account in this sense, is not an abstraction from sense reality but a <u>construction</u> of such a reality; it constructs its own sense reality. It does not proceed by implication and analogy, but constructs itself, by formal deduction, into an analogue of the reality it accounts for.[17]

Of course, in castigating, thus de-valuing, pseudo-systems, Hartman was promoting his own project of developing a true science or formal system of value that would go beyond traditional philosophical approaches, one that would revolutionize our understanding of the value domain in something like the way the systematic discoveries of Galileo and Newton revolutionized our understanding of the physical world. He wrote that:

Today's moral reality is still philosophical; it is not <u>fundamentally</u> different from that of antiquity or the Middle Ages. We have the same fundamental values and disvalues, even though we practice them with greater refinement, including torture. A moral <u>science</u> ought to revolutionize moral understanding itself and hence moral practice, in the same way that natural science has revolutionized our understanding of nature and our sensitivity to it. For this reason it is of fundamental importance to distinguish science from pseudo-science in the social disciplines. Pseudo-science, pseudo-systems, here obstruct moral progress.

Most of the so-called social sciences today are pseudo-systems consisting of sets of secondary properties and descriptions in everyday language. Usually, what is called "system" in social "science" is nothing but short-hand symbolizations by which words referring to secondary properties, say "rational" or "fat," are put into letter form, say "R" or "F". The resulting concatenation of letters is no different in structure from the original concatenation of words, and no new insight has been gained. Due to this fact, much of social "science" today has the same kind of humbug character that was had in earlier times by natural philosophy, e.g. alchemy, with its impressive but senseless symbolic apparatus. A true system must be axiomatic, not stenographic; an entirely new beginning must be made with it, and the investigator must have integrated the entireness of the material at his disposal into exact quantitative form which as such has nothing directly to do with the original observational material, but which mirrors its structure...

A truly new thought is an axiom, which means, an entirely new setting for a problem, that is, for a set of phenomena previously distorted. The scientist who creates an axiom, in transforming secondary into primary properties, steps, like Alice, through the looking-glass, putting his whole world of phenomena into an entirely new medium. A good example is the difference between Aristotle and Galileo. Aristotle used many words such as "transition from potentiality to actuality," "the movable qua moveable" and the like to describe, in secondary properties, the movements of all kinds of things - cars, animals, stars, things, thoughts, the soul, God, and so on - making movement the central theme of the world and creating the most gigantic pseudo-system of history. Galileo, instead of describing all kinds of secondary properties, defined motion as a simple arithmetical relation, that of division, his formula for velocity being the quotient of the space and time in question, $v = s/t$. This was the first step: stepping through the looking-glass, by producing an arithmetical function for a set of observational phenomena. Continuing his looking-glass logic, and without any further recourse to observation, Galileo went on arguing: If $v = s/t$, then $vt = s$, and if this is so, then s is a rectangle consisting of the sides v and t; what is needed then, is to investigate this rectangle, its angles, diagonals, etc. Consequently, he proceeded to draw rectangles, triangles and the like, and produced a miniature geometry which became the science of mechanics.[18]

To get back to our original problem, if there are both systems proper and pseudosystems, does this mean that there is more than one kind of systemic value, or that we need to make a place for both systemic and pseudosystemic values? Do pseudosystemic values really belong to the domain of the systemic? Since they are measured by analytic concepts, do they not really belong to the domain of extrinsic values? Are they perhaps something intermediate between systemic values and extrinsic values, raising the possibility that Hartman's three-tiered value hierarchy might need four or more tiers? What, if anything, could systemic and pseudosystemic values have in common?

In reply, it appears that pseudosystemic objects really are systemic values in the sense that they consist of extremely limited sets of purely conceptual elements. <u>All finite and definite sets of intensions are systemic objects</u> and thus are systemic values. However, sets and systems of sets of analytical or empirical intensions should not be confused with <u>their referents</u> or extensions, for these are extrinsic objects and values.

The objects known in the sciences differ from that knowledge itself in many important ways. Consider, if you will, the value of the stomach in the digestive system. Both "stomach" and "digestive systems" are concepts which may be defined in finite sentences, but their referents are empirical objects. They are not conceptual constructs. They cannot be described exhaustively by a few properties; their intension is not exceedingly finite. Their referents are not identical with their defining properties; they exist in the physical world, not merely intramentally; and they exemplify innumerable expositional properties in addition to those few which define them. Their value is not an all or nothing affair; they are good, average, fair, or worthless by degrees. Thus, they would seem to be extrinsic rather than systemic objects. It is only our knowledge of them that is systemic. These things are true of all pseudosystemic objects, whether they belong to digestive systems, family systems, political systems, economic systemic, ecological systems, and all empirical or worldly systems.

Of course, some empirical entities and our concepts of them resemble each other in one important respect; <u>they are what they are because of their relations</u>. They are not themselves in splendid isolation. In some very important and obvious sense, their internal relations with other things make them what they are. A stomach would simply not be a stomach apart from a digestive system. As Aristotle noted, a hand is not really a hand apart from a human or living body. Having just the relations that it has with the body is integral to its being a hand that functions as a hand. The internality of the relations of pseudosystemic objects to their larger context is <u>not</u> sufficient to transform them into systemic <u>values</u>. Even here, we must keep track of the distinction between <u>concepts of relations</u> and what Whitehead called "<u>concrete facts of relatedness</u>." The former are systemic entities, the latter empirical.

Systemic Valuation

Robert S. Hartman was as much interested in the topic of <u>valuation</u> as in that of values, and he made important contributions to our understanding of both. Let us remind ourselves that <u>value as such</u> is concept or standard fulfillment, and that <u>valued objects</u> are intentional objects (or logical subjects) which fulfil their concepts or standards. We valuate values, and <u>valuation</u> is the process or activity of being consciously involved with valuable objects. Valuation is how we attach value to things, and in the broadest possible sense valuation is conscious involvement. (This definition is more fundamental than Hartman's, as expressed in the bottom paragraph below.) Normal consciousness is always intentional, i.e. it is inescapably involved with its objects of awareness. Thus, consciousness is valuation. Every form of conscious involvement, including conscious sensation, is valuation; and to study valuation we must simply study consciousness in all its dimensions.

Obviously, there are many forms of conscious involvement. There are many kinds of objects with which consciousness is involved. We now understand the nature of systemic objects of value. Next, we must try to comprehend the forms of conscious involvement that are typically associated with systemic concepts and objects. We must try to understand the nature of systemic valuation.

There are cognitive, operational, and affective dimensions to valuation, including systemic valuation, according to Hartman. In describing the cognitive aspect, Hartman wrote that valuation is the "combinatorial arrangement of the things properties,"[19] that is, it "arranges and re-arranges the properties of things."[20] Hartman defined value sensitivity as "the capacity of matching a set of predicates one has in mind with a set of properties one recognizes in an actual thing or situation."[21] In this sense, valuation is "an act of value subsumption."[22] Insisting that both cognitive and affective aspects are essential, Hartman affirmed that "Valuation is no more nor less a matter of feeling than is music. It is a matter of feeling structured by laws--feeling following definite laws. The feeling of value is nothing arbitrary."[23] In recognizing that we create values when we act to combine values, Hartman also recognized a dynamic dimension to valuation.

Cognitively, systemic valuation is a habit of mind that measures by systemic standards, makes wholesale "all or nothing" judgments and focuses exclusively on finite sets of properties in its objects. Dynamically, it is the combination of systemic objects with other objects. Emotionally it is deliberate detachment or objectivity, originally designed for purposes of conceptual clarity and fair mindedness. Let us examine these in greater depth.

(1) Cognitively systemic valuation is the measurement of an object by a systemic standard. As such, it is an all or nothing mode of conceptual measurement. Remember that systemic objects either perfectly exemplify their properties, or they are of no systemic value at all. The proper counterpart of systemic values in consciousness is a certain mind-set, a certain mode of conceptual measurement. Just as systemic values are all or nothing,

so systemic valuation is a sweeping "all or nothing," "either/or," "black or white," "absolutely for or against" mentality. Cognitively, systemic valuation is a habit of mind that finds positive worth, indeed perfection, in things as long as they are <u>everything</u> that they should be; but it finds worthlessness, non-value, wherever there is the tiniest flaw.

Where it positively enhances the value with which it is combined, the "all or nothing" feature of systemic valuation is most appropriate and useful. I, and I alone, either have or do not have <u>my</u> Social Security number or my numerical slot on the waiting list; and I am quite happy about that. Hartman wrote that

> Not all systemic valuation is evil. It is evil only when it is a transposition - when applied to situations where it is inappropriate. Many things in our individual and social life <u>must</u> be valued systemically. Scientific constructs must be valued this way, and the rigorous discipline of systemic valuation in general is necessary for modern society and is precisely what we saw American education is lacking, as against European education. There are even life situations where systemic valuation is necessary: all situations where no play is allowed and it is a matter of either being or not being. Thus, when meeting a deadline, when making a train, when stopping at a redlight or before a railroad crossing - you either do or you don't - and when you don't you miss, and sometimes (lose) your life. The saying that a miss is as good as a mile expresses systemic valuation. Systemic valuation is necessary in all situations that demand discipline...It is necessary in all situations of emergency...Where numerical order is important, as in tagging the right baby of the right mother, there is no badness in systemic valuation.[24]

Systemic valuation may be and often is applied to other things besides systemic objects. It may be applied to people, to things, to beliefs, to anything. When the "all or nothing" feature of systemic valuation is used to detract from the value of the entity valuated, it can be pernicious. "Since it belongs to constructions of the mind it is obvious that when applied to actual beings it 'prejudges' them."[25] It is the mind-set of totalitarianism, reductionism, perfectionism, dogmatism, ideology, and prejudice. When the systemic valuation of non-systemic objects so detracts from their worth that they are reduced to systemic objects, systemic valuation is always disvaluation or transposition. Of course, many of the systems we actually use to devalue persons are pseudosystems that involve finite empirical elements integrated into abstract patterns which are employed to impose order--elements such as color of skin (racism), gender (sexism), national origin (nationalism), biological classification (speciesism), or social class or status (snobbery). Here, only those who fit the system have value, and those who do not are worthless.

Systemic valuation is often the first step of our conscious involvement with something new as we try to make sense of it by giving it some place in a pre-existing conceptual scheme, and in that sense pre-judgments (prejudices) are not always objectionable. However, we must be careful not to continue to treat persons or things as if they are nothing more than what our initial prejudices judge them to be, careful to use our pre-judgments, not to degrade, but as building blocks for further exploration and enrichment.

(2) <u>Dynamically</u>, systemic valuation is the activity of combining systemic objects with other objects. These objects themselves may be either systemic, or extrinsic, or intrinsic. Adding (or performing any mathematical operation on) two numbers is the systemic valuation of a systemic value, as is the identification of two formal concepts, as in the Whitehead/Russell definition of "number" as "the class of all similar classes."[26] Designating a piece of clothing as a uniform is an example of the systemic valuation of an extrinsic object. Clothing belongs to the perceptual world; but in identifying it as a uniform, we turn it into the symbol of a military system, a medical system, a police system, etc. Only when the system has been added does clothing become a uniform, which is the systemic valuation of an extrinsic value. When we grind lenses according to the science of optics to create eyeglasses or when we introduce computer guidance systems into projectiles to make "smart bombs," we combine the systemic with the extrinsic. Again, when we philosophize about intrinsic value, we combine the purely conceptual with the inherently precious; and the result is the systemic valuation of intrinsic value.

(3) <u>Affectively</u>, systemic valuation is emotional detachment, objectivity, disinterestedness; but it should not be confused with uninterestedness. Emotionally, systemic valuation is a form of conscious involvement that approximates non-involvement without being non-involvement. Intrinsic valuation is the richest and deepest form of conscious involvement; by contrast, systemic valuation is a form of shallow involvement. It is not as shallow as total indifference or uninterestedness, for it is not oblivion. Rather, in its native and most proper home, it is deliberate detachment for purposes of cognitive clarity and fair-mindedness. Instead of being uninterestedness, it is open-minded interestedness. In relation to systemic objects, it is a commendable form of relatively uninvolved involvement. In the pursuit of knowledge, it is indispensable in both the formal and non-formal sciences. Hartman wrote that "natural science measurement is that of systemic value, or rather of a species of systemic value, the application of system to exten-

sions... Systemic measurement is the abstract, formal kind of measurement used by the scientist, objective and detached."[27]

Outside of the quest for knowledge, the objectivity and detachment of systemic valuation may be an unacceptable form of emotional involvement, though it is certainly a possible one. Hartman discussed Ortega y Gasset's treatment of the degrees of emotional involvement in the death of a dying man by the man's wife, by a reporter who has come to record and report the event, by the attending physician, and by a painter who has come merely to paint a picture and who sees only "lines shapes, colors, systemic aspects of an event whose intrinsic meaning escapes him and indeed does not interest him." Here the painter's detachment makes him "aloof" and "unconcerned," and gives him "a maximum of distance with a minimum of feeling..."[28] Of course, as Hartman noted, Ortega's unconcerned painter is a very atypical artist, for painters are usually intensely involved emotionally with (i.e. they intrinsically valuate) what they paint.[29]

In discussing the topic of pain, Hartman indicated that we are very much involved with our own pains, but in dealing with the pains of others we may become professionally aloof and express our emotional distance by saying something like: "The patient in (room) eighteen has a referred pain in the sternocleidomastoid." In such circumstances the pain is "not of a person but of a certain physiological and medical entity, a unit in a certain hospital room with a certain pathological symptom. Here pain is precisely determined within a network of relations and belongs to systemic value language."[30]

Hartman noted that forms of valuation are very fluid in the human psyche, that we are never stuck where we are, and that one form may lead to another as consciousness is successively enriched (or impoverished). By a process of enrichment, systemic valuation may lead to extrinsic, then to intrinsic valuation.

> The relationship between systemic, extrinsic and intrinsic value corresponds to a process of continuous enrichment with definite leaps from one value dimension to the next. Thus, if I buy a package of cigarettes from a saleslady I am in a legal, a systemic relationship with her. If I take her out for dinner I am in an extrinsic relationship, and if I take her to church and marry her I am in an intrinsic relationship with her: my total being is joined with here in a common intrinsic Gestalt. This Gestalt grew through successive enrichments, out of the first tenuous bond, the original sales contract.

All intrinsic relationships, except those of the family, grow out of systemic and/or extrinsic relations through processes of enrichment; and such processes are as common as is intrinsic value itself.[31]

Systemic Disvalues and Devaluation

Hartman's "value exponentation" allows for values and valuations to be positively combined in many ways, as we have seen. Systemic values may be positively valuated systemically, extrinsically, and intrinsically; and there may be systemic valuations of systemic, extrinsic, and intrinsic values. Values and valuations may be negatively combined as well. Systemic values may be disvalued systemically, extrinsically or intrinsically; and there may be systemic devaluations of extrinsic, intrinsic and even of systemic values.[32] Hartman called such combinations "value transpositions," which he understood to be the negative valuation of one mode of value (or valuation) by another.[33] They are combinations that reduce or destroy value. He defined <u>disvalue</u> or <u>negative value</u> in terms of "ought," i.e. "the negative value (of a thing) is that which it ought not to be," just as its positive value is "that which the valued thing ought to be."[34]

Each dimension of value sets its own "oughts." Our present interest is in systemic "oughts" and "ought-nots." Presumably a <u>systemic disvalue</u> would be either (1) the failure of a systemic object to fulfill a systemic intension that ought to be fulfilled, or (2) the combination of a systemic with a non-systemic object (i.e. one that is more, and ought not to be excessively finitized or trivialized) that reduces it to a mere token within a system (or pseudosystem). Let us examine these in more detail.

(1) Since systemic objects always fulfill their intensions, it seems doubtful initially that there could be any systemic objects that fail to fulfill their systemic intensions. However, we often <u>try</u> to do the impossible with concepts, either deliberately or inadvertently; and <u>that</u> will generate systemic disvalue. <u>The product of any formal mistake in conceiving or reasoning is a systemic disvalue.</u> Hartman identified <u>contradiction or counter-sense</u>[35] as a paradigm of systemic disvalue. When we generate contradictions, we attempt futilely to do the impossible with concepts by producing concepts which cannot possibly be fulfilled, concepts which cannot possibly fulfil their "ought" for they have no intelligible "ought."[36] Hartman explained that:

> In the statement that "a thing can be and not be at the same time," we have a new transposition: <u>counter-sense</u> (<u>Widersinn</u>). In this kind of transposition subject and predicate are coherent; the addition of "not" to the proposition would give it perfect sense. Similar

contradictions are committed in the following examples: "a pentagon has twelve sides"; "physical being is immeasurable"; "two bodies may occupy the same place at the same time"; "houses cannot be lived in"; "bachelors are married"; "war is peace." In all these propositions the predicates contradict the meaning of the subject. It can be demonstrated that they are false, they are formally false. The transposition is systemic; what is transposed are systemic values.[37]

In the fictional world envisioned by George Orwell's 1984 where "War is Peace," and "Freedom is Slavery" contradictions which have no intelligible fulfillment create an impossible way of life. Besides logical contradiction, there are many other kinds of systemic disvalue. Any false definition, any mathematical miscalculation, any erroneous programming, any purely conceptual error, is a systemic disvalue.

(2) Some systemic disvalues are actually non-systemic objects, rich in properties, but made to be poor in properties by shrinking them to the finite significance that they have as mere elements in a system. Systemic value is finitized value, and systemically disvalued extrinsic and intrinsic objects are inordinately finitized by ignoring all their non-systemic properties.

If we create systemic disvalues by trying to do the impossible with concepts, or by reducing valued objects to their functions or positions in a system, how do we create systemic disvaluations? Let us recall that cognitively, systemic valuation is the measurement of objects by finite conceptual intensions. Dynamically, it is the combination of a systemic object with some other that diminishes its worth. Affectively it is detached or dispassionate involvement. What could the contrasting notion of systemic disvaluation possibly be?

There are at least two forms of systemic disvaluation, depending upon whether the objects disvalued are, or are not, systemic objects. The systemic disvaluation of systemic objects is the activity of annihilating conceptual meaning (or value) in a cool and detached frame of mind, of dispassionately generating conceptual error or unintelligibility. The systemic disvaluation of extrinsic and intrinsic objects is either the cold, calculating reduction of their significance to finite elements in a system or the cold calculating combination of them with systemic objects which diminish their value. It is pervasive and pernicious, and we must explore it in greater depth.

Hartman was convinced that "in most life situations...systemic valuation is out of place."[38] When applied to persons or things, systemic valuation can be reductive if it coldly disregards or diminishes their richness, reducing their significance to that of minimal finite factors in a system. He wrote that "The world of systemic valuation is not only that of systems as in science, but also in other fields: ideologies, slogans, rituals, psychological illusions and delusions, imaginings, and orders of all kinds, from monastic and military orders to the routine of the household."[39] He explained that:

> This is the model of black and white valuation of things, the simplest kind of valuation there is. Since it belongs to constructions of the mind it is obvious that when applied to actual things it "prejudges" them--it is the model of prejudice. This kind of thinking is based on the logical category of limitation; the variety of the world is limited to only two distinctions: A and non-A (e.g. white and non-white, Communists and non-Communists). Such persons are limited, <u>bornées</u>, value blind, in the same sense that a person is unmusical who only knows two tunes, the one that is the Star-Spangled Banner and the other that is not. Systemic valuation is the model of schematic and dogmatic thinking.[40]

Systemic disvaluation suffers from <u>two obvious flaws</u> when applied to non-systemic objects like persons or things. <u>First</u>, it recognizes no shades of gray, and it treats all things as worthless that have even the slightest imperfections (as all things have except formally constructed concepts.) Systemic disvaluation is the mentality of:

--a Biblical Inerrancy which says that either the scriptures are flawless or they are worthless.
--a perfectionism which says that a new car with its first dent is totally ruined or that the person who makes a small social mistake is utterly humiliated.
--a dogmatism which says that either you are totally for me or totally against me.
--an authoritarianism which makes a place for only true believers and the damned.
--a totalitarianism which says that either you conform or you die, you are nothing.

<u>Next</u>, just as systemic objects have only a definite few properties, so systemic disvaluation is a habit of mind that focuses upon a limited set of properties in its objects and is blind to all else. There is nothing wrong with positive systemic valuation that enhances value. However, when we systemically devalue, we degrade and diminish value; and serious problems may arise. Systemic devaluation is a mind set that habitually disregards the richness of its objects. The systemic devaluation of extrinsic and intrinsic objects grotesquely distorts, underestimates and depreciates their worth. It refuses to see and to appreciate the richness that is there to behold. Socrates

systemically depreciated all the magnificent but non-philosophical features of human life when he claimed that "The unexamined life is not worth living." Hartman gave the reason why the systemic valuation of persons easily degenerates into their devaluation. It is because

> The subjects of <u>logical or systemic</u> valuation are things in a minimum relationship: as elements of a system or as schemata. A schema is less real than any empirical thing. When human beings are valued systemically they are less real than, say, a piece of paper. In a bureaucratic procedure a person does not exist unless he has a birth certificate. At the border he does not exist unless he has a passport.[41]

"Better dead than Red" says in effect that unless persons are non-communists, their lives are utterly worthless. Human relations are regularly poisoned by such systemic distortions, underestimations and trivializations, of human worth.

Hartman was keenly aware of the pervasiveness of the systemic devaluation of persons in the modern world. He wrote that

> Any bureaucratic procedure that sees not humans but instances of a rule, any authoritarian person that tries to impose his will by using the rules of a system, any procedure that imposes conformity is guilty of this evil of transposition of the logical and the axiological. It is the use of a system which gives evil the power to extend its range, and at the same time, to assume the resemblance of good. All great evil is systemic evil.[42]

In his previously unpublished paper titled "The Nature of Valuation," Hartman explained that systemic valuation, with its potential for immense systemic evil, manifests itself in such things as:

1. War, where persons are reduced to numbers, as on dog tags or in body counts and casualty statistics.[43] (In our most recent 1991 war in the Middle East, civilian casualties were disguised as "collateral damage," and military casualties were covered by "bomb damage assessments.")

2. "The love of the uniform in Europe, Asia, and South America which cancels individuality and gives anonymity and prestige in uniformity."[44]

3. Impressive looking passports which gain special treatment for their bearers.[45]

4. The reduction of prisoners to penal serial numbers.[46]

5. The reduction of patients to "cases."[47]

6. Treating a corpse as "number 2,432," whose funeral is "scheduled for parlor 43 for a certain day at a certain hour, with preacher number fourteen, singer number 87, rendering music number 174, and flowers and decorations class B."[48] (From Ralph Borsodi's This Ugly Civilization.)

7. The "pure specialist" who becomes a learned ignoramus because he "only knows systems; as a specialist he looks at the world itself as a system. In doing so the world is distorted."[49]

8. Dictators that arise initially to create systems out of chaos, for "the age-old prescription for tyrants is first to manufacture emergencies and then appear as savior."[50]

9. Nazi Germany which reduced people to "elements of the system, and all their intrinsic and extrinsic differences are erased; they are, as individuals, unavailable. There is nothing but a mass of interchangeable, formless elements: chaos numbered and indexed. The culmination of such systemic organization was Nazi Germany."[51]

10. The theological concept of God as "the perfect being...the prototype of all systemic things."[52]

Reductionism in such disciplines as psychology and metaphysics is another pernicious and misleading form of systemic devaluation. Consider the thesis of behaviorism that the whole human psyche is nothing more than externally observable human behavior, or the dogma of mechanistic materialism that persons are nothing more than matter in motion in accord with deterministic laws.

Systemic Confusions and Errors

Intrinsic relationships may grow out of systemic relations through progressive enrichments of involvement. Nevertheless, systemic values should not be confused with intrinsic values, and we should not systemically disvaluate intrinsic values. Hartman believed that we are often confused and make value mistakes, and that the study of and application of formal axiology could help us avoid value confusions and errors. Psychologically, it is possible to confuse systemic value with any form of value; but, Hartman thought, the most commonplace value confusion is that of systemic with intrinsic value. He explained that:

> our capacity for valuation all but breaks down as soon as systemic or intrinsic valuation is required. Then there appear confusions both in practice and in theory. The most fundamental, most consequential, and most prevalent such confusion is that between systemic and intrinsic value--both equally unknown theoretically--which appears, in practice, in the confusion of systemic value with "spiritual" value, in the hypostatizations of national, social, theological, and other ideologies as demanding man's supreme loyalties...[53]

The exact basis of the confusion of the intrinsic with the systemic is not clear from what Hartman says, but we can develop an axiological analysis that will help us to see the point. The confusion of the intrinsic with the systemic seems to result when (1) we intrinsically valuate mentally constructed systemic objects, which like intrinsic objects are non-sensory or non-empirical and (2) then mistakenly believe that these systemic objects are far richer in properties than they actually are, that they are as rich in properties as intrinsic entities.

To valuate an object intrinsically is to be maximally involved with it both emotionally and conceptually. To be an intrinsic object to be maximally rich in properties, and to be a systemic object is to be minimally rich in properties. Now, there is no confusion in maximal conscious involvement with minimal objects, as long as we know what we are doing. At times, however, we do not know what we are doing. We become maximally involved with minimal objects, forget what they are, and muddle-headedly identify or confuse them with maximal objects. Examples of the intrinsic valuation of minimal objects, as if they are objects of far greater value, are not hard to find. Consider, if you will, the muddle-headed confusion of:

1. The Flag (as a symbol, not as a physical object) with the rights and freedoms of the Constitution, or with the Republic for which it stands.

2. The Bible with the God to which it testifies.

3. Maps with the territory that they represent .

4. Words with the things that they denote.

5. Ideologies with the people that are sacrificed in their promotion.

6. Dogma with divinity.

7. Slogans and shibboleths with principles.

8. The 30 second commercial with the politician.

Can you think of other circumstances in which systemic value is confused with intrinsic or extrinsic value?

Hartman's theory of systemic values and valuations may itself be valued systemically, extrinsically, or intrinsically. I have learned so much from it that I tend to value it intrinsically, while operating systemically within it, and while not confusing it with intrinsic value. I hope that many others may come to do the same.

NOTES

1. Robert S. Hartman, The Structure of Value, Carbondale, Southern Illinois University Press, 1967, p. 252.

2. Ibid., p. 330, n. 29. See also p. 295.

3. Ibid., p. 154.

4. Hartman repeatedly affirmed that systemic entities are mental constructs. See The Structure of Value, pp. 38, 79ff, 82ff, 112, 116, 194, 252, 253, 254.

5. Ibid., p. 275.

6. Ibid., p. 253.

7. Ibid., p. 194. On p. 112 Hartman used the terminology of "perfect" versus "nonvalue."

8. Robert S. Hartman, "The Value Structure of Creativity," The Journal of Value Inquiry, Vol. VI, Winter 1972, p. 253.

9. Hartman, The Structure of Value., pp. 85, 87, 88, 250, 253.

10. Ibid., p. 79.

11. Ibid., pp. 19, 112, 222, 257, 359 n. 41.

12. Ibid., p. 81.

13. Ibid., p. 349, n. 8.

14. Robert S. Hartman, "The Logic of Value," The Review of Metaphysics, Vol. XIV, March 1961, pp. 392, 398.

15. Hartman, The Structure of Value, p. 32. See also pp. 31-54, 79-92.

16. Ibid., p. 47. See also his unpublished paper titled "System and Pseudo-System in the Social Sciences."

17. Hartman, "System and Pseudo-System in the Social Sciences," unpublished paper, p. 1.

18. Ibid., pp. 6, 7, 8.

19. Hartman, The Structure of Value, p. 215. See also pp. 19, 216, 217.

20. Hartman, "The Value Structure of Creativity," p. 252.

21. Robert S. Hartman, The Hartman Value Profile (HVP) Manual of Interpretation, Muskegon, MI, Research Concepts, 1973, p. 30.

22. Robert S. Hartman, "The Nature of Valuation," p. 7.

23. Hartman, The Structure of Value, p. 129. See also Hartman's discussion of the importance to valuation of approval and disapproval, pp. 246f, 248, and pro-attitudes, p. 345, n. 20.

24. Robert S. Hartman, "The Nature of Valuation," a previously unpublished manuscript that appears for the first time in this volume, pp. 33, 34.

25. Hartman, "The Value Structure of Creativity," p. 254.

26. Hartman, The Structure of Value, pp. 17, 51.

27. Hartman, "The Value Structure of Creativity," pp. 250, 251.

28. Ibid., pp. 261, 262.

29. Hartman, The Structure of Value, p. 357, n. 27.

30. Ibid., pp. 255, 256.

31. Ibid., pp. 223-224.

32. See Hartman's examples, Ibid., p. 273.

33. Ibid., p. 268.

34. Ibid.

35. Ibid., p. 269.

36. Ibid., pp. 271-272.

37. Ibid., p. 270.

38. Hartman, "The Nature of Valuation," this volume, p. 33.

39. Hartman, "The Value Structure of Creativity," pp. 253-254.

40. Hartman, The Structure of Value, pp. 112-113.

41. Hartman, "The Nature of Valuation," this volume, p. 25.
42. Ibid., p. 20.
43. Ibid.
44. Ibid., p. 25.
45. Ibid.
46. Ibid., p. 32.
47. Ibid.
48. Ibid.
49. Ibid., pp. 26-27.
50. Ibid., p. 20.
51. Ibid.
52. Ibid., p. 34.
53. Hartman, The Structure of Value, p. 252.

Chapter IV

EXTRINSIC VALUE AND VALUATION

John W. Davis

Robert S. Hartman's task was to turn moral philosophy into moral science, and he provided at least the foundations for such science in his writings, especially his major work, The Structure of Value; Foundations of a Scientific Axiology.[1] This work offers both a formal frame of reference, a logic of value, for value sciences and a beginning for the application of this logic, especially with respect to extrinsic value, our present topic. Let us start by placing Hartman's efforts within the context of Twentieth Century ethics.

The Problem: The Relation of Value to Natural Properties

The direction of his work was strongly influenced by G. E. Moore, who, according to Hartman, was the Galileo of value science. In terms of the nomenclature of contemporary ethics, Moore was a cognitivist, a non-naturalist, and an intuitionist. He believed that there can be moral knowledge, but that value, whether moral or some other, cannot be defined in naturalistic terms. Moore's Principia Ethica, first published in 1903, gave impetus to a theme, "What is good?" that captured the interest of many later philosophers, including Hartman. Moore began by proclaiming that many of the difficulties and disagreements in ethics are mainly due to a very simple cause: "namely to attempt to answer questions, without first discovering what question it is which you desire to answer."[2] Philosophers talk about the nature of good, right, duty, and so on, but the basic question, which must be answered first is "What is good?" Until this question is answered, Moore believes, we cannot know either what things are good or what acts are right. But Moore reaches an astonishing conclusion:

If I am asked 'What is good?' my answer is that good is good, and that is the end of the matter. Or if I am asked 'How is good to be defined?' my answer is that it cannot be defined, and that is all I have to say about it.³

But not quite. He went on to say that good is something simple, unanalyzable, non-isolatable, not in space and time, analogous to number and truth, dependent on natural (descriptive) properties but is not itself such a property, and, moreover, that while we cannot prove that something is intrinsically good, if it is, then most of us will "see" that it is--hence his intuitionism.

Hartman, like many of his contemporaries, was struck by Moore's insight that while a thing's goodness is not one of its descriptive properties yet its goodness depends only on these descriptive, or natural, properties. How goodness, a non-natural, non-descriptive property could depend on natural, or descriptive, properties was a problem that Moore wrestled with, especially in his chapter on the concept of intrinsic value in his Philosophical Studies, but did not resolve. Moore concludes that if a thing is good, then it must have the descriptive properties it has. But why must it? What is the connection between good and the other properties? Moore rejects the answers given by others: this connection is neither definitional, psychological (emotional), causal (empirical), nor logical. For naturalists and traditional subjectivists like E. A. Westermarck (Origin and Development of Moral Ideas, 1906; Ethical Relativity, 1932) and Ralph Barton Perry (General Theory of Value, 1926; Realms of Value, 1954) this connection is one of definition. If a thing is good, then it is an object of positive emotion (retributive kindly emotion, for Westermarck; positive interest, for Perry). This is a statement of definitional implication. Good means positive emotions or interest. Moore rejects their explanations as instances of the naturalistic fallacy: it is fallacious to identify good, which is not a natural property, with any natural property what-so-ever. John Dewey's position (Theory of Valuation, 1939), a more objective form of naturalism, is rejected for the same reason. For Dewey emotion is a necessary but not a sufficient condition for value. It is raw material for evaluation. Intelligence must be added. That something is good means not merely that it is liked, desired, or enjoyed, but that it will do; that it has serviceability, as determined by intelligence, in fulfilling the requirements of a situation involving an organism in interaction with its environment. But this, too, is to identify good with natural, or descriptive, properties.

The newer subjectivists, emotivists like A. J. Ayer (Language, Truth, and Logic, 1936) and Charles Stevenson (Ethics and Language, 1944), accused Moore of confusing intuitions of non-natural properties with emotional responses. The connection between some supposed property, good, and descriptive properties is psychological or emotional. Beliefs concerning descriptive properties cause emotional responses; such beliefs are persuasive. As Ayer might say, to attribute goodness to something is to vent positive emotion in response to it. The word "good" is nothing more than an ejaculation of warm feeling.

Other philosophers, more in the mainstream of contemporary analytic philosophy, argued that the clue to Moore's puzzle was to be found in studies of the use of the word "good" in a wide range of contexts, even in those in which little, if any, emotion is involved. Thus J. O. Urmson in a classic article, "On Grading" (Mind, 1950), looks at good within the wide framework of general evaluation and concludes that its non-natural character is that of a grading label. "Good" as a grading label is like "fair," "bad," "extra fancy," "prime," and so on. Assigning a grade is a matter of neither subjective liking nor intuition; rather it is a formal matter of meeting grading criteria. The assignment of "good" to a thing, like the assignment of the grade "A" to a student, or the grade "extra fancy" to an apple, is objectively decidable. But not objectively decidable in the sense that a grade is a sensible property. Just as one does not see, smell, taste, hear, or touch the student's grade or the extra fanciness of apples, one does not have sensible impressions of good. If an apple has been given the grade "extra fancy," then it has certain natural, or descriptive, properties of size, color, texture, etc. that can be sensed and are required for that grade. So too for things graded as good. Urmson concludes that "'good' is a grading label applicable in many different types of contexts, but with different criteria for employment in each." Hence Urmson's solution to Moore's puzzle is that if a thing is good, it has the descriptive properties corresponding to those of the criteria for that grade in a specific context. The connection between good and the properties is both formal and conventional; criteria must be met, but these are a matter of convention.

R. M. Hare (The Language of Morals, 1952) agrees with Moore and Urmson that good is not a natural property but that it depends on natural properties. It is not a natural property, for "good" is a commending word, and if a thing is said to be good, then it is being commended for having the properties it has. It's goodness depends on natural properties in the sense that good is a "supervenient" or "consequential" property of such properties. Good follows from those descriptive, "good-making," properties in that the thing possessing them is praised for having them. We commend things, according to Hare, in order to guide choices, and because of this purpose there is a certain logic with respect to the use of the word "good." If an apple is said to be good then any apple like it would be good. If this were not so, then choices would not be guided through the use of "good." Hence for Hare value judgments are covertly universal; a class of comparison is implied and criteria are prescribed. Here, as for Urmson, the connection between good and the natural properties is both formal and conventional: the commendation is entailed by the correspondence of the thing's properties to those prescribed for its class of comparison, but these requirements are a matter of convention and of preference.

Hartman's Solution: Value as Concept Fulfillment

At first glance, Robert S. Hartman's account of value is similar to that proposed by Urmson and Hare. "If a thing has all the properties which it is supposed to have," says Hartman, "then it is good." As we have seen, the "properties which it is supposed to have" are, for Urmson, those that fit the criteria for the grade, and, for Hare, those good-making properties required for commending a thing of its kind. But for Hartman "the properties which it is supposed to have" are, generally speaking, those properties designated by its concept. If a thing has all the properties corresponding to the attributes of its concept then it is good. Thus Hartman defines value in terms of concept fulfillment.

Hare appears to reject this. He states that the process of making known a standard for judging a thing good has "certain features in common with the process of defining (making known the meaning or application of) a descriptive word, though there are important differences."[4] Since the function of the word "good" is to guide choice, the properties commended through its use may not be those referred to in the meaning of the concept. "Good" may be used to change this meaning. Evaluative force may alter descriptive meaning. For Hartman, "good" and other value words are used to indicate how well things exemplify concepts. They are measures of exemplification, of degrees of meaning. Thus the word "good" indicates that a thing has the full meaning of its concept. Choices may be guided, but this is incidental. Hartman attributes to value words a much more formal character than does Hare. For Hare, users of value words have a common intent, namely guiding choice, and the logic of such words follows from this. For Hartman, the logic of value is not one of intention of persons but of intension of concepts. It is a logic of the intensional meaning of concepts, as we shall see.

Like G. E. Moore, Hartman is a non-naturalist, for he rejects the belief that good is a natural, descriptive property, and he believes that good depends only on these natural properties; but unlike Moore, he shows how good depends on these properties and how, as a consequence, good can be defined. Moore was concerned with defining good philosophically, or analytically, as an abstract concept, and this, Hartman agrees, cannot be done. But Moore's conclusion that a thing's goodness depends only on it natural properties suggests to Hartman that good can be defined synthetically, as a technical, scientific term. The key to the meaning of good is to see it as a logical operation: when good is attributed to a thing the properties of a concept are combined with the idea of the thing; a concept is exemplified by the thing. Good is a logical term that indicates that a concept is fully exemplified by a thing. Good is thus defined in terms of the logical relationship of class and member. If a thing has all the properties which it is supposed to have as a class member, then it fully exemplifies its class concept, and is a good such class member. Good is not a property of a thing, but is a property of the properties of a thing. It is not a first but second order property. Actually, it is a property of a thing's properties insofar as these properties are seen as reflecting class membership. It the property of completeness with respect to the set of the expositional properties of the relevant class.

Speaking precisely, the descriptive properties upon which the value, "good," as defined by Hartman, depends are the "expositional" properties of an abstract concept. As we shall see, Hartman distinguishes between definition and exposition. The expositional meaning of a concept designating a group of empirical things is obtained by abstracting, one by one, the descriptive properties common to the group, and, theoretically, there is no limit to the number of properties that could be abstracted. The definition of the group's concept is a minimum statement of this exposition. Thus Hartman argues that belonging to a class is definitional fulfillment, but being a good member of the class is expositional fulfillment. He writes, "The definitional properties must in all cases be fulfilled; the value differentiations adhere to the expositional properties exclusively."[5] Hence, for example, a thing must first be an apple before it can be a good one, but its being an apple is no assurance that it is a good one.

Good is a property of concepts rather than objects, says Hartman. A thing is good not as an object, but as an example, as an exemplification of a concept. A thing, x, is not good as x but as a good C--where C stands for a concept. Thus Hartman says that knowing that a thing is good requires a knowledge of the concept of which it is an instance. If I am told that Smith has a good wife, I need not know Smith's wife with all of her properties in order to understand her goodness. But I must know what is a wife. The word "good" indicates that Smith's wife is fully what she is as a wife, that she has the full, expositional meaning of "wife." Not all wives are fully wives. Some are only fair, and some are bad. Value words are notations of the different degrees in which a thing can be what it is. Such words are measures of class membership, measures of degrees of meaning, or degrees of value.

The goodness of Smith's wife is not a natural property but depends on the descriptive properties which she has. It is a consequence of these properties as they are seen as corresponding to the attributes of the concept "wife." Her wife goodness does not depend on all of her descriptive properties, but only on those designated in the intension of the concept "wife." She has a multitude of properties and these may be seen as exemplifying many concepts. She is not only a wife, but is, let's say, a mother, a lover, a physician, a gardener, and so on. She is good, fair, or bad in all the ways in which she can be seen as fulfilling the intension of concepts.

According to Urmson and Hare, and for Dewey as well, that good which is a consequence of a thing's natural properties is in the last analysis extrinsic good. Value, for these philosophers, is always extrinsic, or instrumental. It is always comparative in that the same criteria for a grade or for a class are applied to several particulars. John Rawls says that they reduce all value to economic value.[6] We agree with Rawls that this is a weakness of their positions. They cannot account satisfactorily for intrinsic value. And, of course, the notion of systemic value, which Hartman introduces, is completely foreign to their theories of value.

The Three Categories of Value

Hartman's insight, the axiom of his formal axiology, that a thing has value in the degree that if fulfills the intension of its concept is rich in comparison with these more narrow accounts of value. Value is concept fulfillment, but there is more than one type of value for there is more than one type of concept. The concepts dealt with by Urmson and Hare are for the most part the names of classes of things in ordinary, everyday experience, apples, strawberries, fire hydrants, motor-cars, cacti, and morally good persons. Concepts of this type are termed by Hartman, <u>abstract</u>, or <u>analytic</u>. They arise as one abstracts, one by one, the properties common to a group of empirical things, things like strawberries and wives, and such concepts are of denumerably infinite content, for theoretically such abstraction of common properties could continue <u>ad infinitum</u>. Hartman is in agreement with Urmson and Hare that the characteristic value of things designated by such concepts is extrinsic. Thus <u>extrinsic value</u> is the fulfillment of an abstract concept. It is the value arising through pragmatic thinking as persons order and classify things. It is the value that one attributes to empirical things (things in space and time) in their empirical aspects. If a thing (object, process, event) is to be subject to extrinsic valuation, then it must have, at least theoretically, an unlimited number of discernable, discrete properties, countable descriptive properties in terms of which it can be compared to other things. Otherwise, there could be no assignment of class membership and no comparison of the thing's properties with those of its concept.

But there are non-empirical things or empirical things in their non-empirical aspects to which persons also attribute value. Smith's wife, Jane, has functional value as a woman joined in marriage to a man. Jane keeps Smith's house, shares his bed, mothers his children. And although she does not fulfill all that one might expect of a wife, Smith yet loves her. She is not fully good as compared to other wives, but to Smith she is precious. She is incomparable. Incomparable not as a housekeeper, bedmate, or mother but as a individual, a person, as Jane.

"Jane" is a proper name designating something in its concreteness, in the totality of its properties. Hartman refers to such a name as a <u>singular concept</u>, or unicept, and the fulfillment of such a concept is intrinsic value. A singular concept is not a concept in the usual sense, since it represents a thing in the fullness of its being; consequently the fulfillment of such a concept is not a matter of matching a concept's attributes, one by one, with the properties of a thing. Rather, the fulfillment of the singular concept is an experiencing of a thing in its concreteness. It is an identification with it. It is a prizing of a thing in its uniqueness. It is in Smith's case, his love of Jane.

A thing is unique because, as Hartman says, it has the properties it has.[7] Its uniqueness is not one of its properties, but is a property of its properties. It is its intrinsic value. And this value escapes both Urmson and Hare. But not Moore. Moore does not confuse the intrinsic with the extrinsic. He concentrates on the <u>experience</u> of <u>intrinsic</u> goodness and sees that such an experience depends on the totality of the good thing's properties. For a thing's value changes as its properties change. Thus for Moore intrinsic goodness is a totiresultant property.[8] In contrast, Urmson and Hare concentrate on the <u>use</u> of the word "good" in various contexts, and they see this use as depending on only some of a thing's properties, namely, those properties relevant to a criterion in a specific context. Thus for them good is a resultant, or consequential, property but not a totiresultant property. And this good is, of course, extrinsic, and never involves the total nature or reality of that to which it is attributed. Consequently, such good is of less value than one that involves all the properties of a thing.

If a thing's value is its richness of properties, as Hartman claims, then a value that involves all of a thing's properties is a greater value than one that involves merely some of these properties, and for Hartman it is infinitely greater. A thing is infinitely more valuable as an intrinsic value than as an extrinsic value. Jane, for example, is infinitely more valuable as Jane than as a housewife. For as an individual, Jane can be valued not merely as a housewife but in an unlimited number of ways, as cook, mother, companion, teacher, etc. Her value as an individual, as Jane, is thus on a higher level of richness, for her individuality is a reflection of her total being and is inclusive of her various functional or extrinsic values as housewife, mother, etc. Consequently, the fulfillment of a singular concept is different from, and infinitely greater than, the fulfillment of an abstract concept.

But these are not the only ways in which Jane is an object of valuation. In addition to her comparative worth as a empirical thing and her uniqueness as a person, Jane as a woman legally joined in marriage to a man has <u>systemic</u> value as an element of a system. The word "wife" is not only an abstract concept of ordinary language; it is a legal term defined in systems of law, both civil and religious. It is a concept constructed in the mind rather than one abstracted by the mind from experience. Hartman terms such a concept a "construct," or a "formal" or "synthetic" concept. Should Smith become indifferent to Jane's infinite richness of properties, and become increasingly sensitive to her failure to fulfill her various functions as a wife, he might seek a divorce. He would find that in spite of her defects she is yet perfect as a lawful wife, for she has a defined place within an institutional system. And so, of course, does Smith as a husband. Consequently, if their union is to be dissolved, it must be done in accordance with the law.[9]

The fulfillment of a formal concept is the least valuable of the three types of concept fulfillment, for few properties are involved, comparatively speaking. For example, there is little meaning in a marriage that is merely systemic. When the union is intrinsic each person takes joy in the sheer being of the other. Each is the other's life. But as love fades the intrinsic gives way to the extrinsic and the systemic. The wife may say of the husband: "He is not a bad husband. He is a good father to the children, and a good provider. But I just don't love him." Each may become increasingly sensitive to extrinsic disvalue. Finally, only the systemic may be left, mere legal relations. As we say, they are married in name only, married only legally, systemically.

Hartman accounts for these value differences more formally in terms of the types of intensions characterizing formal, abstract, and singular concepts. The procedure for constructing a formal concept is <u>definition</u>, and a definition involves a finite and definite number, "n," of properties, or predicates, with a minimum of two. For example, "wife" defined in terms of the genus, "woman," and differentia, "married". In contrast, the procedure for establishing an abstract concept is <u>exposition</u>, as we have seen, and this is a matter of abstracting, one by one, properties common to a group of empirical things. Since such abstraction may continue <u>ad infinitum</u>, the expositional intension is discursive and denumerably infinite, which Hartman represents by the transfinite number "$\aleph_0$". Thus the intension of the concept "wife" as an abstraction from experience includes, theoretically, all those properties common to all wives, whether dead, living, or yet to be. While in theory the establishment of the abstract intension can continue ad infinitum, in practice it obviously does not, for the purpose of such concepts is to enable us to deal pragmatically with the empirical things of our world. All extrinsic valuation is in practice finite. Nevertheless, an abstract concept is richer than a formal one, for a formal concept must have a definite and finite number of properties. Yet the intension of the singular concept is richer than both of the above. The procedure that yields the singular is termed by Hartman, "description," or "depiction," and this is as we have seen, a matter of experiencing, of total involvement of valuer with that valued. The intension of the singular is a non-discursive, nondenumerable infinity of properties. It is a continuum, an uninterrupted whole, a Gestalt, which numerically may be represented by the transfinite number "$\aleph_1$."

The fulfillment of the formal concept is, as we have seen, systemic value; and the values are either perfection or non-existence, since a construct is just as it is defined to be or it is not such a thing. The fulfillment of the abstract concept is extrinsic value; and, unlike systemic value, extrinsic value admits of degree, since an empirical thing can have more or less of the attributes of an abstract concept. Thus the values here are good, fair, poor, and so on. The fulfillment of the singular concept is intrinsic value; and here too there are degrees of fulfillment depending on the depth of the intrinsic experience. Such experience is indicated by terms like "unique," "authentic," "unauthentic," "sincere," "insincere," "honest," "dishonest."

The more concept fulfillment, the more value; and the richer the concept, the more value possible. Thus systemic value is of less value than extrinsic value, and extrinsic value is of less value than intrinsic value; for the intension of the formal concept is finite, that of the abstract concept is denumerably infinite, and that of the singular is nondenumerably infinite. Thus, as Hartman says, the dimensions of value, systemic, extrinsic, and intrinsic, form a hierarchy with intensional cardinalities of n, $\aleph_0$, $\aleph_1$, respectively.

Axiology as a Formal Science: A Logic of Value

Hartman, like many of his predecessors in moral philosophy, wanted to make value inquiry scientific, but unlike most of them he emphasized the formal aspects of science. In general, recent philosophers have thought that to make ethics scientific one must imitate the natural sciences, and for them, this meant making value inquiry empirical. Hence the attempt by various philosophers like Perry and Dewey to define value as a natural, or descriptive, property or a set of such properties open to observation, experimentation, public verification. But modern natural science has both formal and empirical aspects. It is both theoretical and applied. Its theoretical side gives emphasis to mathematics and logic, the applied gives more stress to experimentation, prediction, observation, verification.

A science, says Hartman, is a frame of reference (some formal pattern of thought) applicable to a set of data. The formal frame of reference for natural sciences is mathematics, and specific natural sciences, like physics and chemistry, arise as various mathematical forms are applied to natural facts. But values are not facts, as Moore has shown. Value cannot be defined in terms of natural properties, but it can be defined in terms of the intensions of concepts, as we have seen. Consequently, if there are to be various applied value sciences, like ethics and aesthetics, then there must be a frame of reference, analogous to mathematics, that can account for the logical structure of intensions. Mathematics, the logic of number, is an extensional logic. What must be developed is a logic of value, an intensional logic; and this is Hartman's goal. His formal axiology is not an applied science on the level of, say, economics and psychology, or physics and chemistry, but is a formal, theoretical pattern, a logic of value, on the level of mathematics. Hence the "value" that is the immediate subject matter for Hartman's theory of value is not a phenomenon of immediate sense experience, a thing like an apple, a wife, or an American flag. Rather, it is that which these and all other values have in common as value, value in the most abstract sense, value as intension, meaning, or richness of predicates. But an understanding of the forms of order for such an abstraction can help us to understand and control the phenomenal values of immediate experience. The organic chemist's formula, C_2H_5OH, represents only a bit of a pattern to be found in the experience of that colorless, inflammable liquid that some Protestants pledge each year to forgo. Nevertheless, as the formula for ethyl alcohol it is an instrument for controlling the occurrence of events on which an experience of this liquid depends. Analogously, when the applied value sciences become well developed, there will be value formulas that enable us to understand and control our experience of values. These formulas will be applications of the logic of the three kinds of intensional structures--finite, denumerably infinite, and nondenumerably infinite--which as norms determine the kinds of value things with corresponding set of properties possess: systemic, extrinsic, or intrinsic value.[10]

Thus formal axiology is a system based upon the logical structure of intension. An intension is a set of predicates, and a set of predicates is a value, "value" in the formal sense. When a set of predicates is matched with a set of properties of some actual thing then the value of that thing can be measured. This "value" is, as Hartman says, scientific value, and is the result of an application of a formal system to the phenomenal values of immediate experience. The value of an actual thing is its richness of properties. But the measure of this richness is meaning, a set of predicates, an intension. Hartman writes: "A standard of measuring is a set of units arbitrarily selected which is applicable to certain phenomena and by comparison with which the nature of these phenomena can be numerically determined."[11] Conceptual intension, or meaning, is the measure that Hartman has selected for value phenomena.

> To measure value by meaning then, means, <u>to use meaning as a measuring rod</u> which fits the thing from which the number of the value of the thing can be read off. Just as the units of the meter are the centimeters, so the units of an intension are the predicates it contains. The set of predicates is compared with the set of properties actually possessed by the thing; and the thing has <u>value</u> in the degree that the set of its properties corresponds to the set of predicates contained in the measure of its value, its intension; just as the thing has length corresponding to the centimeters contained in the measure of its length, the meter.[12]

Each kind of thing has a measure appropriate to it. Solids, liquids, and gases can all be measured in various ways. There are measures for temperatures, speed, and time. But the extent, dimensions, quantity, and so on of one kind of thing cannot be measured the same way as another. So too for value. Just as the yardstick is inappropriate for measuring room temperature, the dollar is inappropriate for measuring the aesthetic worth of a painting or the moral worth of a person.

"Good" and "bad" are words measuring meaning, and, as Hartman explains, are logically no different from "meter" and "half a dozen." Such value words allow us to indicate that things are what they are in various degrees. The statement "Old Fred is a horse" tells us quite a bit about Old Fred. But "Old Fred is a good horse" is a more precise description, for "good" indicates that Old Fred has the full measure of "horse."

Not only does each kind of thing, whether a mental construct, an empirical thing, or a person, have a value measure, a type of concept, appropriate to it, but each thing has its own value measure; and this measure is the specific meaning indicated by its name. Its name is its norm, for its name is the indicator of what or who it is supposed to be. But as we have seen, a thing, whether Old Fred, Jane, or something else, may have many names, and thus be subject to various value measures within the three dimensions of value.

Applying the Logic: Measuring a Thing's Value

Although Hartman's attention was given for the most part of the development of the formal aspects of scientific axiology, value science also has an applied side, which in the case of extrinsic value concerns the development of intensional patterns applicable to specific types of empirical things. As we have seen, the value of a thing is measured when a set of predicates is compared with the thing's set of properties. Conception, perception, and application are all involved, as Hartman explains:

> The application of the combinational calculus of intensions brings about the exact measurement of value. Value sensitivity may be exactly defined. It is the capacity of matching a set of predicates one has in mind with a set of properties one recognizes in an actual thing or situation.[13]

Value errors can also be exactly defined, for these are errors of conception, perception, and application. The concept one has in mind may be incorrectly defined, the thing may be incorrectly perceived, and the concept may be incorrectly applied. It is easy to go wrong.

But who is it that knows what a thing is supposed to be? When this has not been established by linguistic usage and custom, it is likely to be the expert. An expert is a person who has special skill or knowledge in some particular field. When one does not know about a particular thing or situation, one turns to a specialist or an authority who has the required experience. If one wants to know the value of a house or a horse, or how a job or a gymnastic exercise is to be performed, one turns to an expert; for the expert knows that for which one should look, and, moreover, can see it. The ordinary person, even with a knowledge of the concept "gymnast," would have difficulty scoring a performance of a floor exercise or an exercise on parallel bars. The performance would likely be over before the properties could be matched with the predicates. As Hartman writes, "The more expert we are at knowing things the more properties we know these things to have. The taste of a glass of Burgundy, for example, has been shown by experts to contain 158 properties."[14] Most unskilled tasters would be hard put to discern 4 or 5.

The abstract concepts of ordinary language are forms of order facilitating our interaction with things in space and time. An actual thing is a set or collection of properties. Concepts are our guides concerning the significance of these properties. They tell us what the properties mean, and they may mean this or that, depending on their correspondence with sets of predicates. The better the match, the more meaning and the more value the thing has as such a thing. To find the meaning of a thing is to find a concept that fits it. But, again, a thing can have many meanings. Its range of meanings, and thus of values, is limited only by the number of concepts that can be applied to it, and for Hartman, there is, theoretically, no limit.

Hartman speaks of valuation as a playing with the properties of a thing. It is "a playing with properties, as music is a playing with sounds."[15] The properties played with are those that lie before us in immediate experience. These properties become meaningful as some thing or fact of sensible experience as they are differentiated into sets. Perceived as a set of descriptive properties, the thing is seen as what it is. It is what it is, but it can be what it is in different ways; or, let us say, it can be more or less what it is, for it can be good, fair, bad, and so on, as such a thing. Thus the thing's values are its different subsets, or combinations, of its set of descriptive properties. "A value predicate is a subset of a description."[16] Hartman's formula for determining all the possible values for an n-propertied thing being what it is is $V_t = 2^n - 1$.[17] Suppose a thing to have five descriptive properties, then the total value possibilities are 31, $2^5 - 1$. If four properties, then the number is 15, $2^4 - 1$.

Let us say that the value <u>good</u> is represented by $\underline{n}$; the value <u>fair</u> by more than one half of $\underline{n}$; the value <u>average</u> is represented by one half of $\underline{n}$; and the value <u>bad</u> by less than one half of $\underline{n}$. In Hartman's words, "the possible <u>values</u> are $\underline{n}$, half of $\underline{n}$, half of $\underline{n}$ plus a number that is less than this half, let us say $\underline{m}$, and half of $\underline{n}$ less the number $\underline{m}$."[18] In sum n, $\frac{n}{2} + m$, $\frac{n}{2}$, $\frac{n}{2} - m$; or in other words, good, fair, average and bad, respectively. As one can easily see by constructing a simple truth table, as below, with four properties there is one way to be good (n=4), four ways to be fair ($\frac{n}{2} + m = 3$), six ways to be average ($\frac{n}{2} = 2$), and four ways to be bad ($\frac{n}{2} - m = 1$). Thus there is a total of fifteen possible values for a thing with four properties. Each value is a sub-set of the set of properties. Hartman refers to the totality of the sub-sets as the thing's total value. "The total value of a thing is the totality of the sub-sets of the thing's set of descriptive properties."[19]

A	B	C	D		
T	T	T	T	-	All properties present - "Good"
T	T	T	F	-	Three properties present - "Fair"
T	T	F	T	-	- "Fair"
T	T	F	F	-	Two properties present - "Average"
T	F	T	T	-	- "Fair"
T	F	T	F	-	- "Average"
T	F	F	T	-	- "Average"
T	F	F	F	-	One property present - "Bad"
F	T	T	T	-	- "Fair"
F	T	T	F	-	- "Average"
F	T	F	T	-	- "Average"
F	T	F	F	-	- "Bad"
F	F	T	T	-	- "Average"
F	F	T	F	-	- "Bad"
F	F	F	T	-	- "Bad"
F	F	F	F	-	

Table of Values for a Four-Propertied Thing

Conceptually, extrinsic valuation is a matter of measuring a thing's properties by means of a concept, as is also the case with both systemic and intrinsic valuations. But some valuations have an affective or emotional aspect. As Edwards explains elsewhere in this book, systemic valuation is objective, impartial, and dispassionate, a wholly intellectual procedure, with no involvement of emotion. In contrast, Carter stresses that intrinsic valuation is emphatic and empathetic. What then of the extrinsic? On the one hand, the process of measuring the extrinsic value of a thing can be characterized like the systemic, as objective, impartial, and dispassionate, for a set of predicates is compared with a set of properties. The evaluator need not take a "pro-attitude" toward the thing being measured. On the other hand, the determination of the set of predicates used as a measure may involve emotion. "Extrinsic valuation is the model of everyday pragmatic thinking," writes Hartman.[20] But such thinking involves human desires and interests. We order and classify the things that we interact with in space and time for all sorts of purposes. Our abstract concepts help us get what we want. However, this is not to say that there is no logic involved in the formulation of such concepts.

Yet, why fix one set of predicates rather than another as the intension of a concept, and if the intension changes over the course of time, what criterion, if any, governs the change? Perhaps at times the establishment of an intension is in part a matter of chance, but generally this appears to be tied to both the conative, or purposive nature, and the intellectual nature of human beings. As John Dewey has said, our ideas are instruments, plans for action, suggested solutions to problems. But as ideas are tested and questions are answered, and insecure situations made secure, new difficulties arise and new ideas are suggested to deal with them. Attention is given to those properties of things which appear to have utility for a purpose at hand. Utility is a matter open to inquiry, and in this sense "science is the norm for extrinsic value."[21] But attention given to properties may also lead to changes in purpose. For example, the concept "luxury car" has undergone remarkable changes in intension during the Twentieth Century. A good luxury car of 1920 would lack many of the properties of a good one of today. A 1991 luxury car would be expected to have an electronic automatic climate control system, a tilt steering wheel, six-way power front seats, air safety bags, power windows, high-level electronic AM/FM stereo with cassette, and so on, to say nothing of the changes in engine and chassis that have occurred since 1920. The evolution of the concept reflects a complex interplay between the developments in science and engineering, on the one hand, and human needs, desires, and interests, on the other. But in 1991 a good luxury car remains, as in 1920, one that has all the properties that such a car is supposed to have, and such goodness can be objectively assessed by comparing the properties of the concept with those of a car, and can be done so even by persons who dislike luxury cars.

For Dewey, and for other philosophers who give a teleological account of extrinsic value in terms of the means-end relation, the goodness of a car rests on its capacity for meeting needs. Dewey argues that valuation is a type of intelligent activity that is called forth only when there is a difficulty; when there is some need, lack, or privation to be made good. It is an effort to modify a problematic situation in the direction of preference. Thus a thing is judged of positive value because it assists a course of action whereby needs are met, desires are fulfilled, ends are attained. The question of a thing's value is the question of whether it will do, as determined by intelligent inquiry, in a continuum of means-ends. It is not enough that the thing is desired, or even enjoyed. The phenomenal values had in immediate experience, likes and dislikes, pleasures and displeasures, are merely the raw data for intelligent evaluation. That which is prized or despised must be appraised, if it is to be judged a value. Appraised in terms of both its more immediate efficacy in relation to a projected end and its long run consequences, as an actual end attained becomes a transition to future experience. A thing's goodness in this sense is fullness of "instrumentality" in a continuum of means-ends. A privation is made good, and this is approved in terms of both cost and consequences, and both are matters of relations.

No thing has value apart from its relation to other things. Thus for Dewey no object has an absolute, intrinsic worth. There are no ends-in-themselves. All value is extrinsic or instrumental. An end enjoyed merely as an end, as something complete, finished, final, is a consummatory experience; and this for Dewey is to treat it not valuationally but aesthetically. A thing in its individuality can be enjoyed or suffered as a had experience, but it cannot be evaluated this way for it cannot be known. Knowing and valuing have reference to general character, standardized and averaged sets of properties and relations. Hartman disagrees, of course, with Dewey, since for him prizing a thing in its uniqueness is a form of knowing and is intrinsic valuation.

The descriptive properties relevant for extrinsic valuation are, of course, those that belong to the exposition of the thing's concept. Extrinsic valuation presupposes that definitional properties are present. For example, before a wife can be good as a wife, she must first be a wife. That is to say, she must at least have the two minimal properties, "married" and "woman," the differentia and genus of the definition. But a person that is married and a woman may not be a good wife. Neither is some one who is a woman but unmarried, nor someone who is not a woman but married, an average, fair, or bad wife. Let us say, as concerns extrinsic valuation, a wife is a married woman with descriptive properties A, B, C, D, E, and so on. These descriptive properties being expositional properties normal to a woman joined in marriage to a man. The possible values of a wife are the sub-sets of the set of descriptive properties A, B, C, D, E, ... This set is regarded as the normal set in terms of which a wife is considered to be a wife, and it is at the same time the <u>normative</u> set for a wife.

> The set is posited as normal by virtue of its normativity and as normative by virtue of its normalcy. As normal, the set determines the thing as <u>fact</u>, as normative, it determines the thing as <u>value</u>. As the former, it is called the description of the thing, as the latter it is called the thing's goodness.[22]

Why accept the normal as the norm? Perhaps because this has proved to be an efficient way of dealing with the things that persons interact with in space and time.

> This analytic set of descriptive properties, the intension, is the set which language and custom have fixed in order to be able to deal with things and not become diverted by the multiplicity of value forms in which things appear. It is the common denominator of these forms.[23]

While, theoretically, abstract concepts are established through a logical procedure of abstracting, one by one, properties common to a group, and this set of properties then becomes the normative set for the group, in practice such an establishment of a normal and normative set may be more psychological, an intuitive funding of experience whereby a composite average is obtained for the members of a group. This seems to be suggested by a recent study by psychologists at the University of Texas concerning the norm for physical beauty.[24] Persons asked to judge pictures of faces for attractiveness found the most attractive faces, both for males and for females, to be those composed of features average for a group of 16 or 32 faces. Thus the norm for faces was discovered to be the normal, the perfect average of all faces. In Hartman's terms, this "perfect average" is the exposition of human face. The best (good) face is the face that not only has eyes, nose, mouth, chin, brow, cheeks, and so on, but has these in a relation and with a size or shape that reflect the group as a whole. No actual face need be the perfect average or contain the full exposition, but this still serves as the norm. It is reported that both infants and adults perceive the same faces as attractive, regardless of the racial or cultural background of the person viewing the face.

The concept "wife" is more variable. The intension of the concept obviously changes from society to society and from time to time. Many of the properties normal to an American wife are not those normal to a wife in Saudi Arabia. Moreover, the criteria that today's all American "girl-next-door" must face upon becoming a wife are not precisely the same as those that shaped the image of "the girl that married dear old dad." Nevertheless, attributes like "shares the husband's bed," "mothers the children," and "gets the food on the table" are probably expectations common to many cultures.

There are experts for cheese and wine, and for cars and horses, but who is the expert for wives and husbands? Who decides which properties are essential, and which are not? Perhaps, ultimately, and within the limits of traditional rights and obligations, the expert is the person who has or is a wife or husband. Yet, there appears to be some order, or logic, with respect to attributes of intensions of more or less vague concepts, like "wife," of ordinary language. This logic may provide the key to the relative value of an attribute within an intension. For example, some attributes of "wife" appear to have a more central role than others have within the chain of meaning of the concept. They share more richly in the concept's total meaning, and thus are more important. Is not "sharing the bed" of more significance in a marriage than "getting the food on the table"? (Even though the closest way to a man's heart may well be through his stomach!) The former is a traditional conjugal right and obligation sanctioned by law. The absence of this attribute from the concept "wife" would appear to change its essential meaning. The latter is less central in the overall meaning of "wife." But can we say that its role is insignificant? While, today, in our society the requirements for being a woman in a marriage are more flexible than formerly, nevertheless, most wives, even those who work outside the home, continue to assume responsibility for meal preparation, and are judged accordingly. Meal preparation in the home remains largely woman's work. Certainly, "prepares the family meals" is not an attribute of "husband," and a male who assumes this role may find himself referred to as a "person who would make someone a good wife." Thus both attributes are part of the conventional meaning of "wife," but the former is a more valuable property for a wife to have than is the latter. A marriage may well survive the wife's defects with respect to "getting the food on the table," but defects with respect to "sharing the marriage bed" are a more serious matter. Moreover, a wife might even be a pretty good wife and never prepare a meal, but one that never shares the marriage bed could hardly be a wife.

Such considerations suggest that number of properties alone is not sufficient to determine value, for two wives may have the same number of properties, but yet have different values. Suppose "wife" to have ten attributes, including the two mentioned above, and suppose of two particular wives, each has nine of the ten properties, but one has missing the "meal preparing" property and the other the "bed mate" property. Their values are not the same. Again, some properties are more valuable than others in determining a particular's value. But how is this to be determined?

Let us conclude by looking briefly at Hartman's solution to our problem. For Hartman the value of a property is determined by its logical position within an intension of a class concept. He explains that the structure of the analytic intension "represents an order of the world of everyday experience; it assigns to each property not only a place but also a value."[25] Let us look at this structure. An analytic definition, for example, that of "wife" consists of four terms: <u>definiendum</u> ("wife"), <u>definitional equality</u> ("is"), <u>genus</u> ("woman"), and <u>differentia</u> ("married")--two subjects ("wife" and "woman") and a predicate ("married"). The subjects are of the same type, which is to say, they are on the same level of abstraction (only one property), because of definitional equality. The predicate is of a higher type, and is on a lower level of abstraction, for it represents a higher degree of differentiation in the process of making specific the meaning of a term. But the predicate, too, has its own definition, a genus and differentia, and while this genus is on the level of the predicate (here a subject) the differentia will be of a still higher type, and on a still lower level of abstraction, and thus reflect a higher degree of differentiation. But this additional differentia will have a definition, and so on, and on, with higher and higher types and degrees of differentiation and lower levels of abstraction, and increasing numbers of properties. Thus the process of specifying the expositional content of an abstract concept is a series of analytic implications, a movement from the highest level of abstraction and lowest level of differentiation, or specification, to the lowest level of abstraction and highest level of differentiation of an intensional structure. It is a process that begins with one property and culminates in increasing richness of properties as meaning becomes more fully determined. Hartman writes:

> The place of a property is determined by its position in the degree of differentiation, and by the type to which it belongs. Likewise, degree and type determine the value of the thing. In the process of abstraction, the higher degree of differentiation potentially contains, or is the base of, the lower degrees, and its fulfillment is that of more properties. It is that from which the lower degrees are abstracted. Hence, a set of properties of a higher degree of differentiation, if actually differentiated, that is, containing the fullness of its determinations, is worth more than a set of properties of a lower degree of differentiation equally fulfilled. . . Conversely, the lack of a set of properties of higher degree of differentiation is a greater disvalue than that of a lower degree of differentiation. The lack, for example, of a horse's foot is a greater disvalue than the lack of his tail, but the lack of his mouth is a greater disvalue than the lack of his foot.[26]

This is to say that for the horse, its mouth is worth more than its foot and its foot is worth more than its tail, since in the series of analytic implications that differentiate the full set of horse properties, the mouth will be seen as having more properties than the foot, and the foot more than the tail. The number of properties contained in a part of a thing is determined by the part's level of abstraction or level of differentiation in the full differentiation of that thing. But the value of the respective parts for the thing that has them is, Hartman says, "proportionate to the number of properties contained in each."[27]

Accordingly, with respect to our concept "wife," the value to be assigned to various properties like "meal preparing," "bed mate," and "mothering" is determined by the place each has in the fully differentiated set of wife properties. The place of each is determined, as we have seen, by its degree of differentiation and by its type within the full set of wife properties. Thus degree and type determine the value each attribute has for a wife. They determine the value for they determine the number of properties contained in each attribute. The value of the various properties for a wife is, then, proportionate to the number of properties each contains.

It follows that being a bed mate is more valuable than being a meal preparer for a wife, since the former contains a higher number of properties. In the case of a wife defined as "married woman," the genus "woman" is of a lower type than the differentia "married;" and while "bed mate" is an essential property of being married, "meal preparer" is a property attributed to a woman not as married but as woman.

In summary, Hartman, like many of his contemporaries was concerned with the relation of value to natural properties, and he concluded, as did many of them, that while value is not a natural property it yet depends on such properties. But unlike them, Hartman saw this dependence in terms of the logical operation of concept exemplification. Value is attributed to a thing to the degree that its properties correspond to the attributes of its concept; and the richer the concept, the more value possible. In this chapter we have concentrated on abstract concepts whose fulfillment yields extrinsic value. We saw how this kind of value can be measured through a comparison of a concept's intension with a thing's set of descriptive properties. We saw that the normal set of descriptive properties for a class becomes the normative set for the class member. Finally, we examined the problem of the relative value of an attribute within an intension, of why one descriptive property is more important than another in determining a thing's value, and we found this to be determined by the logical position of the attribute within an intension.

NOTES

1. Robert S. Hartman, The Structure of Value: Foundations of a Scientific Axiology (Carbondale: Southern Illinois University Press, 1967).

2. G. E. Moore, Principia Ethica (Cambridge: University Press, 1954), p. vii.

3. Ibid., p. 6.

4. R. M. Hare, The Language of Morals (Oxford: Clarendon Press, 1952), p. 132.

5. Robert S. Hartman, The Structure of Value, p. 179.

6. John Rawls, A Theory of Justice (Cambridge: Harvard University Press, 1971), p. 434.

7. Robert S. Hartman, "Sputnik's Moral Challenge," Texas Quarterly, III, No 3 (Autumn, 1960), p. 15.

8. Moore, Principia Ethica, pp. 206-207.

9. In India recently two couples in their haste and because of the heavy veils of the brides were distressed to find themselves married to the wrong persons. Nevertheless, the village elders concluded that, since they had gone six times around the sacred flames, nothing could be done. Intrinsic commitment had here been confused with systemic conformity.

10. Robert S. Hartman, The Structure of Value, p. 193.

11. Robert S. Hartman, "The Value Structure of Creativity," The Journal of Value Inquiry, Vol. VI, No. 4 (Winter, 1972), p. 251.

12. Ibid., p. 251.

13. Ibid., p. 253.

14. Ibid., p. 253.

15. Robert S. Hartman "The Science of Value: Five Lectures on Formal Axiology," (unpublished essay), p. 37.

16. Robert S. Hartman, The Structure of Value, p. 218.

17. Ibid., p. 216.

18. Ibid.

19. Robert S. Hartman, "The Science of Value," p. 36.

20. Robert S. Hartman, The Structure of Value, p. 113.

21. Robert S. Hartman, "The Nature of Valuation," this volume, p. 16.

22. Robert S. Hartman, The Structure of Value, p. 217.

23. Ibid., p. 219.

24. Reported in the Knoxville News-Sentinel, Dec. 3, 1990.

25. Robert S. Hartman, The Structure of Value, p. 200

26. Ibid., p. 202.

27. Ibid., p. 205.

Chapter V

UNIVERSALS, INDIVIDUALS, AND INTRINSIC GOODS

Rem B. Edwards

Most traditional philosophers, whether Utilitarian or non-Utilitarian, have regarded only universals, i.e. repeatable properties, as intrinsic goods. I will examine this opinion and contrast it with the view of Robert S. Hartman and others that individuals, non-repeatable entities, are intrinsic goods. Then I will propose that the truth involves a synthesis of these extreme positions.

Intrinsic goods are things that are desirable for their own sake, ends in themselves, inherently worth actualizing and preserving in existence. What sorts of things are intrinsically good? Are they individuals or universals? To decide we must first determine what counts as a universal and as an individual.

Universals are things which can occur concretely more than once within the universe, and individuals are things which occur only once, in their full immediacy and concreteness. Concrete or fully definite instances of universals are capable of repeated instantiation. However, concrete or fully definite individuals are not repeatable in their fullness, though they can be partly repeated in the experience and constitution of other individuals.[1] Individuals are unique, one of a kind.

Intrinsic Goods as Universals

Traditional hedonistic or pluralistic theories of the good have identified only universals, only repeatable properties, as intrinsic goods. Hedonists offer pleasure, or happiness--as involving a surplus of pleasure over pain, as the good. Obviously, there are many instances of pleasure or happiness in human and animal experience. If pleasures differ qualitatively, as Mill believed,[2] there are still many instances of "lower" pleasures derived directly from the sensory qualities of things like food, drink, and sex; and there are many instances of "higher" pleasures derived from things like philosophy, music, art, and literature. In addition to happiness, pluralistic views also cite other repeatable properties as intrinsic goods--rationality, knowledge, autonomy, virtue, beauty, creativity, love, freedom, preference or desire fulfillment, etc. Yet, all such goods are universals by definition, for there are many instances of each. Traditional accounts have generally subscribed to the view that only universals have intrinsic worth and, by implication, that individuals do not.

Individuals as Intrinsic Goods

There is another philosophical position, a minority view, represented by Emerson and Kierkegaard in the 19th Century and Robert S. Hartman in the 20th, which maintains that individuals have intrinsic worth. John Stuart Mill may have toyed with this possibility in his chapter "Of Individuality, As One of the Elements of Well-Being" in On Liberty, as we shall see. Despite all his talk about respecting persons as ends in themselves, I do not regard Kant as representative of the individuality tradition. When he explained what he meant by the enigmatic phrase "respecting persons," it is clear that Kant valued only the universal law: "Respect for a person is properly only respect for the law (of honesty, etc.) of which he gives us an example."[3] For Kant, individuals are mere receptacles for the instantiation of universal categorical imperatives, just as they are mere receptacles for the instantiation of pleasures for hedonistic Utilitarians.

In our century, Robert S. Hartman developed a highly sophisticated version of the view that individuals have intrinsic worth in many articles and in his book titled The Structure of Value. I will not plumb the depths of his formal axiology,[4] but I will explain briefly some of the relevant features of his position.

Hartman recognized three kinds of value, intrinsic, extrinsic and systemic, as fulfillments of three kinds of concepts. (I assume that entities can fulfill concepts even when no one is applying concepts to them, just as trees can fall in forests even when no one is watching.) Hartman believed that all intrinsic goods are individuals. However, as I shall explain, he did not think that all individuals are intrinsic goods. Extrinsic and systemic goods clearly are universals involving repeatable or universal features of class membership. An entity is extrinsically good if it fulfills the definitional and expositional properties of an empirical class, whether physical or social.[5] For example, a machine is an automobile if it exemplifies the definitional properties of being a passenger vehicle and being propelled by its own engine. Yet a car that is merely (i.e. only definitionally) a car is not much of a car. If it is a good car, it must also have such good-making expositional properties as having safe tires and brakes, comfortable seats, a quiet ride, a quality stereo system, a sound body, a fuel-efficient engine, etc. Hartman did not give an adequate account of how good-making expositional properties are originally chosen, but it seems to me that they are selected by what other philosophers have called "pro-attitudes." They are those properties of empirical objects toward which someone, not necessarily the valuator, takes a positive attitude because of their function or utility. Eventually, conventions with respect to such pro-attitudes become established which can guide our practical choices. Thus, we can make the right practical choices simply by applying standards, as do apple graders, without taking pro-attitudes ourselves. We can also challenge a popular consensus in light of our individual preferences, and we can be challenged to change them by trend-makers, moguls and reformers.

A systemic good fulfills either the minimal defining properties of an empirical class or those of a highly abstract constructed concept. Persons are "good Communists" in China if they support the existing economic system and do not espouse democratic ideals. Ideologists who cherish systems, not individuals, often zealously sacrifice individuals for systemic universals that exist only in thought. According to Hartman's hierarchy of values, however, this is a great mistake because ideologists rate entities poorer in properties higher than those richer in properties, and because degree of value depends on richness in properties. In terms of richness in properties, "The universal has the lowest, the unique the highest value...Formal axiology confirms the radical value reversal of existentialism, in particular Kierkegaard: its highest value is the individual, its lowest the system, with classes--of individuals or things--in the middle."[6]

Hartman claimed that "intrinsic value is the value of uniqueness."[7] Did he believe that all unique things are intrinsically good or merely that all intrinsically good things are unique? He explained that the category of "intrinsic value" could be applied to individual persons, to groups of persons, to individual things, to groups of things, to concepts, and to words.[8] This suggests that all things considered in their uniqueness are intrinsic goods. Yet, as his writings disclose, he really believed only that all intrinsic goods are unique, that the only intrinsic goods are individual persons (whether human or Divine). In his "Four Axiological Proofs of the Infinite Value of Man," Hartman argued that human persons are intrinsic goods because they have an infinite capacity for combining concepts with objects,[9] they have their own definitions or concepts of themselves in themselves,[10] they can conceptually mirror or represent all things in themselves,[11] and they are consciously self-actualizing beings.[12] Individual non-persons cannot do these things and thus are not intrinsic goods. As Hartman noted, "A chair does not know that it is a chair but I know that I am I."[13] The same would be true of any individual painting, concept, group, or word. Every sea shell, every grain of sand is unique and may be intrinsically valuated; but is it thereby an intrinsic value?

Hartman's distinction between intrinsic <u>value</u> and intrinsic <u>valuation</u> may be used to resolve the question of whether all unique things are intrinsic goods. A unique entity occurs only once with just its properties. All unique things may be intrinsically valuated, but not all unique things are intrinsic values. Hartman's writings are somewhat confusing because he did not strictly observe the distinction. Sometimes, as in the reference preceding Footnote 8 above, he wrote "intrinsic value" when he should have said "intrinsic valuation."

An <u>intrinsically valuable entity</u> is something good in itself; and only unique persons are intrinsic values, Hartman believed. He also believed that individual persons exemplify a nondenumerable infinity of actual properties. Contrary to Hartman, persons could be intrinsically valuable because of the quality, not simply the quantity, of the universal properties that they actually exemplify, even if the number of these properties is only immense and practically incalculable, but still finite. <u>Intrinsic valuations</u>, by contrast, are intense positive conceptual, dynamic, and affective personal involvements of unique conscious individuals with valued objects. Intrinsic valuation is maximal conscious involvement. Individual persons may be valuated intrinsically, but so may extrinsic and systemic objects. Hartman wrote:

> Since I do not abstract in intrinsic valuation, I concentrate on the thing as it is, I am fully concentrated on this one thing. For this reason, intrinsic valuation when applied to things brings about aesthetic valuation: the artist is fully concentrated on the thing he creates. He and the thing are empathically related; they form one unit. Applied to persons this valuation is ethical; it is complete involvement of one person with another, complete concentration of one person on another; the persons are sympathetically related and form one unit. We may call this relationship between persons <u>Community</u>.[14]

We may intrinsically valuate a person, a painting, a concept, a holy word, a flag, a sea shell, or a grain of sand by appreciating it for what it is. A physical object such as a painting is an extrinsic value which is valuated intrinsically when deeply appreciated as a unique work of art. Concepts or words are systemic or extrinsic values which can be intrinsically valuated when we have intense positive conceptual, dynamic and emotional involvements with them as special sacrosanct symbols. Yet, strictly speaking, none of these things become intrinsic values merely because we intrinsically valuate them.

The maximal conscious personal involvements of intrinsic valuation may take many forms, but they are all universals that can and do occur many times. Hartman identified universals such as love,[15] enjoyment,[16] appreciation,[17] emphatic and empathetic personal involvement,[18] mystical union,[19] conscience,[20] and creativity[21] as forms of intrinsic valuation (though he sometimes called them intrinsic values.) We may love a flag or a car, but that does not make it an intrinsic good. This is only the intrinsic valuation of an extrinsic value. By contrast, when we love a unique person, we intrinsically valuate an intrinsic value. All of these forms of intrinsic valuation are universals, for they may and do occur again and again. The intrinsic valuation of an intrinsic value is the combination of a universal with an individual, as will be explained later.

For the moment, let us note an important implication of Hartman's view that only unique persons are intrinsic goods. The distinctive things about persons, we should recall, are that they can combine concepts with objects, they have their own concepts of themselves, they can conceptually represent things to themselves, and they are consciously self-actualizing. This means, when taken seriously, that other conscious beings such as animals and even newborn human babies which totally lack these abilities are not persons. Are they therefore of no intrinsic worth? Hartman's position on this is not clear. He used "a baby" (a newly created person) as the example of the intrinsic valuation of an intrinsic value on the "Hartman Value Profile;"[22] but he did not treat individual animals as intrinsic goods.

Hartman apparently accepted the view of Pico della Mirandola that because animals are incapable of doing so, God created man "to ponder the plan of so great a work, to love its beauty, and to wonder at its vastness."[23] Lacking these abilities, animals seem to lack intrinsic worth, on Hartman's view. (His views on animals are further explored more sympathetically in the articles in this volume by Robert E. Carter. For a less sympathetic view, see the article in this volume by Frank Forrest, particularly his analysis of "killing a deer for food," where he treats a deer as having only extrinsic worth.)

Hartman may have thought that human infants are intrinsic goods because they have the potential to become persons in his sense while animals lack such potentials. However, this solution unjustifiably equates potential properties with actual properties and confuses potential intrinsic worth with actual intrinsic worth. The only kind of value that correlates with potential properties is potential value. Actual value requires actual properties.

Unfortunately, Hartman's thinking about values often seems to confuse the actual with the potential. This was particularly true of his "proofs" for the infinite value of man based on the claim that we can think an infinite number of thoughts, that we could think about <u>all</u> of the things in the world, i.e. an infinite number of things. Because we have these capacities, human persons are supposedly infinitely rich in properties, nondenumerably so, according to Hartman. However, since it takes time to think even a finite number of thoughts, none of us can <u>actually</u> think an infinite number of thoughts in a finite span of years; and none of us can <u>actually</u> know <u>all</u> of nature, or all there is to know. Even if it is claimed that we can do so <u>potentiality</u>, these are not <u>real</u> potentialities of concrete individuals. When each of us dies, we will still know only our little corner of the world, the universe. None of us will ever <u>actually</u> come anywhere close to realizing infinite potentials for knowing and thinking in our three score years and ten. Hartman claimed that we are literally infinite in properties,[24] but at best this may be only metaphorical speech.[25] If so, it would be a mistake to tie intrinsic worth to transfinite mathematics, taken literally, as Hartman tried to do.

Nevertheless, taken metaphorically, the uses of transfinite mathematics in axiology can be most important as a way of expressing formally our considered <u>qualitative</u> judgments that a thing is more valuable than our idea of it (e.g. the blueprint of a house versus the house itself) and that conscious individuals are immensely and incommensurably more valuable than non-conscious things. Assigning higher transfinite cardinalities to conscious individuals than to empirical and conceptual objects may not be based so much on the <u>number</u> of actual properties possesses, however important that may be, as on the <u>kind</u> of entities that they are and the types of universal <u>qualities</u> that they exemplify. Once applied, however, transfinite set theory can be a powerful instrument for expressing the qualitative insights that conscious valuing beings are better than non-conscious entities, and that their respective values are incommensurable. As Frank Forrest shows in this volume, set theory is an immensely powerful tool for calculating worth and resolving problems. It is not without problems of its own, however, as Mark Moore also shows in his following essay.

If actual worth does not correlate with merely potential properties, basing the intrinsic worth of human infants on properties possessed only potentially rather than actually is precarious business. This implies that babies possess no actual intrinsic worth since they are not actually persons in

Hartman's sense. Human infants and animals can have intrinsic worth, however, if (1) at least some individual non-persons that can valuate intrinsically are intrinsic goods, whether infants or animals, and (2) if intrinsic goods are finite and are actualized by finite degrees--even though we assign transfinite cardinalities to them to express their incommensurability with non-intrinsic goods.

The enrichment by degrees of the lives of individual human adults by universals is an integral part of our self-concepts. Yet, the added value that the finite realization of such universal goods as happiness, creativity, and virtue bring to our lives cannot be accounted for in conventional transfinite mathematics, because the addition of a finite number to an infinite number always yields the same infinite number that was there to start with, nothing more. However, as Robert Brumbaugh has suggested, conventional transfinite mathematics may be extended to allow for mathematical operations of ordinal addition and subtraction <u>within</u> cardinalities.[26] Thus, if we assign the cardinal value of nondenumerable infinity to individual consciousness, we can still add ordinally within that infinity to account for the enrichment of any human's life through maturation, education, intellectual development, moral growth, creativity, empathy, affection, happiness, etc. Yet, no sum of universals will ever override the value of individuals since no additions within cardinalities can surpass those cardinalities themselves.

Back to animals, our last cat, Samantha, was a real character, a rich and delightful center of conscious experience and activity who had her own standards of acceptability and unacceptability. Though she was not a person, she helped me to appreciate the worth of conscious individuals. I am convinced that her life had great intrinsic worth and that our love for her was the intrinsic valuation of an intrinsic value. What reasons might there be for such a conviction?

Intrinsic Goods as Syntheses of Universals and Individuals

It is possible that intrinsic values, i.e. intrinsically good things, are neither universals alone, as traditional theorists have believed, nor individuals alone, as Hartman appeared to maintain. Considered in complete abstraction from one another, neither individuals nor universals are good in themselves. Rather, intrinsic goods involve a synthesis of universals and individuals. <u>Intrinsic values consist in the realization of certain kinds of universal and repeatable properties by certain kinds of unique and unrepeatable individuals</u>, i.e. those kinds of unique individuals that are capable of consciously actualizing the relevant universals. Hartman himself actually took this position, for he regarded as intrinsic goods only the synthesis of individuals with the repeatable properties of combining concepts with objects, having self-concepts, etc.

Implicit in Hartman's position is the suggestion that another repeatable property or universal, the capacity for intrinsic valuation, is a defining trait of intrinsic value. Intrinsically valuable entities thus consists of the actualization of valuations by those unique individuals who have conscious capacities for valuations, especially for intrinsic valuations. (I shall leave the question open whether individuals have intrinsic worth who have merely systemic or extrinsic capacities for valuation, e.g. computers or utterly heartless persons. I shall also leave open the question of the exact metaphysical status of consciousness.[27])

If the general capacity for intrinsic valuation, another universal, is emphasized, both human infants and at least some animals count as intrinsic goods because of properties actually possessed, not merely because of unrealized potentials. Flags, sea shells and grains of sand, no matter how unique, are not capable of consciously measuring by standards, actively combining values, loving, enjoying, appreciating, synthesizing, creating, or being emphatically and empathetically involved. Babies, animals and paradigm persons actually have some of these conscious capacities in varying degrees and are the relevant kinds of individuals. Affective and dynamic capacities are sufficient for intrinsic valuation in the absence of cognitive capacities. Although human infants and most animals have no language-dependent concept of self, they nevertheless seem to have a sense of being conscious centers of experience and valuational activity that are distinct from the rest of the world. Degrees of intrinsic worth correlate with the degrees to which individuals actually exemplify various capacities for intrinsic valuation.

More developed persons can have a concept of self that calls for the actualization of cognitive as well as dynamic and affective capacities for intrinsic valuation. Deliberate self-fulfillment creates the highest intrinsic worth only to the extent that the self realized is an intrinsic, not merely a systemic or extrinsic, self. Most adult humans have far greater intrinsic worth than most babies or animals because they have a greater self which includes greater capacities for intrinsic valuation.

Individuals and Universal Capacities for Valuation

Individuals who know themselves, who have a correct concept of themselves, understand that they are unique centers of conscious experience and activity who actualize universal potentials of selfhood in their own distinctive ways. Intrinsically valuable entities would seem to be conscious individuals who actualize their general capacities for valuation, particularly for intrinsic valuation.

According to Hartman, intrinsic value involves the fulfillment by themselves of the concepts which unique individuals have of themselves. This can be true only of human selves who have matured beyond infancy, so a slightly broader notion is required if infants and animals are intrinsically good. Knowing and fulfilling capacities for valuation, for conscious involvement, is an important aspect of the concepts which mature individual persons have of themselves. Some of these capacities belong to the systemic self, some to the extrinsic self and some to the intrinsic self, as follows:

The Systemic Self is the most abstract conceptual self. It consists of one's actual or potential:

a. Knowledge and application of mathematics, logic, computer programs, rules, regulations, laws, symbols, the formal aspects of music and the arts, and the formal aspects of the sciences, including the natural sciences and axiology.
b. Knowledge of and obedience or conformity to ideal constructs such as rituals, institutional regulations, positive laws, moral rules, principles.
c. Offices, memberships or positions in institutions, organizations.
d. Non-empirical formal, theoretical, philosophical and religious concepts, beliefs, doctrines, dogmas, ideologies.
e. Capacity for systemic valuation, i.e for measuring objectively by constructed concepts and for combining systemic values with others.

The Extrinsic Self is the public and practical self, i.e. one's actual or potential:

a. Perceptions, sensations, relations with perceptual objects--including one's possessions, physical environment, nature.
b. Mastery of facts, including the use of means-ends, cause-effect relations.
c. Bodily structures, functions, behaviors.
d. Physical skills, talents, abilities, habits, disciplines.
e. Social skills, talents, abilities, habits, discipline, i.e. abilities to relate to others.
f. Knowledge of and conformity to the ideal demands or expectations of others (parents, peers, society).
g. Knowledge of and conformity to manners, customs, conventions, dress codes, and social morality.

h. Social roles, such as student, teacher, parent, sibling, child, citizen, spouse, employer, employee, producer, consumer, etc.
i. Social status, reputation.
j. Management of one's practical affairs, such as career or work, ambitions, financial affairs, property or possessions, meeting physical needs, health habits, amusements, hobbies, athletics, etc.
k. Competitiveness with others.
l. Comparisons between oneself and others.
m. Proneness to accidents, to good or bad luck.
n. Analytic, empirical, factual and social concepts and beliefs.
o. Capacity for extrinsic valuation, for measuring practically by empirical class standards and for combining extrinsic values with others.

The Intrinsic Self is the total self, the self with all its properties. As such it includes the systemic and extrinsic selves. But to them, the inner or primordial self is added.

The Inner or Primordial Self consists of one's actual or potential:

a. Experiential self-awareness, paying attention to one's internal psychological states, processes, activities, experiences.
b. Awareness (and appreciation) of oneself as a unique center of conscious activity and experience.
c. Attention, concentration, choice, decision, self-control, free will, autonomy.
d. Emotions, feelings, desires, interests.
e. Enjoyments, pleasures, delights, happiness.
f. Empathetic identification and compassion.
g. Imagination and creativity (in any field of human interest or endeavor.)
h. Religious experience and devotion.
i. Conscience, i.e. the ideal demands or expectations that one places upon oneself, including one's deepest moral sense of right and wrong.
j. Authenticity, being true to oneself.
k. Moral virtues, such as honesty, sincerity, truthfulness, courage, integrity, temperance, fidelity, gratitude, justice, wisdom, benevolence, non-maleficence, etc.
l. Self-acceptance, self-respect, self-esteem, self-love, and delight in one's own being.
m. Aesthetic sensitivities and creativity.
n. Faith (in Kierkegaard's sense of the knowledge and acceptance of oneself as a unique individual living out one's life before God.)

o. Deepest hopes for oneself and others, one's long (and short) range plan of life.
p. Love of and identification with others.
q. Cooperation and intrinsic unity with others.
r. Singular and metaphorical concepts and beliefs, including one's concept of oneself.
s. Capacity for intrinsic valuation, for the foregoing forms of self-identification and measurement and for combining intrinsic realities with others.

Conceptually, intrinsic valuation involves measuring valued objects by individual concepts, seeing things in their uniqueness, as one of a kind, as in a class by themselves. Our intrinsic value as individual persons is determined as we are measured by our own concepts of ourselves. We may live up to and thus fulfill our concepts of ourselves, or we may not. Our self concepts always include an awareness of our actual properties and of the ideal properties that we ought to exemplify. Notice that many if not most of our properties are relational properties, for we are what we are largely through our relations. Hartman greatly admired Kierkegaard's definition of the self as "a relation that relates itself to itself."[28]

According to Hartman, conscience is that part of ourselves through which we set ideal norms for ourselves. It determines the properties that we ought to possess.[29] If we allow others to set all the standards which we think we ought to fulfill, we have no conscience or are out of touch with conscience. However, the requirements of conscience may (or may not) coincide with what others require of us. Conscience is that core of the inner intrinsic self that should determine how we ought to develop ourselves systemically, extrinsically and intrinsically. Through conscience we establish many different kinds of standards for ourselves, including moral norms.

Suppose, however, that some of us agree that our intrinsic goodness consists in fulfilling the ideal norms that we set for ourselves, but we find that we set only non-moral or downright immoral norms for ourselves. We find that we conceive of ourselves as persons who:

--always obey the authorities, no matter what, or
--are racists, members of a master race, who set racist norms for ourselves, or
--are male chauvinists who set sexist norms for ourselves, or
--are worldly manipulators, exploiters, and users of others for material and social gains for ourselves, or
--are sadists who delight in inflicting pain and suffering on others.

Hartman could say that if we make such claims, we are out of touch with conscience and are judging ourselves by norms that have been set for us by external and extrinsic segments of society. Skeptics and relativists, who believe that conscience is always merely a social product, would doubt that there is an independent primordial conscience in each of us that tells us all the same thing, especially in matters of morals.

Hartman actually assumed that all of us has a conscience that sets the same moral norm or imperative for each of us, an inner ethical compass, which tells us all that we should intrinsically valuate all persons, ourselves and others; and that we should not evaluate any persons merely systemically or merely extrinsically. I take it that this is what Hartman had in mind when he claimed that ethics is the application of intrinsic valuation to individual persons.[30] A well developed intrinsic self will be a richer self, will enrich the lives of others, and thus will be a better self. If conscience fails to give us this common moral imperative, then my intrinsic value consists not so much in my fulfillment of my concept of myself as in my fulfillment of Hartman's concept of myself! (There is a tension in Hartman's thought between objective and subjective norms of self-realization.) Hartman was convinced that all mature individuals who are truly in touch with conscience will find that it makes some universal requirements. A synthesis of universals with individuals is necessary for intrinsic worth.

How can we know whether Hartman got it right (or wrong) when he identified intrinsic values with individuals? What pre-systematic considerations support the thesis of this paper that intrinsically valuable entities are a synthesis of universals and individuals? An appeal will be made to the principle of isolation identified by G. E. Moore, and of replaceability, to be explained shortly. According to G. E. Moore, the proper method to be used to decide what things have intrinsic value is "to consider what things are such that, if they existed by themselves, in absolute isolation, we should yet judge their existence to be good."[31] Moore was the first to label it, but the method of isolation is as old as Plato's Philebus and Aristotle's Nicomachean Ethics. Considerable imagination and experience is involved in the application of the methods of isolation and replaceability. Their application should show that individuals and universals are necessary for any organic wholes which we judge to have intrinsic worth after careful, knowledgeable, impartial, disinterested (systemic) consideration, and that intrinsic worth is lost or absent if either the relevant individuals or universals are destroyed or absent.

Isolating Individuals from Universals

Do human individuals have any intrinsic worth when totally bereft of all conscious capacity for such universals of valuation as love, appreciation, enjoyment, compassion, empathy, conscientiousness, creativity, concentration, self-knowledge, etc.? Correspondingly, do those universal qualities involved in valuations have intrinsic worth when divorced from individuals? Would individuals in isolation, or universals in isolation, be the sorts of things which, on careful consideration, we would judge to be ends in themselves? After due consideration we may conclude that neither individuals nor universals in total separation have intrinsic worth, that only synthetic wholes incorporating both are intrinsically good.

Let us first consider individuals that lack both consciousness and actual intrinsic valuational capacities. Then we will consider conscious individuals in the absence of intrinsic valuations, then intrinsic valuations divorced from conscious individuals. Are they valuable in themselves?

First, do individuals totally and permanently bereft of all conscious capacity for valuation, especially intrinsic valuation, have any intrinsic worth? We have already considered individual grains of sand, sea shells, and works of art and have concluded that they are not intrinsic values though they may be intrinsically valued. Let us now consider those individual persons who are irreversibly comatose, who are definitively deprived of all conscious capacities for valuation simply because they are definitively deprived of consciousness itself. Do their individual lives have intrinsic worth? (This question should not be confused with: "<u>Did</u> their lives have intrinsic worth?") My considered judgment is negative. So it seems was Hartman's, for he wrote that "those who only vegetate and do not live "fully" do not fulfil the intension of "life" and are not good "livers," not living the good life."[32] Readers must judge the worth (or worthlessness) of purely vegetative existence for themselves after careful consideration. Determinations of intrinsic worth are so basic that we can only invite careful, informed, unfettered, and impartial (systemic) judgment under conditions of isolation or replaceability.

Again, some human individuals, e.g. developing fetuses, have not yet attained a capacity for conscious involvement. The capacity for consciousness seems to emerge between 27 and 30 weeks after conception, i.e. near the beginning of the third trimester of pregnancy. Only then do those types of brain waves manifest themselves that are indicative of the presence of consciousness, and premature infants sleep all the time till then. If we abort a first or second trimester fetus, have we destroyed an actual intrinsic good?

If actual value correlates with properties actually possessed, the answer must be negative. This question should not be confused with: "<u>Will</u> their lives have intrinsic worth after normal development occurs if not aborted spontaneously or artificially?"

About 40 to 50 percent of all human conceptions end in spontaneous abortion, so a significant number of embryos fail to have a real potential to become newborn babies. Pre-conscious fetuses have the potential to develop into conscious human individuals if all goes well; but so do all human ova and sperm. With cloning, so do all the genetically complete cells which constitute most of the tissues and structures of every human body. Are all of these potential persons also actual persons? Furthermore, if potential persons are equal in value to actual persons, then contraception and good old fashioned conservative abstinence will be morally equivalent to murder since they deny existence to potential persons. The implications of equating potentiality and actuality are absurd, and we may conclude that potential properties do not equal actual properties, that actual value does not equal potential value, and that potential value does not equal actual value.

The synthesis hypothesis is that an intrinsically good thing involves a fusion of (1) unique centers of conscious experience and activity with (2) universal valuational capacities like love, appreciation, enjoyment, empathy, conscientiousness, creativity, etc. Irreversibly comatose and pre-conscious individuals satisfy <u>neither</u> of these conditions, and in considering them we are not reflecting on (1) in isolation from (2). Irreversibly comatose and pre-conscious individuals <u>are not individuals</u> in sense (1), i.e. they simply are not unique centers of consciousness; and they are not evaluators. They lack both (1) and (2). They satisfy <u>neither</u> necessary condition for intrinsic worth.

The possibility must now be considered that either (1) alone or (2) alone is sufficient for intrinsic worth.

Can we consider the value of individuals who actually are (1) unique centers of conscious experience and activity but who are devoid of (2) all universal valuational goods? Perhaps so. Let us consider A. a certain form of mystical experience, and B. a form of consciousness so dominated by evil universals that good universals are excluded, or nearly so.

A. There are many types of mystical experience, some of which have content, some of which do not. There is a form of purely monistic introspective mystical experience that is said to be a state of pure consciousness which is not conscious of anything, i.e. which has no object, no content, whatsoever.[33] If normal consciousness is always intentional, always involved with an object, the pure consciousness of monistic mysticism is not. To reach this state of radically altered consciousness, the mystic practices meditative techniques which involve the progressive detachment of consciousness from the external sensory world, from all features of one's body, from all emotion and feeling of every kind, from all awareness of time and plurality, and finally from self itself. What is left? Monistic mystics answer metaphysically and after the fact that what remains is the pure cosmic consciousness of God or the Brahma itself. A more plausible interpretation, however, is that the mystic simply established contact with herself or himself as (1) a pure center of conscious activity and experience to the total exclusion of (2) all content whatsoever, especially of reflective self-awareness, and of all other universal goods. The mystic experiences the consciousness of a self that is not self conscious; and in this sense, what remains is a self that is not a self.

What is the value of a conscious individuality that is so pure that it excludes self-consciousness, all awareness of individuality? Monistic mystics seems to prize it very highly, but why they do so is most puzzling, especially to us non-mystics. What they prize so highly is the poorest, not the richest, form of consciousness. They do not always mean what they say, however. Their writings disclose that the consciousness they cherish is never so poor, so devoid of all content as some of their pronouncements would indicate. Sooner or later, pure monistic consciousness is described as "bliss," as "ecstacy." Thus a consciousness with no content has content after all, that of ecstatic, orgiastic delight! One suspects that mystics who profess to cherish pure consciousness never really do so. Consciousness of bliss, of high quality pleasure, remains. But it is not recognized as being anyone's pleasure!

If it were truly devoid of all content, including bliss, the pure monistic mystical experience would be a consciousness poorest in properties; but it should not be confused with other forms of mystical experience. Many mystical experiences are infinitely rich in content, not infinitely poor. As Robert S. Hartman described such an infinitely rich "mystic exaltation":

> In such experiences, as reported by some, the subjects, on progressing from one infinity to the next, find that a previous infinity is limited and shrinks to insignificance when seen from the vantage point of a higher infinity. Thus, subjects experienced the entire world, with its infinity of events, actions, things, relations, and then rose to a higher state of awareness, where the whole world shrank and a new world infinitely richer than the one just left opened up to their marvelling consciousness. One subject experienced the totality of all works of art, tons and tons of sculpture, acres and acres of paintings, miles and miles of lace-- only to see all this later from a distance as one great activity of a divine

spirit. Such experiences often appear intolerable, for they seem to burst the limited human frame.³⁴

We should not confuse the mystical experience of a divine spirit, infinitely rich in properties, with the mystical experience of one's own <u>pure</u> consciousness, so infinitely poor in content that it lacks even bliss. It is the intrinsic worth of the latter that we may doubt.

B. Finally, let us consider another type of situation in which individual consciousness remains, but its universal capacities and opportunities for intrinsic valuation are almost completely excluded. Here, of course, the isolation is not complete; but it may be sufficient for informed judgment. Some conscious persons are so overwhelmed and diminished by the evil universal of excruciating and unrelievable pain, both physical and emotional, that almost all other resources for positive cognitive and affective involvement are excluded. Does their unique consciousness have intrinsic worth during those agonizing moments, or is it, together with their life, a liability rather than an asset? If such moments of horror will endure until death brings relief, is conscious individuality worthwhile and worth preserving for its own sake under such conditions? I have my doubts. In this country, under such conditions, multitudes now choose either to be drugged unconscious or to refuse lifesaving medical care, either directly or through Living Wills. In the Netherlands each year, more than two thousand persons voluntarily request and receive active euthanasia when their physical and mental suffering becomes unbearable. Thus, many others reach the same conclusion after thoughtful consideration. If individual conscious life has some intrinsic worth under these conditions, it is judged not to be enough to be worth preserving at the price of such great and hopeless suffering.

Isolating Universals from Individuals

Do intrinsic valuations have intrinsic worth when totally divorced from individuals? It is impossible to apply Moore's method of isolation to decide this question. In the real world, repeatable intrinsic valuations always occur in conscious individuals and never in isolation. Metaphysicians like Aristotle and Whitehead plausibly maintain that universals cannot exist apart from individuals. We could, of course, verbally hypostatize worlds of pure love, pleasure, empathy, or creativity, etc., totally separated from individual conscious subjects; but this is hardly to imagine or experience such worlds in a manner sufficient for our purposes. We are always there reifying such worlds.

Amazingly, most traditional ethicists have affirmed that only universals, but not individuals, have intrinsic worth. This is true of quantitative hedonists, qualitative hedonists, and pluralists who answer the question: "What things are good?" Have these philosophers arrived at their position by isolating away individuals, or by ignoring them, i.e. by not seriously considering the question of their worth? The latter seems to be the case. Traditional ethicists have adhered so blindly to the tradition of universals-alone-as-goods that they have not taken seriously the idea that unique individual centers of conscious experience, activity, and valuation have an intrinsic worth that is not reducible to the value of happiness or some other universal good which they contain. Those who regard only good universals as intrinsic goods have never considered them in isolation from individuals, for they cannot be found apart from individuals.

Contrary to tradition, the synthesis hypothesis affirms that good universals like happiness, knowledge, conscientiousness, creativity, empathy, compassion, virtue, etc. have <u>no value in themselves</u>. We can never <u>find</u> them in and by themselves. Since they exist only in individuals, there is no way to judge that they have intrinsic worth in isolation from individuals. Rather, they have intrinsic worth only because and to the extent that they enrich the lives of unique conscious beings. They have value <u>only in others,</u> only in conscious individuals who infuse them with their own worth, and <u>not in themselves</u>. This is a radical break with the dominant philosophical tradition.

The Replaceability of Individuals

Do good universals have intrinsic worth when completely divorced from unique conscious individuals? We cannot answer by the method of isolation, for universals exist only in individuals. However, the method of replaceability provides another approach to separating the value of the universals of intrinsic valuation from the value of unique conscious individuals. In my <u>Pleasures and Pains</u>, I pointed out that to determine whether some non-hedonistic good is an intrinsic good, not merely an instrumental good, we should replace it in thought, experience, or imagination with something equally efficient in generating pleasures, and then consider whether such a replacement results in loss of any intrinsic worth.[35] Similarly, to determine whether the universal goods contained by an individual conscious person exhaust the value of that individual consciousness, we should consider whether something essential to intrinsic worth would be lost if he or she could be replaced by another person who exemplifies the same kind and degree of desirable universals.

Are individual persons replaceable by other individual persons without loss of intrinsic worth, assuming that no universal goods are lost in the process? Utilitarian theories, which regard only universals as intrinsic goods, are frequently criticized for making individuals replaceable. Peter Singer was particularly daunted by this objection, though he finally accepted its implications. As he expressed it:

> Essentially, the problem is that classical utilitarianism makes lives replaceable. Killing is wrong if it deprives the world of a happy life, but this wrong can be righted if another equally happy life can be created without any extra cost. Classical utilitarianism has this consequence because it regards sentient beings as valuable only insofar as they make possible the existence of intrinsically valuable experiences like pleasure. It is as if sentient beings were receptacles of something valuable, and it did not matter if a receptacle got broken, as long as another receptacle were available to which the contents could be transferred without any getting spilled in the process. The reasonableness of the classical utilitarian position turns on the reasonableness of this consequence.[36]

Of course, some individuals <u>are</u> replaceable without loss of intrinsic worth. It is reasonable for prospective parents to abort a first or second trimester fetus with grotesque birth defects and replace it as soon as possible with another normal pregnancy because the defective infant is not, i.e. has not yet become, an intrinsic good. Nothing is lost and much is gained, not merely because the later infant will be happier, more loving and creative, etc., but also because the defective individual has no actual intrinsic worth. It has no actual capacities for valuation, enjoyment, or any other universal goods. It is not even a conscious receptacle.

The situation is very different, however, when we contemplate the loss and replacement of a third trimester fetus, a healthy newborn, an older child who has been killed in an automobile accident, or a wife, husband, or friend who has died a sudden and painless death. If in some magical world a loved one could be instantly replaced with another person who is equally happy, loving, autonomous, knowledgeable, creative, etc., so that neither the universe nor our own experience of it is impoverished with respect to these highly desirable universals, would not something of great intrinsic worth be lost nevertheless? Of course, nothing like this could ever happen in the real world; but if the answer is yes even for a magical imaginary world, then all traditional Utilitarian theories of intrinsic good are suspect.

In the real world, traditional Utilitarian theories fail to capture the fact that love and grief are directed to individuals, or rather to the synthesis of universals with individuals, and not merely to universals alone. When we love other persons, we cherish them as individuals and not solely as receptacles for the instantiation of pleasure, love, conscientiousness, creativity, etc. At the same time, of course, we want them to be happy, loving, conscientious, creative, etc. So, what we really prize is the synthesis of universals with individuals. The addition of just the right universals enriches the lives of individuals. Similarly, when we grieve for the loss of a dear one, we are not consoled if told that "you can get another one soon who will be equally happy and who will make you equally happy." In situations of grief, something essential to intrinsic goodness, i.e. the individual, has been lost; and no quantity of universal-good-replacements can compensate for that loss. Traditional utilitarianism cannot adequately account for love and grief.

Could there be a revised and non-traditional Utilitarianism that sees individuals as essential to any synthetic whole that counts as intrinsically good? I think so and indeed suspect that Utilitarians have occasionally sponsored this view without fully realizing it. For example, in a recent article titled "Utilitarianism and Respect for Human Life," T. L. S. Sprigge avowed in an early paragraph that "the only rational view" is that "to think of anything as good or bad is precisely to think of it as having qualities of which the only conceivable actual species are pleasure and pain."[37] Yet, without seeing the discrepancy, he later claimed that:

> To the extent that our attitudes are of this desirable sort we will have some appreciation of the special quality of feeling contributed to the totality by each particular individual we know (and realization that there is some such special contribution made by individuals we do not know). Thus we will no more want to see one individual's special contribution to the total cut short earlier than need be than we would want to destroy works of art. Human happiness requires a taste for particular sorts of good, and each human individual is a particular good.[38]

Now, assuming no equivocation, it cannot be the case that only universals like pleasure are good and that each human individual is a particular good. However, their synthetic unity may be such.

John Stuart Mill also may have affirmed the intrinsic worth of universals-in-individuals in his chapter "Of Individuality" in On Liberty. For Mill, the value of individuality consists primarily in the realization by individuals of such repeatable properties as spontaneity, originality, choice, self-control, conscience, impulse, self-development, character, disposition, etc. The important point is that individuals must place their own unique stamp on the realization of these universals. It is essential for happiness, according to Mill, that it be *my* (or any individual's) originality, choice, character, etc.

Furthermore, Mill insisted that "In proportion to the development of his individuality, each person becomes more valuable to himself, and is therefore capable of being more valuable to others."[39] Here, of course, is the problem: in what sense do we become more valuable to ourselves? Do we view ourselves merely as better receptacles, better extrinsic means to the realization of happiness (or other universal goods)? Or do we see ourselves as essential features of intrinsically good states, believing that something necessary to the good would be lost or lacking if we are lost? After due reflection, the answer should be the latter. (As a former qualitative hedonist, I have not always subscribed to this view![40] I am deeply indebted to Robert S. Hartman for the change, though I made it under his influence many years after his death.) Self-respect involves more than valuing ourselves as receptacles. Just as traditional views cannot account properly for love and grief, so they cannot account for self-respect.

Individuals vs. Individuality

I will conclude with a few comments on individuals vs. individuality. We have seen that Hartman's forms of intrinsic valuation (enjoyment, appreciation, creativity, love, etc.), are universals; yet he affirmed officially that only individuals have intrinsic value. Mill also, we saw, regarded repeatable properties (originality, choice, self-development, impulse, character), as forms of individuality, i.e. as forms through which individuals realize themselves. Upon close examination, both Hartman and Mill believed that intrinsic good is actualized as the foregoing universal forms of individuality are synthesized with individuals. This raises the question of whether individuality is itself a universal; and the answer is that individuality is, but individuals are not.

I once heard a colleague facetiously console another concerning his impending divorce with the words: "Don't worry; you will soon find another wife, and she will be equally unique." Uniqueness or individuality is itself something that all individuals share, something repeated by each individual; thus, oddly enough, it seems to be a universal. However, uniqueness is a very peculiar universal, the universal of not being a universal, which is true of every individual. Hartman resolved this difficulty by pointing out that uniqueness is not a property of individuals but is rather a property of their properties.

> What could unique things possibly have in common? If they have something in common they are not unique, and if they have nothing in common they cannot be known by any generic concept--this argument rests on a simple logical fallacy, namely that of confusing levels of thinking. Axiological science solves the paradox of the knowledge of uniqueness in the same way that it solves the Moorean paradox of the

knowledge of "goodness": the concept of uniqueness is on a higher logical level than are the properties of the thing that is called unique. The thing is unique because it has all the properties it has. But the property "having all the properties it has" is not itself one of the properties the thing is said to have. Thus, things can have uniqueness in common and yet be different things, that is, have different sets of properties; just as they can have goodness in common and yet have each its own different kind of goodness. Uniqueness, in other words, is not a property of things but a property of properties of things.[41]

Thus, what unique centers of conscious experience and activity share is that they are different, that true statements may be made about them that cannot be made of any other individuals, that they possess properties that no other individuals possess, that the total set of their universal properties is different from that of everyone else, that they exist in such a way that the universe exemplifies them only once, and that intrinsic good is diminished by their loss.

Of course, in many human relationships, persons are replaceable without loss of worth; but it is always extrinsic or systemic worth, not intrinsic, that is expendable. Football players are replaceable without loss by other football players as long as we view them merely as extrinsic means to winning games. Systemically, a coach can order: "Take out number 84, and send in number 16." Students are replaceable without loss by other students, professors by other professors, salesmen by other salesmen, prostitutes by other prostitutes; for in these relationships, more than one person can exemplify the relevant good-making properties. However, any relationship in which one person is replaceable without loss of value by another person is an extrinsic or systemic relationship, not an intrinsic one.

Once we develop an intrinsic relationship with another person--a friend, a relative, a spouse, a child--we know that he or she cannot simply be <u>replaced</u> by <u>another</u> friend, parent, relative, spouse, child without loss intrinsic worth. To be sure, if death intervenes, we can get another friend, wed another spouse, or conceive another child; and each of these will also be unique. Yet, we will never have a unique <u>replacement</u> for the singular individual who has been lost. A new <u>intrinsic</u> relationship is never a replacement relationship. Even with new gains, lost individuals are still lost; and we are cognizant of their loss. To think that one unique person could ever <u>replace</u> another is simply to fail to understand the concept of uniqueness and its value.

NOTES

1. I agree with Alfred North Whitehead on this. See his Process and Reality, New York, The Free Press, 1978, p. 48. Axiologically, the repetition of individuals within other individuals occurs within the experience of intrinsic valuation.

2. I tried to make sense of Mill's views in Rem B. Edwards, Pleasures and Pains: A Theory of Qualitative Hedonism, Ithaca, Cornell University Press, 1979.

3. Immanuel Kant, Fundamental Principles of the Metaphysics of Morals, New York, The Liberal Arts Press, 1949, p. 19, n. 3.

4. I have done this already to some extent in two articles: (1) "The Value of Man in the Hartman Value System," The Journal of Value Inquiry, Vol. 7, 1973, pp. 141-147; and (2) "Intrinsic and Extrinsic Value and Valuation," The Journal of Value Inquiry, Vol. 13, 1979, pp. 133-143.

5. Robert S. Hartman, The Structure of Value, Carbondale, Southern Illinois University Press, 1967, pp. 194-198.

6. Ibid., p. 254.

7. Ibid., p. 195.

8. Ibid., pp. 308-309.

9. Robert S. Hartman, "Four Axiological Proofs of the Infinite Value of Man," Kant-Studien, Vol. 55, 1964, pp. 431-33.

10. Ibid., pp. 433-34.

11. Ibid., pp. 434-35.

12. Ibid., pp. 435-36.

13. Ibid., p. 433.

14. Robert S. Hartman, "The Nature of Valuation," a previously unpublished manuscript that appears as the second chapter of the present book, p. 23.

15. Robert S. Hartman, The Structure of Value, p. 113, 259-60.

16. Ibid., pp. 114, 251.

17. Ibid., pp. 291, 299.

18. Ibid., pp. 114, 260, 299, 224.

19. Ibid., pp. 224, 251, 272, 274.

20. Robert S. Hartman, "A Logical Definition of Value," The Journal of Philosophy, Vol. XLVII, No. 13, 1951, pp. 415-417.

21. Robert S. Hartman, "The Value Structure of Creativity," The Journal of Value Inquiry, Vol. VI, Winter 1972.

22. This is an extremely powerful psychological test which takes the structure of a person's values as being the key to the structure of that person's personality.

23. See Robert S. Hartman, "Four Axiological Proofs of the Infinite Value of Man," p. 434.

24. Robert S. Hartman, "Applications of the Science of Axiology," this volume, p. 194; and see the long quote on p. 388.

25. I have developed this critique in Rem B. Edwards, "The Value of Man in the Hartman Value System."

26. Robert S. Brumbaugh, "Formal Value Theory: Transfinite Ordinal Numbers and Relatively Trivial Practical Choices," Journal of Human Relations, Vol. 21, 1973, pp. 211-215 and "Robert Hartman's Formal Axiology: An Extension," The Journal of Value Inquiry, Vol. 11, Winter 1977, pp. 259-263.

27. For axiological purposes, it is not necessary to give a fine-tuned metaphysical analysis of what is involved in being a unique center of conscious valuational experience and activity. It would make no axiological difference whether such entities are enduring Kantian or Cartesian subjects, or enduring Whiteheadian societies of personally ordered actual occasions. Nor would it matter whether they are metaphysically in space/time (as in mind/brain identity theories) or out of it (as in Cartesian or Kantian theories.) I have explored some of these deeper metaphysical problems of consciousness in my "Process Thought and the Spaciness of Mind," Process Studies, Fall 1990, pp. 156-166. When Hartman claimed that intrinsic values and value experiences are not in space/time (this book, p. 13), this makes more sense to me if I understand him to be talking phenomenology, not metaphysics. Intrinsic experiences of intense love or creativity are phenomenally self-contained, and

for practical purposes they do not exist in any obvious way in the external sensory world of public (extrinsic) space/time.

28. Søren Kierkegaard, The Sickness Unto Death, Princeton, Princeton University Press, 1980, p. 13.

29. Robert S. Hartman, "The Nature of Valuation," this book, pp. 15, 16.

30. Ibid., p. 2.

31. G. E. Moore, Principia Ethica, Cambridge, Cambridge University Press, 1959, p. 187.

32. Robert S. Hartman, The Structure of Value, p. 160.

33. This is described and discussed by W. T. Stace. See his Mysticism and Philosophy, Philadelphia, J. P. Lippincott, 1960, pp. 110-111, 162.

34. Ibid., p., 224.

35. Rem B. Edwards, Pleasures and Pains: A Theory of Qualitative Hedonism, pp. 50-53.

36. Peter Singer, "Animals and the Value of Life," in Tom Regan, ed., Matters of Life and Death, New York, Random House, 1980, p. 249. The replaceability argument against utilitarian theories of intrinsic goodness is now quite commonplace. See, for example, R. G. Frey, ed., Utility and Rights, Minneapolis, University of Minnesota Press, 1984, pp. 7-8, 121-22, 142.

37. T. L. S. Sprigge, "Utilitarianism and Respect for Human Life," Utilitas, Vol. 1, Number 1, May 1989, p. 2.

38. Ibid., p. 21.

39. John Stuart Mill, On Liberty, Ch. 3, para. 9.

40. See the concluding paragraph of my "Intrinsic and Extrinsic Value and Valuation," p. 143.

41. Robert S. Hartman, "Sputnik's Moral Challenge," The Texas Quarterly, Vol. III, Autumn 1960, p. 15.

Chapter VI

THE NORM OF INTRINSIC VALUATION

Robert E. Carter

While Robert S. Hartman's <u>formal</u> axiological system stands as a major contribution to the field, the care that he took to understand and to deal with the practical real-life valuations which actual people make is of no less importance. He would often speak of people whom he worked closely with as having <u>great</u> character, and this meant that they were sensitive to all three value dimensions, that they were well integrated with respect to them and within themselves, and he inevitably emphasized the <u>importance of their sensitivity to intrinsic valuation</u>. Sensitivity to intrinsic values is what allows us, as centers of consciousness, to interact with each other soul to soul, or heart to heart, in sincerity, honestly, and with compassion and tenderness. It is our capacity for intrinsic valuation which makes us most recognizably human, at least in the sense of being human-as-we-ought-to-be, and not necessarily as we are. He lamented the fact that North American culture was so limited in terms of sensitivity to intrinsic values, for excessive materialistic concern focuses attention on the <u>extrinsic</u> value dimension in particular. Had I known my Heidegger better when I consulted with Bob over several months, both in Mexico and in Tennessee, I would have asked whether he thought that North Americans conceived of the empirical world of space and time as consisting of mere material-at-hand, available for use but not worthwhile for its own sake, and not intrinsically good in itself. I have no doubt about his answer, for he would have responded that Heidegger did well to see this without a formal axiology to help him sort things out.

Axiology

The <u>axiom</u> on which formal axiology is based, which makes the "science" of Axiology possible, is that "a thing is good if it fulfils the intension of its concept."[1] An alternative way of saying this is that "anything is good (or valuable) if it is what or as it is supposed to be."[2] Thus, an automobile is good if it has all of the properties which are contained in your <u>concept</u> of an automobile.

Hartman recognizes three kinds of concepts, and therefore, three possible ways in which a thing can fulfil its conceptual intension, with one such fulfilment yielding intrinsic value. There are synthetic (or constructive) concepts, analytic (or abstractive) concepts, and singular concepts (which he sometimes called "unicepts," or proper names). Fulfilment of the definition of the first results in systemic value, of the second extrinsic value, and of the third intrinsic value. Fulfilment of abstractive concepts ("good" as a member of a class) yields extrinsic value, and fulfilment of singular concepts refers the judgment "good" to the <u>thing in itself</u>--i.e., the thing valued is to be thought of as a class by itself. A singular thing is a member of that class of which it is the only member. Intrinsic valuation is valuation of unique existents. Rem B. Edwards has pointed out that if persons are each of them unique, then the only thing which they can be said to have in common is that they are "different." He writes that "what unique individuals share is that they are different, that true statements may be made about them that cannot be made of any other individuals, that they possess properties that no other individuals possess, that the total set of their properties is different from that of everyone else, that they exist in such a way that the universe exemplifies them only once, and that intrinsic good is diminished by their loss."[3] Of course, we do possess many properties in common with other beings and things, starting with the basic chemical composition of our bodies. But we are also different and distinct in being unlike any other physical and/or psychological entity in the world. No two personal histories are exactly the same, nor are any two human bodies. Axiological uniqueness is not, of course, a natural property, but it is a second order property which--as both Hartman and G. E. Moore held--is dependent on those first-order "natural" properties. In this sense, a person's uniqueness is the totality of properties belonging to that thing, including its potentiality. Thus, it is "unique" which applies to intrinsic values, rather than "good," for "good" is applied in the extrinsic sense of "good of a kind," and the appropriate systemic thing is "perfect," as precisely defined by the exceptionless system of which it is a part.

Consciousness

If "value" (or "good") refers to a logical operation of comparing a <u>norm</u> to an existing thing to be evaluated, then it would seem that values do not exist independently of human consciousness. That which is valued may exist empirically, of course, but its value is necessarily the relational result of its being an object of consciousness for someone. Or perhaps it is better to simply say that valuation is necessarily the relational result of a logical operation <u>for</u> <u>some</u> <u>consciousness</u>. It is true that Hartman never attempts to determine whether forms of consciousness other than human consciousness may value intrinsically, or qualify as being of intrinsic value, but I think this is because he thought that he had undertaken enough in attempting to analyze the structure of <u>human</u> <u>consciousness</u>. Nevertheless, he did not close the door to animals and other forms of consciousness (someday) being shown to possess the capacity of self-consciousness, or at least the sort of consciousness which would allow the possibility of <u>intrinsic</u> valuation. I assume that he did assume that animals were capable of pursuing ends, and that some of them were capable of choosing or establishing those ends. Dogs decide to chase squirrels, run away to avoid punishment, and deliberately eat from the cat's dish even after repeated scoldings. But it does appear--or at least it did for Hartman--that human beings alone can "select their own ends, devise their own ends."[4] Human beings <u>can</u> and <u>do</u> determine their own ends, seek their own goals upon reflection and apart from habits and drives. There is a further issue concerning the nature of the ends selected. Human beings can pursue ends of an intrinsic nature, such as always treating others as being of intrinsic worth. But is the same true of animals? Are they ever capable of intrinsic valuation? Again, I would not rule this out, for just as "simple" people are sometimes more transparent and caring than are more worldly and sophisticated people, so, too, may animals be capable of spontaneous valuation of the whole "other." It is impossible to say with certainty, of course, but I would want to be included amongst those who think that animals are conscious, affectively aware even to the point of remarkable sensitivity, and sometimes are even socially concerned creatures, and therefore ought <u>not</u> to be excluded from whatever claims are made on behalf of human consciousness. With respect to Hartman, however, it remains at least a legitimate claim that only humans are incontrovertibly known to be able to determine their own ends, seek their own goals, etc., and if such freedom is essential to intrinsic valuation, as Hartman argues, then "intrinsic values are only [<u>demonstrably</u>] possible for human beings. Or, let us say, for conscious beings, whatever we call them."[5] This qualification was added in response to a question about whether humans alone were capable of setting goals, and performing the required logical operations to qualify as beings who were <u>of</u> intrinsic value. In fact, I recall that Bob Hartman had no strong feelings about this one way or the other, and his point was simply that there was insufficient empirical data to confirm of what non-human consciousness was actually capable. I take comfort from the fact that he left the door open to animals being of intrinsic value, even though one must go beyond his conclusions in claiming that they do possess the required properties of conscious awareness and decision making.

Be that as it may, "to say that something is of intrinsic value, is to say that it is so from a human perspective."[16] A human being values something intrinsically when he or she "incorporates that particular thing into his or her own end. It is the identification of the human being with that particular thing."[7] The singular concept of intrinsic valuation has the richest intension of the three kinds of concepts and, correspondingly, the most limited extension. It is in a class by itself, a class in which it is the only possible member. Its extension is of the barest minimum, and its intension, which is neither selective, nor abstractive (i.e., some selection from the range of natural properties attended to), includes a non-denumerable infinity of properties, as is the case with any other singular thing. Nothing else in the universe has exactly this infinity of properties, and, hence, singular things are apprehended as unique existents. The singular thing "forms one uninterrupted whole or Gestalt."[8] It is referred to as a non-denumerable infinity because it is "everywhere dense"--i.e., between any two members of this infinity there is an infinity of other members.

Singular things are apprehended in their full concreteness:

> [The] singular thing is apprehended by either perception or intuition (the latter the Platonian or the Husserlian noesis). The first is the case if the singular thing is a spatio-temporal thing, the latter if it is not. In the former case, the thing is called a concrete thing, in the latter case it is called an ideal thing. In both cases, it is axiologically real.[9]

There is no selection of properties here. There is no separation of thing and concept. There is no separation of object and observer: "Thing and observer are one continuous entity; for, if the thing is to be apprehended in its concrete totality ... the thing must be apprehended in toto, in itself, grasped as one in its total Gestalt."[10] The singular thing is apprehended through involvement of the subject in the object, by identification or compenetration,[11] by interpenetration.[12] Involvement varies from occasion to occasion, and person to person, but the singular thing "in itself is the totality of all these aspects."[13]

"For Its Own Sake" and "In Itself"

One of the alternate expressions for "intrinsic value" is "worth having for its own sake." In my four-day long dialogue with Bob Hartman on <u>intrinsic value</u>, he often went to the dictionary in order to clarify the meaning of a term. "What does it mean to say that something is worthwhile, or worth having, or valuable for its own <u>sake</u>?" he would ask. Dictionary in hand, he pounced on the meaning of "sake" as "end, purpose, motive, goal." That something is worthwhile for its own sake, he too took to mean being worthwhile to the extent to which it realized its <u>own</u> purposes, or goals. The <u>prima facie</u> meaning had shifted from the object valued as being worthwhile for itself, to the human valuer and the realization of his or her purposes. It is the realization of one's own nature that yields experiences of intrinsic value. This needs elaboration in some detail.

The formula, "<u>anything is good (or valuable) if it is what or as it is supposed to be</u>," is intended to refer <u>both</u> to the object of valuation, and to the valuer. An object is valuable to the degree to which it fulfils the intension of the concept of that thing, which serves as its norm. But intrinsic valuation necessarily requires that the thing valued be valued not comparatively, but "in itself," in its uniqueness. Intrinsic value, as the fulfilment of the singular concept, is called "intrinsic" because the value inheres in the thing itself, and not in its membership in a class (extrinsic value). Only <u>persons</u>, however, have in themselves their own concepts of themselves and, therefore, only persons have within themselves the <u>standard</u> or <u>norm</u> of themselves.

Person, self, and Self

An object, then, may be judged to be <u>what</u> it is supposed to be, but a conscious person alone may be said to be <u>as</u> he or she is supposed to be. As was evident from the analysis of the meaning of "sake" above, intrinsic valuation necessitates that the valued is a part of the <u>end</u> or <u>goal</u> of a human being: "In other words, a human being incorporates that particular thing into his or her own end. It is the identification of the human being with this particular thing."[14] And it is valued "in itself," in the sense that "there can be nothing else under consideration at the same time. It must be one's whole world."[15] Putting the "for its own sake," and "in itself" characteristics of intrinsic valuation together, Hartman concludes that "intrinsicness is exactly defined by us as something which belongs to the human being, for its own sake, because he/she has consciousness, and which is in itself, namely, exclusive of any other consideration."[16] Since intrinsic valuation means that an object is incorporated into the self of the human being, then it must be something which fits into this self. Thus, "we next have to ask, what is the human self?"[17]

In one sense, it seems odd to ask what ought to be intrinsically valued, since "anything can be intrinsically valued, because anything can be incorporated into the consciousness of a human being."[18] On the other hand, if every intrinsic valuation is apt as it stands, then whatever is so valued is ipso facto valuable. This makes no sense, however, for it collapses the distinction between the valued and the valuable, between what is valued and what ought to be valued, between me as I am, and me ideally, or as I ought to be. It means that whatever a person values intrinsically, is what he or she ought to value. All normativity is lost, since there is no longer a distinction to be made between the normative and the non-normative. Yet the whole point of a theory, or a system of values and value applications is to make normative distinctions possible. Hartman resolved this issue by distinguishing between two senses of "self":

> Let us see what things are intrinsically valuable, and which are not. Since intrinsic value means that an object is incorporated into the very Self, with a capital S, of the human person, it must be something which fits into this Self.
>
> The human being is a being conscious of itself. It is this self-consciousness which makes it possible for him or her to have value experiences, to have an end in him or herself, to define his or her own end, to have his or her own purpose. So it is the capacity of having a purpose (a characteristic of consciousness), which is the defining property of the Self.[19]

Intrinsic value exists wherever a human being, or a consciousness with the requisite powers of intrinsic valuation, as an end in him, her or itself, "incorporates the object valued into him or herself, and the person and the object valued fuse into one."[20]

For Hartman, then, the norm is a Self. Since a human being is a being having an end within him or herself, we have to find out what is appropriate to that being, i.e. what that end is that is within it, and what it is that will enrich it. The problem is that "there are good selves, and bad selves, selves which are as they ought to be, and selves which are not as they ought to be."[21] It will follow that anything at all is of (genuine, or normatively speaking) intrinsic value if (and only if) it ought to be incorporated into human consciousness. "The only other things that, by nature, have the same degree of value as my consciousness, are other persons. This is why you must never use persons, yourself or others, as anything other than ends in themselves. My consciousness, and others' consciousness are on the same level of worth."[22] Yet, it is perhaps intuitively easier to conceive of other consciousnesses as being of intrinsic value than it is of objects. Nevertheless,

> ... non-persons can be of intrinsic value, if lifted up by a valuing consciousness. But we must decide which things ought and ought not to be lifted up by consciousness into intrinsic value. We need a hierarchy of value, in order to see what things would and would not diminish consciousness by being lifted into the realm of intrinsic valuation.[23]

The point is that, so long as there is a normative distinction to be made at the valuational level of the intrinsic, then there may be objects of intrinsic valuation which, rather than being lifted up by the valuing consciousness, pull that consciousness down to them. The Self itself would be diminished, rather than enhancing or enriching the object and itself. More must be said about the self and the Self, in order to resolve this issue.

The self and the Self

To be conscious includes being conscious of yourself. Consciousness is the capacity to introspect, to "split" the self, so to speak, such that the same self can look at itself, and can look at itself looking at itself, ad infinitum, at least in theory. Consciousness of oneself requires that the "self" in "oneself" be a small "s" self, and that the "I" which is conscious of the small "s" self is "Self" with a capital "S". Full consciousness arises only in that consciousness which is the subject of the judgment, "I am conscious of myself," i.e. which is capable of being the subject of its own self-knowledge and self-understanding, but which can never itself be the **object** of self-knowledge or self-understanding. The Self can never be an object of consciousness, but only that which is conscious of something, for example, the self. The Self is that out of which the specifiable conceptual objectification of Self as self arises, as a distinct focus or form. It is the objectification of the unobjectifiable, the form of the formless, a conceptualization of that which is not itself conceptualizable. There is the self, and there is the Self which is conscious of the self, and the self (not the Self) can have extrinsic value experiences, but never intrinsic value experiences: "Only the Self which is conscious of the self can have an intrinsic value experience."[24] The reason why will become clear shortly.

The Transparent and the Opaque

The self, or "I' which is the object of self-reflection, is always a different "I", i.e., is at each moment in a different time and/or space, and from one year to the next, or at one stage of development to the next, has characteristics and memories of an incredibly different sort and combination. Thus, as Hartman saw it,

> ... you need some concept which pulls together all of the stages of yourself in space and time. The "I" is a concept which pulls together all of the stages of the empirical. And the concept is always in quotes. The concept "chair" is in quotes, but the chair you are sitting on is not in quotes, as I speak of the chair. This is very important, because we need it later on for the determination of the nature of a norm. Only a concept can be a norm. Now this conceptual "I" consists of all of the empirical "I's" of you.[25]

While everybody has a self and a Self, they do not have them in the same degree, or in the same way, or as clearly as do others. The terms which Hartman adopts to express this difference in degree and clarity of self-awareness, are "opacity" and "transparency." These are terms which appear in both phenomenological and existentialist writings, e.g. Heidegger, and Kierkegaard, amongst others.[26] You are opaque when you assume that the empirical self is the only self, i.e., when you conflate the two at the expense of the Self. But the Self can "differentiate" itself to the point of nearly complete transparency. The degree of transparency is the norm of intrinsic valuational capacity:

> The self must become more and more transparent. This means that only those can have the full experience of intrinsic value who have a transparent consciousness. And those who do not, cannot have it. The degrees of the capacity for intrinsic valuation depend on the transparency of the self. ... The normative measure of intrinsic value is the transparency of consciousness. Thus, when consciousness is opaque, it is very close to the empirical. ... And what does it mean to say that consciousness becomes more and more transparent, and less and less empirical? Bergson gives the correct answer when he says that consciousness is as large as what it comprehends. So, when it comprehends the whole universe, then it is as large as the universe. Man is as large as the whole universe, because he/she is defined by the range of his/her consciousness.[27]

Only those can have the full experience of intrinsic value who have transparent consciousness, and those who do not cannot have it, or at least may have it only to the extent of their transparency: "The degrees of the capacity for intrinsic valuation depend on the degree of the transparency of the Self."[28] An opaque consciousness is one which identifies itself with the empirical, more or less exclusively.

Transparency is not itself a fixed and final state. Hartman, like so many others, observes that even the most transparent consciousness has still further infinite depth, or further transparency.[29] A similar recognition of the infinite depth of the Self is found, for example, in the work of the Japanese philosopher, Nishida Kitaro: "The bottom of my soul has such depth; Neither joy nor the waves of sorrow can reach it."[30] The soul, or Self is not only infinitely deep, it is immune to the destruction and insensitivity of the empirical world, or at least it can become so. This is because for Hartman, it is not in the empirical space-time world, but transcends it. As with all other concepts, and reason itself, the Self is not in space and time. It is in a world of its own, with different laws and a different logic:

> A transparent consciousness means that you are not in space and time, because it is not empirical. It is a pure concept. Yet it is you, so it is really you as a concept. ...So if you have an experience of something that is neither here nor there, or that is somewhere else in space, and you have that experience very clearly, then this is an experience of pure consciousness. ...
>
> Pure consciousness is not at a certain time, because it is not empirical, and therefore, it has an immediate awareness of everything. So you can write about the whole universe, you can feel what is going on anywhere, past and present. You are just away, and that is transparency.[31]

It is not that the Self does not affect and even control the self and the body, but only that it is not controlled by the self and the body. It is in, but not of this world, affects, but need not be determined by the empirical world.

Knowing and Feeling

While the system of value and valuation which Hartman devised is a formal structure, and as such is a logical and conceptual account of the nature of value and valuation, the emphasis placed on the involvement of the "whole person" makes evident that he did not wish to exclude the affective and volitional dimensions of human valuation. Indeed, in a telling passage in the

Structure of Value, reference is made to Jose Ortega Y Gasset's essay, "A Few Drops of Phenomenology."[32] An accident scene is recreated through the eyes of four different people, each with a different perspective; a painter, a reporter, a physician, and the injured and dying man's wife. All four are actively involved in the incident, but the degree and nature of the emotional involvement is different. The painter is interested only in "a constellation of spatial and optical elements (S^S)," of light and shadow; the reporter concentrates professionally on the facts of the everyday event (E^S); the doctor views the event of the dying 'patient' professionally (I^S); the wife values intrinsically the life of her dying husband, himself of infinite worth (I^I).[33] Ortega measures these four perspectives by "the emotional distance between each person and the event they all witness."[34] Hartman goes on to observe that Ortega's measure coincides with his own value system and value hierarchy: "the intrinsic valuation involves the valuer completely; 'for the wife of the dying man the distance shrinks to almost nothing.'"[35] The other participants are progressively less emotionally involved, and removed. The greatest intensity of valuation, which includes the greatest intensity of feeling, namely love, to the extent of identification with the beloved, is found with the intrinsic valuer, the wife. Intrinsic valuation is an act of identification, and identification involves the entire person, and it involves all of him or her with the greatest of intensity. Intrinsic valuation is an emotionally intense identification with and appreciation of that which is valued, and is often termed ecstasy, or joyful, or beatific, or wonderful, or is expressed only through metaphor, e.g. "you are my whole world," or by means of non-linguistic human pointers at the distant moon of the inexpressible, such as "Ahhh," or "Wow."

Given even this much evidence from Hartman's writings, it is obvious that he does not ignore the affective aspect of valuation. Of course, as he used to warn, physicists need not "spark," nor botanists "bloom," in order to study electricity and the flowering of plants, nor need axiologists qua formal axiologists need to feel in order to structure, analyze and clarify the feeling aspect of human valuation. The "science" of Axiology is an intellectual, conceptual activity, but valuation itself is much more than its measure, as the weather outside is much more than the thermometer on the wall. And this "more" includes, for the transparent self, the Self, that capacity to reach out and to embrace what is beheld, to empathize, love, and sympathize with the other. You are not aware that you are aware of the other, for there is only the awareness. There is no subject, no object, no intellectual distancing, but only involvement, intense emotion, enjoyment. There is only this, and outside of this event, there is no time, no continuity with the past, no space. When you become totally "lost" in loving, or in writing or inventing, or in painting, or in watching a bamboo grove sway in the summer breezes, or in listening to the "hot" sound of a cicada buzzing in warm summer sun, then you are in the intrinsic realm. You are "all there," you live in the now for there is no other time of which you are aware, and you are here for there is no other place. You see everything as though for the first time, afresh, and with a totality of awareness that achieves the most complete concentration. Indeed, Hartman describes this complete "co-presence" in a passage which displays both his insight, and the well-remembered twinkle in his eye as he said something which verged on the naughty:

> I identify myself with the other without giving up myself but, on the contrary, deepening myself in the degree that I penetrate in the other. In this sense, the universe of intrinsic value could be called, were it not for the unfortunate yet significant ambiguity of the expression, the universe of intercourse. ... Sexual intercourse is indeed an example of such a self-enclosed world out of this world; but any intrinsic value experience has the same structure.[36]

It is little wonder, then, that Bob Hartman told me that the transparent person is so wide open to what is happening around him or her, that such "a person feel[s] very deeply."[37] He added that "compassion is one of the properties" of the transparent person, for such a person lives both with and as every other entity.[38] Hence the awareness of a St. Francis that the sun was "brother sun," of Albert Schweitzer that the blacks, and even the black lepers of Africa were his brothers. To ease their suffering was to ease his suffering, and to enhance their lives was to enhance his own. Such universal empathy, universal affinity, or universal concern is a characteristic of the transparent man or woman who is open to and capable of intrinsic valuation. Thus, "you can actually gauge a person's transparency of consciousness by his/her compassion."[39] The opaque consciousness implodes, withers and shrinks until the ego becomes its whole world, and little else is of interest, whereas the transparent consciousness explodes, until the ego embraces the universe, and everything encountered is of supreme interest, such that the sighting of a dewdrop on a rose can set off an intensity of feeling that seems to transform the entire universe of experience.

The Language of Intrinsic Valuation

It is little wonder that the language of intrinsic valuation is the language of metaphor and poetry.[40] The intension of the singular concept must be constituted by individual words, i.e. must be discursive, and yet the set of such words must form a continuous non-discursive whole in order to represent the continuum which is its object. This means that the singular intension must be constituted by discursive elements which are understood non-discursively, or by non-discursive elements which are understood in such a way that they are used to refer to that which is in (or which may be said to constitute) a class by itself. Only persons have their own concepts of themselves; therefore, only persons have within themselves the standard or norm of themselves. A person is intrinsically valuable to him or herself if he or she fulfils his or her own concept of him or her Self. Those who fulfil or actualize their Selves are in accord with their own concepts of themselves. They are true to themselves, authentic, real, genuine, integral, etc. Non-persons have no concept within themselves of themselves; they become of intrinsic value only when persons identify with them. You love a person because he or she is the way he or she is. You love a beautiful flower just the way it is. But whereas the person is already a non-denumerable richness of meaning, value, and potential in him or herself, the flower can become so only within some (human) consciousness. The nature mystic feels oneness with the universe because it is the sort of universe it is, and because he or she is able to open to it, and to embrace it. The religious mystic identifies with the wondrous nature which is God. The opposite of involvement is indifference, and being indifferent to the uniqueness of things is intrinsic badness.[41] This is not to say that hatred and malice are nothing but indifference, but that it is indifference or insensitivity to the intrinsic worth of another that allows ill-will and evil to arise and to become operational. Evil is clearly more than emotional, or intellectual indifference, but it is valuational indifference that allows these to arise in the first place. One who is aware of the intrinsic worth of another would not think of doing harm to that person, for there would be no reason, and no impulse to do so.

Insofar as a metaphor is a word in ordinary language which is used non-discursively, it is able to express in language the total involvement of intrinsic valuation. The language used is the language of identification. Ordinary language is the language of separation, of distinction, of exclusion, of me perceiving it, of this and that, of here or there, of now or later. Separation is indifference to whatever is not me, or is not a part of my valuational concern. Evil arises because we are unable to perceive the value of that to which we are indifferent, and this constitutes the possibility of the arising of evil, which is the destruction or injury of that to which we are indifferent. Hatred, ill-will, or disgust are more than indifference, but it is indifference to the positive worth of someone or something that allows negative valuations to arise in the first place.

The language of intrinsic valuation is the language of "lovers and artists, mystics and prophets."[42] In short, it is the language of those who become totally involved in what they are apprehending, who identify with their object. The language of identification reveals a capacity for empathy, or compassion. "Compassion is one of the properties of the transparent person, because he/she lives with every other being. He/she lives not only with every other person, but with every other thing, or animal, as was exemplified by Albert Schweitzer, and expressed by him as 'reverence for life'. Empathy is one of the properties of transparency: empathy with everything, universal empathy."[43]

Good, Bad, and Evil

Since people are not always compassionate, they need "rough stimulations" in order to feel anything intrinsically:

> The experience of intrinsic value, for which you need a transparent consciousness, and the intrinsic experience of disvalue, which consists of very strong jolts to your opaque consciousness, causes you to look for an intense experience. You can't get it otherwise, because you are too dull. It is like a blind man who wants to see something. So you give him the greatest nuclear explosion possible, and maybe he sees something then of the flash. But if you just light a candle, that wouldn't be enough. A sensitive eye will not even see a nuclear explosion. So, to an insensitive consciousness, an opaque consciousness, hardly anything makes an impression. But he/she has the desire for an impression, so then he/she has to have these disastrous things in order to receive any impression at all.[44]

Nothing else can get through. But the transparent person is able to identify with a tree, with a raindrop inching its way down the incline of a velvet blossom, with a baby, and with the achievements and the grief of another. He or she appears to be virtually surrounded by opportunities for intrinsic valuation. His or her sensitivity is so great that the slightest occasion imprints itself upon his/her consciousness as though it were a nuclear explosion. As the old saying has it, when a Zen man laughs, even the moon shakes! The entire universe is rocked to its foundations, transformed by a subtle smile, or by an encounter with an oak tree.

How the opaque individual might be educated so as to make him or her more transparent is the subject of my later chapter in this volume. For the moment, it is imperative that the distinction between kinds of "badness" be addressed. Strictly speaking, Hartman uses the term "bad" only when speaking of extrinsic experience, and "evil" only when identifying negative intrinsic valuation. He notes that while it is the case that all badness ought not to exist, nevertheless, given the fact of the existence of badness, there is more good in the world as a result. In order to overcome extrinsic badness, you have to transform it somehow. A home tinkerer might take a pile of junk and turn it into a lawn chair, or the students of a driving instructor might benefit from a horrible wreck by using it as an example of the consequences of drinking and driving for a whole class of young drivers.

By contrast, evil is <u>intrinsically</u> bad, and simply ought <u>not</u> to exist. Whereas a bad wreck can be thought of as a good example of an accident, and, hence, may bring about some or even a great deal of good, evil simply <u>ought</u> <u>not</u> to exist. Evil does not exist as a positive force, for Hartman, but only as the absence of intrinsic valuational sensitivity and valuing. Whereas intrinsic goodness is consciousness expanding even to such an extent as to embrace the entire world, intrinsic evil blocks the rest of the world out. "Intrinsic evil contracts space."[45] In one respect, the time and space of intrinsic goodness and intrinsic evil are similar. In both, you have these experiences as though they were your whole world. It is just that the metaphor of an explosion outward describes the intrinsically good experience, whereas a contracting implosion inward depicts the intrinsically evil. In both cases, the "whole world" description applies, for there is only the embraciveness of the whole, but in one case it is an explosion of meaning and value, a reaching out to embrace the entire world, and in the other it is an implosion which constricts meaning and value. Evil is intrinsically bad, and not just bad, even though it is true that opaque persons need the experience of evil to get an artificial kick, simply because their sensitivity is so low.

> But the evil person is not only not empathetic, but is destructive of other people, and of her or himself. Whatever exists, ought to exist, except for evil, which, since it is worse than nothing, ought not to exist. It is contradictory to consciousness and its characteristics. It is nonsensical. Evil is the destruction of Self, and the destruction of other selves and Selves, and so is in direct contradiction with self-preservation. In logical terms, this amounts to claiming that "I am not I." And the result is that the body is harmed, or dies, and the mind breaks down.[46]

The space-time implications of evil are of importance to a thorough understanding of the comparison Hartman is making. Whereas intrinsic value is experience as <u>eternity</u>, intrinsic disvalue, or evil is a "pseudo-eternity," precisely because of its own self-destructiveness:

> The time span of evil is intolerable, whereas the time span of the intrinsically good is infinite. It is interminable time. When you are in an evil situation, then the time in that situation is not infinite, but <u>interminable</u>. You want it to stop. You can't stand it any more. It is negative time. <u>It makes a hell, not a spell</u>. You would do anything to

have it stop. Whereas for intrinsic value experience, on the other hand, you would do anything to have it go on and on and on. ...

With regard to space, whereas intrinsic goodness is consciousness expanding to embrace the entire world, intrinsic evil blocks the rest of the world out. It just shrinks our awareness. Intrinsic evil contracts space.[47]

Intrinsic valuation requires the empathetic interpenetration of valuer and valued, whereas intrinsic evil harms, reduces or destroys both valued and valuer. It is both self (Self) and other destructive, since insofar as it is intrinsic, it, too, is a seamless blending into one of valuer and valued. And it can only be overcome by intrinsic goodness, i.e. by that which operates within the same non-space, non-time dimension. To kill the body is to do nothing to dispel the evil already done. To kill Hitler may or may not stop Nazi evil from continuing, but it does nothing to overcome the evil already done. Only intrinsic value, compassionate identification, or love can undercut or overcome evil. "Response, sheer transparent response, is one of the easiest and surest ways of undercutting an evil personality, and transforming it, and/or its effects."[48] The death of a loved one is transformed by attending to the intrinsically valuable memories of the life lived together, and apart, and while these do not make up for the empirical loss, they last an eternity each time we recall those wondrous events, and each of them opens us to the intrinsically valuable in ourselves, and in our world to which we might otherwise be closed. It is the best we have, and the most we can do in the wake of evil. Death is normally a "natural," and not a _moral_ evil; but whether natural or moral, the only way to overcome it, however difficult and partial the overcoming may be, is to turn it into some good, by allowing whatever value is attainable to arise from the ashes of evil. In this way you not only decrease the power of evil over you, but you also encourage good rather than evil from others. Revenge, self-pity, and hatred are not only self-destructive, but encourage revenge and hatred in a continuing cycle of evil.

The Fruits of Transparency

Hartman held that transparency of consciousness makes it possible for consciousness to "transluce" everything there is, "like an X-ray." The transparent consciousness is not only more sensitive valuationally, but is more adept perceptually and conceptually, as well:

Transparency makes everything translucent. The less transparent consciousness is, the less translucent will the world itself be. In other words, when consciousness is very opaque, it is not able to transluce the world. Now to transluce the world means to make it understandable. So the less transparent the consciousness is, the less it is able to understand the world. To understand means to actually become one with something, to know it so well that one becomes it. So, in this respect, an opaque consciousness stands on one side, and the world is a chaos for him on the other side. Only at a certain stage of transparency of consciousness, does the world become translucent. And that is intrinsic experience.[49]

An opaque self can obtain a very clear view of a small area of interest, or a very confused and dim vision of the whole. But only the transparent consciousness can have a clear vision of the whole, "and the measure of his/her transparency...is the extent and the intensity of the vision and its encompassing."[50]

Transparency requires the sluffing off of the empirical order, for Hartman, such that "consciousness does not stumble over its own matter."[51] To the extent to which it does this, it lessens the distortive factor of concentration on the material, and the controlling emotions, etc. Consciousness must become like glass, something to be looked through, and which might even intensify or magnify what is looked at, the more transparent it is. But the more opaque it is, the more it distorts, and the more it is in the way because one looks at it, in part, rather than through it. Nevertheless, Hartman does not abandon the physical, the body, but only wishes to advise that it must not control consciousness. The body, too, must become transparent in that it records the intrinsic, rather than impedes it. An experience of intrinsic value does not exclude the body. Rather,

> The body must be taken into the experience. In the intrinsic value experience, there is a "thrill" component. Now what is a thrill? A thrill is a bodily transparency. You take the body into the transparency of the experience. If you had no body, you would have no thrill. You would be a disembodied experience, and that would not even be an intrinsic value experience. In this way, you are unique, for each one of us has his or her own thrill. ... That is why an intrinsic value experience has an accompaniment of emotion. But you can't make the emotion the essence of the experience, as some do.[52]

The thrill is the natural bodily aspect of an experience of intrinsic value. It does not control the experience, but "transparently" results from the experience, the bodily component of the event in consciousness. Yet it is no less a part of the experience, and is, as often as not, the carrot that leads us to seek out the sort of life which is rich in intrinsic awareness. As human beings, we are not just conscious, for we are conscious bodies, as well.

NOTES

1. Robert S. Hartman, The Structure of Value: Foundations of Scientific Axiology (Carbondale: Southern Illinois University Press, 1967), p. 103.

2. Robert S. Hartman, "A Logical Definition of Value," Journal of Philosophy, Vol. XLVIII, no. 13 (October-December, 1951), p. 423.

3. Rem B. Edwards, "Universals, Individuals, and Intrinsic Goods," this volume, p. 101.

4. Robert S. Hartman, and Robert E. Carter, "Dialogue on Intrinsic Value," MSS, 1970, p. 30.

5. Ibid.

6. Ibid., p. 30.

7. Ibid, p. 31. See also Robert S. Hartman, The Structure of Value, pp. 250, 331, 199, 224, and 267.

8. Robert S. Hartman, "The Logic of Value," Review of Metaphysics, XIV (March, 1961), p. 408.

9. Hartman, "The Logic of Value" MSS, p. 32.

10. Ibid.

11. Ibid.

12. Hartman, "The Logic of Value," p. 408.

13. Ibid.

14. Hartman, Carter, "Dialogue," p. 31.

15. Ibid.

16. Ibid., p. 32.

17. Ibid.

18. Ibid., p. 36.

19. Ibid., pp. 32-33.

20. Ibid., p. 36.

21. Ibid., p. 47.

22. Ibid., p. 49.

23. Ibid.

24. Ibid., p. 53.

25. Ibid., p. 61.

26. While Martin Heidegger actually employs the German term Durchsichtigkeit, which is translated as "transparent" in English, Søren Kierkegaard writes of becoming self-conscious, reflective, and authentic. In a study by Adi Shmueli, Kierkegaard & Consciousness (Princeton: Princeton University Press, 1971), p. 118, which Hartman often praised, we find the following: "We have seen that the objective world, the world that direct communication reflects, is not qualitatively articulated. It is oddly opaqued and neither personal consciousness nor qualities can be distinguished, for everything 'fuses and coagulates' in it. In introducing negativity into consciousness, indirect communication dissipates the opaqueness of objectivity." And then, as though thoroughly in tune with Hartman's insights, Shmueli writes on p. 119, "The vast horizon and richness of inwardness constitutes human distinction. The richer the consciousness and the personalities of subjective thinkers respecting even everyday objects, so the greater the qualities and differentiations that will single out those things from the anonymity of objectivity. ... Kierkegaard's point is that richly developed personalities, because of a richly differentiated consciousness, begin to see and to apprehend the world in a rich variety of ways" (p. 119).

In Psychology, Sidney M. Jourard, in his work on "Self-Disclosure and Well-Being," writes at length about the physical, psychological and spiritual importance of the transparency of genuine self-disclosure. One book, actually entitled The Transparent Self: Self-Disclosure and Well-Being (Princeton: Van Nostrand Co., Inc., 1964), is an application of existential psychology, and another, Self-Disclosure: An Experimental Analysis of the Transparent Self (New York: John Wiley & Sons, Inc., 1971), contains a chapter (#24), entitled "The Transparent Way." He writes, "To be transparent is a twofold action, with consequences for self and others. It is to let the disclosure of the world, including our own embodied being, stand forth before our consciousness. It is to be accepting and nonselective toward the ceaseless disclosure of the changing being that is the world. And it is to be an active discloser to the world, which includes one's fellow beings. If I make myself transparent, I suspend my concepts, my expectancies as to how things and people are, and let myself perceive (that is, receive the transmissions of) their being. I suspend my concept of my own being (my self-concept) and let my changing being present itself to my experience, thus necessitating a changed concept of myself, with attendant changes in my behavior. ... My aim, in disclosing myself is to be known, <u>to be perceived by the other as the one I know myself to be</u>" (pp. 180-181).

27. Ibid., pp. 64-66.

28. Ibid., p. 63.

29. Ibid., p. 67.

30. Nishida Kitaro, <u>Intelligibility and the Philosophy of Nothingness</u>, tr. with an Introduction by Robert Schinzinger (Honolulu: East-West Center Press, 1958), from the <u>Frontspiece</u>.

31. Hartman, Carter, "Dialogue," pp. 69-70.

32. Jose Ortega Y Gasset, <u>The Dehumanization of Art</u> (Doubleday & Co., an Anchor paperback, 1956), pp. 13-18.

33. Hartman, The Structure of Value, p. 260.

34. Ibid. Taken from Ortega, The Dehumanization of Art, p. 14.

35. Ibid.

36. Robert S. Hartman, "The Axiomatic Structure of Intrinsic Value," <u>The Journal of Value Inquiry</u>, Vol. VIII, no. 2 (Summer 1974), p. 98.

37. Hartman, Carter, "Dialogue," p. 70.

38. Ibid., p. 73.

39. Ibid.

40. Hartman, The Structure of Value, pp. 266-67; "Logic of Value," pp. 412-23.

41. Hartman, "The Nature of Valuation," this volume, p. 23.

42. Ibid., p. 54; The Structure of Value, pp. 113-14.

43. Hartman, Carter, "Dialogue," p. 73.
44. Ibid., p. 79-80.
45. Ibid., p. 112.
46. Ibid., p. 105.
47. Ibid., p. 110-112.
48. Ibid., p. 114.
49. Ibid., pp. 122-23.
50. Ibid., p. 141.
51. Ibid., p. 150.
52. Ibid., p. 151.

Chapter VII

VALUE COMBINATIONS

Frank G. Forrest

In the previous chapters we saw that the person in modern times who made an important advancement in value theory was Robert S. Hartman. His breakthrough was a general theory founded on a definition of value in strictly logical terms. This definition serves as a basis for the elaboration of a system of logic utilizing set theory applicable to social science and ethics, similar to the way conventional mathematics is applicable to natural science, namely, physics. In this chapter we, first, will examine briefly the nature of science. Then we will study an interpretation of Hartman's axiology called valuemetrics developed by the author of this chapter (Forrest, 1988). Most of the material in this chapter comes from the text on valuemetrics. Valuemetrics essentially is a working model of Hartman's formal axiology applied to ethics. Without the groundwork and foundation he provided the construction of this model would not have been possible.

1.0 The Nature of Science

As a result of the way many people use the word "science," we may incorrectly think of it as a subject. Science is not a subject, it is a _method_ of developing and acquiring knowledge about a subject. Another misconception about science is that this method is applicable only to physical phenomena as in physics. There are different types of sciences. One type is called descriptive science. Geography is an example. Another type of science involves the use of a system of logic such as mathematics that has the same structure as the phenomenon under study and hence models it. Under this conception any number of sciences are possible provided a method of modeling the phenomenal field of a subject is available. Robert S. Hartman has shown us how to do this with the subject matter of moral philosophy. This effort has resulted in the transition of philosophic ethics to scientific ethics. The sequence of events in this accomplishment was: (1) identifying the fundamental phenomenon of ethics, (2) developing a method of measuring this phenomenon, and (3) finding a mathematical system that modeled it.

2.0 What is the Fundamental Phenomenon of Ethics?

Identifying the fundamental phenomenon of ethics involved asking the question, "What is to ethics, for example, as aerodynamic lift is to the theory of flight, or as force is to mechanics?" As described in the chapter, "Extrinsic Value and Valuation" by Professor Davis, Hartman found the reply to this question among the writings of an English scholar, George E. Moore (1873-1958). Moore visualized a science of ethics similar to the natural sciences, and he believed that the study of ethics, whether philosophy or science, was a quest for knowledge of "goodness"--not knowledge of good things but of goodness itself. Evidence that goodness is the fundamental phenomenon of ethics is given in many of the various moral theories. While not all of these theories are stated in terms of goodness, they all can be interpreted in terms of this phenomenon. In any case there are moral principles that command us to be good and achieve goodness. If one is to do this, then obviously he or she must know what is goodness. While Moore postulated that goodness is what ethics is all about, he never defined it such that it would be accessible to measurement. Hartman did. He used semantics as a tool for this purpose. He saw that a concept, one of the elements of semantics, is both a name of a class of objects and a name of the set of properties or attributes possessed by a member of this class. The concept "tree," for instance, is the name of a certain type of plant. This word also is the name of the set of tree attributes, namely, plant, roots, trunk, bark, branches, limbs.... This set of names of properties comprises the definition or meaning of the concept "tree" which in semantics terminology is the concept intension. If one were to ask if goodness is ever a member of this set of properties, Moore's reply would have been, "No, but goodness depends on them." This insight gave Hartman the clue to an objective definition of goodness, which as given previously is: degree of concept intention fulfillment. Hence, concept intension (meaning) is the standard of measure of goodness. An immediate inference from this proposition is: the greater meaning that is fulfilled, the greater the corresponding goodness.

Let us summarize what has been said so far.

(1) Goodness is the fundamental phenomenon of ethics, i.e., goodness is what ethics is all about.

(2) Goodness is not a natural property of anything, but it depends on the natural properties of things. A natural property is an attribute inherent to something such as bark is to a tree.

(3) The collection of the names of the properties of anything comprises a set. This set gives the meaning of the thing's concept. In semantics terminology this set is known as the concept intension.

(4) Goodness is degree of concept intensional set fulfillment.

(5) Concept intension is the measure of goodness. The larger the intensional set that is fulfilled the greater the goodness.

A reading of Hartman's writing will disclose that he tended to use the words "value" and "goodness" synonymously. In this chapter we will see that these words are closely related, but have different meanings. Goodness, as given in (4) above, is degree of concept intension (meaning) fulfillment. There are variations in the size of concept intensions and there are differences in their fulfillment. In order to account for these variations and the myriad gradations of concept intension fulfillment, a construct is required that functions in a manner similar to number. This construct is value. A value and a goodness gradation are the same. Hence, value serves in goodness (quality) accounting as number serves in quantity accounting. The relation between goodness and value is analogous to the relation between temperature and degrees Fahrenheit. We think of certain degrees F as being hot, and another range of degrees F as being warm. The words "hot," "warm," "cool," and so on denote degrees F which are gradations of temperature. The words in the goodness-value relationship that correspond to hot, warm, cool, cold, etc. are excellent, very good, fair, poor, etc. These words denote gradations of goodness, and in this context they are values. Also, in this context the word "value" may be construed as a certain subset of an intensional set, in the same way the word "warm" is a certain subset of all the degrees F. This conception of value is quite different from the meaning of this word in other disciplines where value is defined as an enduring belief that a specific mode of conduct or end-state of existence is personally or socially preferable to an opposite mode of conduct or end-state of existence (Rokeach, 1973).

These conceptions of goodness and value are the foundation of the science of ethics analogous to the way a certain definition of a ray of light is the foundation of the science of optics. Defining a ray of light in a homogeneous medium, "as a straight line" enables us to use various components of the logic of geometry to model the behavior of the fundamental phenomenon of optics. Analogously, defining good and value in terms of sets enables us to use various components of the logic of set theory to model the behavior of the fundamental phenomenon of ethics. These components and certain unique features of its own constitute the subject matter of valuemetrics. Thus, valuemetrics is the framework for the explanation of ethical phenomena just as conventional mathematics is the framework for the explanation of natural phenomena.

According to these definitions anything can be good if it fulfills its concept intension. Things that we dislike such as a skillful thief, a vicious rapist, or pollution all can be good. How do we justify this apparent perversion of the truth? The answer is simply this. We usually define goodness by giving examples of things believed to be good. The criteria for assigning goodness to anything are subjective. This type of definition is unsuitable as a basis for a system of logic. Science must be based on construct concepts defined intensionally and objectively. Application of the system will show us that thieves, rapists, or pollution are bad. These are things that we already know. We do not need a mathematical system to aid us in seeing that these things are of low value. There are, on the other hand, many things about value and disvalue that are not known or about which there is no consensus, as any observer of the state of the world today must agree. Valuemetrics, as will be demonstrated, is an aid in distinguishing right from wrong, good from bad, and in recognizing bad things in the world sometimes disguised as good.

3.0 The Measurement of Goodness

A standard of measure is a unit arbitrarily selected applicable to a specific dimension of some phenomenon. A tree, for example, is so many feet high depending on how many foot long units are contained in its height dimension. If we view goodness as another dimension of a tree like height or weight, and if we see the properties or attributes of a tree as things which correspond to units of measure, we have established a basis for a measurement relationship between meaning and goodness. In order to see this relationship, one must simply understand that in valuemetrics as well as in semantics, the definition or meaning of anything consists of a set of words that name the natural universally understood properties or attributes of the thing being defined. Therefore, just as we can determine the height of a tree by counting off the number of units of measure, such as a foot, from the bottom of the tree to the top, we also can determine the goodness of the tree by counting off the natural properties possessed by the tree that are given in the definition (meaning) of a tree. A tree that has all the natural properties given in the definition or meaning of its concept is a good tree, and one that lacks some of these properties such as bark, limbs, and leaves is not so good. The world in which we live contains many intangible things, justice for example, that do not have natural properties like the roots of a tree. These things still have a meaning, but these meanings are sets of given properties instead of natural properties. The goodness of these things also is a function of the correspondence between the properties they possess and the properties given in their meanings. All meanings have the structure of a set. Sets are mathematical entities and meaning sets are no exception. Sets come in different sizes and so do meaning sets. If goodness is defined as degree of concept meaning fulfillment, we are justified in assuming that the greater the meaning that is fulfilled, the greater the goodness. This conclusion provides the basis for objective differences in the goodness of things depending on the magnitude of the meaning set of the thing's concept. Numbers are associated with the different types of sets. The mathematics of these numbers, called cardinal number arithmetic, is given in set theory. These numbers and their arithmetical operations find practical application in accounting for varying degrees of goodness among the meanings of concepts and concept combinations.

4.0 Accounting for Goodness Mathematically

When we define goodness in terms of the meanings of concepts, we establish three classifications of goodness because there are three types of concepts. The names of these concepts are: (1) construct concepts, (2) analytic concepts, and (3) singular concepts. The meanings of the concepts in these three categories, of course, comprise a set, but the structure of these sets are different. The three types of concepts also are the basis for the three value dimensions described in the previous chapters of this book. This perspective permits us to see systemic value, extrinsic value, and intrinsic value as three discrete realms of goodness. In order to visualize the differences among these three realms, we must take time to review a few things about sets.

4.1 Some Properties of Sets

The two general classifications of sets are finite and infinite. A finite set is a set containing elements (members) such that if one were to count these elements the counting would eventually come to an end. In instances where the counting would never end, the set is infinite. The set of all the countries in North American exemplify a finite set; they can be counted. However, all the possible natural numbers, the set N, starting with 1, 2, 3, and on and on is a set where the counting would never end. For every member of this set another member can be named. Hence, this set is infinite. Within these two classifications, there are two subtypes of finite sets and two subtypes of infinite sets. The two finite subtypes are:

(1) Fixed finite sets--in this type of finite set all the members are known. The set of all the numbers between 5 and 10 is an example of a fixed finite set.

(2) Limited open-end finite sets--there are certain finite sets of properties which have various unknown members. The set of all properties of a tree is an example. We may be able to identify sufficient properties of a tree to define the concept "tree" adequately, but we have no way of knowing all the possible minute parts of a tree. Trees are not man made. As the poet, Joyce Kilmer, wrote "Poems are written by fools like me, but only God can make a tree."

The two subtypes of infinite sets are:

(1) Denumerable infinite sets--set N is an example. Each element of this set is discrete and can be counted, but the counting would never end.

(2) Nondenumerable infinite sets--in this type of infinite set the elements are not discrete. A line of separate holes in the ground is denumerable. A trench connecting these holes is nondenumerable. An example of a nondenumerable infinite set is the set N and all the possible decimal numbers between the members of N. In fact all the possible decimal numbers between 0 and 1 is a nondenumerable infinite set.

There are three kinds of relationships among sets of interest to us-- equal sets, equivalent sets, and subsets. Sets are equal when the elements of one are the same as the elements of the other. For example, Jack and Jane are the parents of two boys, Joe and Jim. Neither Jack nor Jane has other children. If set A is the set of children of which Jack is the father, and set B is the set of children of which Jane is the mother, then sets A and B are equal. In set theory equal sets mean more than having the same number of members. Equal sets have the same members. Sets having the same number of elements, but not the same elements are equivalent. These sets have a one-to-one correspondence. If set A is the set of whole numbers between 1 and 10, and set B is the set of whole numbers between 21 and 30, then set A is equivalent to set B. But if set B is the set of numbers 4, 5, and 6, then set B is a proper subset of set A. A set is a proper subset of another if it has some but not all of the members of the other.

The final feature of sets that concerns us is set cardinality. The cardinality of a set simply is the number of elements it contains. The cardinality of set B in the example just given is the number "3," that is, card B = 3. Both finite and infinite sets have cardinalities. The cardinal number of any finite set is the natural number that corresponds to the number of elements in the set. However, in valuemetrics we use a general number to denote the cardinality of any finite set. Two general finite numbers are required because fixed and limited open-end finite sets have unique cardinalities. The symbols "n" will be used as the cardinal number of the set having the fewer elements and "k" the larger. In valuemetrics, if set A is finite, then card A = n or k. How to choose the proper cardinal number for a given finite set is explained in the next section. Infinite sets have transfinite cardinal numbers. The mathematician who originated set theory, Georg Cantor (1845-1918), used the first letter of the Hebrew alphabet, aleph ($\aleph$) as the symbol for these numbers. This letter is pronounced "al-ef" with the accent on the first syllable. Use of an embellished upper-case "a" (A for aleph) is permissible. In Cantor's system aleph null ($\aleph_0$) is the symbol that denotes the cardinality of a denumerable infinite set. Higher orders of infinity are designated by aleph sub-one ($\aleph_1$), aleph sub-two ($\aleph_2$), etc. The Cardinality of the set of natural numbers (N), therefore, is $\aleph_0$, and the cardinality of a nondenumerable infinite set such as the set of real numbers (R) is $\aleph_1$.

4.2 Types of Concepts and Types of Sets

We will enhance our understanding of the relationship between concepts and sets if we first review a few things concerning the nature of concepts. A concept simply is the name of something. A concept has a meaning and it has examples or referents. In semantics terminology, the meaning of the concept is called the intension. All the examples of the concept is the concept extension. Both concept intension and extension are sets. Another set of interest to us is the set of actual properties a particular referent possesses. The relationship between this set and the intensional set of the thing's concept, incidentally, is the essence of goodness.

There are, as we saw at the start of this section, three types of concepts. The basis for the difference among these types of concepts is the structure of their intensional set. We saw also in the previous subsection that there are four different types of sets. The types of sets that correspond to the types of concepts are:

Type concept	Type Set	Cardinal Number
Construct	Fixed-finite	n
Analytic	Limited open-end finite	k^1
Singular	Nondenumerable infinite	$\aleph_1$

Construct concepts: The collection of attributes of things named by a construct concept is a fixed-finite set, and, as noted in the previous subparagraph, the cardinality of this set is the number "n." The referents of construct concepts for the most part are intangible things invented by mankind. They are the names of ideas. The word "contract" is a construct concept defined as follows--contract: (1) a binding agreement or pledge, (2) written or unwritten, (3) between two or more persons or parties, (4) containing all pertinent terms and conditions. The intension of this concept is a set of four members. For a contract to be a contract, all of these elements must be fulfilled, but no more. If we add another property to this last, we would not have a contract, but would have something else or nothing. Hence, this intension is a fixed-finite set. Caution: do not make the mistake of thinking that because contracts often are written on paper that they are tangible. The tangible thing is the paper. The intangible idea is the contract. Referents of construct concepts are intangible, but not imaginary. They are quite real. The concept intensional set and the set of actual properties of a referent are equal. For this reason only one gradation of goodness is associated with this type of concept. Other examples of construct concepts are:

(1) the names of all mankind's institutions--government, business, education, war, etc.

(2) the names of all geometric figures--circles, squares, triangles, etc.

(3) the names of all numbers

(4) terms used in scientific formulas

---

[1]This is a variation from information given in the chapter "Extrinsic Value and Valuation." The following discussion of analytic concepts contains reasons for this change.

(5) the names of all positions in an organization or institution--janitor, president, captain, secretary, etc.

Analytic concepts: Analytic concepts are the names of things that exist in nature like trees or things mankind builds such as a house using trees. The intension of the concept "house" contains all the names of the properties of a house such as: building in which people reside, rooms, foundation, windows, porch, and on and on. For purposes of communication we can adequately define the concept "house" by naming only a few of a house's most well known features. However, the complete definition of this concept in the valuemetrics context includes the names of all the parts of a house down to the smallest detail, and all the known and unknown properties of the materials used in construction of the house. Each property is discrete. The intensional set of the concept "house" and all other analytic concepts is denumerable. Is this set finite or infinite? Robert S. Hartman took the position that while this set potentially is infinite, for practical purposes it is finite. If we assume that this set is infinite, this assumption leads to solutions of problems in human affairs which he says, "outruns ordinary understanding" (The Structure of Value, p. 278). Therefore, we will assume that the intensions of analytic concepts are finite sets, but not fixed because they contain unknown elements. The type of set that meets these criteria is the limited open-end finite set of cardinality "k". Under these circumstances, a house, for example, can exist without possessing all the possible properties named in the intension of the concept "house." A house without a porch is still a house. Hence, there are various gradations of goodness of houses. Some houses are better than others because they posses a greater number of properties.

In addition to the names of natural objects and things mankind builds using these objects, analytic concepts include the names of all types of actions, and all types of roles. The names of various actions are verbs such as walking, talking, moving, etc. Many words that name a role also name a position in an organization. The concept "manager," for example, as a role is an analytic concept, but as a position in an organization it is a construct concept. The role "manager" may be fulfilled if a certain number of attributes or functions are satisfied. But these minimum attributes are not the limit. A variable number of other managerial functions may be fulfilled some of which at a particular point in time may be unknown. Therefore, the attributes of a specific referent of the concept "manager" will be a proper subset of the intensional set of this concept. Hence, as role models we can compare managers with each other or with an arbitrary standard. However, if we define manager as a duly established position in a organization, this is not the case. As a position in an organization all managers are the same. The meaning set of this word used in this context and the set of properties of a referent are equal. Knowing how these types of words are used is important because fulfillment of an analytic concept is a greater good than fulfillment of a construct concept.

<u>Singular concepts</u>: All known things in the universe are named by a construct or analytic concept except a person and God. The latter are singular concepts. This includes all the derivatives of person and people such as human beings, human life, man, woman, girl, boy, child, and all the singular and plural pronouns. When the article "a" precedes the name of a role or position in an organization, for instance "a soldier," this is a person. All the proper names of persons like "Henry Jackson," "Abu Ben Adam," "Mary Smith," etc. are singular concepts. The concept "Mary Smith" has a meaning like any other concept. However, the person Mary Smith is the only referent of this concept. Hence, the intensional set of the concept "Mary Smith" and the set of properties of the referent are the same. What type of set is this intension? The elements of this set are all her physical attributes and much more. She has a brain, a spirit, and a self. She and all other person have an infinite number of properties. Is this set denumerable or nondenumerable? The logical answer goes like this. If we consider a particular thought as a property of a person, the cardinality of this set is at least $\aleph_0$. Mary will not live long enough to think all these thoughts, but they exist in the same sense as the set of natural numbers (N) exists. When we established the set N, we simultaneously constituted an infinity of thoughts. Each member of this set is a thought which Mary and any other person capable of thinking possesses. Hence, if Mary has the capacity to think of any member of set N, she, a priori, has a denumerable infinity of thoughts just on the basis of the existence of this set. However, Mary has many other possible thoughts all of which can be combined with each other to include all the subsets of set N. This situation can be accounted for in transfinite number arithmetic. The arithmetical operation in this situation results in $\aleph_0$ increasing to $\aleph_1$ (Lin and Lin, 1985). Accordingly, the meaning of Mary Smith and every one else, not in a permanent coma, constitutes a nondenumerable infinite set--"a spiritual Gestalt" the structure of which is that of a continuum[2] (Hartman, 1967). This result is a mathematical accounting for one of the moral postulates of philosophy, that is, the infinite value of a person. It also accounts for one of the principles of democracy pertaining to the equality of all persons under the law.

---

[2] A set with the same transfinite cardinal number as the set of real numbers, i.e., $\aleph_1$. (Webster's Seventh New collegiate Dictionary, 1976).

4.3 Value Dimension

Value dimension is an expression Hartman adopted to identify a realm of goodness. The three realms of goodness are: (1) the goodness associated with construct concept meanings (systemic value), (2) the goodness associated with analytic concept meanings (extrinsic value), and (3) the goodness associated with singular concept meanings (intrinsic value). Within these three realms there are gradations of goodness. In our discussion of the difference between goodness and value, we mentioned that values are goodness gradations, and that they have such names as excellent, very good, fair, poor, and any other evaluative words one would care to employ. The relationship among value dimensions, concepts and values is shown as follows:

Value Dimension	Associated Concept	Number of Possible Values	Names of Values
Systemic	Construct	1	Excellent, or perfect or superior
Extrinsic	Analytic	1 or more depending on the number of known elements in the intension of the associated concept	Excellent, very good, fair, poor, etc.
Intrinsic	Singular	1	Good (axiologically)

Unlike construct and analytic concepts which have any number of referents, a singular concept has only one referent, and one degree of goodness. There is no difference in the number of properties Mary Smith possesses and the number of elements in the intensional set of the concept "Mary Smith." Both of these sets are nondenumerably infinite having a cardinal number of $\aleph_1$. This condition exists with respect to all persons in the universe regardless of their national origin, religion, skin color, sex, physical or mental dexterity, or behavior. Thus, in this realm there is only one goodness gradation. How then can we account for differences in people and classify some as good, some bad, and some better than others? As persons of intrinsic value, there are no differences among people. Mary Smith, be she an adulteress, thief, and abject liar, is just as good axiologically as is Mother Teresa. What is bad is her behavior. But as previously shown, if the concepts "adultery," "theft," and "liar" are fulfilled that is goodness. If Mary as a person

136 *Forms of Value and Valuation: Theory and Applications*

is intrinsically good, and if she cheats on her husband, steals, and lies skillfully is she not good all around? If so, something seems to be wrong. How do we eliminate this confusion? The mathematics of concept conjunctions and combinations provides the answer.

4.4 Concept Conjunctions and Combinations

The logic of concept conjunctions and combinations is a mathematical system that accounts for the outcome of linking and merging concept intensional sets. The cardinal numbers n, k, and $\aleph_1$ represent the three types of concepts in this system. In this capacity these numbers are called value indexes. Thus, the value indexes of the three types of concepts are:

Type Concept	Value Index
Construct	n
Analytic	k
Singular	$\aleph_1$

Robert S. Hartman conceived of the application of the arithmetic of cardinal numbers to concept conjunctions and combinations. In recognition of his profound idea, we will call this mathematical system Hartmanean algebra. He used the words "calculus of value" for the name of this system.

The difference between concept conjunction and concept combination can be illustrated using chemical processes as an analogy. Chemical mixtures, salt and pepper, for example, retain their properties when intermingled and are analogous to concept conjunctions. However, the combination of such substances as sodium and chlorine produces something new or different (salt). This process is analogous to concept combinations. The latter method of associating concepts is the more important and, hence, is of primary concern to Hartmanean algebra. Concept combinations are people's thought creations which find expression in language. In certain respects, concepts are like geometric figures. Just as rectangles, triangles, and circles have different structures, so construct, analytic, and singular concepts have different intensional structures. Geometric figures may be combined in any number of arrangements and patterns. So may concepts. Geometric figure combinations offer a method of visualizing concept intension combinations. The combination of a right triangle and a rectangle in a certain manner produces a trapezoid as shown in Figure 1.

Value Combinations 137

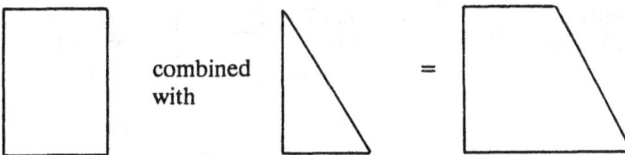

Figure 1. Formation of a Trapezoid

The combination of the concept "person" and the concept "marriage" in a similar manner produces the concept "spouse." If we use the symbol "C_1" for the first concept, the symbol "C_2" for the second, and the symbol "R" for the resultant of the concept combination, then,

$$C_1 \text{ combined with } C_2 = R$$

Many single words such as "spouse" are a combination of two or more underlying prime concepts. These words give the meaning of the resultant concept, and they modify each other, or one concept modifies the other. A prime concept, on the other hand, is a word the meaning of which is given by concepts that do not modify each other. The trunk and leaves of a tree, for example, are part of the meaning of a tree, but the word "trunk" and the word "leaves" do not modify or transform each other. They augment each other. Prime concepts are analogous to chemical elements and resultant concepts are analogous to chemical compounds.

Geometric figures have areas. The corresponding feature of concepts are their value indexes. When two geometric figures are combined, so are their areas. Computation of the new area is possible using certain procedures and conventional arithmetic. When two concepts are combined so are their value indexes. Computation of the resultant concept value index is possible using the arithmetic of general finite and transfinite numbers and other procedures. Various operations with the numbers n, k, and $\aleph_1$ in accordance with this arithmetic are the essence of Hartmanean algebra.

The most basic combination consists of two prime concepts and attendant value indexes which combine as a composition or a transposition. The diagram of an open system, Figure 2, depicts this process.

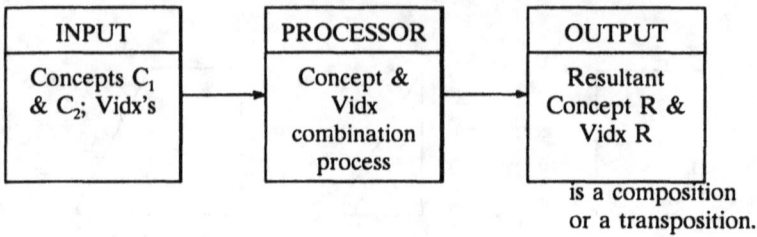

is a composition
or a transposition.

Figure 2. Concept Combination Process

Concept combinations are compositional or transpositional depending on how the combination affects the intensions of the input concepts directly or indirectly, immediately or long term.

If the input intensions are complementary and promote fulfillment of one or the other, a value enhancement has occurred. Value enhancement is compositional. If the input intensions are incompatible and inhibit fulfillment of one or the other, a disvalue has occurred. Disvalue is transpositional. Concept intensions essentially are meanings. When the meaning of at least one input concept is broadened or deepened, the combination is compositional. When it is depleted, fragmented, or degraded, the combination is transpositional. The following illustration reveals how this works. A brand new <u>car</u> is placed in a beautiful <u>show-room</u>. These two concepts complement each other. The combination is compositional. The dealer sells the car but while it is being delivered it collides with a truck resulting in a major accident. Even though this is an example of a "good" accident in that the intension of the concept "accident" is fulfilled, the intension of the concept "car" is depleted. The concept "car" and the concept "collision" are incompatible. Therefore, we have a transposition.

Concept combinations are transpositional when the concept combination is nonsense or a contradiction. A resultant intension containing incoherent subsets is nonsense. The combination of the concept "female" and the concept "mountain" is an example of nonsense. The union of the intensional sets of these two concepts has no referent. The proposition "a mountain is female" cannot be shown to be either true or false. This is the language of jokes. Concept combinations of this nature are transpositional.

The concept combination "married-bachelor" is an example of a contradiction. The relationship of the input concepts in this example is such that if either one is true or false, the other is false or true. This type of combination, like the nonsense combination, has no referent because it is impossible for a thing to be and not to be at the same time.

Later in this chapter we will see how to account for compositions and transposition mathematically. At this point, however, we have the key that unlocks the paradox of how something we consider evil, detestable, or wrong, such as unfaithful spouse, can fulfill its definition, and hence, be good. Whereas a good "unfaithful-spouse" is plausible, these concepts are transpositional, and that is bad. This suggests that the logic of composition and transposition is a reliable and consistent guide for differentiating good from bad, and right from wrong, as well as for making value judgments in general. The following list contains words that connote composition or transposition as indicated.

Composition		Transposition	
advance	facilitate	antitheses	illusion
aid	help	artificial	inconsistent
ameliorate	increase	cheat	incompatible
augment	improve	contradiction	incorrect
beautify	justice	counterfeit	injury
benefit	mend	death	injustice
better	perfect	deception	invalid
build	promote	degradation	impractical
complement	raise	deleterious	imprecision
correct	rectify	depreciation	misfit
develop	rectitude	deterioration	negate
endow	righteousness	destruction	nonsense
enhance	repair	dysfunction	paradox
enlarge	restore	fake	pervert
enable	strengthen	false	perversion
enrich		farce	ruin
		fraud	travesty
		hypocrisy	wrong

When a concept combination involves a human being, composition or transposition occurs depending on how the combination affects the person's physical being, mental health, and self. Physical being refers to all features that comprise the human body and a person's physical needs such as food, water, shelter, sleep, comfort, and clothing. The resultant of a concept combination is compositional when the combination indicates the proper configuration and functioning of a person's body necessary for sustained health. The resultant is transpositional if any of the following is indicated:

disease, pain, sickness, loss of parts of the body, failures of systems within the body, death, or deprivation of physical needs.

Mental health is the state of a person's freedom from debilitating forms of neurosis and psychosis. Resultant concepts are compositional when they reflect happiness, joy, emotional control, and the ability to cope with anxiety, tension, stress, nervousness, depression, and hostility. They are transpositional when they indicate psychological disorder.

Compositions and transpositions related to the self depend on how the concept combination indicates enhancement or depreciation of self-fulfillment. Self-fulfillment refers to a person's drive to realize his or her greatest potential, and the satisfaction of one's continuous need for respect, self-esteem, human dignity, and love. Resultant concepts are compositional with regard to self-fulfillment of a person when the promotion of such conditions as the following are indicated.

(1) Existence of a calling, work, or activity that gives happiness and meaning in life.

(2) Developing awareness of the need to be responsible for one's actions.

(3) Opportunity to acquire knowledge and develop one's skills.

(4) Participation in decisions affecting one's life and welfare.

(5) Avoidance of dishonesty, equivocation, hypocrisy, selfishness, and self-indulgence.

(6) Attaining peak experiences in life.[3]

(7) Developing a harmonious and integrated personality.

Concept combinations indicating things that deny or inhibit these conditions are transpositional.

---

[3]Peak experiences are ecstatic, joyous, happy, blissful moments in a person's life, Maslow (1971).

4.5 General Finite and Transfinite Number Arithmetic

Hartmanean algebra consists of various operations with the value indexes n, k, and $\aleph_1$ These operations involve the mathematics of general finite and transfinite numbers. The fundamentals of this system of logic are contained in that segment of set theory known as cardinal arithmetic. Our interest in cardinal arithmetic will be limited to those operations associated with concept conjunction and combination. These operations are addition and exponentiation.

<u>Addition</u>: In order to show the logic of general finite and transfinite number addition, we will use an operation with sets not previously explained. This operation pertains to the union of two sets, denoted by A ∪ B, where A is any set and B is any other set. A ∪ B also is a set defined by:

A ∪ B = the set of elements "x" such that x is a member of set A or B.

EXAMPLE

Let sets A = {1, 2, 3} and B = {7, 8}. In set theory the symbols { } are used to denote a set.

A ∪ B = {1, 2, 3, 7, 8} and card (A ∪ B) = card A + card B.

The union of sets permits us to see how general finite and transfinite numbers are added to themselves and to each other.

EXAMPLE
Let A and B be any two fixed finite sets. Then

card A = n and card B = n   [By previous definition]

card (A ∪ B) = n + n.   [Definition: union of sets]

But, A ∪ B also is a fixed finite set. Thus,

card (A ∪ B) = n. Hence,

n + n = n   which means that the sum of any two finite numbers is a finite number

Similarly, we find that k + k = k. The sum of k and n (k + n) equal k because the union of a limited open end finite set of card k and a fixed finite set of card n is still a limited open end finite set.

We will use the union of sets to determine the results of adding two alephs and an aleph with n or k.

EXAMPLE

Let N_o and N_e be the sets of all possible odd and even numbers. Then

card $N_o = \aleph_o$

card $N_e = \aleph_o$ and

card $(N_o \cup N_e) = \aleph_o + \aleph_o$

However, the union of the sets of all possible odd and even numbers is the set N, i.e., $N_o \cup N_e = N$. But,

card $N = \aleph_o$. Therefore,

$\aleph_o + \aleph_o = \aleph_o$.

Adding higher order alephs, however, requires theorems and procedures in addition to the union of sets operation. These operations are of such complexity as to render an explanation herein impractical, but they are given in the set theory texts--Lin and Lin, or Zuckerman--used as references. Therefore, we will use these references to establish that:

$\aleph_1 + \aleph_1 = \aleph_1$ [Lin & Lin, p. 211, Ex. 6.4 5]

$\aleph_1 + \aleph_o = \aleph_1$ [Lin & Lin, p. 141]

$\aleph_o + $ (n or k) $= \aleph_o$ [Lin & Lin, p. 141]

$\aleph_1 + $ (n or k) $= \aleph_1$ [Lin & Lin, p. 141]

The union of a nondenumerable infinite set, e.g., set X, with a lower order infinite set or a finite set does not alter the structure of X. Hence,

$\aleph_{x+1} + \aleph_x = \aleph_{x+1}$ and

$\aleph_x + (n \text{ or } k) = \aleph_x.$

The general rule for addition in cardinal arithmetic is:

> The sum of any combination of general finite and transfinite numbers equal the highest number being considered, e.g., $\aleph_1 + k + \aleph_0 = \aleph_1$

Exponentiation: Exponentiation is an extension of multiplication, and multiplication is an extension of addition. We saw in the previous section that $n + n = n$. The expression $n \times n$ means that n is added to itself n times, i.e., $(((n + n) + n) \ldots n)$. The sum of the first two n's is equal to n, and that n added to the third n is equal to n and so on. Hence, $n \times n = n$ which means that a finite number multiplied by a finite number is a finite number. Next, n^n means that n is multiplied by itself n times, i.e. $(((n \times n) \times n) \ldots n)$. Since $n \times n = n$, by the process of iteration $n^n = n$. By the same procedure $k^k = k$ and $k^n = k$. What about n^k? If we can demonstrate that $n^k > k^n$, then we would be justified in assuming that n^k also equal k. We will make this determination by the method of empirical evidence. The relationship between k^n and n^k may be established by substituting specific finite numbers in these expressions where $n < k$ as shown in Table A.

Table A
Comparison of k^n and n^k

n	k	k^n	n^k
2	3	9	8
2	4	16	16
2	5	25	32
3	4	64	81
3	5	125	243
4	5	625	1024
4	6	1296	4096
5	6	7776	15625

An examination of this table reveals that for all possible exponential pairs of finite numbers where $n < k$, $n^k > k^n$ except when $n = 2$ and $k = 3$ or 4. In valuemetrics n and k are the value indexes of the meanings of construct and analytic concepts. In these capacities a specific finite number for n can be known, and we know that $n < k$. The most simple of all construct concept intensions is an operational definition of the nature $A = B$.

The specific value index of a concept defined by A = B may be determined as follows.

Let the formula A = B be the intension set (IN) of the concept X.

Then, $IN_x = \{A, =, B\}$ and card $IN_x = 3$.

In Table A all exponential combinations of n and k when $n \geq 3$ indicate that $n^k > k^n$. Therefore, if $k^n = k$, we may assume that in valuemetrics

$n^k = k$.

$\aleph_x$ raised to the n or k power i.e., $\aleph_x^{(n \text{ or } k)}$ means that the aleph is multiplied by itself n or k times. The results of these operations, by iteration, are equal to $\aleph_x$.

Let $\aleph_x$ be any transfinite number. Then

$(((\aleph_x + \aleph_x) + \aleph_x)\ldots \aleph_x) = \aleph_x$. Thus,

$\aleph_x \times \aleph_x = \aleph_x$, and

$(((\aleph_x \times \aleph_x) \times \aleph_x)\ldots \aleph_x) = \aleph_x$. Therefore,

$\aleph_x^{(n \text{ or } k)} = \aleph_x$

When we raise n, k, or $\aleph_x$ to the $\aleph_y$ power the process of iteration is not applicable. Instead we use mathematical functions and the Aleph Hypothesis. These operations also are beyond the scope of materials in this book, but may be found in our reference tests. The results of these operations reveal that:

$\aleph_x^{\aleph_y} = \aleph_{y+1}$ when $y \geq x$, and $\aleph_x^{\aleph_y} = \aleph_x$ when $x > y$ \qquad [Zuckerman, p.356]

and

$(n \text{ or } k)^{\aleph_y} = \aleph_{y+1}$. \qquad [Lin & Lin, p. 146]

The following rules pertain to exponentiation of n, k, and the alephs.

(1) n, k, $\aleph_0, \aleph_1 \ldots$ raised to the nth power equal n, k, $\aleph_0, \aleph_1$

(2) n, k, $\aleph_0, \aleph_1 \ldots$ raised to the kth power equal k, k, $\aleph_0, \aleph_1$

Value Combinations

(3) $n\aleph_x$, $k\aleph_x$ and $\aleph_x^{\aleph_x} = \aleph_{x+1}$

(4) $\aleph_x^{\aleph_y} = \aleph_{y+1}$ when $y > x$, and $\aleph_x^{\aleph_y} = \aleph_x$ when $x > y$.

4.6 Hartmanean Operations

Basic Equation: The key aspect of a concept combination is the compositional or transpositional nature of the resultant. The mathematical operation that reflects the behavior of value indexes in concept combination is exponentiation because it reveals possible value improvement or depreciation as a consequence of the combination. In applying this operation, we let C_x and C_y be any two prime concepts and R be the resultant of their combination. If these concepts combine in such manner that C_x is the base and C_y is the exponent,[4] the resulting combinations are:

$C_x^{C_y}$ if they combine compositionally, and

$C_x^{-C_y}$ if they combine transpositionally.

If the combination of C_x and C_y produces R then,

$$R = C_x^{\pm C_y}.$$

This expression is the basic equation of Hartmanean algebra. Concept combinations produce value index combinations. Therefore, by the principle of substitution the basic value index (Vidx) equation of Hartmanean algebra is:

$$\text{Vidx } R = \text{Vidx } C_x^{\pm \text{Vidx } C_y}.$$

If the value index of C_x is k and the value index of C_y is n, then

$$\text{Vidx } R = k^{\pm n}.$$

There are three types of concepts, each of which may be paired with another compositionally or transpositionally. Thus, the total possible number of forms of the basic value index formula as shown in Table B is 18.

---

[4] Rules for making this determination are given subsequently.

TABLE B

Basic Vidx Formula Forms

Base Vidx	Composition			Transposition		
	n Exponent	k Exponent	$\aleph_1$ Exponent	n Exponent	k Exponent	$\aleph_1$ Exponent
n	n^n	n^k	$n^{\aleph_1}$	n^{-n}	n^{-k}	$n^{-\aleph_1}$
k	k^n	k^k	$k^{\aleph_1}$	k^{-n}	k^{-k}	$k^{-\aleph_1}$
$\aleph_1$	$\aleph_1^n$	$\aleph_1^k$	$\aleph_1^{\aleph_1}$	$\aleph_1^{-n}$	$\aleph_1^{-k}$	$\aleph_1^{-\aleph_1}$

Earlier in this section we saw how concept combinations produce something new or different and how the input concept intensions are either fulfilled or depreciated. We saw also that exponentiation of concept value indexes suitably reflects the outcome of a concept combination. Concept conjunctions, on the other hand, do not yield anything different from the input concepts. Neither composition nor transposition is involved. One concept simply is coupled with the other. The mathematical operation that accounts for this process is general finite and transfinite number addition. Concept conjunctions appear in the basic equation as augmentations of one or both of the input concepts. The equation

$$R = C_x^{\pm C_y},$$ for example, might be augmented to include a

concept conjunction in lieu of C_y. The equation then would read

$$R = C_x^{\pm (C_{y1} + C_{y2})}.$$

4.7 Transfinite Fractions

One method of looking at a proper fraction is to see the denominator as the total number of equal subdivisions of any unit, and the numerator as any number of these subdivisions from 1 to the total. Hartmanean algebra is concerned with proper fractions having a numerator of 1 and a denominator of one of the general finite or transfinite numbers. In conventional arithmetic both the numerator and denominator of a proper fraction are specific finite numbers. Are proper fractions having transfinite denominators conceivable?

Answer: let g--h be any line segment in Figure 3 containing a unit bounded by 0 and 1.

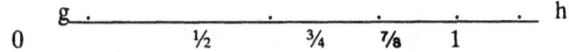

Figure 3. Infinite series Converging to Zero

If we go half the distance from 0 to 1, and then half the remaining distance to 3/4, and half the remaining distance to 7/8, and on and on, each interval becomes smaller (1/2, 1/4, 1/8, 1/16, . . .) but the process never ends. In this process the denominator of the series of fractions increases <u>ad infinitum</u>. If $\aleph_0$ is the number representing denumerable infinity and if $\aleph_1$ represents a greater infinity, we have the series:

$$1/2, 1/4, 1/8, 1/16, \ldots 1/n, 1/k, 1/\aleph_0, 1/\aleph_1, \ldots$$

4.8 Solution of Basic Value Index Equation

The value index combination framework developed to this point and the arithmetic of general finite and transfinite numbers provide a means for solving any basic value index equation. For example,

if Vidx $R = k^n$, then Vidx $R = k$ [Rule 1 p.144]

Table C shows the corresponding resultant value indexes of the 18 basic formulas given in Table B.

TABLE C
Vidx R for All Combinations of n, k, and X_1

Base Vidx	Composition			Transposition*		
	n Exp Vidx R	k Exp Vidx R	X_1 Exp Vidx R	-n Exp Vidx R	-k Exp Vidx R	-X Exp Vidx R
n	$n^n = n$	$n^k = k$	$n^{X_1} = X_a$	$n^{-n} = 1/n$	$n^{-k} = 1/k$	$n^{-X_1} = 1/X_a$
k	$k^n = k$	$k^k = k$	$k^{X_1} = X_a$	$k^{-n} = 1/k$	$k^{-k} = 1/k$	$k^{-X_1} = 1/X_a$
X_1	$X_1^n = X_1$	$X_1^k = X_1$	$X_1^{X_1} = X_a$	$X_1^{-n} = 1/X_1$	$X_1^{-k} = 1/X_1$	$X_1^{-X_1} = 1/X_a$

*Any quantity with a negative exponent may be written as the reciprocal of the quantity with a positive exponent (Parson 1961).

Consolidation of the data in Table C reveals that:

$$n^n = n \qquad n^{-n} = 1/n$$
$$n^k = k^n = k^k = k \qquad n^{-k} = k^{-n} = k^{-k} = 1/k$$
$$X_1^n = X_1^k = X_1 \qquad X_1^{-n} = X_1^{-k} = 1/X_1$$
$$n^{X_1} = k^{X_1} = X_1^{X_1} = X_2 \qquad n^{-X_1} = k^{-X_1} = X_1^{-X_1} = 1/X_2$$

The application of Hartmanean algebra to solve valuemetrics problems is for the purpose of determining the value index of concept combinations. Hence, we start with the resultant. If R is a binary concept, that is, if it has two prime underlying concepts, then seven steps are required to find the value index of R.

<u>Finding the Value Index of R</u>

Steps:
1. Determine the underlying concepts C_1 and C_2.

2. Identify the value indexes' of C_1 and C_2.

3. Determine the base concept in the exponentiation of C_1 and C_2. This step is required only when the value indexes are different --See Step 3 in the following Example.

4. Determine whether the combination is a composition or a transposition.

5. Write the basic equation for R; i.e., $R = C_x^{\pm C_y}$.

6. Write the basic value index equation substituting the value indexes of C_x and C_y for these terms in the equation.

7. Perform the indicated arithmetic. The outcome is the value index of the concept combination R.

EXAMPLE 1. Find the Vidx of the concept "spouse."

GIVEN

R: spouse

150   *Forms of Value and Valuation: Theory and Applications*

SOLUTION

Step 1. If the underlying concepts are neither specified nor evident, refer to the dictionary or other pertinent authentic reference material. In this instance C_1 is the concept "married" and C_2 is the concept "person."

Step 2. C_1 is a status in society, a construct concept, having a Vidx of n. C_2 is a singular concept the Vidx of which is $\aleph_1$.

Step 3. In order to determine which input concept in the basic equation is the base and which is he exponent, apply the following exponentiation rules -- ER's.

ER 1. Ask which concept names the thing valued and which indicates how or why it is valued? The name of the thing valued is the base, i.e.,

$R = (\text{what is valued})^{\pm \text{how or why}}$.

The concept valued, the what, is the concept whose fulfillment is enhanced or depreciated as a consequence of the combination. In certain instances both concepts enhance or depreciate each other. If this is the case, go to ER 2 or 3.

ER 2. Ask which concept is the means with respect to the resultant as the end? The means concept is the exponent, i.e.,

$R = C_x^{\pm(\text{the means})}$.

ER 3. If one concept modifies the other grammatically as an adjective modifies a noun, ask which concept is modified? The concept modified is the base, i.e.,

$R = (\text{concept modified, e.g., a noun})^{\pm(\text{modifier})}$.

Value Combinations 151

Marriage contributes to the fulfillment of a person physically, mentally, and spiritually unless there are indications to the contrary. In this example no such indications exist. Therefore, by ER 1, C_2 is the base, and C_1 is the exponent.

Step 4. Any one of the following composition rules (CR's) justifies assigning a positive (+) exponent.

CR 1. When the input concepts are compatible, agreeable, consistent, or harmonious.

CR 2. When C_x and C_y complement each other.

CR 3. When C_x enhances fulfillment of C_y or vice versa.

CR 4. When one input concept broadens or deepens the meaning of the other.

CR 5. When either input concept is a person, a situation that benefits, comforts, helps, improves, promotes, or strengthens the person's physical, psychological, social, or spiritual being.

Any of the following transposition rules (TR's) justifies assigning a negative (-) exponent.

TR 1. When the input concepts are incompatible, conflicting, disagreeing, discordant, incongruous, or inconsistent.

TR 2. When they produce a deficiency, deficit, detraction, destruction, or something unlawful.[5]

---

[5]Unlawfulness is a transposition provided the law violated is not a transposition.

TR 3. When one input concept hinders, impedes, or obstructs fulfillment of the other.

TR 4. When C_x narrows, restricts, or limits the meaning of C_y.

TR 5. When the resultant concept has no referent.

TR 6. When either input concept is a person, a situation that results in hurting, injuring, or weakening the person's physical, psychological, social, or spiritual being.

By reason of CR 2 and 5, C_1 is a positive (+) exponent.

Step 5. $R = C_2^{C_1}$

Step 6. Vidx $R = \aleph_1^a$

Step 7. Vidx $R = \aleph_1$

These seven steps are consolidated in the following format for the solution of a problem.

SOLUTION

C_1: write the word for the first concept; and its Vidx.

C_2: do the same for the second concept.

$R = C_x^{\pm C_y}$

Vidx R = Vidx $C_x^{\pm \text{Vidx } C_y}$

Vidx $R = ?$

The solution to the problem in this example according to the consolidated format reads as follows:

C_1: married; n

C_2: person; $\aleph_1$

$R = C_2{}^{C_1}$

Vidx $R = \aleph_1{}^n = \aleph_1$

The following problem involves a transposition.

EXAMPLE 2. Find the Vidx of the concept combination "illegal rule" in the context of the rules and regulations of an organization.

GIVEN

(1) R: illegal rule

(2) The law involved in this matter is just.

SOLUTION

C_1: rule; n

C_2: legality; n

$R = C_1{}^{-C_2}$ TR 2

Vidx $R = n^{-n} = 1/n$

Hartmanean algebra goes beyond finding the value index of a combination of two prime concepts. The resultant of a concept combination can be combined with a third concept to form a second order combination as depicted in Figure 4.

154   *Forms of Value and Valuation: Theory and Applications*

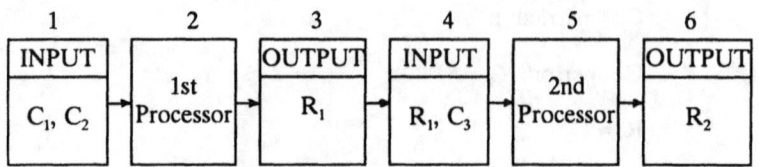

Figure 4. Second Order Concept Combination

The output of Stage 6, Figure 4 may be combined with a fourth concept, the resultant of which may be combined with a fifth concept and so on indefinitely. Resultant concepts also may be combined provided that one of the R's in the combination has not been an input concept for the other. In Figure 4, R_1 and R_2 may not be combined, but R_2 may be combined with R_3 provided R_3 is a combination of concepts not involved with the production of R_2. Example 3 illustrates the effect of combining more than two concepts.

EXAMPLE 3. Find the Vidx of the concept combination "faithful spouse."

    GIVEN

        R_x: faithful spouse

SOLUTION

        R_1: spouse; $\aleph_1$ Example 1

        C_3: faithful; k   In this instance the concept "faithful" denotes a form of behavior. The Vidx, therefore, is k.

        $R_2 = R_1^{C_3}$

        Vidx $R_2 = (\aleph_1)^k = \aleph_1$

Value Combinations 155

4.9 Concept Combination Topology

In Figure 4 and Example 3 we saw how a resultant R, can become a factor in the basic equation of Hartmanean algebra. The resultant of a combination of a resultant and a prime concept is a second order combination. A third order combination occurs when an R_2 combines with a prime concept or another R. Theoretically, the number of resultant orders is limitless. The rules for exponentiation, composition, and transposition-- ER's, CR's and TR's--previously given apply to the combination of R's and C's, and R's with other R's. The following recapitulation pertains to the various types of combinations that are possible with two, three, or more prime concepts.

First Order Combination: As stated previously, the symbol C_X where X is any whole number, designated a concept having a value index--n, k, or $\aleph_1$. The first concept is C_1, the second C_2, and so on sequentially. The resultant of the combination of any two prime concepts is a new concept designated as R_1 having a value index derived by exponentiation of the input concept value indexes. In terms of index numbers there are 18 different forms of first order combinations such as $\aleph_1^n$, k^k, n^{-k}, ... (See Table C).

Second Order Combination: This type of combination contains three prime concepts. The resultant of the combination of any two of them is combined with the third. This may be achieved in two ways. In the first method R_1 is the base and C_3 the exponent. The second is vice versa. These two sub-types are designated as R_{2a} and R_{2b} respectively. The basic equation and examples of the value index relationships for this type of combination are shown below.

Sub-type	Basic Equation	Example	No. Possible Forms
a	$R_{2a} = R_1^{\pm C_3}$	$= (k^n)^k$	108
b	$R_{2b} = C_3^{\pm R_1}$	$= \aleph_1^{(k^n)}$	108

Third Order Combinations: A third order combination consists of four prime concepts having 648 possible forms. Examples of this type and higher orders will not be illustrated because they are cumbersome and in practice are not required. Higher order combinations generally will consist of combinations of R's. The combination of two R's anywhere in the network of a large complex of concepts has the same format as a first order combination. In Section 4.11 we will see how a network of several concept combinations is constructed.

4.10 Concept Conjunctions in the Basic Equation

Incorporation of concept conjunctions in the basic equation does not alter the various frameworks in the topology given in the previous section. However, concept conjunctions might produce a change within a given combination depending on its content. In a sub-type "a" of a second order combination, assume that:

$$\text{Vidx } R_1 = n^n, \text{ and}$$

$$\text{Vidx } C_3 = k, \text{ and that the combination is compositional.}$$

Under these conditions,

$$\text{Vidx } R_{2a} = (n^n)^k = k, \text{ and if}$$

$$\text{Vidx } C_3 = (k + k + n), \text{ then}$$

$$\text{Vidx } R_{2a} = (n^n)^{(k+k+n)} = k.$$

However, if

$$\text{Vidx } C_3 = (k + \aleph_1), \text{ then}$$

$$\text{Vidx } R_{2a} = (n^n)^{(k+\aleph_1)} = n^{\aleph_1} = \aleph_2$$

4.11 Concept Diagram

Finding the final value index of a complex idea given in a sentence requires translating the sentence from a string of words to a network of concept combinations. The structure of this network reflects the manner in which the various prime concepts and resultant concepts are related. Concept diagrams as shown below are useful in developing and displaying this network.

Value Combinations

Equation	Concept Diagram
$R = C_1^{C_2}$ $^*R = k^k = k$	$\overset{k}{C_1} \quad \overset{k}{C_2}$ joined to R
$C_1 + C_2$	$[C_1 \; C_2]$
$R_{2a} = R_1^{C_3}$ $R_1 = \aleph_1^{k} = \aleph_1$ $R_2 = \aleph_1^{-k} = 1/\aleph_1$	(diagram with $\aleph_1$ indicating base concept, and (-) indicating transposition; nodes C_1, C_2, C_3 combining to R_1 then R_2)
$R_{2b} = C_3^{R_1}$ $R_1 = \aleph_1^{k} = \aleph_1$ $R_2 = k^{\aleph_1} = \aleph_2$	(diagram: $\aleph_1$ on C_1, k on C_2, k on C_3; $C_1, C_2 \to R_1$; $R_1, C_3 \to R_2$)
$R_{2b} = (C_3 + C_4)^{R_1}$ $R_1 = k^n$ $R_2 = (\aleph_1 + \aleph_1)^k = \aleph_1$	(diagram: k on C_1, n on C_2, $\aleph_1$ on C_3, $\aleph_1$ on C_4; $C_1, C_2 \to R_1$; $R_1, [C_3 \; C_4] \to R_2$)

*Henceforth, the symbol R will be used to denote both a concept combination resultant and Vidx R.

EXAMPLES

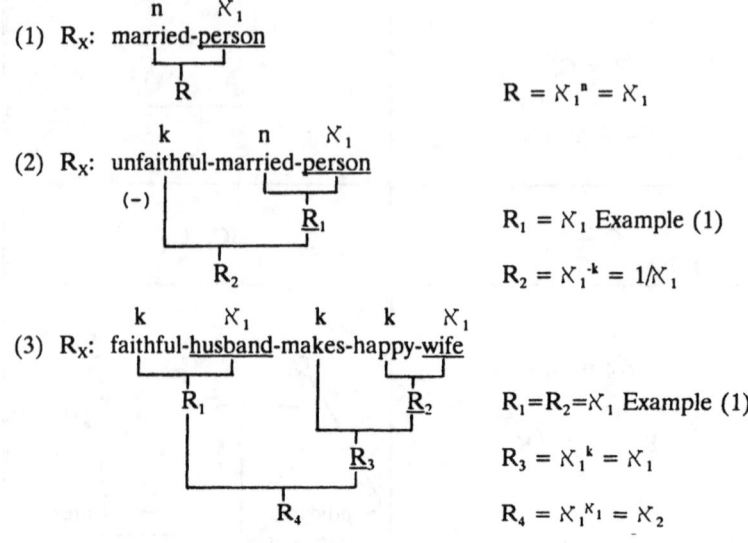

4.12 Interpretation

In order to interpret the solutions to problems using Hartmanean algebra ask "How does the combination of concepts in the situation under consideration affect the generation of value?" There are three possible modes: (1) value creation, (2) value neutral, and (3) value depreciation. When the value index of the combination or combination network exceeds the largest input concept value index, value has been created. When the final resultant value index is less than the smallest input concept value index, value has been depreciated. All other relationships between the final value index and the input value indexes are value neutral. Example (2) in the previous section is an instance of value depreciation and Example (3) is value creation. These two situations are easy to evaluate and a mathematical system is not required to show that faithfulness and happiness are better than unfaithfulness. Neither are a principle in physics and the arithmetic of finite numbers required to indicate that running 100 yards at eight miles per hour will take less time than walking it at five miles per hour. However, the same scientific principle and mathematics that will solve this simple time-rate-distance problem also solves complex problems such as those encountered in supersonic intercontinental navigation. Similarly, the same mathematical system which shows us that Example (3) is better than Example (2) will provide insight for the resolution of more complex problems. The purpose of these examples at this point is to illustrate a process and validate the results, not resolve a complicated issue.

5.0 Value Creation

The relation between the final value index and the input value indexes of a concept combination network is the basis for a principle usable as a guide in making value judgements and decisions. This principle, the Value Creation Principle, reads as follows:

> Select courses of action, ideas, or forms of behavior that result in value creation or that, secondarily, are value neutral. Avoid those that depreciate it.

The following statement is a corollary of this principle.

> When two or more courses of action, ideas, or forms of behavior having different value indexes are being considered, choose the one having the highest value index.

5.1 Application

The two ways to create value are: (1) go beyond $\aleph_1$, and (2) transpose transpositions. Our examination of these two methods will consist of a glimpse of the mathematics involved, and a look at an example of each method.

Going Beyond $\aleph_1$ We saw in Table C and subsequent illustrations that

$\aleph_1^{(n \text{ or } k)} = \aleph_1$. However, $(n \text{ or } k)^{\aleph_1} = \aleph_2$,

and, hence, the latter is the arithmetic of value creation. $\aleph_1^{(n \text{ or } k)}$ means that a person has been benefitted systemically or extrinsically. For example, Mary Smith is a computer systems analyst with Bell Mid-West Corp. She recently received a pay raise. In this situation the key concepts are "Mary Smith," and "pay-increase." The concept diagram for the combination of these two concepts is as follows:

160   Forms of Value and Valuation: Theory and Applications

$$\text{R: } \underbrace{\overset{n}{\text{pay-increase for}} \overset{\aleph_1}{\text{Mary Smith}}}$$

$$R = \aleph_1^n = \aleph_1 \qquad \text{ER 1, CR 5}$$

Repeated pay increases do not change the relationship between n and $\aleph_1$. If we add a second pay increase we get $\aleph_1 + \aleph_1 = \aleph_1$. In order to create value, the relationship between n and $\aleph_1$ must be reversed.

There is an expression "identify with" which means to become the same. For this expression to properly denote the relationship between a person and his or her position, the person must do more than produce the minimum expected results. If Mary Smith identifies with her position at Bell Mid-West, the position becomes part of her self. She give herself to the position. It becomes part of her. She does more than occupy it. The concept combination of this situation is:

$$\text{R: } \underbrace{\overset{\aleph_1}{\text{Mary Smith}} \overset{C/T}{\text{identifies-with}} \overset{n}{\text{corporation-position}}}$$

$$R = n^{\aleph_1} = \aleph_2 \qquad \text{ER 1, CR 5}$$

Note that the symbol C/T appeared in the concept diagram. C/T means composition/transposition indicator. It indicates the relationship between the subject concepts "Mary Smith," and "corporation-position."

Another method of going beyond $\aleph_1$ is for two persons to interact such that both obtain some degree of self fulfillment through such conditions as love, respect, or kindness. This, of course, includes a person identifying with another, but this close relationship is not always necessary. The value index equation that reflects this situation is:

$$R = \aleph_1^{\aleph_1} = \aleph_2.$$

<u>Transposing Transpositions</u>: The second method of creating value is to convert 1/n, 1/k, 1/$\aleph_1$, and 1/$\aleph_2$ to general finite or transfinite whole numbers. In valuemetrics terms, this method of creating value is called transposing transpositions. In ordinary language this means redressing

Value Combinations 161

injustice, wrongs, and badness. Transpositions occur mathematically as a result of a negative exponentiation, for example:

$k^{-n} = 1/k$ Any quantity with a negative exponent may be written as the reciprocal of the quantity with a positive exponent.

The inverse of this expression is:

$(1/k)^{-n} = k$ by the same rule.

This means that a transposition combined with another concept transpositionally is a composition. Disvaluing a transposition changes the transposition to a composition. The transposition "1/k" must be disvalued--abhorred, condemned, rejected, spurned--not valued. The mathematics of valuing a transposition is shown in the following example.

$$(1/k)^n = (1^n)/(k^n) = 1/k$$

Valuing a transposition virtually deepens it. In order to transpose a transposition, it must be disvalued.

EXAMPLE 4

Earlier we saw that R_2: unfaithful-married-person is an instance of a transposition. One of the ways to transpose this transposition is to combine R_2 with the concept C_4: reformed.

The concept diagram of this combination is:

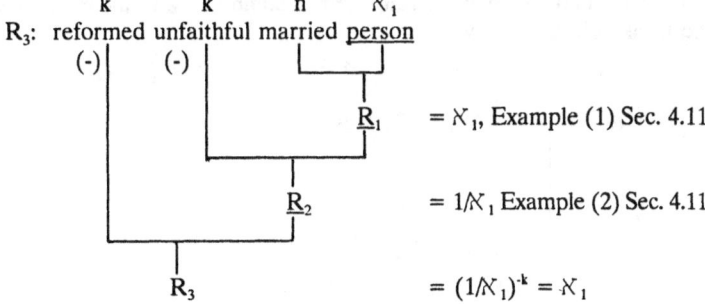

162   Forms of Value and Valuation: Theory and Applications

Another way to transpose the transposition R_2 is to combine it with the concept C_5: kill. The concept diagram of this R_3 is:

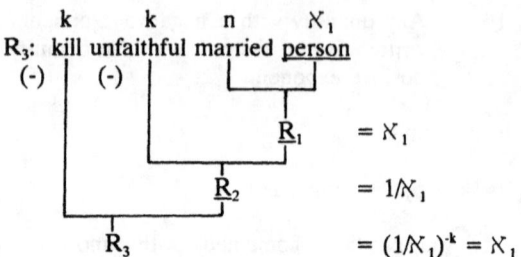

According to this line of reasoning killing an unfaithful spouse has the same value as reforming an unfaithful spouse. Intuitively, this does not seem right. It is not right in the valuemetrics system either because this system involves another step which shows that these two situations are not of equal value. This step consists of combining the concept which transposes the transposition, which in this instance is "kill," with the base concept of the transposition which in this instance is "married person." Let this concept combination be:

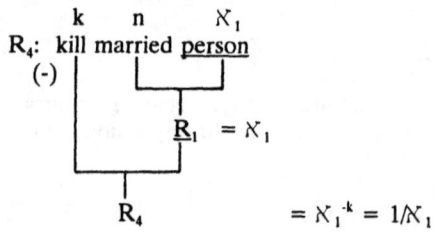

However, when the concept "reformed" is combined with the base concept of the transposition we have:

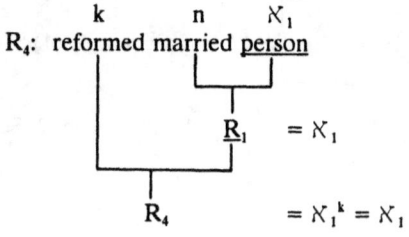

This illustration provides the basis for a rule for selecting a course of action to redress injustice, wrongs, and badness.

The Transposition Correction Rule

When transposing a transposition for the purpose of redressing injustice, wrongs, and badness select a course of action concept which if combined directly with the base concept of the transposition is not also a transposition for reasons other than a nonsense concept.

6.0 Justifying Transpositions

Transpositions abound in nature and in human affairs. Animals kill each other. Lightening causes forest fires and destruction. People go to war. Are transpositions ever justified? In valuemetrics anything is justified to the degree that value is created or held neutral. Can a transposition be used to create value? In the previous section we saw how transposing transpositions created value, but this is not an instance of using a transposition to create value. When we transpose a transposition, the transposition is the base in the exponential expression. When we use a transposition, it is the exponent. Our examination of the question, "Are transpositions ever justified?" will begin with a review of the arithmetic involved. Then we will look at real world examples.

When a transposition is the exponent in the basic equation of Hartmanean algebra, the exponent is a fraction. Fractional exponents are roots. The arithmetic of general finite and transfinite roots is given in Table D. The relationship between whole number exponents and fractional exponents, i.e., roots is similar to the relationship between addition and subtraction. One is the inverse of the other; for example $5^2 = 25$ and $25^{1/2} = 5$. Table D shows the results of this process with the numbers n, k, $\aleph_o$, $\aleph_1$, $\aleph_2$, $\aleph_3$, and $\aleph_4$.

Table D
Exponents and Roots Relationship

Exponent	Root	Exponent	Root
$n^n = n$	$n^{1/n} = n$	$\aleph_2^{\aleph_0} = \aleph_2$	$\aleph_2^{1/\aleph_0} = \aleph_2$
$k^n = k$	$k^{1/n} = k$	$\aleph_3^{\aleph_0} = \aleph_3$	$\aleph_3^{1/\aleph_0} = \aleph_3$
$\aleph_0^n = \aleph_0$	$\aleph_0^{1/n} = \aleph_0$		
$\aleph_1^n = \aleph_1$	$\aleph_1^{1/n} = \aleph_1$	$n^{\aleph_1} = \aleph_2$	$\aleph_2^{1/\aleph_1} = n$
$\aleph_2^n = \aleph_2$	$\aleph_2^{1/n} = \aleph_2$	$k^{\aleph_1} = \aleph_2$	$\aleph_2^{1/\aleph_1} = k$
$\aleph_3^n = \aleph_3$	$\aleph_3^{1/n} = \aleph_3$	$\aleph_0^{\aleph_1} = \aleph_2$	$\aleph_2^{1/\aleph_1} = \aleph_0$
		$\aleph_1^{\aleph_1} = \aleph_2$	$\aleph_2^{1/\aleph_1} = \aleph_1$
$n^k = k$	$k^{1/k} = n$	$\aleph_2^{\aleph_1} = \aleph_2$	$\aleph_2^{1/\aleph_1} = \aleph_2$
$k^k = k$	$k^{1/k} = k$	$\aleph_3^{\aleph_1} = \aleph_3$	$\aleph_3^{1/\aleph_1} = \aleph_3$
$\aleph_0^k = \aleph_0$	$\aleph_0^{1/k} = \aleph_0$		
$\aleph_1^k = \aleph_1$	$\aleph_1^{1/k} = \aleph_1$	$n^{\aleph_2} = \aleph_3$	$\aleph_3^{1/\aleph_2} = n$
$\aleph_2^k = \aleph_2$	$\aleph_2^{1/k} = \aleph_2$	$k^{\aleph_2} = \aleph_3$	$\aleph_3^{1/\aleph_2} = k$
$\aleph_3^k = \aleph_3$	$\aleph_3^{1/k} = \aleph_3$	$\aleph_0^{\aleph_2} = \aleph_3$	$\aleph_3^{1/\aleph_2} = \aleph_0$
		$\aleph_1^{\aleph_2} = \aleph_3$	$\aleph_3^{1/\aleph_2} = \aleph_1$
$n^{\aleph_0} = \aleph_1$	$\aleph_1^{1/\aleph_0} = n$	$\aleph_2^{\aleph_2} = \aleph_3$	$\aleph_3^{1/\aleph_2} = \aleph_2$
$k^{\aleph_0} = \aleph_1$	$\aleph_1^{1/\aleph_0} = k$	$\aleph_3^{\aleph_2} = \aleph_3$	$\aleph_3^{1/\aleph_2} = \aleph_3$
$\aleph_0^{\aleph_0} = \aleph_1$	$\aleph_1^{1/\aleph_0} = \aleph_0$	$\aleph_4^{\aleph_2} = \aleph_4$	$\aleph_4^{1/\aleph_2} = \aleph_4$
$\aleph_1^{\aleph_0} = \aleph_1$	$\aleph_1^{1/\aleph_0} = \aleph_1$		

The relationships in Table D are the basis for the following rules concerning fractional exponents.

(1) $n, k, \aleph_0, \aleph_1, \ldots$ raised to the 1/nth power equal $n, k, \aleph_0, \aleph_1, \ldots$

(2) $k, \aleph_0, \aleph_1, \ldots$ raised to the 1/kth power equal n or $k, \aleph_0, \aleph_1, \ldots$

(3) $(\aleph_{x+1})^{1/\aleph_x} \leq \aleph_{x+1}$.

(4) $n^{1/k}$, $n^{1/k}{}_x$, $k^{1/k}{}_x$, $\aleph_x{}^{1/k}{}_x$, and $\aleph_x{}^{1/k}{}_{x+1}$ are indeterminants, symbolized as "d," i.e., $n^{1/k} = d$, $n^{1/k}{}_x = d$, $k^{1/k}{}_x = d$ . . . .

The symbol "d" is similar in nature to the mathematical factor "i," the symbol for $-1^{1/2}$ ($\sqrt{-1}$). Both i and d are different from any other number.

According to the value creation principle, all the cases that come under rules (1), (2) and (3) are justifiable transpositions, and those cases to which rule (4) applies are not. This includes cases where $R = 1/d$.

The following is an example of rule (2).

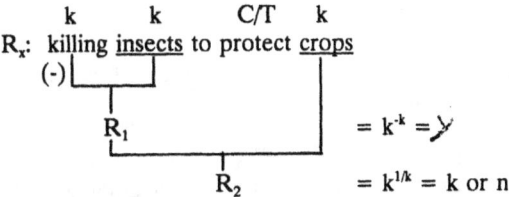

Examples of referents of the concept combinations under rule (4), i.e., unjustified transposition are:

(1) $n^{1/k}$: sacrifice of an animal to fulfill a religious ideal.

(2) $n^{1/k}{}_1$: killing a person for revenge.

(3) $k^{1/k}{}_1$: harming a person in a medical experiment.

(4) $\aleph_1{}^{1/k}{}_1$: scapegoat (a person suffering incarceration, pain, or death for the benefit of another).

(5) $\aleph_1{}^{1/k}{}_2$: father sells daughter to buy jewelry for himself.

7.0 Induced Transpositions

The resolution of transposition justification problems ought always be examined in light of the long range consequences of the justification. Does the transposition promote or induce other transpositions?

EXAMPLE 5

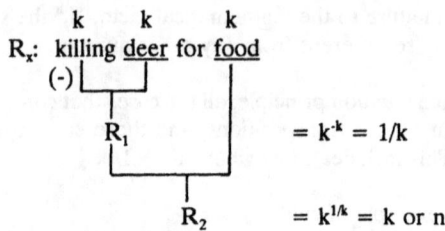

R_x: killing deer for food (with k, k, k)

$R_1 = k^{-k} = 1/k$

$R_2 = k^{1/k} = k$ or n

R_x is justified by rule (2).

Examination of this justification with respect to its effect on the deer population involves two possible cases.

Case 1 k or n k C/T k
R_x: killing deer for food maintains proper deer-population-balance

$R_2 = k^k = k$

$R_3 = k^{(k\ or\ n)} = k$

Case 2 k or n C/T k n
R_x: killing deer for food will cause deer-population extinction (-)

$R_2 = k^{-n} = 1/k$

$R_3 = (1/k)^{(k\ or\ n)} = 1/k$

INTERPRETATION

Under the conditions of Case 2, killing deer or any other animal for food is not justified provided sufficient other types of food are available.

8.0 Concept Combination Syntax

Syntax is the way words are put together to form phrases, clauses, and sentences. The valuemetrics application of syntax is the way concepts are put together to form value index equations. The examples in our study of Hartmanean algebra consisted of concept combinations which were given. However, in the application of this system of logic to life in the real world, very often we will have to create concept combinations which represent situations of various complexity. This will require that we condense the narrative of the situation to a factual irreducible concept combination or network of combinations without the loss of or alteration of meaning. The statement must be capable of being translated to $R = C_1 {}^{\pm C_2}$. In order to offset the diversity and lack of precision in our language, the following rules of syntax should be observed.

Within the general rule of expressing an idea using the least number of words:

(1) Think in terms of newspaper headlines.

(2) Use construct concepts whenever possible.

(3) Keep the number of singular concepts to the absolute minimum. Although a person or people may be involved, if it is possible to express an idea without a singular concept, do so. For example, the expression "book" may be used instead of "my book." On the other hand, if murder is the thing under consideration, then two singular concepts must be employed. "Murder" is a concept having underlying concepts, namely,

$$R = \underbrace{\overset{\aleph_1}{\text{person}} \text{ with-malice-aforethought-killing a } \overset{\aleph_1}{\text{person}}}_{\text{C/T}}$$

$$R = \aleph_1{}^{\aleph_1} = 1/\aleph_2.$$

The situation where a person is killed by accident, a car crash for instance, would involve only one singular concept. The concept combination in this case would be:

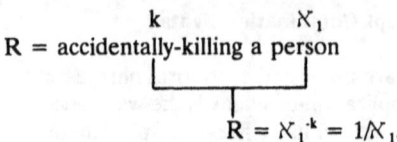

$$R = \aleph_1^{-k} = 1/\aleph_1.$$

Here is where knowledge of the facts is particularly important. If a person is killed as a result of a pure accident, then the transposition vidx is $1/\aleph_1$. However, if the accident was no accident, but the result of malice by another person, then the transposition vidx is $1/\aleph_2$.

(4) Whenever practical identify words in a statement that are C/T indicators, and use them for this purpose.

(5) Do not game the problem. This means avoid manipulating concept combinations to arrive at a preconceived outcome. Let logic control the results.

(6) Avoid the use of euphemisms, figures of speech, and half truths. Name things for what they are.

(7) Consult the dictionary.

9.0 Concluding Remarks

The truth of the outcome of a properly completed Hartmanean algebra problem depends on the correctness of the concepts used and the truth of the relationships that are given. This system, like all mathematical processes, exists independently of any other phenomenon and, hence, has no way of discriminating incorrect inputs relative to a given situation. When valuemetrics is used as a basis for value judgments, it is essential that the input concepts and their relationship reflect truth and reality, otherwise the results will be valueless. If one is ignorant or unsure of the facts in a situation, consulting authentic reference material or an expert on the matter is advisable prior to applying valuemetrics.

Whereas Hartmanean algebra is universal, the meanings of all concepts are not. Construct concepts are subject to this condition. The concept "marriage," for example, in the Judeo-Christian culture might have a different meaning from the word used to denote entering into the husband and wife relationship in another culture. This does not invalidate valuemetrics because meanings (intensional sets) in the final analysis are the items of interest to us, not the concepts.

The tenor of the remarks and explanations concerning the works of Robert S. Hartman in this and previous chapters has been more than laudatory. However, Hartman's works neither are without critics, nor is all of the criticism unwarranted. The principal sources of justifiable criticisms of scientific axiology are: (1) the inconsistencies and contradictions in set theory where we define a set as any collection of objects, yet we can prove mathematically the existence of the empty set, and (2) the peculiarity of cardinal number arithmetic where a part is equal to a whole. The results of these enigmas are reflected in Hartmanean algebra making it a blunt instrument as compared to the arithmetic of conventional numbers. In Hartmanean algebra, for example, the concept combination "humiliation of a person" has the same vidx as "killing a person." Both are $1/\aleph_1$. In this situation the arithmetic of transfinite numbers tells us that they are transpositions, and in and of themselves they are bad, but it is unable to provide guidance for determining which is the worse. On the other hand, we have seen in this chapter how Hartmanean algebra, despite its obtuseness, provides a system of logic for the analysis of value phenomena by the method of science. Whereas various criticisms of this system are justified, this does not mean that scientific axiology has no application in the real world as some critics tend to indicate. Therefore, one of the purposes of this book is to reveal those aspects of Hartman's works which promise to yield useful information on how to find new solutions concerning what is good and right in the affairs of mankind. If we permit the strangeness of the scientific method to deter us from the actions indicated, then the relation of our technological ability and our axiological ability might remain perilously disproportionate, possibly to the detriment of ourselves and future generations.

REFERENCES

Forrest, Frank G. "Valuemetrics: The Science of Personal and Professional Ethics" Daytona Beach, Fla., 1988.

Hartman, Robert S. The Structure of Value: Foundations of Scientific Axiology. Carbondale, Ill.,: Southern Illinois University Press, 1967.

Lin, Shu-Yeng T., and You-Feng Lin. Set Theory with Applications. Tampa, Fla.: Book Publishers, Inc., 1985.

Maslow, Abraham H. The Further Reaches of Human Nature. New York: The Viking Press, 1971.

Person, Russell V. Essentials of Mathematics. New York: John Wiley and Sons, Inc., 1961.

Rokeach, Milton, The Nature of Human Values. New York: The Free Press, 1973.

Zuckerman, Martin M. Sets and Transfinite Numbers. New York: Macmillan Publishing Co., Inc., 1974.

Chapter VIII

HARTMAN'S VALUE THEORY: FORMAL MODELS

Mark A. Moore

Introduction

The value theory of Robert Hartman represents a very interesting attempt to bring formal or mathematical thinking into a realm which is often described as subjective. Values, it is frequently said, are very personal feelings which each individual holds uniquely. We think of our values as a personal right and are obliged to resist attempts at changing or molding our values for us. The very idea, then, of a mathematical or formal treatment of values is inherently contrary to the personal view.

Nonetheless, Hartman believed that (1) values are (in some cases) objective phenomena, and (2) our understanding of them needs to become a formal discipline. But does the predicate of (1) apply to the subject of (2) and the predicate of (2) apply to the subject of (1)? Hartman argued persuasively that many problems with man's relation to man and nature are examples of values gone crazy.

There is much to be said for this view. Few would question that the practice of slavery is a debasement of the human person, the human spirit, and surely a grim exploitation of human freedom and potential. Even though we may want to say that values are personal, there is a part of us which tends toward the view that some actions are right or wrong in themselves and that is the end of it. But this implies that at least some values are not subjective. Who would argue that the practice of slavery is a personal value like choosing how to style one's hair? Of course, the value of slavery and any claim that it is merely part of the personal inventory of one's chosen values was not always challenged the way it is today. The practice of slavery, if it really is wrong in any objective sense, is a practice which can and should be outlawed, which means that society has both the right and duty to see to it that slavery is never practiced. The use of force to prohibit some practices is not only allowed but, in fact, is the only responsible action. The history of social conflict may indeed be a history of value conflicts and their resolution by debate, legislation, and force. What today is assumed without argument was not always accepted; and controversial responses to issues being debated today concerning relations between man and the environment, preservation of animal species, conservation, alternative uses of energy, and the like, may someday be accepted as sane and responsible behavior. At present, we vigorously debate these issues, just as once it was debated whether one had the personal right to buy and sell other persons.

So, there is a double focus to our understanding of values. On the one hand, we want to say that values are personal and unique to each individual; and yet we also want to say that at least some actions are really right or wrong in themselves and that merely believing that some act is "right for me" is not sufficient. Therefore, there may be reasons for treating values as the sort of things which can be measured, analyzed, and rank ordered. To make explicit the objective nature of values, Hartman utilized a formal model. In this chapter we shall examine this model.

What is a Formal Model?

We are already familiar with many formal models. Geometry, which we study in school, is a formal model of surfaces or space. Chemistry, which, among other things, calculates how different elements combine, is also a formal model. Physics, which calculates motion and forces in the large and sub-atomic world, is also a formal model. Biology, with its new understanding of the gene, is a formal model. Clearly, the success of these sciences is dependent upon formal models. In fact, the importance of formal models is so accepted that research in other disciplines, such as sociology and psychology, is aimed at developing their own formal models.

But what exactly makes a formal model a formal model? What are the differences between describing something, say motion in physics, by a formal model rather than in other ways? We must begin with the idea of measurement. Somehow formal models measure things in ways that ordinary descriptions do not--for example, a forward pass in football.

We can easily imagine the radio or television announcer describing the play in great detail; how the quarterback receives the ball from the center, how he drops back and looks over the field of play to select the receiver, how he scrambles to avoid being tackled, then throws a long pass which wobbles in the wind only to be well over the receiver's outstretched hands. In contrast, a physicist would describe the same event in terms of formulas and diagrams for the mass, momentum, and shape of the ball along with factors for air resistance and density (it may be a very rainy day) and the like. The end result will be an entirely different description of the event.

Formal models, then, require mathematics or logic to describe events and relations, while our ordinary words are used to describe richly similar events. But why use mathematics to describe anything? The answer is that mathematics allows us to observe relations and predict events which are beyond the capacity of ordinary language. Mathematical models allow a physicist accurately to predict that the pass would be too far down field for the receiver to catch. Moreover, formal models allow a scientist to observe relations to which other descriptions blind us. For example, with the creation of a formal model for space (geometry) one could not only prove that the earth is round (and not flat), but also measure the circumference of the Earth. This was done by Erastosthenes (among others) in approximately 200 B.C. This could have been accomplished by observing relations which only geometry could provide. Erastosthenes did this by observing the difference in the zenith of the sun while standing at the bottom of a well at two places of known distance (Alexandria and Syene). His measurement of the Earth's circumference was correct to within 5 percent. The point is that without geometry the concept of zenith has insufficient definition to make possible such calculations.

Even more dramatically, physicists are today working with elements which can only be observed in their geometrical "shadows." Sub-atomic elements really cannot be directly observed at all. Yet with knowledge of physics, it is possible to observe the shadows or tracks of these entities. Without science, we would never know that these entities exist let alone be able to describe them. Today, physicists are using geometries of many dimensions to describe entities called "super-strings." This is an attempt to describe fundamental "objects" of nature which are many dimensional but "rolled up" into a few dimensions. Our language, which describes the everyday world of football games, is not only of no help in describing such entities, but is, in fact, counterproductive. Scientific investigation depends upon formal models, and the language we use to describe the everyday world is of no assistance. The "objects" of super-string theory are pure formal constructions and can only be described mathematically.

Finally, we must also be aware that formal models themselves are never final, complete, and without criticism. The history of science is the history of the replacement of one formal model with another more accurate one. No matter how revealing and accurate a formal model may be, there will always be found "blind spots." Plane geometry, for example, cannot do an accurate job of describing space of three dimensions. For that we need solid geometry or, better still, analytic geometry. But remember, it was literally hundreds of years between the simple two-dimensional geometry of Euclid and the sophisticated geometry of Descartes and the very sophisticated calculus of Newton and Leibniz. Science uses its formal models, but when a model is found to be inadequate, a new one must be constructed.

By analogy, the use of formal models in our understanding of values would allow us not only to measure values but also to see value relations that heretofore have remained unknown. Hartman's formal theory of value is a good example.

Hartman's Value Theory

In reality, Hartman's theory of values actually consists of two formal models which are quite independent of each other. To do his theory justice, we must treat these two models separately. The first model is what we shall call the **Ordinal Model** and the second is the **Cardinal Model**. To understand what this means, we must take a short time to review the language of formal models, mathematics.

Cardinal and Ordinal Numbers

Mathematics consists of many types of numbers: real, irrational, rational, whole, ideal, etc. Two of the most important, however, are "ordinal" and "cardinal" numbers. The difference between these two types of numbers is really quite simple and easy to understand. Cardinal numbers refer to the size of a collection or set of numbers. For example, if I write down the numbers from 1 to 10, then I have a small set of numbers. I would describe the size of this set as **finite**. This means that the set of numbers in my collection is limited. In fact, any collection of numbers which is limited, even though it may be quite large, is finite. Mathematicians tell us that some collections of numbers are larger than finite, and these are called **infinite**. So, now we have two types of cardinal numbers: finite and infinite. Finite sets are collections which are limited and infinite sets are collections which are not limited. The natural number system in its entirety is an example of an infinite set.

But now something strange occurs. Mathematicians tell us that there are infinities which are larger than the natural number system; in other words, some infinities are larger than others. While the natural number system is unlimited and therefore infinite, each element in this infinity, each individual number, is countable. The natural number system consists of an infinite number of individual elements. However, there exist sets of numbers which can not be counted by the natural number system. These numbers are larger than our infinite natural number system. The numbers in the natural number system are called a **denumerable infinity**, while these other numbers are called a **nondenumerable infinity**. We will not bother with the details of the reasoning mathematicians go through to arrive at this conclusion, but it is essential in our analysis of Hartman's value theory to know that such larger infinities do exist.

In summary, then, we can say that there are three types of cardinal numbers: **finite, denumerably infinite, and nondenumerably infinite**. We will visit these three concepts again when we discuss Hartman's cardinal formal model for value. The system of ordinal numbers, on the other hand, is used to describe priority or sequence. This number system consists of terms such as first, second, third, etc. Since we often think of values as placing varying importance on things, it would be natural to think of values as an ordinal process. For example, we say that a Jaguar is first in our esteem of automobiles, a BMW second, an Audi third, etc. Here, we are not interested in the absolute measure of the differences, only the order.

In values, we need both types of numbers. Hartman utilizes both systems of numbers in his value theory. Let us look at Hartman's ordinal formal model first, and then we shall look at the cardinal model.

The Ordinal Model

Hartman begins by contrasting three types of fundamental values. These are the building blocks for all value relations. They are called **Intrinsic**, **Extrinsic**, and **Systemic** values. As with most formal models, these value types are based on differences which we can describe with ordinary language, and we can readily find examples of them. Systemic values are formal or mathematical values. If I say that "2 + 2 = 4," then I have correctly summed "2 + 2". If, on the other hand, I sum "2 + 2 = 5," then I have made a mistake. Systemic values, then, are the values of correct logical deductions and formal relations. Systemic disvalues are incorrect formal statements. For example, a correctly written computer program is systemically good, while a program with errors or "bugs" is systemically bad. Systemic values, while real, exist in a realm of abstract thought. We correct mistakes in a computer program by changing the computer code; it is as simple as that. In the late 1960's, hippies criticized Systemic values as "irrelevant," and those who were concerned with such values were regarded as persons who had no grasp of the real world. While surely overstated, we can certainly agree that Systemic values by themselves are indeed hollow and empty compared with the rich variety of the world in which we live. It is to the values of this world to which we next turn.

Extrinsic values are the values of the real or living world. They are the values of cause and effect, of means to ends, of action and consequence, of life and death. When we act, our actions have consequences, and it is fair to ask about the worth of these actions. This "worth" is just another way of asking about the extrinsic value of our actions. An automobile accident, regardless of the motives or conscious state of the driver, is bad; and the degree of badness will, in part, be determined by the amount of loss. Putting aside possible consequences of injury, we can say that automobile accidents can be valuated for their degree of disvalue or badness by the size of the loss. Insurance companies deal almost exclusively with extrinsic values and not merely with auto accidents. Features of our bodies also are extrinsic values. When we eat well, exercise, do not smoke, and in general do what our doctor tells us, the quality or well-being of our lives increases. Healthy living is an extrinsic good, which may also result in a reduction in health insurance premiums.

Finally, we come to the third category which Hartman calls Intrinsic values. Intrinsic values are our personal life. They are often the motives or intention behind the act. This fundamental realm of values not only has a basis in our experience but also has a basis in law. Our legal system is very quick to distinguish actions which cause unintended harm from those actions which were intended to bring about harm. For example, the charge of manslaughter, while a serious charge, is not nearly so serious as first degree murder. The latter charge requires the proof that the murder was intended, and for that reason the seriousness of the crime and its negative value are much higher. But in both cases, the Extrinsic value of the act, the loss of human life, is the same. In fact, well-intended acts which unhappily have undesired consequences are quite forgivable in our society. The expression "but he intended well" goes a long way in excusing unfortunate consequences.

The same is more or less true for unintended actions which have desirable consequences. If things turn out better than intended, then the Extrinsic value is quite high, but the Intrinsic value is very low. If I park my car on a street beside a sidewalk to go shopping, and my car happens to protect a pedestrian from certain injury or perhaps death from a runaway truck, this is surely extrinsically good; but it does not make me a hero. My only intention was to go shopping, but the consequence of my action was to save a life. If I had intentionally driven my car into the path of the runaway truck to protect pedestrians, the deliberate action to save life would be highly valued in our society. Intrinsic values, then, are personal. They pertain to individual character. They are the values of honesty, good intentions, kindness, forgiveness, etc. In a religious context, they are the values of the great religious thinkers. Their disvalues are evil, and consist of deceit, dishonesty, exploitation, and corruption. They are the values of Satan.

To summarize, then, Hartman has three basic values: Systemic, Extrinsic, and Intrinsic. He uses an ordinal scheme to give priority to each value. Not surprisingly, Hartman rates Intrinsic value as the highest value, Extrinsic as second, and Systemic as third. As for disvalue, he rates intrinsic disvalue (evil) as highest in disvalue, extrinsic second, and systemic third. This is Hartman's basic ordinal scheme, and please notice that, so far, nothing formal has been done. All our descriptions and accounts of the three types of values are done in ordinary language with no attempt to bring in a formal model. But it is not difficult to take this step, and Hartman does it with an ingenious scheme.

Since we have an ordinal ranking of the three values, we can express them in the following way:

> First: Intrinsic value;
> Second: Extrinsic value;
> Third: Systemic value;
> Fourth: Systemic disvalue;
> Fifth: Extrinsic disvalue;
> Sixth: Intrinsic disvalue.

Hartman adds a very nice complication to the scheme. Each value, he argues, can itself be the object of appreciation or value. So, not only does an action have a value (say the bank makes an error in my account in their favor), but this action can itself be evaluated by me. In other words, I can view this action from one to three value perspectives: systemically, extrinsically, or intrinsically. I may say that the bank error was merely a computer error and in a rational way call the bank to reconcile the difference. This would evaluate the systemic error in a systemic fashion. However, I may choose to value the error extrinsically, especially if there are returned checks which cause problems with creditors and additional costs for reprocessing checks. Finally, I could opt to evaluate the bank's mistake as an intentional act designed to hurt me. So, each of the six elements above may be viewed in three different ways. This makes eighteen different ordinal combinations of value. (Of course, each of the eighteen could be viewed three ways and thereby explode our ordinal combinations, but we certainly need not bother with this.)

Of the eighteen value combinations, nine are positive and nine are negative. The nine positive values are all examples of what Hartman calls **value composition,** and the nine negative combinations are what Hartman calls **value transposition.** If we use the convention of exponents to represent value compositions and subscripts to represent value transpositions, then we would get the following eighteen combinations, each of which is associated with an example supplied by Hartman. (The Structure of Value, pp. 272-273.) The ordinal listing of the items below corresponds to the degree of value associated with each item. The first item receives the highest value and the last item the lowest value.

Positive Value Relations: Composition

I^I A Baby; Mystic Experience; Creative Act

E^I My New Car; "Peach"; Creative Engineer

S^I Corporate Personality; Morale of Army; Maxim; Creative Thinker; Hypostatization

I^E "Mr. Republican"; Materialist God; Selling Favorite Painting

I^S "Elizabeth II"; Axiological Value; Philosophy of Creativity

E^E Ice Cream Sundae; Binding of Book; Easy Chair

S^E "By This Ring I Thee Wed"; Application of System; Popular Science

E^S Production Line; Game; "Legal Tender"; Abstraction; Corroborating Witness

S^S Technical Improvement; Deduction; Corroboration

Negative Value Relations: Transposition

S_S Puzzle; Existentialist Depreciation of Thought; Jabberwock; Logical Paradox; "Red Tape"

E_S Uniform; Pedant; Policeman Stopping My Car

S_E Bad Popularization; Bribed Judge; "Egghead"; False Application of System

E_E Chocolate and Sawdust; Inkblot on Book; Chair Smashed by Hammer

I_S Paranoia (Systemic Self); Color Line; Menotti's The Consul; The Metaphysical Fallacy; Killing in War

I_E Person as Function ("Alienation of Self"); Idol; Jesus tempted by Satan (Matt. 4:1); Metaphor Taken Literally; Christmas Shopping and Merchandizing; Act of Killing

S_I Argumentum ad Personam; Burning Heretics; Strategy in War; "Intelligenzbestie"; Rationalization

E_I Lovesick Truant; Building an Ugly Bridge; Train Running over Suicide

I_I "We'll Always be Friends" (Friendship used to terminate love); Nazi Irma Greese (tied women's legs in labor, used life to kill)

This arrangement represents a simple but elegant formal model. It is a formal model because: 1) it utilizes an ordinal mathematical arrangement; and 2) it identifies precise relations of which we are, at best, only dimly aware. Remember, formal models make all relations clear and obvious. Anyone who examines the above list would conclude that there are eighteen combinations; while, if we only had a discussion about value combinations, this would not seem so obvious. It is not essential that we agree that values can or should be treated in the above manner; it is only important that we understand that the above represents a formal model.

We have every right to ask what the model can do for us. Formal models can have applications; and if they do, then there should be a

180   *Forms of Value and Valuation: Theory and Applications*

clarification of what would otherwise be obscure. In the next section we must inquire about the consequences of this formal model.

What Does the Ordinal Model Do?

When we inquire as to the purpose of a formal model, we must be careful since utility is not always a criterion used to evaluate a formal model. Mathematicians often construct formal models which represent no particular function at all. These "pure systems" make no reference to the real world. However, they have been found to be useful after they were constructed. So, while mathematicians play these purely formal games with no attempt to describe anything, other scientists often find an application. Similarly, we do not need to find an application of a formal system in order for it to be valid; but it certainly helps to justify the usefulness of the model.

Does Hartman's scheme have a use? Indeed, it does; one of great importance. Hartman constructed an ingenious application for his eighteen element ordinal array. He proposed that the array represents a scheme for value norms, a kind of ideal ordering of values. If values are properly assigned, then they will follow the same sequence as the formal array. If values are not properly assigned, then the incorrect list will be different from our ideal. Furthermore, the degree of divergence from the ideal can be measured.

For example, imagine that we construct a list of eighteen items which are, in fact, examples of the ideal model. Now we ask persons to use their own judgment and arrange the list of items in the way that they feel represents a listing of best to worst. We can then check to see how similar the two lists are. It is possible (but very unlikely) that an individual will exactly match the ideal list; and it is possible (but again very unlikely) that an individual will exactly mismatch our ideal list. At any rate, the degree of deviation can be measured. This imagined experiment has, in fact, been done; and from it has grown a very subtle profile of an individual's strengths and weaknesses at valuation. The results of thousands of tests have been correlated with several important psychological profiles which have a known reliability of predicting certain human behavior tendencies. The correlations with the Hartman profile are very clear.

The formal model has a clear application. There are practitioners of the Hartman technique around the world. These individuals, who have been trained to administer, score, and interpret the results, have found applications for the Hartman profile in a number of personal and business situations. As a result, we have to give Hartman's Ordinal Model very high marks for its formal structure and its applicability.

Critique of the Ordinal Model

As we noted earlier, it is a mistake to think that formal models, once they have shown usefulness in application, should remain unchanged. The exact order of the eighteen items Hartman has identified is, of course, subject to inspection and change. (Later on in this chapter, I shall present an alternative list.) Further, it can be asked, why only eighteen? Hartman arrives at eighteen by simply looking at the number of ways that the three base values (Intrinsic, Extrinsic, and Systemic) can be combined in positive and negative ways. The math expands these three base values into eighteen combinations. If other base values were added, the list would be larger. Or, if other ways of combining the values were identified, then the list would expand. So, there is a lot of room for speculation on ordinal lists of values. The progress of value theory as a science will depend upon challenging Hartman's list in hopes of finding formal models with greater applicability. While one formal model is as good as any other, so long as some principle of logic is not violated, we certainly prefer models which have greater application to our real world. Creation of models which have greater application is exactly the work of science, and value science is certainly no exception. Hartman's scheme is the first, and it has proven to be very useful in application; but it should not be looked upon as the final model.

The Cardinal Model

We have reviewed the Ordinal Model of Hartman's science of values and have found the model both interesting and useful. We must now turn our attention to the Cardinal Model. Before doing this, I must provide a brief apology and explanation. If you were to pick up Hartman's major work, The Structure of Value, you would nowhere find his speaking about two models, one ordinal and one cardinal. I have separated Hartman's work into two models because there seems to be some serious problems with the Cardinal Model. These problems are so severe that we might be tempted to reject the entirety of Hartman's work, and that would be a pity. Rather than throw the baby out with the bath, I have chosen to separate Hartman's work in such a way that all aspects can be examined without complete acceptance or rejection. This is important because if there are flaws in Hartman's work, then the nature of his use of formal models makes it very easy for critics to reject the entirety of what he has accomplished, and this would be shameful. With my apology given, let us turn to the review of the Cardinal Model.

182   *Forms of Value and Valuation: Theory and Applications*

During the presentation of the Ordinal Model above, no justification was given of the exact arrangement of the eighteen items. The possibility of other arrangements was mentioned, but there was no account of how Hartman came to arrange the eighteen in just the way he did. Hartman does offer an explanation for this, and this involves the use of cardinal numbers. You will remember that we identified three cardinal numbers: finite, infinite, and nondenumerably infinite. Each of these numbers has a mathematical symbol to identify it. These symbols, as presented below, are:

$$\text{Finite} = n;$$

$$\text{(Denumerably) Infinite} = \text{Aleph-0};$$

$$\text{(Nondenumerably) Infinite} = \text{Aleph-1}.$$

Mathematicians have developed ways of combining types of numbers. For example, cardinal numbers may be divided, multiplied, raised to exponents, etc., much the same as any other numbers. Hartman uses these techniques cleverly to arrive at the ordinal array. He assigns to each a base value and a particular cardinal number, as follows:

$$\text{Finite} = n = \text{Systemic Value};$$

$$\text{(Denumerably) Infinite} = \text{Aleph-0} = \text{Extrinsic Value};$$

$$\text{(Nondenumerably) Infinite} = \text{Aleph-1} = \text{Intrinsic Value}.$$

Next, the value combinations may be used as exponents to arrive at the following scheme:

I^I means Aleph-1 to the Aleph-1 power;

I^E means Aleph-1 to the Aleph-0 power;

I^S means Aleph-1 to the n power.

This is no different from taking a certain number, say '2', and raising this number to three different powers:

2 power 2: $2^2 = 4$;

2 power 3: $2^3 = 8$;

2 power 4: $2^4 = 16$.

The exact arithmetic for the Aleph series works as follows:

$$n \text{ to the n power: } n^n = n;$$

$$n \text{ to the Aleph-0 power: } n^{\text{Aleph-0}} = \text{Aleph-1};$$

$$n \text{ to the Aleph-1 power: } n^{\text{Aleph-1}} = \text{Aleph-2};$$

$$\text{Aleph-0 to the n power: Aleph-0}^n = \text{Aleph-0};$$

$$\text{Aleph-0 to the Aleph-0 power: Aleph-0}^{\text{Aleph-0}} = \text{Aleph-1};$$

$$\text{Aleph-0 to the Aleph-1 power: Aleph-0}^{\text{Aleph-1}} = \text{Aleph-2};$$

$$\text{Aleph-1 to the n power: Aleph-1}^n = \text{Aleph-1};$$

$$\text{Aleph-1 to the Aleph-0 power: Aleph-1}^{\text{Aleph-0}} = \text{Aleph-1};$$

$$\text{Aleph-1 to the Aleph-1 power: Aleph-1}^{\text{Aleph-1}} = \text{Aleph-2};$$

By replacing the base values for their proper 'n' and Aleph symbol, we get the following array of elements:

$$\text{S to the S power: } S^S = n;$$

$$\text{S to the E power: } S^E = \text{Aleph-1};$$

$$\text{S to the I power: } S^I = \text{Aleph-2};$$

$$\text{E to the S power: } E^S = \text{Aleph-0};$$

$$\text{E to the E power: } E^E = \text{Aleph-1};$$

$$\text{E to the I power: } E^I = \text{Aleph-2};$$

$$\text{I to the S power: } I^S = \text{Aleph-1};$$

$$\text{I to the E power: } I^E = \text{Aleph-1};$$

$$\text{I to the I power: } I^I = \text{Aleph-2};$$

This accounts for the nine positive values, but what of the negative values? To arrive at their values, Hartman simply takes the above products and divides them into "1".

S to the S disvalue: $S_S = 1/n$;

S to the E disvalue: $S_E = 1/\text{Aleph-1}$;

S to the I disvalue: $S_I = 1/\text{Aleph-2}$;

E to the S disvalue: $E_S = 1/\text{Aleph-0}$;

E to the E disvalue: $E_E = 1/\text{Aleph-1}$;

E to the I disvalue: $E_I = 1/\text{Aleph-2}$;

I to the S disvalue: $I_S = 1/\text{Aleph-1}$;

I to the E disvalue: $I_E = 1/\text{Aleph-1}$;

I to the I disvalue: $I_I = 1/\text{Aleph-2}$;

This is a very clever scheme. Not only does it begin with an intuitive idea about how base value types (Systemic, Extrinsic, and Intrinsic values) are distinguished, but it goes much farther by relating each of these types to a cardinal number. In this way, Hartman is able to show how different value combinations are calculated to form distinct mathematical values. While this is a clever scheme, it is not without its difficulties. In the next section, we shall critically evaluate Hartman's Cardinal Model.

Critique of the Cardinal Model

The first question that we ask of any formal model is: does it do what we want it to do? Imagine a group of objects which we find to be distinct and separable. For example, consider looking into an office where we find both tables and chairs. If we do not wish to distinguish these items individually, we may choose to refer to them by their generic name, "furniture." This is fine so long as we do not lose the ability to refer to the items separately. Now, if we use a formal model, the model must be able to make all the distinctions which we ordinarily make. In fact, one of the important criteria for formal models is that they should allow us to make distinctions which ordinarily we cannot make. We saw how the use of geometry allowed early scientists to prove the Earth round without having the benefit of a view of the Earth from

Mathematical Models and the Science of Values 185

Space. This demonstrates that the power of geometry, like any formal model, expands our ability to "see."

Notice what happens to Hartman's use of cardinal numbers to describe the base values and their relations. First, as we have seen, Hartman identifies each base value with a distinct cardinal number:

$$\text{Finite} = n = \text{Systemic Value};$$

$$\text{(Denumerably) Infinite} = \text{Aleph-0} = \text{Extrinsic Value};$$

$$\text{(Nondenumerably) Infinite} = \text{Aleph-1} = \text{Intrinsic Value}.$$

So far, so good. We begin with three base values, and each has a distinct cardinal number to represent it. But when we get to the combinations and transpositions of these values, then things are not so well-ordered. Notice that in the Ordinal Model, there are eighteen combinations, each of which has its own rank. No two of the items are of the same rank. It is reasonable to assume that the Cardinal Model will likewise distinguish the eighteen items so that no two are of equal value. This however, is not the case. When we rearrange the table according to the Aleph value, then we find that several of the combinations have the same value:

S to the S power: $S^S = n$;

E to the S power: $E^S = $ Aleph-0;

S to the E power: $S^E = $ Aleph-1;

E to the E power: $E^E = $ Aleph-1;

I to the S power: $I^S = $ Aleph-1;

I to the E power: $I^E = $ Aleph-1;

S to the I power: $S^I = $ Aleph-2;

E to the I power: $E^I = $ Aleph-2;

I to the I power: $I^I = $ Aleph-2;

The problem gets no better when we look at disvalues:

S to the S disvalue: $S_S = 1/n$;

E to the S disvalue: $E_S = 1/\text{Aleph-0}$;

S to the E disvalue: $S_E = 1/\text{Aleph-1}$;

I to the S disvalue: $I_S = 1/\text{Aleph-1}$;

I to the E disvalue: $I_E = 1/\text{Aleph-1}$;

E to the E disvalue: $E_E = 1/\text{Aleph-1}$;

E to the I disvalue: $E_I = 1/\text{Aleph-2}$;

I to the I disvalue: $I_I = 1/\text{Aleph-2}$;

S to the I disvalue: $S_I = 1/\text{Aleph-2}$;

In effect, where there were eighteen distinct, ordinal items, there are now only eight. Four value compositions:

$$S^S = n;$$

$$E^S = \text{Aleph-0};$$

$$S^E, E^E, I^S, I^E = \text{Aleph-1};$$

$$S^I, E^I, I^I = \text{Aleph-2}.$$

And four value transpositions:

$$S_S = 1/n$$

$$E_S = 1/\text{Aleph-0};$$

$$S_E, E_E, I_S, I_E = 1/\text{Aleph-1};$$

$$S_I, E_I, I_I = 1/\text{Aleph-2}.$$

This is unfortunate. In the example above, where we imagined furniture in the office, we saw that even if we refer to all the items generically as "furniture," the option is still available to us to distinguish tables from chairs. However, in the case of Hartman's Cardinal Model, we are rather like Humpty Dumpty. What a formal model obscures simply cannot be distinguished within the formal framework by any number of the King's horses and men. If we cannot formally distinguish S^E from E^E at the very foundations of the model, then the distinction is hopelessly lost. This would be disastrous for the entirety of Hartman's science. What we so nicely distinguished within the framework of the Ordinal Model has now become scrambled Humpty Dumpty eggs, and they will never be separated again. This is why it is useful to look at Hartman's work as really two models rather than one. What does Hartman have to say for himself on this issue? In fact, he was aware of this problem, so let us get his response. In <u>The Structure of Value</u>, he writes: "Although some compositions and transpositions have the same axiological value, for example S_I and I_I both have the value 1/Aleph-2, this axiological value covers a difference,..." (p.275)

I'll say it covers a difference, and it is a difference which makes a difference! As a formal model, the Cardinal Model is surely a disaster for a science of value. Again, what the formal model has failed to distinguish cannot be differentiated. Despite its nice beginning of distinguishing Systemic, Extrinsic, and Intrinsic values, the Cardinal Model simply obscures our understanding of the ways in which these values can be combined. This does not mean that the issue is futile; but it does mean that Hartman's formal model, based on cardinal numbers, is not a complete success.

There is also another serious problem with Hartman's Cardinal Model. Notice that the value transpositions are all expressed as "1/number". In other words, value transpositions are expressed as fractions. Let us suppose that we want to look at a value relation which has three value components, for example: $S_S{}^S$. This is a systemic value, systemically disvalued, and then systemically valued. Although this may seem complex, it really is not. It could be something as simple as an error in a computer program which has been corrected. Now, since the error has been found and corrected, the overall value of the three-part scheme ought to return to neutral. But this cannot be. The problem is simple arithmetic. Once you create a fraction, raising the fraction by the power of an exponent will never result in a number greater than 1. This means that once you create a value transposition (a fraction), then no amount of value composition will ever change the negative value into a positive one. In fact, as the size of the exponent grows, the size of the fraction gets smaller. This means that an extrinsic or intrinsic evaluation of the error in the computer program would result in an even greater disvalue than merely the systemic valuation. This seems to be far too great a restriction on how value combinations can interrelate. From the point of view of our intuitive understanding of values, this means that no amount of positive value which we may receive from realizing that we have made a mistake will ever overcome the disvalue of the mistake, no matter how minor. In other words, we can never positively profit from our mistakes. Moreover, and perhaps more seriously, from a religious perspective, forgiveness of sins (value mistakes) can never lead to a positive value. The system of cardinal numbers will never allow a transposition and its subsequent compositions ever to go above the number (1). No positive good emerges in the story of the prodigal son, or Jesus' forgiveness of Mary Magdalene.

It should be pointed out that this problem could be nicely solved by making the exponent the fraction rather than the entire expression. In other words, instead of expressing S_E as 1/Aleph-0, express it as $S^{1/E}$. In this way, the relation of transposition is seen as a root rather than an exponent. This is probably closer to reality since roots are the opposite of exponents. But is this the end of the matter? Let us approach this question from the following perspective. Why would Hartman want to use cardinal numbers in the first place? The answer to this question is revealing. Cardinal numbers express an intuitive qualitative difference. Cardinal numbers are not so much quantitatively dissimilar as they are qualitatively dissimilar. This is useful for Hartman because with the cardinals he wants to express his intuition that Systemic, Extrinsic and Intrinsic values are qualitatively different and incommensurable. Extrinsic value is not different from Systemic value because it has more properties, but because it is qualitatively different. The same is true of Intrinsic value. Intrinsic value is sometimes described as a wholeness, or oneness. Mathematically, a nondenumerable infinity is a continuum. This is very close to our intuitive notions of intrinsic value. So, cardinal numbers have a natural appeal. Unhappily, the cardinal numbers ultimately collapse the differences in the combinations of the base values, which the Ordinal Model is so keen to distinguish. Is there no way to save the Hartman program? Is there not a more suitable way to capture the intuitive differences in the base values and at the same time honor the ordinal rankings and preserve the incommensurability of the systemic, the extrinsic and the intrinsic? There may exist such models, and in the final section of this chapter we shall briefly explore another possibility.

Ought Value Ordinal Model

The approach we shall consider is an expansion of a concept developed by Hartman called "ought value." Ought value is defined by Hartman as follows:

Since a thing ought to be good, that is, ought to be n, its value of ought is n less that which the thing is. Hence, the value of ought is determined by the formula $o = n - x$, where x is the value the thing has at the moment of valuation. (The Structure of Value, p. 233)

Ought value, then, is the measure of what a thing lacks in value. If ought value = 0, then the thing is all it should be; while if ought value > 0, then the thing is not all that it should be.

There are three ways in which a thing can have an ought value of null (or 0). They are:

Ought value = 0: I^I, E^E, S^S.

Also, we can imagine three cases where ought disvalue = 0. They are:

S_S, E_E, I_I.

Apart from these six combinations, there are two other types of relations. One type of relation has the exponent or subscript being a greater value than the base. For example, E^I or S^E are cases where the superscript is a greater value than the base. Let us call these cases of "value enrichment." When this occurs with disvalue, we shall call it "disvalue limitation." For example, when E_S occurs, then the base value E is not fully disvalued but only partially disvalued. On the other hand, there are cases where a base value may be "constrained," that is, cases where ought value > 0. This occurs any time the subscript or superscript is of a less value than the base value. For example, I^E and I^S are such cases. There are, then, three cases of ought value = 0, three cases of value enrichment, and three cases of ought value > 0. Similarly, there are three cases of ought disvalue = 0, three cases of disvalue limitation, and three cases of ought disvalue > 0. The two tables below summarize these relations. Numbers in parentheses refer to rankings in Hartman's original scheme.

Ought Value Composition

		(3)S^I		+2 LEVELS
VALUE ENRICHMENT:		(2)E^I	(6)S^E	+1 LEVEL
OUGHT VALUE = 0:	(1)I^I	(5)E^E	(9)S^S	0 LEVEL
OUGHT VALUE > 0:	(4)I^E	(8)E^S		-1 LEVEL

                    (7)I^S −2 LEVELS

Ought Disvalue Transposition

                              (12)I_S +2 LEVELS

DISVALUE LIMITATION: (11)E_S (15)I_E +1 LEVEL

OUGHT DISVALUE = 0:   (10)I_I (14)E_E (18)S_S 0 LEVEL

OUGHT DISVALUE > 0:   (13)S_E (17)E_I −1 LEVEL

           (16)S_I −2 LEVELS

This scheme provides the following ranking:

HARTMAN ORDINAL SCHEME	OUGHT VALUE ORDINAL SCHEME
Composition	Composition
1) I^I	I^I
2) E^I	E^I
3) S^I	S^I
4) I^E	I^E
5) I^S	E^E *
6) E^E	S^E *
7) S^E	I^S *
8) E^S	E^S
9) S^S	S^S

Transposition	Transposition
10) S_S	S_S
11) E_S	E_S
12) S_E	I_S *
13) E_E	S_E *
14) I_S	E_E *
15) I_E	I_E
16) S_I	S_I
17) E_I	E_I
18) I_I	I_I

Notice that the two schemes agree in all but six places, which have been indicated by an "*." The conclusion is that the Ought Value Model is different from Hartman's Ordinal Model, but at least there is a rationale for the Ought Value Model. Does this mean that Hartman is wrong and the Ought Value Model is correct? No, it only means that the scheme derived from our analysis of ought value is justifiable. This stands in contrast to Hartman's Ordinal Model, which loses its justification when we realize that his Cardinal Model will not support his Ordinal Model. The real proof lies in empirical testing to determine which of the two competing models is more applicable in the real world. While this testing has not yet been completed, there has been some concern on the part of practitioners of the Hartman Value Profile that the particular ordinal arrangement of the eighteen elements may be in need of adjustment. In fact, Evert Schildt found the Ought Value Model's ordinal arrangement of the eighteen elements more similar to statistical distributions he gathered in giving the Hartman Profile to citizens of Sweden. The point here is not to draw conclusions, but to understand how models are derived and justified.

In conclusion, two things are obvious. First, Robert Hartman has taken a giant step in bringing orderly thinking into a most esoteric and difficult subject, values. Second, while a giant step has been taken, there remains the formal problem of his utilization of cardinal numbers to justify his ranking of value relations. These problems, however, do not so much represent a stopping point to Hartman's work, but an invitation to continue.

Chapter IX

APPLICATIONS OF THE SCIENCE OF AXIOLOGY

Robert S. Hartman

It is my intention, in this lecture, to discuss in detail the application of the Science of Axiology to three fields which will illustrate the impact that axiological thinking has, and can have, on contemporary problems of our world. The three fields are: 1) political economy, 2) international political affairs, and 3) personal ethics. The first example, which concerns the economic system, will illustrate the relation between morality and economics. The second, which concerns the political system, especially with respect to war, will illustrate the relation between individual morality and collective immorality. The third, which concerns the relation between fathers and sons, will illustrate the relation between two different moral values. It is my hope that these examples will provide a concrete view of formal axiology.

The relation between moral and economic value has been discussed in books many times over but always categorically rather than axiomatically and, consequently, has failed to lead to a new economic system. The axiom of Axiology shows that moral value has primacy over economic value. The question is how, in the face of economic reality, can this primacy be imposed? If formal axiology is correct then we should be able to observe that, in practice, economic systems function better when they are more moral and worse when they are less moral. Since the function of an economic system is the creation of wealth, then, according to our definition of "good," a good economic system is one that creates wealth and a bad economic system is one that does not create wealth. In other words, a bad economic system gives rise to poverty rather than wealth. In political economy the word "poor" is the counterpart of the word "bad" in formal axiology, and conversely, the word "rich" is the counterpart of the axiological word "good," and "wealth" the counterpart of the axiological word "goodness."

Further, since according to formal axiology, moral value has primacy over economic value, we should be able to observe in economic reality that the lack of morality in an economic system leads to impoverishment, while the existence of social morality leads to enrichment, economically called wealth.[1]

What is the meaning of morality in an economic system? We have defined morality as the application of intrinsic value to persons, and have shown that the human being has literally infinite value. Economic value has been defined as the application of extrinsic value to things and it was shown that things viewed extrinsically have infinitely less value than persons. Consequently, it is clear that an economic system combined with morality means the combination of the extrinsic value of things with the intrinsic value of persons.

The combination of persons and things in economic activity is called the process of production. Defined by John Locke, production is the conjunction of human labor with nature. In a factory, the raw materials enter on one side and get out the other as finished products. What has happened meanwhile? In a special manner, the raw materials have combined with human labor. The moral factor, then, in production, ought to be grafted on to human labor.

In applying the dimensions of value to human labor, it will be observed how well they fit the facts and how easily they not only order the facts but also provide an understanding of the core of economic activity.

Systemically, the acts of labor are part of an exact, calculated system in which each act is paid in accordance with its capacity and function within the system. This is labor as viewed by the Taylor system which divided work into minute acts calculated to the second and paid in fractions of cents. To this was added the army of indefatigable time-study engineers, efficiency experts and resultant industrial managers. What does man derive from such a system? Considered as no more than a bundle of fragmented elements it is not possible for him to put his heart and soul into his work. In enterprises of this type, when a worker is asked what he is doing his pathetic and ironical reply is usually: "Nothing, I just work here." It is natural for him not to be interested in the progress of the business, for he only works for his pay which is by the hour, although more accurately by the second, and he will try to do the least work for the most pay. He is alienated both from himself and from the economy, and he rebels against this alienation, by deadening split-up work a la Chaplin's "Modern Times" or by strikes, as in the most modern but actually antiquated new Vega factories of General Motors.

As the worker holds back his labor in this kind of work - up to 40% and more of his capacity - so the owners of the industry hold back his wages: both compete in giving as little for as much as the traffic will bear. So we have two diametrically opposed forces, in the deadly struggle of the classes. This is the theory of traditional economics which culminated in Karl Marx and which treats of economic man in two opposing roles, as two opposing classes struggling only for gain; the management side has been described by Adam Smith and Ricardo, the proletarian side by Karl Marx. This is what we call the old capitalistic system. It is the application of systemic value to work. Its science is classical economics and its man is homo oeconomicus.

In this system there is no room for morality and therefore, according to our formal hypothesis, it should be a relatively poor system.

The application of extrinsic value to labor does not divide work into minute elements but considers work a class of functions executed by workingmen. As such, each worker is a function within a class of workers ("class" in the logical and, hence, social sense), and the fulfillment of his function, using his own skill, is complemented by the functions of other workers using their skills. This system of economy and of labor is characterized by job evaluation, merit systems, and pay not for special, minute fractions of labor but for the worker's skill and ability. What is valued here are not minute acts of labor, but the worker as a member of the class of workers. Man is paid for his work without the consideration of specific jobs, as in the guaranteed annual wage, in job rotation and the like. This is part of the present capitalistic system and is a more advanced economic system than the former. Man is now considered a social, rather than merely an economic being. We call the science of this system social economy and its man homo socialis. In this system there are two opposing classes, labor and management, and the conflict between these classes is on the social rather than economic level: the great collective bodies of unions and industries, and a precise balance between the two.

According to our hypothesis, this system should create more wealth than the former: and it is quite clear today, since the two systems exist side by side, that the old capitalistic system based on the exploitation of labor is poorer than the newer system. The United States and other countries which have advanced in economic development are richer than the countries with economies based on the predatory capitalism of systemic value, such as South Africa, Brazil and the pseudo-feudal countries and colonies, where fewer and fewer rich become richer and richer, and more and more poor become poorer and poorer.

More advanced, still, than the second or social stage, of the economic system, is the moral stage: the application of intrinsic value to labor, out of which grows a new science, <u>moral economics</u> and its man, <u>homo moralis</u>.

The application of intrinsic value to labor means that the laborer is considered not as a Taylorian construction nor as a function within a class of laborers, but as <u>a moral person of infinite value</u>. This means that the worker gives his complete self to his work, with a sense of responsibility not only for himself but also for his colleagues, the company and the total economy. His interest in the business will be as intense as the owner's, who also is a person of infinite moral value; and with the disappearance of the division between capital and labor, we will have a collaboration between individuals which will result in an economy that surpasses anything that we know today. To some extent, this has already occurred in North America, especially in the profit-sharing industries which in all economic statistics are the wealthiest and best managed in every country. Moreover, they completely reverse the <u>division</u> of labor in a process of <u>integration</u> of labor: small groups of workers are responsible for whole assemblies and subassemblies, including their own quality control. The prototype of this new kind of industry is the Lincoln Electric Company in Cleveland, Ohio. Examples in Europe include the Saab automotive works in Sweden.

Labor leaders of this new moral economy, such as the late Walter Reuther and his successors, are more interested in the productivity of the economy than in the fight of wages. For progressive management, in the United States today, high wages - after the revolutionary pioneering of Henry Ford sixty years ago, - the participation of labor in management, job security and pensions are obvious requirements. Only the old-style businessman in the U. S. is primarily interested in profits and secondarily in supplying the market. His labor counter part, the old-style labor leader, is primarily interested in wages and the class struggle. What the profit motive is for the old-style businessman, the struggle between the classes is for the old-style labor leaders. The modern labor leaders and modern businessmen agree that they are economic and social partners with a common interest in high production and high wages, that is, in Prosperity.

This new economic procedure based on mutual interest on the part of labor and management, introduces a community of human relations between management and labor, heretofore unimagined. The human dimensions becomes a new dimension in administration, as important as skill; and without the understanding of it a modern businessman will not be able to fulfill his task.

This view of human relations in business takes us into a completely new realm, far different from the old theory of industrial management and its calculations, or from viewing the economy as a whole in a mathematically finite manner. It takes us into the realm of intrinsic value whose mathematics is infinite, or, more accurately, transfinite. It can be said that the more finite mathematical calculations are applied to the field of human relations and the more narrowly correct they are, the greater the falseness of the result. The new science of human relations presupposes a transfinite analysis provided by formal axiology.

A number of examples prove this. When the establishment of a ten-minute rest period each morning and afternoon was proposed in a factory in Baltimore several years ago, the management engineers got to work with their slide rules and calculating machines in order to determine exactly the loss of production as a result of these twenty minutes of rest daily, five days a week, twenty times per month, multiplied by twelve per year, for 1,200 workers, paid by the hour. On the basis of these calculations they reported that the production loss would ruin the company. However, the rest periods were established anyway, and instead of loss of production, production increased. With twenty minutes less "work" each day, more was produced than formerly. The same result was recorded in the famous Hawthorne experiments of Elton Mayo and others. The old psychotechnic methods of Taylor, which did not consider man even as a pure economic function but as a fragment of labor subdivided into sub-fragments, without taking into account the man behind these fragments, have brought about results in which the calculations play no part. The object of the Hawthorne experiments was the study of human workers; and it was found, in general although not in particular, that no matter what methods were applied to a group under study, whether higher wages were paid nor not, more hours of work required or less, whether working conditions were better or worse, the production of each group increased in every case. The reason was that the workers were being considered as human beings and they responded accordingly. The experiments also indicated that there existed a reserve of energy previously unused, good-will and the desire to cooperate on the part of the workers. Many other examples can be given but one more, concerning a foundry in Ohio, will suffice. This foundry operated on the following formula: 100% minus 50% equals 170%. The owner said that he stayed awake nights thinking about how he, in his "small way could do something to better the world." He finally decided to give his workers 50% participation in the profits of his company. As a result of their greater cooperation, greater punctuality, less absenteeism, greater savings in materials, less accidents among them, production increased 40% and the profits 340%. These profits were divided in half: 170% for the workers, 170% for the owner who received 70% more than before he gave away 50% of his profits. At the same time, he lowered his price 40%.

What made all of this possible was the inclusion in the equation of the resource of human cooperation. It was an investment made in people, the employment of a previously unused economic resource, the willingness to work. This and other similar formulae are valid from some 120,000 plants in the United States and thousands in Europe, Asia, Australia, and Latin America, which have given the workers a share in the profits. All of these experiments have shown that, if human cooperation is mobilized, it is the most powerful economic resource at our disposal. Labor, viewed intrinsically, is not a commodity to be brought and sold at a price, wages, but rather the worker's investment of his own self in the company, as a true partner, and his corresponding participation in the success of the firm.

That profit-sharing, a moral system of economics, leads to greater riches than the traditional and social systems, is exemplified by the trust plan or deferred plan by which a certain percentage of the income of a company is set aside in a trust fund from which an employee receives his share on retirement. Of these, both qualitatively and quantitatively, Sears Roebuck has the most outstanding plan, with more than 200,000 members participating in its trust fund. When a Sears Roebuck employee retires after twenty-five or thirty years of service, a sort of graduation ceremony is held. I was present at a graduation in the old non-inflationary years. The employees were divided into three groups: those who had been earning up to two thousand dollars a year, those who had been earning up to three thousand a year, receives as much as sixty thousand dollars. And those who had been earning up to four thousand a year received up to $120,000 - and these were honest to goodness dollars. Today the results are multiplied but the large numbers are less significant. Of course, these amounts are not paid in one lump as the U. S. government and not the retiring employee would get most of it. What makes possible such amounts as these is the increase of the fund by means of interest and investments over the course of time. The average of the individual funds of Sears Roebuck employees in the United States at that time was $40,000! In Mexico, Sear Roebuck employees had, after a number of years, more money in their individual funds than did the U. S. employees after the same length of time, because of the higher increment of the fund due to higher interest rates. When these employees retire or leave the company and take out their money, they will be, relatively speaking, rich people.

Here is a system, economically good, which creates riches for all and which already exists in many parts of the world. It is based on the infinite value of the human being and the transfinite logic of intrinsic value.

This system has nothing whatever to do with the oppositions within the old systems of capitalism and communism. It is an entirely new system, and both these old systems are developing in its direction. The methods, mentioned above, are not limited to the capitalistic system because the line dividing capital and labor no longer exists. All of these methods can be applied and are being applied within the socialist and communist systems. The change has already begun in Russia and is operating on a large scale in Yugoslavia. The difference between Russian Communism and Yugoslav Communism is precisely the difference in the degree to which the workers share in the profits and in the administration of the enterprises. There is little practical, though a legal, difference between a Yugoslav company and a cooperative in the United States in which the workers are the owners, and there are many such companies both in the United States and in other parts of the world. Neither is there much difference between the management of a Russian enterprise and an American company operating within the socio-economic system. "Man does not live by bread alone," and the Organization Man of Dudintsev's book, may just as easily be American as Russian. Axiologically, old-style Capitalism and Communism have many characteristics in common and, from different points of departure develop in the same direction. Axiologically, we can also see how correct are the revolutionaries when they say that poverty is unnecessary. However, the revolution that will abolish poverty is not a political but a moral revolution. From the axiom of axiology follows the theorem that the degree of poverty in a society is the measure of its lack of moral and social responsibility; the wealth of a nation is a direct function of its social morality. It is no accident that during the Nixon Administration with its moral scandals the economy of the United States and its currency hit rock bottom. And the Soviet economy, throughout its 50 year history, has been plagued by crucial shortages, most recently of wheat, so that only massive foreign purchases avoided a famine. These two countries were victors in World War II. Germany and Japan, on the other hand, were the losers. But they went through a crucible of moral regeneration. They are today the most prosperous nations after the two giants--and without suffering their internal contradictions.

Social morality is closely connected with political morality. That morality is the prime factor in the goodness of an economic system, that is, for the creation of wealth, has already been demonstrated. We shall now show the need for morality for the goodness of a political system. Such a system is called a state. What, then, is a good state? According to the axiological axiom, a good state is a state which fulfills the definition of "state." But what is the definition of "state" and what are the properties that govern it? It was simple to define the function of an economic system, i.e. to create wealth. The definition of a state appears to be more difficult. Nevertheless, we can arrive at this definition easily if we do not recall all that has been written on this subject, but use our common sense and powers of observation, that is, the scientific method in the Galilean sense of observing the phenomena and penetrating to the essence of the subject. What is a state?

When we walk along the street or drive along the highway, it is quite clear to us what element in our surroundings belongs to the state. It is found neither in the trees nor the stores, for example, for although there are state trees and stores, they are not essential to the state. The element that belongs to the state is found in the organisms of public order, especially the police and the military. The police are in charge of keeping public order; and if I am assaulted by a thief or involved in some other kind of serious emergency, the police will help me. As a rule, we do not think of the police in terms of the function of assistance but rather in terms of the function of arrest, that is, we consider the police from the point of view of the thief and not of the peaceful citizen. From the viewpoint of the peaceful citizen, the police protects him in case of emergencies, disasters and catastrophes, and for their services he pays through taxes. Curiously enough, the citizen pays for these services in the hope that he will never require them, that never will a situation arise that will make it necessary for him to utilize the services that he pays for throughout his life. He hopes with all his heart that others will benefit by these organisms which he pays for and that neither will he have to make use of these apparatuses nor will they be concerned with him in any way. In short, he pays in order not to receive anything. The State, then, is the maintenance of an apparatus by citizens who want to have as little to do with this apparatus as possible. With the money they work so hard for, they finance the less fortunate in cases of emergency, even with the fervent desire of helping them. What is most curious is that this altruistic behavior stems from the most profound egotistical motives, somewhat like the statement I once read on a house in Bavaria: "Saint Florian, protect our town, don't burn my house, burn others down." This profound egoism leads to a most profound altruistic action in which the state exemplifies this curious situation. The principle behind this, however, is not at all curious, being one that we employ constantly in many different ways in our life. It is the principle of insurance. We pay an insurance company for exactly the same reason we pay for the police, with the fervent hope that we will never have to use it; and there is nothing we would like better than to arrive at the end of a year having lost our money. We pay the premium for the following year again in the hope that we will lose it. The principle of the state is the principle of insurance - a theory of the state rarely found in books devoted to this subject. It is a principle profoundly moral and widely used. For example, another curiosity, it is the same principle as that of lottery, except that in the case of a lottery we finance those more fortunate than we. A lottery thus is no more nor less gambling than is insurance.

In what respect is the principle of insurance, one type of which is the state, a moral principle? Simply insofar as all power channelled in the public order is focused on a person in trouble, on a person who is neither part of a system nor member of a class, but himself alone, this human being in adversity. The state and insurance are really the principle of all for one. Unfortunately, this simple situation has never been seen clearly, as has its contrary, one for all, the conformity of one to a group, or being one among many to produce collective unity. The latter is the general theory of the state today and even the emblem of the United States contains the words E pluribus unum, one from many, instead of Omnes per unum, all for one. Today, we are living in the epoch of collectivity, and the individual does not firmly exist either in the theory or the practice of the state. Formal axiology should rescue him.

The bitterest consequence of this notion of collective unity with respect to the state is war, which leads to the greatest tension between the intrinsic value of moral man and the systemic value of the immoral state. The raison d'etat, the Reason of State is amoral and usually immoral. In war, values are turned upside down. In time of war, the most honorable man is the one who kills the greatest number of people while in time of peace if he kills only one he gets the electric chair, is hung or shot or will spend a lifetime in prison. The war hero is the criminal during peacetime and vice versa. If one contends, as has been done on many occasions, that it is not people but soldiers that are killed in war, then one simply is saying that soldiers are not people, which happens to be the crux of the problem of war. Unfortunately, soldiers not only kill soldiers, but also murder people, as In My Lai.

The difference between soldiers and people is illustrated by the following little story from "Humor in Uniform" of the Readers' Digest.

> We and two other families in our neighborhood gave a party to welcome our new neighbors, a retired Army colonel and his wife. The evening was a great success, and our guests of honor expressed their appreciation over and over. "Really, this has been just wonderful, they exclaimed again as they were leaving. "We do these things for each other in the Army, you know, but we didn't know that people did!"[2]

People are educated to be good citizens and then, as soldiers, trained by their governments to use the most diabolical instruments of torture, taught by means of sacks filled with straw to slit open the maximum number of abdomens in the minimum amount of time. Our sons have been in such situations, good young men who until now had never slit open abdomens and hated the very idea - and we ourselves had taught them to hate it. What then is this sinister power that forces good people into this diabolical predicament? It is the absolute sovereignty of the nation to which we belong. Sovereignty is the expression of the principle of collectivity that makes one out of many, but there is more to it, which formal axiology explains. Sovereignty means "Superiority": it means that the nation is superior to, above and beyond, the moral law, indeed, that no law applies to it except the ones it accepts voluntarily. It is the expression of a jungle of collectivities where might is right. This is a principle completely in opposition to all existing morality - the soldier principle as against the people principle - and in opposition to all axiological definitions of good. Indeed, it corresponds to the axiological definition of evil. And its consequences are both evil - and insane.

This becomes clear when we compare the behavior of sovereign states with that of states and organizations that lack sovereignty. Each formally structured group is a whole, be it a corporation, a town, a city or a state. Obviously, it would be considered mad if the state of Montana declared war on Idaho or if Idaho and Montana organized the rest of the states of the Union into opposing confederations with the object of their warring against each other. It would also be considered insane if the citizens of Newark, N. J., were called up for military service to invade the territory of New York City - but this sort of thing was not considered insane during the Middle Ages when cities made war on each other with the same avidity that nations make war today. It would be equally insane if the General Motors workers in Detroit were given arms in order to conquer the Ford Motor Company. The competition between these two companies is economic and based on co-existence. On the other hand, it is not considered insane, say, for the people of France to be armed to make war against Algiers, the people of Germany to make war against Russia, the people of Russia against the people of America, the people of America against the Indochinese, or the people of Honduras against San Salvador. Nevertheless, as concerns real power, General Motors is more powerful than Algiers, Indochina, Honduras or San Salvador; its annual production is greater than any of these countries, greater than all of Scandinavia and almost half that of West Germany.

National wars appear not insane if one accepts the notion of national sovereignty - as do most people - and it does appear insane if one does not - as does an ever growing group of people. The former do not recognize, the latter do recognize the moral evil of sovereignty, its being above and beyond the law.

What we have seen in the economic field we now see in the political field: the morally insensitive will extol sovereignty, that is, the military, while the morally sensitive will extol society, that is, the people. The former are impelled by fear, the latter by good will and faith. The division between these attitudes separates, in every nation today, neighbor from neighbor, parents from children, hardhats from teachers, town and gown, and political parties within itself. Indeed, it split the Nixon Administration straight through the middle.

If the axiological analysis is correct, then a good state, in which the insurance principle, good will and compassion prevail, will be a better organized, economically richer, and individually more concerned society than a bad state which is victim to sovereignty, the military, and cuts down social welfare. Again, we have the dramatic examples of Germany and Japan on the one hand, and Russia and the United States on the other. The former two were by the victors constitutionally forbidden to have a military establishment; that is, their sovereignty was limited. They could channel all their resources into the civil society, and as a result soared ahead in political savvy and economic growth. The victors on the other hand, both the United States and the Soviet Union, suffer from extreme military expenditures, a lethal nuclear race, economic shortages and dislocations, racial strife, a drying up of the civil society - e.g., the United States is in 13th rank among the peoples of the earth in infant mortality - and contradictions which can only lead to chaos.

What is the difference between the insanity of arming General Motors against the Ford Motor Company and the rationality of arming Germany against Russia or Honduras against San Salvador? The reason is that these last are sovereign nations and that sovereignty is something more than mere unity. The nation considered as sovereign is not just seen as a unit but is endowed with that strange kind of power which disregard of the law gives the criminal. The sovereignty of the democratic collectives is a fiction masterfully constructed by Rousseau, as the general will, la volonté générale, whose properties are neither more nor less than the same properties that belonged to the absolute monarch. In the great democratic revolutions in France, the United States, Russia and other countries, the absolute sovereignty of the autocratic Sovereign was crushed as far as domestic matters were concerned, but remained intact as far as foreign relations were concerned. The new democracies which succeeded the absolute monarch claimed national sovereignty as had their erstwhile King or Emperor. But since there was no longer a sovereign as a single physical person, sovereignty had to be constructed, and any connection with concrete reality had to be ignored. Therefore, it remained as a fiction, as a construction and axiologically it is a systemic value.

As a result, all nations today, democratic or totalitarian, have, as refers to their foreign relations, that is, their relations with each other, all the characteristics of the autocratic prince of ancient times. According to the theories of Hobbes and the practice of those times, the prince had totalitarian rights over his subjects. He was above the law, the sole moral judge, and it was sinful for the subject to make judgments based on his own conscience. Further, the sovereign prince had absolute power over all property and his subjects owed him total obedience. Rousseau transferred all of these characteristics to the prince-less collective, the collective that arose out of the revolution. This being the case, as regards external relations, all the revolutions of the past from the American, French, the African and South American up to the Russian, were futile; and the international situation is exactly the same as if these revolutions had never taken place.

The natural expression of this state of things is war. In time of war, the force that is imposed by a republican, quasi-democratic sovereignty, is the same as that of autocratic and monarchic sovereignty: the citizen owes complete obedience to the collective of the nation as his sovereign, in exactly the same way his forebears owed obedience to the absolute monarch. What was criminal in terms of his personal and moral life, was heroic in terms of this disobedience and is still, even though the sovereign is no longer a single monarch but a national collective.

Nevertheless, from the point of view of axiology the transference of sovereignty from the person of the prince to the popular will, is of utmost significance; for, as has been said, the popular will is a fiction, a construction and therefore is subject only to systemic valuation. Axiologically, sovereignty has infinitely less value, in the exact meaning of our definition of infinite, than the moral value of the individual person. This leads to the inevitable conclusion that the individual person must reject the exigencies of a fiction which works against him and which is contrary to what he is, a moral being, the being which contains the infinite of intrinsic value. Axiologically, it is infinitely evil to kill another human being or to use violence against him for the sake of an idea, a system or any other abstraction. This represents the systemic devaluation of intrinsic value as symbolized by the formula I_s, which was mentioned earlier. The alternative is, of course, a moral view of sovereignty in which the volonté générale is focussed on the moral person, as in the principle of insurance.

Another extremely important aspect is that to kill a human being for the sake of an idea means that the end justifies the means. This proposition, axiologically, is infinitely bad because the means are concrete and the end is a thought. The concrete, as we have seen, as intrinsic value or even as extrinsic value, is infinitely more valuable than a thought, which has systemic value. What counts exclusively is the means and not the end. This is the doctrine of Ghandi which led to his method of satyagraha or non-violence. It is also the doctrine of Jesus Christ: we should conquer evil by good, not by another evil.

Formal axiology helps us understand these often misunderstood words which mean that against one value must be pitted a better value and that only a better value can surpass a worse value. In other words, it means that systemic value must be overcome by extrinsic and intrinsic values. This further means that we should be creative in all situations and perceive the germ of good even in the worst situation. It is precisely what Abraham Lincoln meant when, asked why he was so kind to his enemies, he replied: "Am I not annihilating my enemies by making friends of them?" It is the doctrine of Castellio who, when Calvin burned Servet in the name of faith, wrote: "To kill a man in the name of faith is not the defense of faith but the murder of a man." In the same way, axiology obliges us to say today: "To burn men, women and children in the name of a cause, is not the defense of the cause but the murder of men, women and children."

Scientific axiology, based on purely formal equations, thus arrives at truly revolutionary results. It ought to be destined, and I believe it is, to bring forth a new moral world. For the real revolutions are not those fought in the streets but those of the spirit.

Two accounts, one imaginary and one real, will serve to show, respectively, the consequences that could result, on the one hand, from our failure and, on the other, from a method towards moral success in this world. The first account can be found in Nevil Shute's novel On the Beach, in which the beach represents the ocean of time, on whose shores the last waves are lapping and dying in the sand. The beach is that of Melbourne, Australia, the southernmost city of the world, where the people are living out the last weeks and months of their lives. Life on earth is about to disappear due to a short, but devastating atomic war in the northern hemisphere, and the polluted atmosphere is slowly moving southward with the winds and currents. In latitude after latitude, in city after city, human and animal life is dying as a result of sickness produced by radiation, a kind of cholera which begins with nausea, vomiting, diarrhea, increasingly violent spasms and, finally, death from exhaustion. Australia, like the other southern nations, distributes cyanide pills to those who want them to help them through their last agonizing hours, so that they may die peacefully in their beds, the whole earth going to sleep, mankind ending "not with a bang, but a whimper" as T.S. Eliot says in the motto of the book.

Some ask themselves, as we certainly would, why life on earth must come to such a ridiculous end. The only answer is "we have been too silly to deserve a world like this." After poisoning their child and about to swallow their own pills, Lieutenant Holmes and his wife, Mary, ask each other if anyone might have prevented the course of events, and the Lieutenant says: "I don't know, some kinds of silliness you just can't stop. If a couple of hundred million people all decide that their national honor requires them to drop cobalt bombs upon their neighbor, well, there's not much that you or I can do about it. The only possible hope would have been to educate them out of their silliness."[3]

Thus, life on Earth ends in a paradox: a race that has reached the acme of intellectual development destroys itself willingly in abysmal stupidity. This paradox must puzzle to the point of mystery any future visitor to this planet, as it does, forty-five thousand years after the catastrophe, the Select Exploratory Mission, whose six-volume report, "The Rise and Annihilation of Earth-Life," fell, by some spatiotemporal wizardry, into the hands of the managing editor of the Washington Post and Times Herald, Alfred Friendly, who reviewed it on June 26, 1955, where you can read it. Forty-five thousand years after the catastrophe, "earth is once again verdant with forest and grass, with even the once devastated areas hidden under dense foliage. In one sense it is a singularly beautiful planet. But in another, more impressive sense it is the ultimate in horror. Over the face of this planetary paradise there is no free-moving life. There is no eye, no ear, no hand, no football, no intelligent thing." Even greater than the horror is the mystery. The more the Mission "discovered about life on Earth the less it was able to explain its extinction."[4]

Each discovery reported, each deduction substantiated, each piece of the puzzle rightly fitted into place only serves to deepen the mystery: Here was a civilization of great advancement, motivated as all life must be by the burning desire to survive, accomplished in engineering and vastly knowledgeable in science, and esteeming the loftiest philosophical standards--which nevertheless knowingly destroyed itself. "Knowingly" is used advisedly. It is at the root of the enigma. A team headed by the Mission deputy himself makes a brilliant and irrefutable proof (Vol. II, pp. 560-719) that Earth-man could not have escaped knowing that the neutron emission from two hundred and forty-odd macro-fission-fusion reactions would fatally empoison virtually all life then extant on Earth. The proof comes from the fact that the knowledge and techniques necessary to create a giant fission and/or fusion reaction necessarily include the knowledge of the degree of radio-activity that results, and its effects on life forms.[5]

So far the Report. That the technically so highly developed Earth-man was morally silly to the point of playing with cosmic devices as a child plays with toys, the Select Exploratory Mission could not imagine. Yet this was the situation.

It is, let us be clear about it, our situation at this very moment. The reason is, again very simply, that there are two entirely different kinds of knowledge, material knowledge and moral knowledge, and that up to this day we have developed the former and neglected the latter. The solution, then, for us humans on Earth, with our destiny still in our hands, our future still wide open, Earth still beckoning to us to continue the grand adventure of life we share with our brothers in the Universe--the solution is simply to close the time lag between material and moral knowledge and to develop the latter as we have the former. It means the creation of a moral science.

The new science is well on the way and is being taught already. We have found that learning these laws changes the character of the young people, makes them more aware, more awake, more sensitive. In fact, we have found that it changes whole families, bringing them happiness and insight. Let me mention only one such case. One of my students told me a week or so before the term papers were due that the writing of that paper was "the most important thing in my life." When I got the paper the title was "Homecoming of a Son." The subject was, in short, that through learning the various value dimensions he had found that he had never loved his parents. He had been ashamed of them for being workers. Learning the true values--that intrinsic value has nothing to do with what a person does, but only with what he is--he had seen the injustice he had done them. He wanted to correct it, but the problem was how to do it without showing them that he had never loved them before. The paper was about the method he evolved to overcome this difficulty, how he showed them his love, and how this changed the whole atmosphere in the home from one of indifference and tension to one of love. "Harmony and continual laughter prevailed." He did all this during the Christmas vacation, and wrote the paper while he acted out its content. To read it was a thrilling experience, like a miracle consciously wrought. About two weeks later he came to me with a letter from his mother. She wrote that such strange and wonderful things had happened during the vacation, that she and his dad had been thinking and talking about what it was, and they had come to the conclusion--that they had never really loved him. "I have felt for years that somewhere along the line Daddy and I failed you in some way. . . Life is sure funny, isn't it? You go through the years while life is passing you by thinking you are doing what's right and yet you are blind to what really is happening around you."

This seems to me a perfect description of our present situation. We are blind to the true values all around and within us. If the whole world would learn the true values the way that young man and his family learned them, our troubles would largely be over, the equilibrium in human affairs would be restored, and the scene on the beach at Melbourne would never take place.

These, then, are the two pictures of the world of the future: a world of life and love, and a world of death and desolation. One or the other of these worlds will and must be ours. Either what I have said is fiction and what Nevil Shute has said is prediction, or what Nevil Shute has said is--and will remain--fiction and what I have said is prediction. The satellites whirling high above us at this moment, spell either our doom or our destiny.

This, then, is our extraordinary opportunity. We may go on spending our money to develop the hydrogen and cobalt bombs and make the scene at Melbourne come true and give the men from Outer Space their opportunity to write the six-volume report, or we may use a fraction of this money - hardly more than the cost of some tiny gadget in an intercontinental missile - to concentrate the energies of a dozen or so people on human survival. The choice is ours, and it may be final.

NOTES

1. Robert S. Hartman, <u>Die Partnerschaft von Kapital und Arbeit: Theorie and Praxis eines neuen Wirshafts-systems (The Partnership of Capital and Labor: Theory and Practice of a New Economic System</u>), Opladen-Cologne, Westdeutscher Verlag, 1958.

2. <u>Reader's Digest</u>, April 1973, p. 33.

3. Nevil Shute, <u>On The Beach</u>, New York, Morrow, 1957, p. 309.

4. <u>Washington Post and Times Herald</u>, June 26, 1955.

5. <u>Ibid</u>.

Chapter X

USES OF AXIOLOGY IN BUSINESS

Vera Mefford

If we ask a random group of business professionals why so many businesses fail every year, the answers will range from personal business philosophy to criticism of politicians and current economic policy. It is notable that the same business phenomenon can produce so many different points of view. In an attempt to explain this, well-known management consultant and author, Peter Drucker, claims that the underlying reason is the lack of a genuine theory of business and an integrated discipline of business management. Drucker's claim is supported by recent statistics of the Better Business Bureau, which cite that 89% of business failures are due to mismanagement. Business owners and supervisors can mismanage in three basic areas which can be clearly defined by formal axiology: funds (systemic value dimension); production processes (extrinsic value dimension); and human resources--personnel and customers (intrinsic value dimension).

Incompetent supervision is a primary source of dissatisfaction and occupational stress for workers throughout corporate America. This is true because individuals are often promoted to managerial positions without sufficient training. The best technical person in the shop or department is promoted to supervisor and has difficulty making the transition from doing to delegating, due to little or no disciplined management training. When they run into trouble, these managers fall back on personal experience for guidance, and this is usually not sufficient to handle the responsibilities they face. Moreover, many managers are given no systematic feedback about the quality of their performance and how to improve it. As our business culture moves further into the information age, it is apparent that new management standards are needed to guide companies toward optimal growth and development. Many books have been written on various aspects of business, but there is no text available that clearly defines and demonstrates what business and its management ought to be. Too much emphasis has been placed on specific kinds of management, or certain aspects of business operations rather than on the general (underlying) concepts themselves. Toward fulfilling this need, this chapter will attempt to organize the broad field of business according to the principles of formal axiology, and discuss several current uses of axiology in business. The foundations for a scientific, formal axiology, as developed by Robert S. Hartman, provide an excellent frame of reference to integrate all specific business operations into an axiological formula that can then be used as an ideal value standard according to which we can measure the worth of actual businesses.

The Value Structure of a "Good" Business

Generally, a business is an organization whose objective is to produce and sell for a profit products and services that satisfy society's needs and desires. In axiological terms, a business is an <u>economic value generator</u>. The value term "good" is defined in formal axiology as "the case where the given thing fulfills all the specifications of its concept." The concept "business" includes the intensions "profit-making," "production," and "people." Therefore, a good business should produce value in all three dimensions: systemically, by making a profit; extrinsically, through efficient production, and intrinsically through moral behavior toward its personnel and customer base.

An ideally "good" business is one that integrates and balances financial, economic and human value, which can be expressed as ($I = E = S$). This means that an axiologically ideal business <u>ought</u> to generate as much profit as it can by means of efficient production, and it ought to generate as much productivity as possible by means of generating the fullest sense of personal achievement in its personnel, and the fullest sense of satisfaction in its customers. This ideal can be used as a norm for measuring all forms of business, from those which emphasize profit values, to non-profit foundations which generally emphasize people values and social service.

A business is a multi-dimensional organization which should continue to unfold its potential and grow in all three value dimensions. If efforts for business development are held to only one or two of the value dimensions, e.g. if a business owner believes the only purpose of his business is to make a profit, then its potential for growth is restricted because it lacks an equal focus on developing people. In fact, labor unions arose because companies paid little or no attention to the intrinsic value dimension of human values. As the preceding article by Robert Hartman shows, giving equal emphasis to human resources has historically proven to increase production (and therefore profit), boosting the economy in general. This is convincing evidence that the intrinsic value dimension is the richest in properties and contains the extrinsic and systemic dimensions. Business value can be progressively gained or lost. To gain a clearer understanding of this principle of containment, let us first analyze in axiological terms how a business is constructed.

Business Value Formation

Systemic values consist of the minimum set of properties to identify a thing as such. For a business, systemic values are the minimum elements required to qualify as a business at all. Companies like AT & T which specialize in providing system values to other business have generally done very well in the marketplace. The reason for their success is that systemic value is a basic necessity for all business. These values include all the systems which prescribe, automate or direct all internal business processes, and all systems which connect the business to the outside world. Systemic values are the logical foundation around which extrinsic and intrinsic values can be built.

Extrinsic values are perceptual space-time properties, characterized by their comparative nature. For a business, extrinsic values expand the systemic business foundation into real space and time through tangible, practical product or service related activity. As soon as business activity begins, the threshold to the intended customer base is crossed by some tangible means. All business processes which are directed toward some specific or general goal are also extrinsic values. In this value dimension, work schedules are created, and personnel are assigned responsibilities. Sales and marketing are the primary goal-oriented business activities at the extrinsic level. Extrinsic business values are identifiable by <u>degrees</u> of fulfillment. Even the first product or sale can be made very well or very poorly. The comparative value term "good" is properly used when the actual degree of fulfillment corresponds to the stated goal, or to the desired degree of production and performance.

Intrinsic values are characterized by their continuous, holistic nature. In business intrinsic value is holistic, tying everything together through the personnel of the company. People provide the cohesion, energy and vision to maintain the business, motivating and driving the company to greater productivity and success. The total fulfillment of the intrinsic dimension is the total fulfillment of business purpose. The internal level of intrinsic value is found in the job satisfaction and in the sense of personal achievement of the employees; and the external level of intrinsic value is achieved in the complete satisfaction of the customer base.

To attain holistic growth, a business needs a strategic plan which integrates the horizons of value growth: the internal horizon (personnel and their competency), the external horizon (expansion of customer base), and the system horizon (innovation and design improvement in all products and services.) If one horizon is overemphasized, one or both of the others suffer some value loss. The axiological ideal is a balanced emphasis, uniting effort in all three growth dimensions.

Business Value Loss

Three categories of value loss, or axiological "transposition," parallel the dimensions of positive, compositional value outlined above. Understanding the process of value loss is essential to analyzing and resolving business problems and deficiencies. The first phase of identifying any business problem should focus on the systemic dimension, because the loss may be due to a change in the system, e.g. a new tax law or judicial ruling, or a new regulation from the Environmental Protection Agency.

A good example of systemic value loss in a business is the often recurring problem when profit has decreased to a level below minimum adequacy (S_S). Profit loss signifies a fundamental negation in the fulfillment of the business plan or purpose; and in most cases, this is a result of value loss in other dimensions.

Extrinsic value loss necessarily includes systemic value loss. For example, if a large number of defective products are produced, contracts will be canceled, resulting in direct income and profit loss. The axiological symbol (E_E) means the extrinsic values of the production process are disvalued by the defective products produced.

Axiologically, any investigation into a business value loss problem should begin with the systemic dimension. First, we should check for a systemic defect in the design of the production process or the product itself (E_S). Then, the functioning of all machines and labor should be reviewed (E_E). Finally, we should focus on intrinsic values (E_I) where the product or service may be rejected by the customer's disvaluation of it. Sabotage by personnel is also possible, which brings us to the human resource dimension of intrinsic value loss.

The case of employee error, intentional or not, is the source of the most serious problem. Intrinsic value loss (I_I) can be expressed as follows: the intrinsic value of the total fulfillment of operations is disvalued by the intrinsic value of the employee through lack of capacity, lack of training, or willful sabotage. A company's reputation is most harmed by poor workmanship. That is why AT & T developed and implemented the "Zero Defects" quality program, with great success. They realized that in order for the program to be successful, it had to be internalized, implemented and managed by the employees themselves, as their own expression of personal pride and achievement. This shows that for an extrinsic value process, like that of production of a product or delivery of a service, to maintain efficiency and consistent quality, it must be integrated with the intrinsic valuation of the people doing the producing. This leads us to consider the role of those whose responsibility it is to manage and guide the business. Formal axiology can provide business managers with a map that will enable them to capture increasing value in each dimension. This is the major task of management.

Axiology Applied to Business Management

Sound organizational management, in axiological terms, means guidance and control of business tasks and responsibilities to produce integrated positive value results in all components of the business: financially (the broadest systemic value), economically, i.e. in goods and services (the broadest extrinsic value), and interpersonally (the broadest intrinsic value).

To establish a discipline for achieving this management ideal in a progressive, step-by-step manner, we can use formal axiology to produce a hierarchy of value distribution which can order management functions into thirteen value formations. The axiological emphasis patterns below are in order of increasing value (stages), associated with common managerial function names. The value retention of each stage prepares the foundation for adding the value in the subsequent stage. The following table shows in progressive order the "13 stages to management excellence." I symbolizes people, E production, and S, systems.

Stage	Pattern	Function
Stage 13:	I = E = S	Balanced, holistic, integrated management
Stage 12:	(I = E) > S	Developing People
Stage 11:	(I = S) > E	Delegating
Stage 10:	I > (E = S)	Communicating
Stage 9:	(E = S) > I	Efficiency
Stage 8:	E > (I = S)	Processing Work
Stage 7:	S > (I = E)	Control
Stage 6:	I > E > S	Listening
Stage 5:	I > S > E	Diplomacy
Stage 4:	E > I > S	Counseling
Stage 3:	E > S > I	Maintaining
Stage 2:	S > I > E	Organizing
Stage 1:	S > E > I	Planning

Stage 1. Planning: Axiologically, the first stage formula indicates minimum capture of value. In a business, this is "planning," which is the absolute starting point and foundation for all other business management values, with highest emphasis on the S dimension, medium emphasis on the E dimension, and low emphasis on the I dimension. The business plan contains the chosen means for establishing all specific values. The management function of this stage is to create an operational design or map that can be followed to achieve all value objectives. This includes the definition of basic policies & procedures for all aspects of the operation. Both long and short-term goals should be defined to maintain progressive perspective. The work is analyzed in terms of these goals, then divided into parts which fit people's abilities. Jobs are defined accordingly and responsibilities assigned in order to fulfill the general value objectives. Cost analyses should be run to check the economic feasibility of the plan and its defined goals. If financial projections are viable, implementation can begin with stage 2.

Stage 2. Organizing: To begin implementing the plan, the value emphasis shifts to favor the necessary (S) values in the intrinsic dimension. High emphasis on System value is maintained to show that all values are chosen according to the necessary priorities of the plan. The Organizing stage emphasizes recruiting and staffing, represented by the medium emphasis on the interpersonal (I) value dimension. The performance goals and how they are to be efficiently carried out of the (E) dimension take lower priority.

Stage 3. Maintaining: The value emphasis in this stage shifts to favor external values (extrinsic). The systemic values are secondary, and the intrinsic values are lowest in priority. The characterizing value of this stage is maintaining adequate production or service to keep the company in business. Customers and the products/services sold to them take highest priority. This stage demands practical solutions to production and market problems to adequately meet customer needs & desires. The management function of this stage focuses on valuing products & services from the customer's perspective; prospective customers are identified and secured as actual customers; the values of organizing (S) are to be maintained until a sufficient client base is built to sustain business operations. The values of this stage are stabilized when a sales threshold is achieved that will keep the company in business.

Stage 4. Counseling: Here, the highest emphasis is the extrinsic value dimension (work, production, sales, etc.), with secondary valuation on the intrinsic, people dimension. The valuation focus is on helping each employee perform better and gain a greater sense of personal achievement from his or her work. The primary management function is to coach and "counsel" personnel with regard to performance. A formal schedule should be established for one-on-one counseling as well as group training sessions. The manager should maintain an open-door policy, and encourage each employee to ask for help or clarification. This feedback opportunity is essential in enabling employees to correct mistakes and better meet or exceed performance standards.

Stage 5. Diplomacy: This stage places highest emphasis on the intrinsic values of interpersonal relations, with a focus on avoiding or resolving conflicts with employees and customers. The goal is to achieve a harmonious group that works together as a team, and harmonious customer relations. Secondary emphasis is on system values (making more money) and lowest emphasis on external values (production). The primary management activity in this stage is resolving complaints or problems while preserving people values: exchanging input and feedback with all people in the organization in an atmosphere of honesty, trust and respect, building personal rapport and raising receptivity with personnel and customers.

Stage 6 . Listening: The values of this stage are well represented by the value "listening." Listening is an empathetic value needed for clearly identifying people's actual needs and desires. Highest emphasis is kept on interpersonal value, with secondary value on action that is/is not taken (E dimension). System values are held in temporary suspension. This stage solidifies personal rapport--empathetic and intrinsic concern for personnel and customer needs and desires. The primary activities in this stage are asking open-ended questions to get sufficient information, and checking for understanding and agreement on all sides. Customer needs and desires should be continually evaluated to ensure market receptivity of products and services and to develop long-term customer loyalty. Employee attitudes should also be reviewed consistently to maintain optimal levels of morale and teamwork. Sensitive listening to employees and customers sets the stage for efficient controls in stage seven, which orders and stabilizes the values established in the previous six stages.

Stage 7. Control: This is a key stage which places highest emphasis on the systemic value dimension with the guiding value of "control," to express the need for defined rules and policies that guarantee the stability of the values produced in the preceding stages. Secondary emphasis is placed on people and production values, which are valued equally. The goal of this stage is to establish objective standards for both people and production values. The primary management function is to measure and refine the actual

218   *Forms of Value and Valuation: Theory and Applications*

performance of current employees. A performance appraisal interview with each employee is one central task for this stage and includes coaching, counseling and goal setting. The results of the performance review summarize the overall quality of operational performance, which requires a balanced concern for people and production. In this stage the manager gains expertise in controlling subordinate needs and performance in terms of written policies and procedures and according to lines of authority and responsibility. The values of the control stage are stabilized when subordinates and supervisors can consistently agree on the performance evaluation and on goals for improvement.

Stage 8.   <u>Processing Work</u>:   This value distribution emphasizes the external value dimension: defining work goals and meeting them in practical time and space, and doing what must be done when it should be done. Secondary emphasis is placed on equally valued people and systems. Goals should be pursued through people in the context of established policies and procedures. The main management activity of this stage is to define work goals operationally, dividing available time into work segments leading to goal fulfillment. The manager guides the work process toward specified goals and <u>follows up</u> to completion. Managers also set an example by doing their own work as it should be done, when it should be done. The values of this stage are stabilized when all segments of the work process interface smoothly to produce high quality results as defined by performance goals.

Stage 9.   <u>Efficiency</u>:   The value distribution of this stage is characterized by the value, "efficiency," indicating high and equal emphasis placed on the S and E dimensions, with people values taking second priority. The objective of this stage is to keep the projections of the business plan and its cost thresholds (S), in harmony with the actual costs of maintaining quantity and quality output (E). This stage focuses on analyzing the work flow to eliminate wasted time, energy and finances with a value focus on operational cost efficiency. The primary management function of this stage is keeping detailed financial records and reviewing them to make changes in the work process to better fit the budget. The goal is to get as close as possible to zero-defects production with the least amount of money and energy expended.

Stage 10.   <u>Communicating</u>:   This value level focuses on interpersonal value, with secondary emphasis on the efficient production of work and the plan for work. This value shift is characterized by the value "communicating," toward better teamwork and cooperation. Primary concern is placed on individual people values in communicating with employees and with customers. Management functions include sharing and explaining carefully why certain changes may be needed, checking for understanding, and seeking personal agreement and commitment from all people in the organization for highest collaboration and cooperation. The higher the quality of communication with co-workers and customers, the more competent and productive the manager's work.

Stage 11. Delegating: The value characterizing this stage is "delegating," which places equal emphasis on developing interpersonal value according to the systemic needs of the organization. Production value is secondary because delegating projects the work tasks into the short or long-range future (assigning responsibility, coaching/counseling, verification). The manager's primary activity in this stage is giving specific directives to personnel concerning what, how and when to do work tasks. Follow-up is important to ensure that directives have been carried out as desired and to improve accountability. The manager also takes on the role of leader to guide the functional abilities of the employees in such a way that actually helps them grow in the direction that best fits their talent and potential.

Stage 12. Developing People: The value emphasis in this stage is on the unity of people values and production values. Developing people aims toward the fullest expression of the employee's energy and creativity, which includes the manager's own development; for in developing others, one develops oneself. The objective of this stage is to guide people toward realizing a high degree of personal satisfaction and achievement from their work. Group meetings provide a forum to seek creative input from all employees to facilitate the work flow and to give all personnel the opportunity to develop their leadership skills. The key to developing and maintaining productive employees and loyal customers is to emphasize the intrinsic worth of all individuals, for their own sake. This leads to the final "ideal" management stage in which the values of all dimensions are balanced and fully engaged.

Stage 13. Balanced Integration: Excellence in management is achieved through developing the potential of all value dimensions in a balanced effort. In a "balanced integration" of management functions, justice and integrity are maintained in all dimensions to ensure steady growth of the cohesive whole. Equal attention and emphasis is placed on the manager's primary resource: other people. The balanced stage is always unstable due to the dynamics of business operations as they change through time. The value distribution in the balanced stage serves as a norm for dealing with change. Change should be managed such that values are as balanced as possible. As soon as a value change is perceived in any one dimension, effort can be applied directly to that dimension to restore balance. The balanced stage indicates openness for positive change in all dimensions. When all previous stages have been properly covered, the management of the business has become stable, in a dynamic disequilibrium which must be continually adjusted according to these valuational stages. The management process may be continually reviewed from stage 4 onward, with new personnel and new customers on a perpetual basis.

The Hartman Value Profile (HVP) in Business

Beyond the difficult task of hiring personnel, the toughest challenge for today's business managers is the full access and utilization of available human resource potential. For the best hiring decisions, the employer needs to know how a person understands and copes with the values of the work-place. The Hartman Value Profile is a logically based personal preferences inventory which serves as an effective evaluation tool for employability at all levels and in all kinds of jobs. The HVP can help assess or measure the development of professional and personal abilities and blocks to development. In this application, the HVP provides a diagnosis of an individual's job-related strengths and weaknesses, as well as offering a prescription--(recommendations for professional improvement). The HVP is not a "test" but rather an expert interview technique for determining how an individual personally evaluates a given set of established values. The information contained in the results from the HVP has proven very helpful to managers for hiring qualified personnel and for defining training needs, improving individual performance, and for resolving interpersonal conflicts among employees.

Building on Hartman's formal axiological foundation, an extended axiological "map" or general system of value space can be generated that combines thirteen cognitive forms with twenty emotional temperaments (David Mefford, The Hartman Value Profile: Professional Manual of Interpretation, 1986.) This system enables us to type a person's coping strategy with the world or with the self in one of 260 (13 X 20) distinct value emphasis patterns. There are 260 patterns for world-coping behavior, and 260 patterns for self-coping behavior. For the scope of this paper, we will limit this discussion to world-related types and temperaments, which have been given work-related names describing the character of professional coping strategies.

The extent of value realized in the person's orientation toward work depends on a combination of intellectual awareness of important work-related values together with a positive emotional responsiveness to that reality. The intellectual awareness of the world and its values is accounted for by the thirteen World-view types listed below. They have been given characteristic names which have meaning in a business context. There is only one ideal,

Type 1, which reveals balanced integration among the three basic dimensions. A brief description accompanies each type. I refers to People Values, E to Performance Values, and S to Organizational Values.

Axiological Type, Name and Description

1. "Balanced" (I = E = S). The balanced type is developed in all areas with equal proportion and is competent in all performance dimensions.

2. "Social" (I = E) > S. The social type interprets situations in terms of people and their social and work roles, with less emphasis on system and organization.

3. "Law-giver" (I = S) > E. The law-giver type understands situations in terms of people values and the integration of human resources with the established organization and the law.

4. "Supportive" I > (E = S). The supportive type places greater value on people in any given situation, with less emphasis on equally valued practicality and established procedures.

5. "Efficient" (E = S) > I. The efficient type focuses on the efficient and productive organization and fulfillment of work, with secondary emphasis on people values.

6. "Practical" E > (I = S). The practical type interprets people values and organizational structure pragmatically.

7. "Systematic" S > (I = E). The systematic type interprets situations primarily in terms of the logical relation to systems and the established order of the organization.

8. "Empathetic" I > E > S. The empathetic type emphasizes people as individuals. The work itself is secondary, and organizational needs are last in priority.

9. "Diplomatic" I > S > E. The diplomatic type emphasizes people values and interprets legal and organizational systems in terms of human freedom.

10. "Counselor" E > I > S. The counselor type understands situations best in terms of work objectives, and well integrates people and their talents into the work process.

222   Forms of Value and Valuation: Theory and Applications

11. "Expedient" E > S > I. The expedient type understands situations in terms of comparative work-objective fulfillment and its relation to the business objectives of the company.

12. "Organizer" S > I > E. The organizer type emphasizes established system and order. People have their place in the system, while the work and its performance are least important.

13. "Analytic" S > E > I. The analytic type understands situations in terms of logic and analysis, and solves problems according to established organizational rules.

The three basic scores which make up these types have three axiological "valence" variables each: positive (+), negative (-), or balanced (o). These three variables yield twenty basic variations (emotional temperaments). The twenty world-value temperaments characterize a person's emotional responsiveness to the context of work, identifying his or her current professional attitudes.

The following list of work-related temperaments are characterized according to specified value dimensional content. The <u>intrinsic temperament</u> reflects the quality of involvement with all people at work as <u>individuals</u>. The <u>extrinsic temperament</u> indicates the quality of involvement with work detail and other people on a <u>social/professional</u> level. The <u>systemic temperament</u> reflects the quality of involvement with <u>established</u> system and order and people in <u>authority</u>.

1. (I-,E-,S-)   "Hostile"
2. (I-,E-,S+)   "Vigilant"
3. (I-,E-,So)   "Reactive"
4. (I-,E+,S-)   "Merchant"
5. (I-,E+,S+)   "Conformist"
6. (I-,E+,So)   "Operator"
7. (I-,Eo,S-)   "Skeptic"
8. (I-,Eo,S+)   "Mastermind"
9. (I-,Eo,So)   "Journalist"
10. (I+,E-,S-)   "Accommodator"
11. (I+,E-,S+)   "Reformer"
12. (I+,E-,So)   "Compassionate"
13. (I+,E+,S-)   "Facilitator"
14. (I+,Eo,S-)   "Collaborator"
15. (Io,E-,S-)   "Independent"
16. (Io,E-,S+)   "Judge"

17. (Io,E-,So)   "Humorist"
18. (Io,E+,S-)   "Consultant"
19. (Io,Eo,S-)   "Objector"
20. (Io,Eo,So)   "Virtuoso"

Using this axiological typology of persons, a company seeking to fill a direct sales position would use the Hartman Value Profile to determine the cognitive type and temperament of the individual and weigh this against its defined ideal. In this case a "Social/Merchant" pattern would be considered close to ideal, while an "Analytic/Conformist" pattern would be more suitable for another position such as accounting or scheduling.

Formal Axiology For Customer Communications: Advertising

Formal axiology provides a scientific foundation on which a company can create a message to its customers about the values of products or services. Axiology can also be used to measure the impact of that message and to refine the message to get across optimal intended value information about the product to the consumer. With most competitors moving rapidly, the race will go to those who listen and respond most intently to their current or intended customers. The axiological application system presented here provides the means to organize product/service information, to separate all potential message channels, and to choose an optimal communication interface between products/services and consumer needs and desires. The 13 axiological value distribution patterns form the core of the framework that can function as the guidance system for creating an advertising message and for choosing how to best communicate it to any given target group(s). This means once the sender and receiver poles of the message are expressed in axiological form, the system of formal axiology can also show how advertising and sales efforts should be constructed for optimal success.

Procedure:

1. <u>Define axiological product profile</u>. This must be done according to the set of all three value dimensions. All essential product features must be listed, then sorted according to the formal I, E, and S dimensions:

   I: How well the product is, in its totality, what it ought to be;

   E: How good the product looks and functions in practical comparison to other products of the same class; and

S: How well the product is designed according to the ideal of perfection.

Then, the axiologically sorted list is reviewed to determine which dimensions have the most value emphasis, defining the relations of value intensity among the three dimensions. This last step produces a product value profile which represents the axiological value structure of the product. The resulting pattern will have to be placed into the same format as the axiological pattern of the customer profile, which is necessary for precision in comparing their similarities and differences.

2. <u>Define axiological customer profile</u>. The Customer Value Profile is produced according to the results obtained when customers sort an axiologically structured list of product values called the Product Value Profile. This is a forced-ranking set of product values in two parts: 18 phrases and 18 quotations. Each list of values consists of a selected set of possible product values which covers the binary axiological range of nine positive and nine negative product attributes. The customer is asked to rank the list of phrases from best to worst, and the list of quotations from most agree with to least agree with. The results of the ranking reveal a precise profile of how the customer perceives the product in the following axiological dimensions:

I: How well the product is perceived in terms of intrinsic strength, durability, quality and uniqueness.

E: How well users perceive the product in terms of what they can see, touch, and put to use practically.

S: How well users perceive the systems, design, and cost/benefit structure of the product.

The results show how well the advertising, marketing and sales efforts of a company are impacting the specific needs and desires of the different customer groups.

3. <u>Overlay profiles of product and customer to define differences</u>. The axiological channels for advertisement message construction are chosen according to the value patterns resulting from an overlay of the product profile with the different customer profiles. Where the product and customer profiles are axiologically equivalent, a channel is chosen which captures and emphasizes this equality. Where the product and customer values are in opposition, a channel is chosen which bridges and unites the differences. For

optimal communications success, both equalities and differences must have their channels of conveyance.

4. Choose value channels (1-13) best linking product with customer. The 13 value concept formations become channels of value communication as shown below.

Channel/Name   **Description**

1. I = E = S   "Integrated" - Meets all needs and desires

2. (I=E)>S   "Mass Appeal" - Imitated by all others

3. (I=S)>E   "Quality/Dependability" - Quality guaranteed

4. I>(E=S)   "Quality/Service" - Comprehensive service support

5. (E=S)>I   "Efficient" - Time, money or energy saver

6. E>(I=S)   "Practical" - Best for the price and quality

7. S>(I=E)   "System-connected" - System controlled value

8. I > E > S   "Personal Satisfaction" - Maintains customer loyalty

9. I > S > E   "Image-Enhancing" - Improves users' image

10. E > I > S   "Function/Quality Anchored" - It keeps on working

11. E > S > I   "Function/Quantity Anchored" -More for the money

12. S > I > E   "Design Anchored" - Designed for durability

13. S > E > I   "Price Bound" - Costs less

Each of these channels can be assigned an axiological "valence" or communication channel amplification, which has three possible variations: overvalued (+), undervalued (-), or perceived in a balanced (o) way (as intended). When all value channels have been chosen and ordered, the <u>cognitive</u> or mental value set has been covered. Then, to complete the analysis, the value amplification is chosen which covers the <u>emotional</u> set of values. As demonstrated in the previous section (HVP) there are 20 standard amplification patterns for real-world based emotional formation, leading up to an ideal of balance in all dimensions. For this application, we will include the 7 non-standard patterns for the super-real (the seven axiological valences which identify <u>imaginary</u> forms of over or super-valuation, where both compositional and transpositional components of a value set are all overvalued). These 7 super-positive valences, as forms of creative imagination, are ideally suited for the language of advertising, which commonly attributes more value to a product or service than it actually contains (David Mefford, <u>Phenomenology of Man as a Valuing Subject</u>, 1989, pp. 119 - 132).

"Super-Positive" Valences   Characteristic Name

1. (Io,Eo,S+)   "Super-Idea"
2. (Io,E+,So)   "Super-Thing"
3. (I+,Eo,So)   "Super-Spirit"
4. (Io,E+,S+)   "Super-Abundant"
5. (I+,Eo,S+)   "Super-Symbolic"
6. (I+,E+,So)   "Super-Spatial"
7. (I+,E+,S+)   "Super-Real"

To give an example of how this system works, we will refer to the product/consumer value analysis done for one of the leading manufacturers of truck bodies. In spite of this company's standard-setting history and quality reputation in the industry, sales levels had been falling for several years when, in 1988, the value analysis was undertaken.

The firm's customers fell into three categories: leasors, distributors, and dealers. Several of each group completed the axiological product evaluation, and the resulting customer profile clearly showed that all users had an objective or positive perception of the product extrinsically and systemically. This means they well perceived how good the truck body looks, how well it functions, how well it is designed, plus the extensive set of user options available $(E = S) > I$. However, users did not perceive the intrinsic dimension of the product as intended: the high quality of construction materials, attention to overall quality control, and the proven durability over time with heavy usage.

This indicated to the company that their advertising and sales efforts should be refocused on clarifying and amplifying the intrinsic perception of their product. Among other changes, company management chose to amplify channels 3 & 4, which focus on the <u>quality</u> that goes into the unique design; and they further backed up their quality claim by extending their warranty. This helped them to reestablish profitable sales levels within the year.

The axiological analysis demonstrated in the above example broke new ground both in formal axiology and in business communications. For the first time in the history of communication theory, the mental and emotional components were accounted for within one single logical frame of reference. The beneficial result to the company of using such a value framework for advertising messages is that the message will be playing a familiar value "tune" which the customer is already conditioned to understand and enjoy. This means that advertising dollars and the expense of marketing and sales are not blindly spent or wasted, and that consumer impact can be optimal.

BIBLIOGRAPHY

Crosby, Philip B., Quality is Free: The Art of Making Quality Free. New York, McGraw-Hill, 1979.

Drucker, Peter F., Management: Tasks, Responsibilities, Practices. New York, Harper & Row, 1974.

Hartman, Robert S., The Structure of Value. Carbondale: Southern Illinois University Press, 1967.

McCarthy, Edmund J., Basic Marketing: A Managerial Approach. Sixth Edition. Homewood, Illinois, R.D. Irwin, 1978.

Mefford, David L., Phenomenology of Man as a Valuing Subject. Doctoral Dissertation in Philosophy, Knoxville, The University of Tennessee, 1989.

Mefford, David L., The Hartman Value Profile: Professional Manual of Interpretation. Knoxville, Tennessee, Value Measurement Technologies,Inc., 1986.

Mefford, David L., and Mefford, Vera, "AXCES Product/Consumer Analysis," Knoxville, Tennessee, Value Measurement Technologies, Inc., 1988.

Mefford, David L., and Mefford, Vera, Value Management. Knoxville, Tennessee, Value Measurement Technologies, Inc., 1989.

Chapter XI

USES OF AXIOLOGY IN STOCK SELECTION AND PORTFOLIO MANAGEMENT

Kurt Kaltreider

It has long been known that professional portfolio managers, on average, have not been able to outperform the stock market (almost universally taken to mean the total return of the Standard & Poor's 500 average, or in the case of smaller capitalized stocks the Over-The-Counter Composite average) on an annual basis, and, more importantly, over time. Indeed, in a recent SEI study, the S&P 500 beat more than half of the professionals for the last ten years (year ending 1988); and a mere 1% beat the market for each of the ten years.

More recently, in an article in Barron's on Index Funds, Edward A. Wyatt stated that many professionals have come to believe "that outperforming the broad averages is improbable if not impossible."[1] Indeed, Index Funds, which attempt to mirror the S&P 500, and hence its performance, arose out of the exasperation with professional portfolio managers and their sub-par performance. In the world of money managers these funds are the quintessential expression of despair; the "put your money where your mouth is" belief is that there exist no decision procedures which can add value to the random average of the Index. In short, the idea is a simple one: if the odds are that one cannot find a portfolio manger who will add value to the Index's performance, then why look for one, and why add the extra expense of management fees to your already underperforming funds? Why not just buy the Index and at least assure yourself that you will come close to equalling it and thus outperform a large percentage of the managers that you could hire? Wyatt gives further evidence of the plight of portfolio managers when he writes: "Although a number of money managers in any given quarter might exceed the S&P 500's performance, only 20 mutual funds tracked by Lipper Analytical Services outpaced the market for the three consecutive years from 1986 through 1988."[2] There are over 1,700 equity mutual funds and over 2,400 mutual funds all told. Indeed, over the last five years, 1986-1990, the S&P 500 has returned +85.43% and the average equity mutual fund +54.47%. Extrapolating from these five year annualized rates of return of approximately 13.2% and 9.1%, respectively, we find that in about fifteen years the Index will double the performance of the average fund.

What we have here is a situation at once both distressing and quite odd. It is odd in that in almost any human activity, when we are in the position to make decisions based on knowledge, and often on well constructed theory, we find that our results are better than random and not worse. It is distressing in that there is no dearth of textbooks, journals, and courses taught on portfolio management in our country. The implication is that they are, on the whole, a failure in practice no matter how fascinating or cerebral they all may be.

Consider that the portfolio manager has access to research and information, the abundance of which is almost overwhelming, and that his access to most information is essentially instantaneous. Consider further that he has been trained to make decisions about the information before him. Now consider that the S&P 500 Index is both non-cognitive and non-decisive, i.e., it knows nothing and it decides nothing. AND IT WINS! This flies in the face of all that we expect when human beings are capable of acting on knowledge and rational decision. Something is terribly amiss, and if history is any guide it lies neither in man's knowledge nor in his rational or decision making capacities based on that knowledge. Rather it rests in his methodologies and/or his beliefs.

If we examine almost any other professional endeavor, save portfolio management, we find very different results; and we expect them. If we take any professional involved in the evaluation of objects, present him with 100 objects in his realm of expertise and then request of him the following:

> Sir, if you would evaluate these 100 objects in terms of their ability to perform (or their goodness) and then, if you will, select for me 30 which will, on average, outperform the average of the entire set of 100 for the next year I would be most grateful. Also, to make things a little more exciting, would you also be so kind as to select the 30 most likely to underperform, on average, the average of the entire set of 100; for surely the same knowledge that allows you to select the best should

allow you to select the worst; after all, avoiding the worst, is often as valuable as selecting the best.,"[3]

it would not be seen as too difficult a task. Indeed, it is the kind of thing that professionals are supposed to be able to do with routine ease. It matters not if they be cardiologists, football scouts for the draft, engineers, college admissions counselors, psychologists, or even twelve year old boys selecting an all-star baseball team from the American and National Leagues. The problem should be that simple with regard to portfolio management also, but it apparently is not if one goes by the actual real time performance of the professionals.

To be an expert[4] in some field of knowledge means simply that one has a far greater or richer and more precise concept, and hence understanding, of that of which one is supposedly expert than the vast majority of others. Thus, the cardiologist's concept of the heart should be far greater, far more meaningful, than that of the average person who has never studied the heart. The richer and more precise his concept, the better will be his ability to evaluate any particular heart. Equipped with his concept and its inherent logic, our cardiologist will be able to play our little game above and select 30 hearts out of a set of 100 which will outperform, for the next year, on average, the average of the 100 in terms of cardiac functioning. Further, he will be able to select 30 which will not outperform, on average, the average of the 100. This does not mean that mistakes will not be made or that unforseen problems will not develop, but it does mean that we can feel confident that, on average, one year latter the selected 30 will have performed better than the remaining 70, and that those selected as the worse 30 will have underperformed the remaining 70. We also know that if he is given essentially the same universe of hearts next year, he will be able to delete some from his best 30 and from his worse 30 and adjust both his best 30 and his worse 30 according to their evaluation at that point in time. Thus, from year to year he keeps himself ahead of the average.

The same that holds for our cardiologist holds for our other experts as well--all, that is, except for our poor portfolio manager, who instead of getting increasingly ahead of the game, gets increasingly behind it.

The principle that allows our cardiologist and our other experts to win our game is always the same: the average of the best will outperform the average of the rest, and the average of the worst will always underperform the average of the rest insofar as they all live in or operate under essentially the same conditions.

According to academics there is a reason for the failure of portfolio managers to add value to the Index. They explain this rather singular phenomenon by the Efficient Market Theory and its primary theorem, the random behavior of stock prices, dubbed the Random Walk Theory. Burton Malkiel of Princeton published <u>A Random Walk Down Wall Street</u>[5] in 1973. For many it has been taken as gospel ever since. Its main argument can be summed up as follows: 1) at any given moment the price of a stock reflects all the known information relative to the stock's performance; 2) any future information is obviously unknown; 3) all future information will be made available in a random and unpredictable fashion; 4) consequently, because the present is fairly valued relative to all available relevant information, and the future is unknown, unpredictable, and random, and because the future price movement of a stock will depend upon the future information as it is made known, stock selection cannot be a rational activity in which one can be somewhat assured of selecting a portfolio of stocks which will outperform the Index. Furthermore, as time goes by, superior performance will become more unlikely because the laws of chance will overcome the managers lucky enough to be outperforming the market in the short run. In fact, most managers who are outperforming the market do tend to regress to the mean. But, is this really necessary, as the Efficient Market Theory states? I think not.

The Random Walk Theory, is logically specious insofar as it is <u>a posteriori</u>; that is, it argues from effect to cause, from the fact of the poor performance by portfolio managers to a cause for that poor performance. It flies in the face of all our experience concerning the influence of knowledge on rational decision making and other rational activity. We expect experts to do better in their field of expertise than a random average. Thus, when an expert intervenes in some human activity involving knowledge and rational decisions, we expect the results to improve. If they do not improve, then we conclude one of two things: either 1) the expert is not an expert at all, or 2) little or no knowledge exists in the area in question. (We do not expect the same success rate from the oncologist that we expect from the bacterial infection specialist.) The Efficient Market Theory, in essence, says that all the information available relevant to the future performance of a stock is unknown and that all the known information is already accounted for in the present price of the stock. Consequently, information or knowledge is a moot point in prediction. It seems that one could argue the same in any other field; yet, it is patently absurd in almost any field that one would care to investigate.

With exceptions, of course, a coach could easily select a team today that would be a winning team a year from now, and a psychologist could select a group of individuals who a year from now will have greater mental health than average, and so on. This does not mean that experts may not wish, at a later date, to drop some of their chosen individuals and add others. However, this would also be a rational decision if based on a knowledge of the current status of the individuals in question. (Of course, the term "individual" refers to any single thing, whether it be a human being, a stock, or a car.) There comes a time, it should go without saying, that any natural object, be it a heart or an athlete, will begin to deteriorate; but the fact that we know this is also a function of our concepts of the things in question. Within some time limit, different for different kinds of things, it is generally true that what I call the axiological laws of inertia hold. These laws, taken in a loose sense of "laws," are as follows:

1. That which is good tends to stay good, and that which is bad tends to stay bad.

2. That which is good tends to get better as a very function of its goodness, and that which is bad tends to get worse as a very function of its badness.

If there were not this kind of axiological stability in the world, then we would be living in chaos; and there would not only be no value judgements, but no factual judgements as well. A basketball coach, for instance, would have no way of knowing that he should keep Michael Jordan on his team, for tomorrow he could be Fat Albert. But from the limited time reference of human activity, there is stability within the over-all dynamism of the universe.

Hartman writes,

...value is rational. I can value a thing only if I know it, that is, if I know its name and its properties. That this is true is confirmed by the fact that when we want to value something precisely we call in an expert. The difference between him and us is that he knows more about the thing than we do. Thus knowledge and valuation go hand in hand. It follows that the world as a whole, if it is to be judged valuationally, must be understood, and this in turn means that if value is possible the world can be understood. In other words, the world itself is rational insofar as it is valuable. This, of course, is the Platonic thesis.[6]

In light of these observations and Hartman's insight that a thing is good to the degree that it fulfills the intension of its concept, it seemed to me that one should be able to create a system of stock selection and, hence, portfolio management, that would show the Random Walk Theory to be wrong not just logically, but wrong in fact and in practice. In the summer of 1976 I created such a system from Hartman's formal axiology.

There are only three concepts which are needed: 1) "investment," 2) "company," and 3) "stock." The crucial concept is "investment," in that the stock of a company is purchased with that end in view. I defined "investment" as "an outlay of money with the intention that at some time in the future one shall have more money than the outlay and precisely because of it." Interestingly enough I found that none of the terms in either the exposition of "company" or the exposition of "stock" were logically sufficient to justify an investment. After about a month of intense thought, I realized there is only one thing which would justify, without reduction or condition, the purchase of the stock of a company as an investment. Oddly enough, this concept had a lot in common with G. E. Moore's paradox about goodness--the same paradox that led Hartman to his formal axiology. Moore's paradox about goodness states that "Two different propositions are both true of goodness, namely, 1) that it does depend only on the intrinsic nature of what possesses it. . .and 2) that, though that is so, it is yet not itself an intrinsic property."

Analogously, there is a concept which could not exist (makes no sense) if there were not both the concept "company" and the concept "stock." It is not part of either concept, yet it is wholly dependent upon them both. Let us call this concept "X."

By taking X as the end-in-view, to use Dewey's term, I could then order the expositions of both "company" and "stock."

I defined "company" as "an economic organization existing for the purpose of selling goods or services with the intent of making a profit." I found that the following exposition was adequate to relate "company" to "investment" as the end-in-view and that using the axiological relation, "It is better that A than that B," the components could be ordered and weighted:

Cash/Current Assets
Cash/Current Liabilities
Current Ratio
Dividend Growth Rate
Earning Growth/Debt Growth
Interest on Cash/Interest on Debt
Leverage
Net Assets
Net Income Growth
Quick Ratio

Return on Equity
Return on Sales
Sales Growth
Sales Growth/Debt Growth

In my analysis of "stock," the following expositional predicates seemed adequate:

Average 5 year, PE Ratio/Current PE Ratio
Cash/Share
Cash per Share/Price per Share
Earnings Growth/PE Ratio
Market Average PE Ratio/Stock PE Ratio
Net Assets per Share/Price per Share
Price/Book Ratio
Price/Earnings Ratio (PE)
Price Relative to 12 Month High
Price/Sales Ratio
Sales Growth/PE Ratio
Sales per Share

Again, as with "company," the exposition can be ordered and weighted using the axiological relation "It is better that A than that B," with "investment" as the end-in-view.

Lastly, it should be obvious that "company" is the primary concept because stock must be issued by a company, and all the "stock" variables depend upon some aspect of the functioning of the company, which are then stated as either functions of price or share.

Now that we have the means for determining the relative "goodness" of both companies and stocks, let us play the same game that we asked our cardiologists to play.

Beginning the 4th Quarter, 1985, we were asked by a multi-billion dollar portfolio management firm if we could take the 100 largest capitalized stocks (those with the greatest market value) in the S&P 500 and order them in terms of their probable future performance for each upcoming quarter. The "100" is very important to large portfolio managers because they have to place large sums of money in the market; and the "Big Cap" stocks, as they are known, allow them to do so without greatly affecting the price, while providing easy liquidity. Furthermore, the "100" represents approximately 70% of the capitalization of the S & P 500 and 54% of the entire New York Stock

Exchange. Obviously, a system which could allow one to avoid holding a majority of underperforming stocks in the "100" while holding a majority of the overperforming stocks would be of great value.

Here are our results since we began doing this work for major institutions.

Year	Top 30	Bottom 30	"100"	S&P 500
4th Qtr. 1985	+20.79	+16.76	+17.47	+17.21
1986	+26.61	+16.26	+23.99	+18.50
1987	+10.36	-.70	+4.75	+5.10
1988	+17.20	+14.66	+17.09	+16.62
1989	+45.25	+34.25	+34.86	+31.69
1990	+3.57	-2,80	-2.60	-3.10
1st Qtr. 1991	+17.11	+6.43	+12.85	+14.51
5.5 Year Summary	+248.48	+114.65	+164.81	+148.88

Notice that the Top 30 beat the "100" every year and that the Bottom 30 loses to the "100" every year. More importantly, every year the gap between the Top 30 and the "100" grows positively, while for the Bottom 30, it grows negatively every year. The performance of the Top 30 is strong evidence against the Efficiency Market Theory. Both the Top 30's much stronger than average performance and the Bottom 30's much weaker than average performance constitute strong evidence for the effectiveness of formal axiology in a field which many have believed to be inaccessible to rational decision procedures. It should be noted also that we are using a relatively short time period here; the results over the past 20 years give even more conclusive support for the relevance of formal analysis, the market being outperformed more than fivefold

To get a better idea of the performance of the Top 30, let us compare it to the five year (1986-1990) results of portfolio managers in general. The "SEI" below is a leading consulting firm involved in the tracking and evaluation of portfolio managers.

Top 30	+146.35
Bottom 30	+72.86
SEI Top 5%	+119.24
Average Equity Mutual Fund	+54.47
S&P "100"	+99.76
S&P 500	+85.43

The Uses of Axiology in Stock Selection and Portfolio Management 237

In line with the Efficiency Market and Random Walk theories, notice the extremely poor performance, on average, of mutual fund managers. More importantly, the Top 30 performs well, into the top 1% of equity managers.

As a final demonstration of the relevance of formal axiology to stock selection and portfolio management, I will point out some facts that are little known in the profession itself

As noted above, the cut-off point for the top 5% of equity managers was +119.24, an annualized rate of return of 17%, for the five years ending in 1990. What is surprising and little known is that if one had a 20 stock portfolio from the "100" for each of the 20 quarters of the 5 year period, such that by chance 10 stocks in the portfolio were the worst performing ten and the remaining 10 were the best ten performing stocks in the "100," then one's return for the period would have been +133.10, or an annualized rate of return of 18.45%. This would have placed the portfolio well above the cut-off point of the top 5% of equity managers. Better yet, if one had a portfolio of 10 stocks from the "100" which by chance included the worst five and the best five performing stocks in the "100," one would have a return of +160.21, or an annualized rate of return of 21%. Clearly, this rate is surpassed by few, if any, equity managers.

However, this phenomenon does not occur if we combine the 2nd Top Ten performing stocks (stocks 11-20) each quarter with the 2nd Worst Ten performing stocks (81-90) each quarter. Indeed, this combination, and the subsequent other Top/Bottom combinations, (the 3rd Top Ten/3rd Worst Ten, etc.), do not outperform the average of the "100". Thus, it is extremely important that any stock selection model be able to generate an above average number of top performing stocks and a below average number of bottom performing stocks. The following table shows the model's ability to select a higher than random number of top performing stocks and a lower than random number of underperforming stocks, along with the ratio of one to the other.

Kaltreider Research's Top 30 Selected Portofolio from the "100"

Average Quarterly Performance	Qtrly Perf. Rank	Top 50 Perf. Stocks each Qtr.	Ratio	Qtrly Perf. Rank	Bottom 50 Perf. Stocks each Qtr.	Average Quarterly Performance
+27.37	1-5	46	1.59-1	96-100	29	-14.29
+23.23	1-10	83	1.51-1	91-100	55	-11.50
+14.57	11-20	79	1.25-1	81-90	63	-4.96
+10.35	21-30	67	1.17-1	71-80	60	-1.51
+8.00	31-40	74	1.45-1	61-70	51	+1.27
+5.61	41-50	68	1.13-1	51-60	60	+3.13
+12.35	Top 50	371	1.28-1	Bottom 50	289	-2.71

Kaltreider Research's Bottom 30 Selections from the "100"

(same as column above)	(same as column above)	21	.60-1	(same as column above)	35	(same as above column)
		53	.84-1		63	
		50	.81-1		62	
		67	.82-1		82	
		71	.91-1		78	
		58	.76-1		76	
	Top 50	299	.83-1	Bottom 50	361	

Notice that, in the Top 30 selections, all the ratios favor the Top 50 performing stocks over the bottom 50 performing stocks, and that the opposite is true for the bottom 30 selections. According to the Random Walk Theory, even a 1-1 ratio would not be attainable, for that would make one even with the market or with the universe of stocks in question.

The power of our axiological model is even more clearly demonstrated, perhaps, by looking at ratios of the "super-overperforming" and "super-underperforming" stocks each quarter, and at the model's ability to select the former while avoiding the latter.

Statistics for stocks from the "100" outperforming or underperforming the S&P 500 by 1,000 basis points, or more per quarter for the period from the 4th Quarter of 1985 through the 1st Quarter of 1991.

	+2,000	-2,000	Ratio
Total number	67	38	1.76-1
Top 30 Selections	24	9	2.67-1
Bottom 30 Selections	13	15	.87-1
	+1,500 to +1,999	-1,500 to -1,999	
Total Number	66	97	.68-1
Top 30 Selections	28	20	1.40-1
Bottom 30 Selections	20	28	.71-1
	+1,000 to +1,499	-1,000 to -1,499	
Total Number	205	185	1.11-1
Top 30 Selections	79	53	1.49-1
Bottom 30 Selections	37	51	.72-1
	+1,000 or more	-1,000 or more	
Total Number	338	320	1.06-1
Top 30 Selections	131	82	1.60-1
Bottom 30 Selections	70	94	.74-1

Clearly, the model works, selecting 38.8% of the super-overperformers while selecting only 25.6% of the super-underperformers in its Top 30 selections. Its Bottom 30 selections garner only 20.7% of the super-overperformers while amassing 29.4% of the super-underperformers.

240   *Forms of Value and Valuation: Theory and Applications*

In science, one often uses probability to test a model or hypothesis. If the results obtained by using the model far exceed those expected by probability, this is taken as evidence that the model has predictive value and that something in the model is reflecting or properly structuring something in reality. According to the Efficient Market Theory, a portfolio manager has less than a favorable chance of selecting a portfolio that will outperform the Index, whereas the probability that our Top 30 Selected Portfolio will have 131 super-overperformers is 1/2,922. This overwhelming probability is further evidence of the power of our axiological model. Furthermore, in a study by the University of Tennessee's Business Statistics Department, the probability of our model's selecting 18 of the top 20 performers from the "100" with only 20 selections was $1.11/10^{15}$. It did this for the five year period 1986--1990.

In conclusion, the formal power of Hartman's axiolology demonstrably shows the Efficient Market and Random Walk Theories to be the a posteriori hypotheses they are, confusing what has been with what must be. There are two very simple reasons why equity managers do not outperform relevant indices. 1) Most of them lack a precise and consistent stock selection model which shows the relative value of companies and stocks; and 2) rather than concentrating their efforts on finding a superior subset (portfolio) of the set (the relevant index) they are trying to beat, they rely on data and techniques outside of the set itself, i.e on market timing, economic forecasting, interest rate trends, and so forth. It is not unlike a football coach spending his time trying to figure out the field and weather conditions for a game six months away, instead of trying to draft the very best players, knowing that no matter what the conditions, the best will outperform the rest.

NOTES

1. Edward A. Wyatt, Barron's, Vol. LXIX, No. 20, "Avidly Average," p. 17.

2. Ibid.

3. I have picked 30 objects here so that when we get to selecting a portfolio one could not claim that the portfolio was too small for practical purposes.

4. The term "expert" is preferred here over "professional," with all of its social innuendos declaring that one cannot have knowledge of something unless some higher power has declared so, as if the physician cannot do his taxes and the accountant cannot diagnose pneumonia.

5. Burton Malkiel, A Random Walk Down Wall Street, W. W. Norton, New York, 1973.

6. Robert S. Hartman, The Structure of Value (Carbondale, Southern Illinois University Press, 1969, pp. 109-110.

Chapter XII

THE HARTMAN VALUE PROFILE (HVP & HVPII)

John Austin

Preface

As mankind's first applied formal axiologist, it was Robert S. Hartman's view that

> today's moral reality is still philosophical; it is not fundamentally different from that of antiquity or the Middle Ages. We have the same fundamental values and disvalues, even though we practice them with greater refinement, including torture. The new moral science, axiology, ought to revolutionize our moral understanding itself and hence our moral practice, in the same way that natural science has revolutionized our understanding of nature and our sensitivity to it. The precise knowledge of the axiological relations ought to make us more sensitive to moral reality. It ought to teach us more profoundly the art of living.[1]

This paper represents the key facets of Robert S. Hartman's thinking about the Hartman Value Profile and his work with the test. The paper is a sincere effort to present, in a condensed version, Hartman's work to advance axiology and axiometric procedure, both as a science and measurement system, so as to further value science.

We have drawn almost entirely from, <u>The Structure of Value</u>, <u>The Hartman Value Profile (HVP) A Manual of Interpretation</u>, and the article, "Axiology As A Science," those portions of Hartman's thinking that we felt would best illustrate his theory and test. Only minor editorial changes and revisions have been made along with limited editorial commentary and additions. It is our purpose to "let Hartman speak for himself"; thus the major content of this paper should be attributed to Hartman. We strongly urge the reader who is not familiar with Hartman's work to study the aforementioned references and the book, edited by John W. Davis, <u>Value and Valuation, Axiological Studies in Honor of Robert S. Hartman.</u>

The Making of a Value Test

When Robert S. Hartman shared his examples of secondary value combinations, which consist of compositions and transpositions, with Mario Cardenas Trigos, a Mexican friend and psychiatrist, it was suggested that he had created a value test as well as a list of value dimensions. Thus the Hartman Value Inventory came into being with Hartman and Cardenas as coauthors. As we will illustrate, the words, phrases and quotations that make up the retitled Hartman Value Profiles have axiological meaning in themselves.

Yes, we are speaking of a special logic that pertains to value language similar to the logic that we apply in determining whether words are antonyms or synonyms. Just as there are words and phrases that are logical opposites and similarities, there also are words and phrases that are value or axiological opposites or similarities. We should keep this in mind when we think of language development in children. With language development comes a refinement which has its own maturational antecedents.

How one learned to value in childhood is usually more easily remembered than how or when one learned to talk. Think for a moment of all of the early events, activities and people that are associated with your values and beliefs. Value preferences are learned more easily and are more lasting than we realize. For instance, think of your preference for foods that taste sweet or sour, that are spicy or bland, that are served very cold or piping hot. We might say that these preferences are part of the realm of your biologically based value analogies. The early development and learning of analogies that are both physical and psychological is how a child becomes a full valuing entity before he or she ever goes to school or learns to count or read. Value development is a fascinating phenomenon. It is for this reason that early beliefs are long lasting and often provide a permanent value compass that is life long in directionality and consequence.

Early childhood values not only are acquired or learned through experiences, but are usually first comprehended and remembered in a visual way. For example, Binet found that pictorial opposites or analogies could be observed in normal children at age four. With a picture card, illustrated with both a pretty person and an ugly person, it is possible for most children to identify correctly which word applies to which picture. Now we know why early childhood teachers place stickers on children's drawings or papers that have a face with a smile, or in some instances a face with a frown. Yes, a pictorial representation that indicates happiness or sadness is early and easily understood. Some communities have even adorned their water towers with a smiling face. The symbolism is both meaningful and communicative. This level of concrete reasoning and judgment soon advances to a more abstract level. At age five children can correctly answer and complete many analogies like: Mother is a woman; Father is a __; or a fire is hot; an ice cube is __. Here we see another basis for likes and dislikes, good or bad, right or wrong, same or different.

The key point that we wish to emphasize is that childhood value development is both a behavioral and sequential process. It is our view that early biosocial interpersonal behavior by a mother and father has a profound effect on a child's value development. From this early physical interaction with parents an infant child can experience love-neglect, security-insecurity, nourishment-malnutrition, comfort-discomfort, pleasure-pain, and many other stimuli which have behavioral-value meaning. In terms of physical growth, movement and mobility are motoric indicators of neuropsychological control. These are fancy words for eating, creeping, crawling, standing, walking and elimination--all activities that have potential to shape value preferences and reality processes. However, it is language development which helps a child to focus, express and connect value behaviors and beliefs with words. The power of "me-you," "yes" and especially "no" as shown and spoken by two and three year olds is simply awesome and is only exceeded by temper tantrums and laughter. Can we see the antecedents here which lead to our interest in philosophy, psychology, axiology, in fact to all human endeavor? Let us hope so.

The Making of a Value Test with Pictures

Here we have two test items from the Hartman Value Profile (HVP) Pictorial Form Research Edition, Part One, World Values. One item is a composition (+); the second is a transposition (-); and together they are axiological oppositions as well as being examples of extrinsic value. Consider for a moment the logical opposites of which we could draw a picture to go with each of our pictures. If you thought of spoiled or bad food as being one possible picture, you are on the right track. A picture of a clean and sanitary place would be the logical opposite of the rubbish heap. The two pictures are examples from thirty six pictures, 18 World Value pictures, and 18 Self Value pictures, that Hartman had drawn so as to test adults and children who could not read. It is our view that much research is possible and greatly needed to demonstrate the meaning of pictorial value testing.

Naturally enough, when one thinks of a test one also thinks of how it is to be constructed, how it is to be scored, and so on. Psychological and educational tests constitute a measurement specialty or field that is often referred to as "psychometrics." To measure value we can think of the term "axiometric," as being parallel to, "psychometric." Methods or ways to quantify what it is that we want to measure have to be devised. Meaning is the outcome of measurement and evaluation procedures.

The theory that a test is based on and is supposed to measure is one of the most important considerations. The theory on which the HVP is based is primarily that of value opposites. Pairs of opposites can be grouped so as to define and represent the three axiological dimensions of intrinsic value, extrinsic value, and systemic value in terms of both a "world" and "self" perspective. This is probably the most simple statement that can be made to describe what the HVP is all about.

If we keep in mind that values can be compositions (positive values) which can be opposed by transpositions (negative values), we then can understand how Hartman and Cardenas approached the task of creating the HVP. Also, remember, words, phrases and quotations can be more clearly defined and will have greater precision than pictures. In this case, "a picture is not worth a thousand words" because agreement as to what the picture represents is open to so many interpretations by people. This variance in perception is normal, and a picture may literally produce a thousand words when it really required at most is only a few words.

Hartman was the seeker of key words, phrases and quotations which could serve as both proof and example for his theory. In this sense, he used psycholinguistic and axiolinguistic procedures to verify his thinking about value science. As we will see, he was also creating a pool of verbal tests items from which the HVP would be constructed.

To understand more clearly the importance of the values that Hartman felt to be evident in the compositions and transpositions which he offered as examples of "world value," we need to consider the value dimensions of systemic, extrinsic, and intrinsic. In his last published article, "Axiology As a Science," Hartman tells us how axiology as a science differs from axiology as a philosophy. He then goes on to state that, "axiology as a science is the development of the definition of value in terms of the logical relationship of class membership; a thing has value in the degree in which it fulfills the concept of its class."[2] In other words the greater the fulfillment, the higher will be the value, i.e., good, better, best.

The Making of a Value Test With Words

As follows are examples of words, phrases and quotations which Hartman and Cardenas considered to have "world" value dimensions.[3]

EXAMPLES OF COMPOSITIONS

A Baby; Mystic Experience; Creative Act; A Lover's Embrace

My New Car; Love of Adventure; "Peach"; Creative Engineer; Love of Nature

Corporate Personality; Morale of Army, Shop, etc; Maxim; Creative Thinker; Justice; Hypostatization

"Mr. Republican"; Materialist God; Selling Favorite Painting; "By This Ring I Thee Wed"; A Token of Love

"Elizabeth II"; Axiological Value; Philosophy of Creativity; Devoted Scientist; A Citation for a Good Deed

Ice Cream Sundae; Binding of Book; Easy Chair; A New Car

Application of a System; Popular Science; Uniform; A Decoration for Bravery

Production Line; Game; "Legal Tender": Abstraction; Corroborating Witness; A Telephone

Technical Improvement; Deduction; Corroboration; A Scientific Experiment

EXAMPLES OF TRANSPOSITIONS

Puzzle; Existentialist Depreciation of Thought; Jabberwock; Logical Paradox; "Red Tape"; A Foolish Thought

A Fine; Pedant; Policeman Stopping My Car; A Blunder

Bad Popularization; Bribed Judge: "Egghead"; False Application of System, A Short Circuit; A False Coin

Chocolate and Sawdust; Inkblot on Book; Chair Smashed by Hammer; Rubbish Heap; A Wreck

Paranoia (Systemic "Self"); Color Line; Menotti's The Consul; The Metaphysical Fallacy; Killing in War; Mad Man; An Idiot

Person as Function ("Alienation of Self"); Idol; Jesus Tempted by Satan (Matt 4:1); Metaphor Taken Literally; Christmas Shopping and Merchandizing; Act of Killing; Slavery; Prostitution

Argumentum ad Personam; Burning Heretics; Strategy in War; "Intelligenzbestie"; Rationalization; Imprison an Innocent Person

Lovesick Truant; Building an Ugly Bridge; Train Running over Suicide; Blow an Airliner up in Flight; Poisoning the City Water

"We'll Always be Friends" (Friendship used to terminate love); Nazi Irma Greise (tied women's legs in labor, used life to kill); Raping a Child

Since "fulfillment" implies "properties," we can easily understand why an increase of properties would be important to valuation theory. Hartman states that

> valuation is a play with properties. It is similar to music which is a play with sounds. Thus the properties of things separated from the things are, so to speak, the sounds of valuation. Formal (scientific) axiology is nothing else but the score of this play with pure properties: it gives us their combinations and their keys. These keys are the dimensions of value.[4]

The following is a brief explanation of the value dimensions ("DIM").

1) The fulfillment of a formal concept is called systemic value. Systemic things have only two values, either perfection or non-existence. "The systemic concept has a finite and definite number of properties."

> DIM-S Judgment of concepts, rules, theories, the logical, the legal, the mathematical, of abstract ideas in general, i.e., schematic thinking.

2) The fulfillment of an abstract empirical concept is called extrinsic value. The number of properties, therefore, which an abstract concept has is between one and infinity.

> DIM-E Judgment of practical circumstances, the concrete, the material and the tangible, of things and objects, i.e., pragmatic thinking.

3) The fulfillment by a thing of a singular concept, such as a metaphor which can also be a continuum, constitutes intrinsic value. The predicates of a singular concept are infinite, but they are infinite in a different way from those of the abstract concept. They do not exist by themselves, isolated; rather they continue one with the other; they form a continuum. Intrinsic valuation is the valuation of poets and artists, lovers and mystics, magicians and advertisers, chefs de cuisine and politicians, theologians and creative scientists.

> DIM-I Judgment of the individuality and inner worth of other persons, i.e., empathic thinking.

Systemic value, extrinsic value, and intrinsic value are the value dimensions. They constitute a hierarchy of richness, with intrinsic value richer in qualities than extrinsic value, and extrinsic value richer in qualities than systemic value. "Richer in qualities" is the definition of "better," "poorer in qualities" is the definition of "worse." The definition in use of "ought" is, "The worse ought to be better." Hence, intrinsic value is better than extrinsic value, and extrinsic value is better than systemic value. Also, systemic value ought to be extrinsic value, and extrinsic value ought to be intrinsic value. The hierarchy of value is a valuation of value.

With this understanding, it is possible to see how Hartman and Cardenas selected the test items, the examples of compositions and transpositions, which make up the HVP World Value Phrases. It is also easy to see the axiological opposition of the first composition I^I with the last transposition I_I and so on throughout the listing.

Phrases[5]

I^I A baby. Intrinsic valuation of an intrinsic value. The intrinsic value is the human being which is valued as coming newly into existence, which is also an intrinsic value.

E^I Love of nature. Intrinsic valuation of an extrinsic value. Nature is the totality of all things and this is intrinsically valued.

S^I A mathematical genius. Intrinsic valuation of a systemic value. A system is valued in terms of a human being. (The Universe, I^S, means that a human being is valued in terms of a system.)

I^E "By this ring I thee wed". Extrinsic valuation of an intrinsic value. The intrinsic value is the wedding. This is valued by the ring, which is a thing, that is, an extrinsic value.

I^S A devoted scientist. Systemic valuation of an intrinsic value. The intrinsic value is the human being who is valued in terms of a scientific system.

E^E A good meal. Extrinsic valuation of an extrinsic value. Food is an extrinsic value. When it is regarded as a meal and a good one, then this extrinsic value is extrinsically valued.

S^E A uniform. Extrinsic valuation of a systemic value. The systemic value is the system (S), which is being represented by a dress or suit (E).

E^S An assembly line. Systemic valuation of an extrinsic value. A collection of things (E) is being put into a system (S).

S^S A technical improvement. Systemic valuation of a systemic value. A technical arrangement is a systemic value. When it is improved, this systemic value is valued by a further systemic value.

S_S Nonsense. Systemic disvaluation of a systemic value. Something which makes no sense is a systemic value which, as making no sense, is systemically disvalued.

E_S A fine. Systemic disvaluation of an extrinsic value. The extrinsic value is the situation for which the fine is given. The fine is given by a representative of a system who, in terms of the system disvalues the situation.

S_E A short-circuit. Extrinsic disvaluation of a systemic value. The electric system (S) is interrupted by a spatio-temporal event (E).

E_E Rubbish heap. Rubbish is some substance, usually inorganic (E), made unusable, i.e. disvalued, by another substance, influence, or event (E).

I_S **A madman.** Systemic disvaluation of an intrinsic value. A person is disvalued, or disvalues itself, in terms of a system or fixed idea (the inverse is S_I, the disvaluation of a system or idea by means of a person, item h).

I_E **Slavery.** Extrinsic disvaluation of an intrinsic value. The intrinsic value is the human being (I) which is disvalued as a merchandise (E).

S_I **Burn a heretic at the stake.** Intrinsic disvaluation of a systemic value. The system for which the heretic stands is disvalued intrinsically by eradicating the person that adheres to it.

E_I **Blow up an airliner in flight.** Intrinsic disvaluation of an extrinsic value. The extrinsic value is the airliner, the intrinsic disvaluation is its annihilation. (An intrinsic value means giving existence, creation, an intrinsic disvalue taking away existence, destruction.)

I_I **Torture a person.** Intrinsic disvaluation of an intrinsic value. Here the existence of a human being (I) is destroyed (I). (Cf. items E_I and S_I, where what is being destroyed is a thing and a system, respectively.)

Each composition should be compared with its opposite transposition so as to clearly see the axiological continuum of 18 items from extremely good to extremely bad. It is also possible to discern quickly and contrast the operational importance of the value dimensions of intrinsic, extrinsic and systemic. One can gain additional insight by identifying the three pairs of inverse compositions and the three pair of inverse transpositions which are, as follows:

Inverse Compositions	Inverse Transpositions
E^I Love of nature	E_I Blow up an airliner in flight
I^E "By this ring I thee wed"	I_E Slavery
S^I a mathematical genius	S_I Burn a witch at the stake
I^S a devoted scientist	I_S a madman
S^E a uniform	S_E a short circuit
E^S an assembly line	E_S a fine

Thus far we have attempted to show you the test rationale which is inherent in the items that were selected for the world value part of the HVP.

It is apparent that an objectivity exists in terms of value language and expression. Just as children, in an informal manner, learn to value and think axiologically, we believe young adults also will be able to learn to do the same, but in a more formal way. There is a parallel for our hope especially for teachers and psychologists who as children learned to behave and value in a way so as to become help providers. With formal preparation and study of education and behavioral science, educators and psychologists are able to learn more or less how to think psychologically about behavior and learning. There is also historical precedent for our hope. Think for a moment about the modern and formal science of bacteriology, which only came into being with the advent of the microscope and the work of Pasteur, 1822-1895, and Lister 1827-1912, and others. However, do keep in mind that for thousands of years there were "informal bacteriologists." They were called vinters, cheese makers, brew masters, and bakers; and they all had some knowledge of yeast and the process of fermentation and how to use this knowledge in a beneficial way. It is apparent that just as there were great numbers of "informal bacteriologists" throughout the centuries, we will find that the same phenomenon exists in terms of formal axiology, the science of value.

Knowledge about axiological principles makes it possible to think about psycholinguistic and axiolinguistic processes. For example, the internalized sentences that Albert Ellis thinks are necessary before one displays emotional behavior, either rational or irrational, are probably rich in psycholinguistic and axiolinguistic value and meaning. Ellis, in using the concepts of intrinsic and extrinsic in his theory of rational-emotive psychotherapy, is in close agreement with Hartman as to the importance of these key value dimensions.

An early study by Lafferty, titled "Values That Defeat Learning," illustrates the negative power of irrational beliefs in children. This kind of thinking, which leads to failure, often can be challenged and changed to bring about learning success. In a follow on study by this writer titled, "Values That Promote Learning," with high school honor students, the HVP and Rokeach Value Survey (RVS) tests revealed the key positive values that are held which promote learning success. We also found that there were differences between boys and girls. Both sexes put high value on the importance of honesty and happiness. However, there were widely disparate feelings on other values. Boys put far greater emphasis on cheerfulness, wisdom and external goals, while girls more highly valued helpfulness, world peace and internal goals. This is a good thing because their differences are complementary and yet their achievement is similar. That tells us that there are two routes to high achievement--the boys' way and the girls' way. This is important because whenever there are alternative paths to the same goal, more people can demonstrate success; and these values can be taught to aspirants of success in school.

HARTMAN VALUE PROFILE (HVP)

General Evaluation Report-Axioscope

Key Variables*

Muskegon High School Honor Society

INTUITION Boys and Girls

The capacity of a person to grasp the totality of circumstances in a situation and to recognize which of these is the most important for a favorable development of the situation.

SELF DISCIPLINE AND SELF ORGANIZATION Boys and Girls

Persons who succeed in developing this capacity have a firm sense of duty. The norms which rule them are an integral part of their personality. There is no need to prescribe to them norms or rules to follow, as their moral code dictates these to them constantly.

KNOWLEDGE OF OTHERS Boys and Girls

The capacity of the person to see his fellow man as a unique being, different from any other, and to grasp him (or her) in his (or her) totality, not by some special feature but in his (or her) authentic self. The capacity of empathy--which makes the person respect and comprehend the other.

THEORETICAL ORGANIZATION AND PLANNING Boys and Girls

The capacity of setting theoretical goals on the basis of the concrete situation, and of projecting them back into practice. The capacity of imagining as abstract what is concrete, and as concrete what is abstract.

PRACTICAL ORGANIZATION AND MANAGEMENT Boys and Girls

The capacity of comprehending practical situations and everyday problems, in particular of classifying things and persons, and employing them efficiently within the given circumstances.

INTELLECTUAL DISCIPLINE Boys Only

The capacity of the person to value system, order ideas, relations and concepts. This score measures the acceptance of established norms, both in an organization and in the world at large.

JUDGMENT Girls Only

This is the capacity guiding the person through the various types of values, both in the world and in herself. It is her valuational intelligence--a kind of gyroscope which enables the person to adapt herself to her environment and to her own self.

AMBITION AND SELF DEVELOPMENT Girls Only

This capacity is determined by the difference between the goals a person sets for herself and the actual situation--the difference, that is, between what she wants or ought to be and what she is. It is based on self-discipline, setting oneself goals difficulty to reach, and thus requiring from herself the full development of her potentialities.

SELF ACCEPTANCE Girls Only

The security one obtains from clear awareness of the various values within herself, and achieving their equilibrium. This leads to self-acceptance, with all one's defects and virtues.

SELF DIRECTION Girls Only

This score combines the person's capacity of self-knowledge with her capacity of projecting herself into the future. It is her sense of responsibility for herself, giving correctness to her conduct and fittingness to her aspiration.

*Key variable was based on an averaged set of scores which produced a rating of Very Good.

ROKEACH VALUE SURVEY MEDIAN RANKS
Muskegon High School Honor Society

PART I TERMINAL VALUES	BOYS (N:20)	GIRLS (N:22)
Sense of accomplishment	7.0	8.5
*A world of peace	11.0	2.5
*Equality	14.0	8.5
Freedom	4.5	4.0
Happiness	2.0	1.0
Inner harmony	3.0	6.0
Salvation	10.0	7.0
Self respect	4.5	2.5
True friendship	6.0	5.0
*Wisdom	1.0	10.5
PART II INSTRUMENTAL VALUES		
Ambitious	8.0	6.0
Broadminded	7.0	9.0
*Cheerful	5.0	10.5
*Clean	18.0	13.0
Forgiving	2.0	5.0
*Helpful	10.5	4.0
Honest	1.0	1.0
*Independent	13.0	8.0
*Intellectual	5.0	15.5
Loving	3.0	2.0
Responsible	5.0	3.0
Self controlled	9.0	7.0

*Significant male-female difference

In summary the real differences then between boys and girls, as supported by the findings on both the HVP and RVS are as follows:

Boys		Girls
Wisdom	vs	World at Peace
Intellectual Discipline	vs	Ambition
Cheerfulness	vs	Helpfulness
External Goals	vs	Internal Goals
Stress	vs	Immaturity

These differences are believed to be mainly positive and complementary.

Along the same line of inquiry, it has been found that there are age differences in value. For example, young children and senior citizens will often overvalue "a good meal" and disvalue "a baby." It is apparent that life stages do have an effect on valuation. What we are saying here is that a theory of value and valuation will have to account for different circumstances and individual differences in people.

Two World Value Tests

Hartman recognized, when he created the HVPII, that there are important axiolinguistic differences. While it is true that the hierarchy of value is a valuation of value, the words that represent values can be a problem. It is for this reason in part why Hartman stated, "that while the HVPII is similar to the HVP it is not equivalent." Others that have created value instruments, Acquaviva, Forrest, Mefford, Carpenter, King, to name a few, who have copied the Hartman format and rationale, have found that new versions may produce different results for some people. However, for other people there may be no overall difference, and this is important. What we have here may be more a difficulty with axiometric method than with axiological theory. Translation of the HVP and HVPII into another language also present similar problems. To date there are HVP translations into Spanish by Hartman, Swedish by Schildt and Hartman, German by Mefford and Hartman, French by Hino, Polish by Hajduga and Japanese by Fujimoto. John Davis, David Mefford, Robert Carter, Rita Hartman and this writer have all supported the effort to promote translations and cross cultural axiolinguistic research.

258   *Forms of Value and Valuation: Theory and Applications*

Let us look at the two tests, the World Value phrases in the HVP and HVPII, and see how the items compare. We have presented the items just as they appear on each format or version. The directions for taking the test are as follows:

PART I: PHRASES

DIRECTIONS: On the right you will find 18 words or phrases. Each of these phrases (or words) represents something on which individuals may place different "values" (good or bad)--depending on their own feelings about how good or bad it is.

Read all of the phrases carefully. (If there is a word that you do not understand, ask what it means.)

Write the number "1" on the line in front of the phrase which represents the highest (most) value as far as you are concerned--that is, the one you feel is the **best**.

Write the number "2" in front of the phrase which represents the next best (second best) value.

Number **all** of the phrases in the same way, to show the order of their respective values to you. Use a **different** number for each of the 18 phrases (3, 4, 5 and so on). The number "18" should be in front of the word or phrase that represents the lowest (least) value to you--that is, the one that you feel is the **worst**.

Do not judge the expressions by the **importance** but **only by the goodness** or **badness** of their content.

Decide quickly how you feel about each of the phrases. There is no time limit, but most people are able to complete numbering all the phrases in about ten to twelve minutes. You may begin.

After you have finished, please CHECK to make sure that you have used all the numbers from 1 though 18, without repeating any. (Start with your number 1 and find each number up through 18.)

Cross out numbers used: 1 2 3 4 5 6 7 8 9 10 11 12 13 14 15 16 17 18

A Suggestion: We suggest that you cover the first test and rank order the second, HVPII, 1 to 18. Then repeat this procedure by covering up your ranked answers and rank the HVP test 1 to 18.

THE HARTMAN VALUE PROFILE (HVP)

by Robert S. Hartman, Ph.D. and Mario Cardenas Trigos, M.D.

THE HARTMAN VALUE PROFILE (HVP II)

by Robert S. Hartman, Ph.D.
Research Edition

HVP	HVP II
A good meal	A new car
A technical improvement	A scientific experiment
Nonsense	A foolish thought
A fine	A blunder
A rubbish heap	A wreck
A devoted scientist	A citation for a good deed
Blow up an airliner in flight	Poisoning the city water
Burn a witch at the stake	Imprison an innocent person
A short-circuit	A false coin
"By this ring I thee wed"	A token of love
A baby	A lover's embrace
Torture a person	Raping a child
Love of nature	A life of adventure
A madman	An idiot
An assembly line	A telephone
Slavery	Prostitution
A mathematical genius	Justice
A uniform	A decoration for bravery

The Value Tests as Applied Formal Axiology

The 18 statements in each of the two tests represent value formulae. Their order is the following, where number 1-9 are compositions of value, or valuations, and 10-18 are transpositions, or disvaluations.

In Part I World Value, of the HVP and HVPII the intrinsic, extrinsic and systemic dimensions are represented by everyday values, Persons (I), Things (E), Systems (S). In Part II Self Value, these dimensions are applied to the person himself: the Self or "I" (I), Work (E), the World (S).

Phrases				
Two Scales of World Axiological Values				
Rank	Formula	HVP Phrase	Position in Test	HVPII Phrase
1	I^I	A baby	k	A lover's embrace
2	E^I	Love of nature	m	A life of adventure
3	S^I	A mathematical genius	q	Justice
4	I^E	"By this ring I thee wed"	j	A token of love
5	I^S	A devoted scientist	f	A citation for a good deed
6	E^E	A good meal	a	A new car
7	S^E	A uniform	r	A decoration for bravery
8	E^S	An assembly line	o	A telephone
9	S^S	A technical improvement	b	A scientific experiment
10	S_S	Nonsense	c	A foolish thought
11	E_S	A fine	d	A blunder
12	S_E	A short-circuit	i	A false coin
13	E_E	A rubbish heap	e	A wreck

14	I_S	A madman	n	An idiot
15	I_E	Slavery	p	Prostitution
16	S_I	Burn a witch at the stake	h	Imprison an innocent person
17	E_I	Blow up an airliner in flight	g	Poisoning the city water
18	I_I	Torture a person	l	Raping a child

Special Note: There are also two scales of Self Axiological Values which consist of 18 quotations each, which are called Part II Self Value. Each scale has the same rationale and scoring procedure as Part I World Value. The HVP Part II Scale has a theme of "work" while the HVPII Part II Scale has a value theme of "health." For the serious reader who is interested in axiometrics and the unique relationships of world axiological values to self axiological values, we suggest that <u>The Hartman Value Profile (HVP): Manual of Interpretation</u> be considered as an advanced text.

We suggested that you cover one test and rank order the other test 1 to 18. Then repeat this procedure by covering up your ranked answers and rank order the second test 1 to 18. How much agreement did you have in ranking the two tests? Keep in mind the question: What effect did your knowledge of the rationale of axiological opposites, compositions and transpositions, have on the way you ranked the items? Even though the phrases are mixed up, did you look for pairs? Did you try to use an elimination system to rank the best item with the worst item and so on? Your answers to these questions and your ideas about intrinsic, extrinsic, and systemic dimensions all will have a conscious effect on your results. How consistent were your answers--the ranks between the two tests? How do you think you would have done if you did not have any information about the theory and the test? Also think about how you might do on a different format, the HVP Pictorial Form, or the HVP Card Form, or if you can read a second language, a translated version. Would these procedures have made a difference in your results? Another variation would be to combine the HVP and HVPII cards into one single procedure so as to have a greater number of items. The importance of method is very apparent in terms of test procedure and expectations. There can be problems with method, especially if we succumb to the idea that "science" is "empirical" in the sense that experimentation, observation and prediction must always be part of "science." Hartman called this problem the "empirical fallacy." He stated that, "mathematics, music and axiology are sciences and they do include experimentation, observation and prediction even though they are not empirical."[6]

Thus far we have tried to acquaint you with words, phrases and quotations which illustrate an axiological frame of reference. In introducing you to value theory by example and through the two tests of world value, which were created by Hartman and Cardenas, we hope that you will recognize that a value science is possible. We have stressed the value logic of words and phrases because it is primarily with language that we think about values and beliefs. It is also with language, which is formed by psycholinguistic and axiolinguistic procedures, that we communicate with one another on a value plane about values.

The Value of a Value Theory in Making a Value Test

Hartman said that the reader of his book, The Structure of Value,

has the task of evaluating the value theory presented. Hence, value theory becomes for him a subject of valuation, and he needs a value theory to evaluate value theory. He may, following so many empirical value "theories", simply say that he likes or dislikes what he has read. On the other hand, he may want to be more analytical and test his own value theory against the one presented and, vice versa, the value theory presented against his own. We shall therefore apply our own theory to the valuation of any value theory.

Such a theory is a mental construct. Hence, in our terms it is a systemic value. Since, however, anything can be considered in all three value dimensions, a value theory can also be regarded as an extrinsic and as an intrinsic value. In the former case, it is seen as a tool functioning in the space-time world among similar such tools, or a member of the expositional class of value theories. In the latter case, it is regarded as unique and incomparable, and some person as fully involved with it.

A value theory regarded as a systemic value cannot be either a good or bad value theory, but it either is theory of value or is not. It is if it fulfills the definition of value theory, and it is not if it lacks an element of that definition. We must therefore first of all define a value theory and determine the criterion or criteria. A value theory, obviously, must be a theory of value, that is to say, it must be theory which accounts for the value world, which in turn is the totality of all the value phenomena. Hence, the one criterion that makes or breaks a value theory is that of universal applicability to values. A theory not universally applicable to values is not, according to this criterion, a value theory.

As the proof of the pudding is in the eating, so the proof of a value theory is in the application. There is an elegant way and there is a less elegant way of making this proof. The elegant way is to investigate the level of abstraction. Since a theory is the more applicable the more abstract it is, the most abstract theory is the most applicable. The "best" theory, then, will be a purely formal one and, indeed, no value theory that is not formal will, by this test, by a value theory.

But this elegant test is only available to minds trained in philosophy and science. The less elegant way is to enumerate all the value phenomena to which a value theory is applicable and cross off from membership in the systemic class of value theories any which does not account for all of the enumerated value phenomena. If there is only one value phenomenon which a value theory A does not account for while a value theory B does, then value theory A is not a value theory in the systemic sense of the word.

In our case, there is indeed one value feature which is new in our theory as against any other value theory: that of systemic value, both in conception and application.[7]

Hartman goes on to provide many features to illustrate and to bolster his contention that, "value phenomena are systematically interrelated and thus constitute a value cosmos."

Hartman concludes his systemic comparison of his theory with any other value theory by stating that

all these features must be taken into consideration and the other value theory must be shown to account for them, and to do so systematically and consistently. On the other hand, our theory must be shown to account for and interrelate all the features presented and exhibited by the other value theory. In such a comparison, our value theory will exhibit one great lack. We speak nowhere of purpose, goals, and other teleological features of value theories, such as rightness of acts. The reason is that we deal with axiology and not with teleology. The latter is one of the applied axiological sciences, and arises when axiology, or to be exact, extrinsic value, is applied to time. Therefore, it is a special axiological science and must be discussed in its own right.

A value theory can also be regarded as an extrinsic value. As such it is one of the tools for the understanding of the value world. In this case, again, universal applicability can be used as a criterion; that value theory will be the better value theory which is applicable to more value phenomena. In extrinsic valuation the degrees of value of the things valued are being taken into consideration, and therefore a value theory lacking some of the criteria of a good value theory will not, for that matter, be disqualified as a value theory, as is the case in systemic valuation. Thus there can be better or worse value theories. The extrinsic valuation of value theories, in other words, will admit more theories with the name of value theories into the class of value theories.

A value theory may, finally, have an intrinsic value. In this case all that counts is the involvement of the valuer in the theory. Here we must distinguish two cases. The involvement may be positive or negative, that is to say, either an intrinsic valuation or an intrinsic disvaluation of the theory -- either S^I or S_I. In the first case, we have the personal appreciation of the theory. It is based on the appropriate valuation of the theory as a theory, that is, its systemic features, and the valuer gives himself to the theory as a rational being, and is as such fully involved. In the second case, the personal involvement is not based on these objective criteria but the personal needs of the valuer. Thus, the creator of a value theory may be so much in love with it that he is blind to all other theories. This, of course, would imply that his own theory is incapable of dealing as a theory, that is to say, systematically and rationally, with other theories, and hence the creator must deal with them unsystematically and irrationally -- epithetically rather than analytically. The same is true for the advocate of any value theory who is so much taken by this theory that he does not consider any other. Such an attitude again, and for the same reason, proves the insufficiency of the theory held.[8]

The Scoring of a Test of Value Capacity[9]

The Hartman Value Profiles (HVP and HVPII) are axiological tests which measure a persons capacity to value. This capacity is a talent which, in one sense, is independent of both intellectual and emotional capacities, but in another sense, is dependent on them in so far as the value capacity is the ability to organize one's intellectual and emotional capacities. For this reason, the test also gives indications of these two capacities, in particular, the presence or absence of emotional existential problems. Hartman wrote:

> A distinction must be made between value in general and specific values (interests, preferences, etc.). The capacity to value in general is to specific value interests or preferences as the capacity to see color is to specific color interests or preferences. Before testing a person as to his preference for, say, green or red, he ought first to be tested as to his capacity for <u>seeing color</u>. A color-blind person, obviously, cannot have a valid judgment as to his preference for red or green. Similarly, before testing a person as to his preference for, say religious, theoretical, economic or political value, it would be good first to test him as to his <u>capacity to value in general</u>. Since his interests are <u>specific</u> values, his capacity to distinguish them depends on his capacity to <u>value in general</u>.
>
> Value in general thus is to specific values, or interests, as color in general is to specific colors. In the degree that a person is more or less sensitive to color in general, his preference for this or that specific color is more or less valid and significant. Similarly, in the degree that a person is more or less sensitive to value in general, his preference for this or that value is more or less valid and significant.[10]

Formal axiology specifies and elaborates systematically an objective scale of valuational richness. The tests are based on this rationale. Its expressions represent hierarchical combinations of systemic, extrinsic and intrinsic values. A person's ordering them, as compared to their objective order, measures the person's value capacity. Both the HVP and HVPII measure the deviation of the person's own score from a theoretical score based on formal axiology, the science of value logic. This logic determines the correctness or incorrectness of value judgments. The tests therefore measure the capacity for making value judgments.

The scores come out in numbers; the lower the number the better the score, the higher the number the worse the score. The numerical results make possible collective applications of the test, statistical calculations, rankings of individuals within a group according to various classifications.

The test consists of two parts, the first measuring the capacity of value the world, the second measuring the capacity to value one's own self.

Each part has three sets of scales.

The first set consists of four measures: the Differentiation Score, for the capacity to differentiate values; the Dimension Score, for the sense of proportion, based on the equilibrium between value dimensions; the Integration Score, for the capacity to solve problems and see the relevant in the complex; and the Dissimilarity Score, for the capacity to distinguish between good and bad.

The second set of scales are the value dimensions: Intrinsic Value, the capacity for discerning values in individuals; Extrinsic Value, the capacity for discerning values in the world; Systemic Value, the capacity for discerning values in systems, in order and theory.

Each of these value dimensions in turn has a dimensional and an integrational score, the former indicating the capacity for discerning the value dimension in question, the latter indicating the capacity for solving problems in that dimension.

While the two sets of scales mentioned are objective, the third set of scales is subjective and refers only to the person tested. They are the Dimension and integration measures mentioned in the first set, but seen as percentages of the Differentiation Score. The better the Differentiation Score, the lower its number, the higher are the corresponding percentage scores; so that even a low number in these measures may mean a high percentage for a person of good value capacity. These are the existential and the psychological index, respectively. They measure effects of the person's value sensitivity.

The test yields many scores for each part (world & self) which can be derived by hand scoring or computer scoring. These obtained scores can be processed further in a manner so as to provide both an axiograph and an axioscope analysis of value capacity. We will offer a more detailed discussion of some of the scores and obtained measures along with examples of our research findings.

The Logical Meaning of Meaning and Intension as Measure and Norm[11]

Hartman wrote:

The meaning of a thing is, logically, the set of properties by which the thing is characterized. This set of properties is called, logically, the "content" of the thing's concept or the intension of the thing's concept.

Formal axiology is based on the logical nature of meaning, namely intension, and on the structure of intension as a set of properties. It applies set theory to this set of properties. Set theory is a certain kind of mathematics that deals with the relationship of sets and subsets in general and of finite and infinite sets in particular.

Since mathematics is objective and a priori, formal axiology is an objective and a priori science, and a test based on it is an objective test based on an objective standard.

Just as each class of things must be measured by the kind of measure appropriate to it -- the circumference of a tree cannot be measured by a meter rod but only by a tape -- so each class of things must be measured by the intension appropriate to it. Pears cannot be measured by the intension of "apple", and apples not by that of "tree". But any kind of intension is a set of predicates as any kind of length measure is a set of centimeters (or inches, etc.).

If a thing possesses the whole set of properties given in the intension it is call a good such thing. It corresponds to the full measure of its value, or it corresponds fully to the measure of its value, the intension. If it does not possess them all, it is not so good a thing, or a bad thing -- as a chair, which lacks a seat or a back or both. Words such as good or bad, then, are nothing but words of measuring meaning, logically no different from words such as meter, dozen, score and other measuring words. Sometime such value words are actually used to measure number, as when we say "the town is lousy with tourists", meaning that there are very many tourists in town. We use lousy, which is a value word meaning "very bad", to signify "very many".

The measure of the value of the thing thus is the logical intension of the thing; and a thing is the better the more elements of the intension can be matched with the set of properties possessed by the thing. In general, the possession of all the intensional properties makes the thing good, of half of them so-so or average, of more than half fair, and of less than half bad. Valuation arranges an re-arranges the properties of things. It sees things fluidly rather than solidly, dynamically rather than statically.

The more expert we are at knowing certain things the more properties we know these things to have. The taste of a glass of Burgundy, for example, has been shown by experts to contain 158 properties. This means that there are $2^{158} = 3.6 \times 10^{46}$ possibilities of taste in a glass of Burgundy, an astronomical figure, considering the number of all particles in the universe is only of the range of magnitude 10^{79}.

Thus, the application of the combinatorial calculus to intensions brings about the exact measurement of value. Value sensitivity may then be exactly defined. It is the capacity of matching a set of predicates one has in mind with a set of properties one recognizes in an actual thing or situation. It is a capacity of conceptual-perceptual matching -- a capacity of qualitative measuring. Formal axiology, thus, is the quantification of qualities.

Since, in formal axiology, the intension or logical meaning of a thing's concept is the value standard of the thing, and this standard is objective, namely the definition of the thing in question -- which is arrived at by the development of human speech and society throughout history -- the correct answers for a test based on the system of formal axiology are known from the system of axiology itself, that is from the mechanism of value thinking. In this respect an axiological test is similar to a mathematical test, in which the correct answers are known from the system of mathematics, and the person's answers are measured against the correct ones. Actually, the capacity of valuation is a talent similar to the mathematical or musical.

The items of the test have their precise axiological order and the ranking by a person has a measurable relationship to that order. His scores from the test are the measures of this relationship, that is, of the subject's deviation from the axiological order. This order is due to the fact that the items are illustrations of formulae arising from the mathematical statement of the value dimensions.

The validation of such a test is verification rather than standardization. The standards are the correct answers given in the system. The statistical validation has to verify whether the theory corresponds to practice, that is, whether, in actuality, the majority of people do value as the theory predicts; in particular, whether in the majority of actual value judgments the items of the test follow in the axiological order of the test.

The Validation of a Value Test[12]

Hartman further explained:

> As has been stated before, validation of the test means verification in practice of the axiological theory. The sequence of the items is objectively determined by the numerical values of the corresponding formulae. By projecting his own value order, the test subject measures his own value scale against the objective scale given by formal axiology. Although the measurement is precise, it is of practically infinite variety. There are, for each test, $1 \times 2 \times 3 \times ... \times 18 = 18! = 6.4 \times 10^{15}$ or 6.4 quadrillion possible answers. This means that for every person in the world there are as many possibilities of answering this test as there are people in the world. For both tests together, there are $1 \times 2 \times 3 \times ... \times 36$ possible answers, or more possibilities of answer than there are atoms in the universe!
>
> The test is extremely sensitive and shows up very subtle deviations from the norm. These deviations have their basis in the person's own value pattern. The pattern expresses itself in specific values, interests or preferences, but the test does not measure the latter; it measures the underlying value pattern. The test does not intend to measure the energy or drive a person has. Two persons with identical axiological endowment may have different ranges of action, depending on their innate energy. It is not a test of professional skill or ability. Two persons with the same professional ability, say, as accountants, may have very different scores. This means that one will have a better and one a worse, general value capacity than the other; and this, in turn, may influence their handling of their respective jobs. But it would indicate, even more strongly, two different ways of handling their respective lives; and of handling their jobs differently only in the total matrix of their lives. Thus, the test is not primarily one applicable to special groups, but to individuals. Its standardization by group performance reflects deeper axiological differences than social classification. Thus, a group of hippies and a group of medical pathologists will exhibit different collective patterns; but the reason is not their different social functions but the different value patterns that underlie these functions. Better scores are usually -- though not necessarily -- made by persons in professions demanding empathy with people or things than by persons in professions indifferent to the full range of valuation.

The capacity of valuation, as was mentioned, is a talent similar to the musical or the mathematical. While there are groups of musicians, however, and of mathematicians, there is no special group or profession of people sensitive to values. Rather, this talent is found in all groups and all professions, as well as in all ages, and both sexes. High and low scores, therefore, are distributed among all groups, and usually, in any large enough group the scores follow the normal frequency curve. The specific value differences of the groups, as well as of the individuals, appear as result of the configurations of these scores.

The test items and scales were tested in various countries, especially the United States, where the following studies were made: empirical indices of reliability, indices of construct validity, and empirical indices of concurrent validity. Among the first were: Test-retest stability of individual scores; correspondence of group mean scores; freedom from influence of sex, age, marital status, and educational background; central tendencies of response to each item. Among the second were: Relationships with the following tests: Rorschach, Minnesota Multiphasic Personality Inventory, Raven, Donimo, Sacks Incomplete Phrases, Allport-Vernon-Lindzey's Study of Values, Leary's System for the "Interpersonal Diagnosis of Personality" (in an adaptation by Austin); Felker's "Philosophic Mindedness (PM) Scales," and others. Among the third are the following empirical studies: Differentiation of normals from underachieving high school students; differentiation of normals from juvenile delinquents; influence of professor's values on changes in students' values; differentiation of successful from unsuccessful college students; relationships with grades in college courses on marriage and family, philosophy, and sociology; relationships with peer-rankings of college students for a hypothetical leadership role; relationships with peer-rankings of college students for a hypothetical counseling role; differentiation of successful from unsuccessful graduate school students; relationships with grades in graduate school courses of philosophy of education and social ethics; and others.

The fundamental studies in every country are those which test the validity of the items. This is implicitly a validation of the scales. Since the test is a theoretical construction it was important to see whether the theory corresponded to practice and whether, with sufficiently large samples, the items would be located by the test persons close to their position on the theoretical value scale. The first such experiment, with the first version of the test was made with 225 volunteers in 1966, of mean age 25 years, 67 of whom were male, 158 female, 99 were undergraduate and 126 graduate students. The results are shown in the following chart which gives the correlation between the theoretical and the actual position of each item. As is seen, in the chart of Mean Position of Items, Part I, Dif is 22 and in Part II it is 34. This means a mean deviation of $\frac{22 + 34}{2} = 28.5$.

This result may be measured in two ways, by the theoretical possible range of deviation, *Dif = 162 of the inverted order; and by the random order in which the 18 items arrange themselves. To this end 18 pieces, of equal weight and form, numbered 1-18, were thoroughly mixed and together thrown in the same direction. The number of each item was then registered on the scoring form according to its distance from the thrower, with the closest item in position 1, the next closest in position 2, etc., and the most distant in position 18. The results were the following Random Distribution scoring forms, for four random throws. The random deviations seem to be between 90 (though this is extreme and rarely observed) as lower and 125 as upper limit; or a mean of 102.5. We shall use this mean, though it makes our result slightly worse, rather than the usually observed mean of $\frac{100 + 125}{2} = 112.5$.

Measuring the mean deviation of the sample, 28.5, as percentage of the theoretically possible deviation of 162, we have $\frac{28.5 \times 100}{162} = 17.59$ percent of a possible 100 percent, or a correctness of 100 percent - 17.59 percent = 82.41 percent. Measuring the sample against the random distribution we have $\frac{28.5 \times 100}{105} = 27.1$ percent, and a correctness of 100 percent - 27.1 percent = 72.9 percent. These are the correlations between theory and practice of the first version of the test used.

---

*Differentiation Score (Dif) - This score measures the subject's Value Sensitivity, that is, his capacity of differentiating the value elements in situations. Differentiation Scores vary in practice between 0 and 150. The score represents the value <u>errors</u> of the subject. Theoretically, the maximum of errors is 162, when namely, the subject numbers the items in the inverse order, instead of 1 to 18, from 18 to 1. The differences in this case add up to $2 (17 + 15 + 13....3 + 1) = 2 \times 9^2 = 2 \times 81 = 162$.

It was found that the coincidence of mean position of items with the theory of the test is so close as to produce in the sample a test of excellent value capacities, with a CQ 55 - 22 (excellent - very good), BQ_a 46 - 18 (excellent - good), and BQ_r 1.2 - 0.8 (excellent - excellent). A more detailed description is provided in The Manual of Interpretation.

The items with the largest deviations were subsequently corrected in order to make the verbal formulation more adequate to the formula as well as to the total context of the formulae. Thus, in the first test, item e was changed from "Mud" to "A rubbish heap" (in Spanish it had the correct formulation from the beginning, "Basura"); item g from "Tear out a fly's wings" to "Blow up an airline in flight," etc.

The Hartman Value Profile (HVP & HVPII)

Measures of Central Tendency on Responses* to Each Item
of The Hartman Value Inventory (Form E-1)

axiological rank	Item formula	position in inventory	Part I mean	Part I position	Part I median	Part I mode	Part II mean	Part II position	Part II median	Part II mode
1	I^I	k	2.3	1	2	2	2.9	1	2	1
2	E^I	m	3.2	3	3	1	5.6	5	5	5
3	S^I	q	5.7	7	6	6 & 7	3.6	2	3	2
4	I^E	j	3.1	2	2	1	5.6	6	5	5
5	I^S	f	4.6	4	4	4	10.0	9	9	9
6	E^E	a	5.5	6	6	7	4.3	3	4	4
7	S^E	r	9.0	8	9	8	6.4	8	6	6
8	E^S	o	9.8	10	9	9	4.9	4	4	4
9	S^S	b	5.3	5	5	6	6.3	7	8	8
10	S_S	c	9.6	9	10	10	11.8	12	12	12
11	E_S	d	11.2	12	11	11 & 12	10.3	10	11	10
12	S_E	i	14.2	14	14	14	13.0	14	14	14
13	E_E	e	10.4	11	10	10	14.4	15	15	14 & 16
14	I_S	n	12.1	13	13	13	11.1	11	11	11
15	I_E	p	15.4	15	15	15	12.6	13	13	13
16	S_I	h	15.9	16	16	16	15.3	17	16	17
17	E_I	g	16.4	17	17	18	15.2	16	16	17
18	I_I	l	17.0	18	17	18	17.0	18	18	18

*Obtained from 225 student volunteers in 1966. (Mean age, 25 years; 67 male, 158 female; 99 undergraduate students, 126 graduate students.)

For more details see The Hartman Value Profile (HVP): Manual of Interpretation, pp 61-66.

The rho-correlations between the theoretical sequence and the actual sequence of the sample is as follows:

Q_I mean = 0.97 Q_2 mean = 0.98
Q_I median = 0.98 Q_2 median = 0.99
Q_I mode = 0.95 Q_2 mode = 0.92

274 Forms of Value and Valuation: Theory and Applications

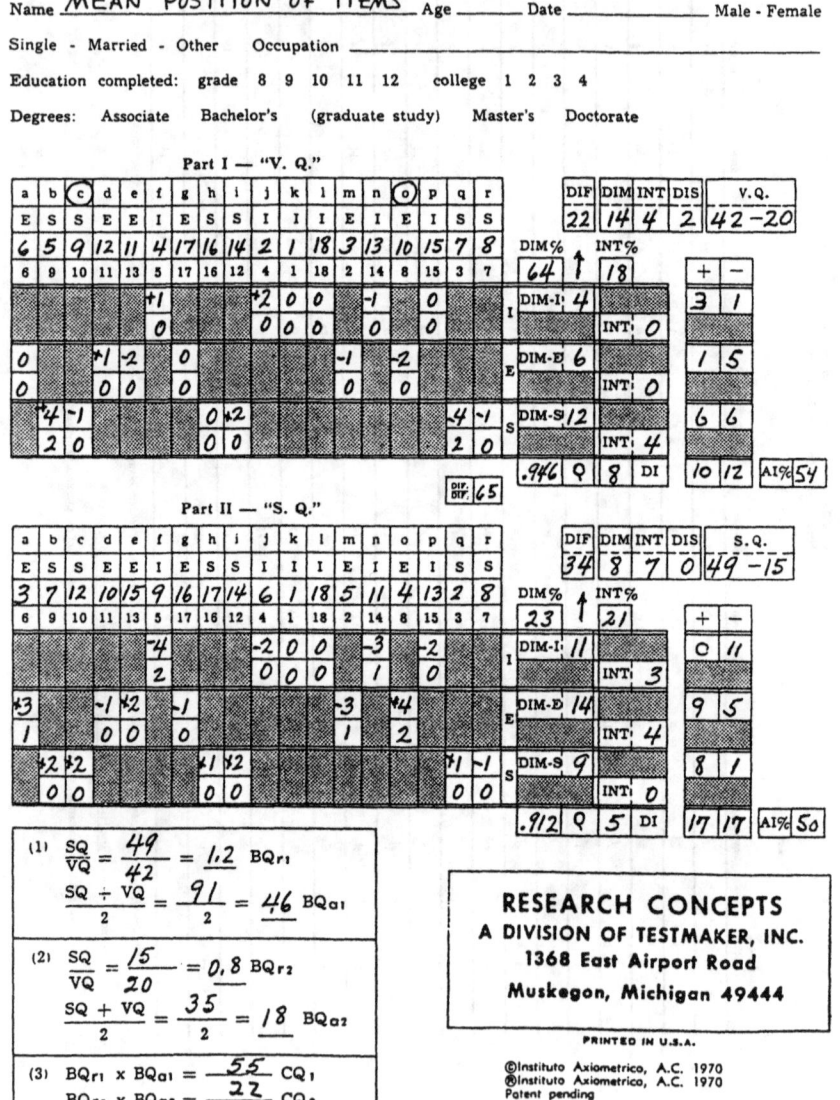

AXIOMETRIC® SCORING FORM

THE HARTMAN VALUE PROFILE

Name **RANDOM DISTRIBUTION** Age _____ Date _____ Male - Female

Single - Married - Other   Occupation _____

Education completed: grade 8 9 10 11 12   college 1 2 3 4

Degrees: Associate   Bachelor's   (graduate study)   Master's   Doctorate

FIRST THROW
Part I — "V. Q."

a	b	c	d	e	f	g	h	i	j	k	l	m	n	o	p	q	r	DIF	DIM	INT	DIS	V.Q.
E	S	S	E	E	I	E	S	S	I	I	I	E	I	E	I	S	S	122				—
10	18	11	4	16	13	15	7	9	12	14	5	17	8	2	1	3	6		DIM%	INT%		
6	9	10	11	13	5	17	16	12	4	1	18	2	14	8	15	3	7					+ —
					8				8	13	13		6		14			I DIM-I 62		INT	
4		7	3	2								15	6					E DIM-E 37		INT	
9	1					9	3							0	1			S DIM-S 23		INT	
																		−.210 Q		DI	AI%

SECOND THROW
Part II — "S. Q."

a	b	c	d	e	f	g	h	i	j	k	l	m	n	o	p	q	r	DIF	DIM	INT	DIS	S.Q.
E	S	S	E	E	I	E	S	S	I	I	I	E	I	E	I	S	S	102				—
6	12	18	8	7	2	13	15	3	17	14	1	11	9	10	16	5	4		DIM%	INT%		
6	9	10	11	13	5	17	16	12	4	1	18	2	14	8	15	3	7					+ —
					3				13	13	17	5		1				I DIM-I 52		INT	
0		3	6	4								9	2					E DIM-E 24		INT	
	3	8							1	9						2	3	S DIM-S 26		INT	
																		.024 Q		DI	AI%

(1) $\dfrac{SQ}{VQ} = \underline{\quad} = \underline{\quad}$ BQ$_{r1}$

$\dfrac{SQ + VQ}{2} = \dfrac{\underline{\quad}}{2} = \underline{\quad}$ BQ$_{a1}$

(2) $\dfrac{SQ}{VQ} = \underline{\quad} = \underline{\quad}$ BQ$_{r2}$

$\dfrac{SQ + VQ}{2} = \dfrac{\underline{\quad}}{2} = \underline{\quad}$ BQ$_{a2}$

(3) BQ$_{r1}$ × BQ$_{a1}$ = $\underline{\quad}$ CQ$_1$

BQ$_{r2}$ × BQ$_{a2}$ = $\underline{\quad}$ CQ$_2$

RESEARCH CONCEPTS
A DIVISION OF TESTMAKER, INC.
1368 East Airport Road
Muskegon, Michigan 49444

PRINTED IN U.S.A.

©Instituto Axiometrico, A.C. 1970
®Instituto Axiometrico, A.C. 1970
Patent pending

The Scores That a Value Test Provides and Their Meaning

The value test is objective and leaves no room for the exercise of the examiner's intuition. It yields its results in exact numbers. These numbers are the test scores, ordered in the test scales. Scores and scales are derived theoretically and have been validated practically. In sufficiently large samples, as we have shown, the scores follow Gaussian normal distribution curve. The value scales are as follows:

Intrinsic Dimension	(Dim-I)	Percentage of Differentiation	(Dif 1- Dif 2)
Extrinsic Dimension	(Dim-E)	Capacity for Valuation World	(V.Q.)
Systemic Dimension	(Dim-S)	Capacity for Self-Valuation	(S.Q.)
Differentiation	(Dif)	Relative Balance	$(B.Q._r)$
Dimension	(Dim)	Absolute Balance	$(B.Q._a)$
Dimension Percentage	(Dim %)	Combined Value Capacity	(C.Q.)
Intrinsic Integration	(Int-I)	Retest Quotient	(R.Q.)
Extrinsic Integration	(Int-E)		
Systemic Integration	(Int-S)		
Integration	(Int)		
Integration Percentage	(Int %)		
Dimensional Integration	(D.I.)		
Dissimilarity	(Dis)		
Rank Order Correlation	(Rho)		
Attitude Index	(AI %)		

From <u>Axiograph: Personal Value Description Chart</u>. Additional derived value capacities:

Self-Integration	Concentration	Self-Direction
Judgement	Practical Solution of Problems	Theoretical Organization
Intuition	Cooperativeness	Practical Organization
Ambition and Self-Development	Self-Knowledge	Sense of Reality
Self-Acceptance	Knowledge of Others	Problem of Valuation
Self-Discipline Self-Organization	Intellectual Discipline	Problems of Self-Valuation

THE HARTMAN VALUE PROFILE (HVP)
by Robert S. Hartman, Ph.D. and Mario Cardenas Trigos, M.D.
Instituto Axiometrico, SA., Cuernavaca, Mexico

AXIOMETRIC® SCORING FORM

Name _____ Age _____ Date _____ Male - Female

Single - Married - Other _____ Occupation _____

Education completed: grade 8 9 10 11 12 college 1 2 3 4

Degrees: Associate Bachelor's (graduate study) Master's Doctorate

Part I — "V. Q."

a	b	c	d	e	f	g	h	i	j	k	l	m	n	o	p	q	r
E	S	S	E	E	I	E	S	S	I	I	I	E	I	E	I	S	S
6	9	10	11	13	5	17	16	12	4	1	18	2	14	8	15	3	7

| DIF | DIM | INT | DIS | V. Q. |

DIM%   INT%

DIM-I INT-I
DIM-E INT-E
DIM-S INT-S

+ − ±

p   D.I.   A.I.%

Part II — "S. Q."

a	b	c	d	e	f	g	h	i	j	k	l	m	n	o	p	q	r
E	S	S	E	E	I	E	S	S	I	I	I	E	I	E	I	S	S
6	9	10	11	13	5	17	16	12	4	1	18	2	14	8	15	3	7

| DIF | DIM | INT | DIS | S. Q. |

DIM%   INT%

DIM-I INT-I
DIM-E INT-E
DIM-S INT-S

+ − ±

p   D.I.   A.I.%

(1) $\frac{SQ}{VQ} = \_\_\_ = \_\_\_ BQ_{r1}$

$\frac{SQ+VQ}{2} = \frac{\_\_\_}{2} = \_\_\_ BQ_{a1}$

(2) $\frac{SQ}{VQ} = \_\_\_ = \_\_\_ BQ_{r2}$

$\frac{SQ+VQ}{2} = \frac{\_\_\_}{2} = \_\_\_ BQ_{a2}$

(3) $BQ_{r1} \times BQ_{a1} = \_\_\_ CQ_1$

$BQ_{r2} \times BQ_{a2} = \_\_\_ CQ_2$

RESEARCH CONCEPTS
A DIVISION OF TEST MAKER, INC.
1368 East Airport Road
Muskegon, Michigan 49444

PRINTED IN U.S.A.

©Instituto Axiometrico A.C. 1973
©Instituto Axiometrico A.C. 1973
Patent pending

HVP-4

From <u>General Evaluation Report - Axioscope</u>

Meaning of Selected Scores

Your scores show, in theory, the extent to which you have developed so far your capacity to value - both when considering the value outside situations, and when considering your own value as a person.

The interpretations of what your scores mean are based entirely on a formal theory of axiological values. (They do not compare your scores with those of any group of people.)[1]

You may be able to increase your capacity to value through appropriate effort (unless it is already very well developed). In addition, you probably can increase the effectiveness with which you make use of your present capacity to value.

"VQ" CAPACITY FOR VALUATION
An indice of the development of the capacity to value the outside world accurately. The number indicates the quantity or the capacity. (Axiological Index).

"SQ" CAPACITY FOR SELF-VALUATION
An indice of the development of the capacity to value oneself accurately as a person. The number indicates the quantity or the capacity. (Axiological Index).

"CQ" CAPACITY FOR COMBINE VALUATION
Your combine capacities to value in the outside world and within yourself, and measured by the value scale you have set yourself in this test.

"DIM-%" DIMENSION PERCENTAGE
Development of the awareness of the reality of the world and the reality of one's own self. (Existential Index) A "poor" score means rich imagination.

"INT-%" INTEGRATION PERCENTAGE
Development of the capacity for organizing one's reactions when confronted with problems in the world and within oneself. (Psychological Index).

"RHO" RANK ORDER CORRELATION COEFFICIENT
A score based on your valuation numbers (ranks) in comparison to a perfect test sequence of valuation numbers.

"AI%"
The AI percentage indicates your positive or negative attitude toward the world or toward one's self. This indice is based on the sums of overvaluation and disvaluation (Attitude Index).

"DIM-I" INTRINSIC DIMENSION
Development of the capacity to discern individuality in others and individuality in oneself. (Capacity for personal valuation, development of the sense of individuality).

"DIM-E" EXTRINSIC DIMENSION
Development of the capacity to discern values in situations in the outside world and in one's own role in the world. (Capacity for practical valuation).

"DIM-S" SYSTEMIC DIMENSION
Development of the capacity of discern system and order in the world and within oneself. (Capacity for theoretical and normative [moral] valuation; for organization and self-organization.)

"DIF" DIFFERENTIATION
Development of the general capacity to judge within oneself. This is one's capacity to size up all three value aspects within oneself: the personal, the practical, and the abstract.

"DIF_1-DIF_2"
Your maturity is measured by the extent to which you make use of your actual value capacity in comparison to your potential value capacity.

[1] Hartman, R. S. <u>The Structure of Value:</u> University of Southern Illinois Press, Carbondale, IL, 1967.

Practical Application of a Value Test[13]

The test may be particularly useful for the following purposes:

In the case of young people, the test shows up not only their general capacity but also their valuational strengths and weaknesses, as well as the value dimensions in which they are particularly gifted. The test thus may serve as a complement to interest, aptitude, personality and other value tests. To help students to learn how to think axiologically, the test will in many instances, aid them in recognizing that there are values that promote learning success.

In the case of executives, the results of the test may serve to channel activities both of themselves and their associates in the direction of their particular valuational strength, and thus to increase their decision-making capacities. It may serve to check activities incompatible with the test results.

In the case of groups, the test shows up the compatibility and incompatibility of the individuals in it and provides a number of classifications comparing individuals in their various functions within the group.

Due to the mathematical nature of the scores and the operations possible with them, groups themselves can be measured as to their homogeneity or non-homogeneity, and intangibles such as "group morale", "group spirit", etc., can be exactly defined and determined.

In the case of matching people, as mates, partners, associates, collaborators, and in all cases of teamwork, the test will indicate compatible and incompatible value patterns. Interpersonal compatibility is the primary basis for positive relationships.

In the case of mental health prevention, the test may help to discover potential suicides and other emotional and intellectual disorders before actual symptoms appear. More recent studies have revealed the value patterns of different types of criminals, i.e. pedophiliacs, atychals, etc.

The test also shows a definite pattern for accident proneness which should be useful for insurance companies, pilot training, etc.

In the case of psychotherapy, psychoanalysis, etc., the test, when given at the first session with the patient, indicates the strengths and weaknesses of the person and thus gives an initial guide for the direction of treatment. Given periodically, it will pinpoint the results of the treatment.

The healthy person who does not require counseling or psychotherapy yet desires new meaning in his life, can be helped by the test to revise and reorder his values. This process is called Axiotherapy. Axiotherapy is similar to other value-directed therapies, such as Logotherapy and Rational Emotive Therapy.

It is obvious that clinical interpretation of the test goes beyond the axiological into the psychological and psychiatric field. This is based on the fact that the valuation capacity is a function of both one's emotional and intellectual organization.

Due to the formal nature of axiology, the interpretation of the scores is not bound to any psychological school but may be made in terms of any psychological theory. While, thus, every psychological school will have its own contribution to make to the clinical interpretation of the test, those psychologies directed toward values will be the most adequate for the full clinical understanding of the data provided by the test. Among these are existential and Being psychologies (Binswanger, Frankl, Rollo May, Maslow), phenomenological psychologies (Merleau-Ponty, Gurwitsch, Erwin Straus) and comprehensively based psychopathologies (Jaspers).

An interesting book, titled <u>Consultation</u> by Blake and Mouton has some parallel ideas with axiological theory. The book encompasses all recognizable forms of counseling, advising, consulting, etc. into a systematic and coherent framework that permits the similarities and differences in assumptions that undergird alternative systems of counseling and consultation to be identified and evaluated.

Blake and Mouton state that

> based upon applying the perspective of searching out comprehensive patterns, we discovered five basically different approaches to counseling and consultation with examples, including: 1) acceptant (Rogers, Roethlisberger, Moustakas, Axline, Gibb); 2) Catalytic (Shein, Super, Bennis, Bird, Kaplan); 3) Confrontational (Ellis, Argyris, Levinson, Ezriel); 4) Prescriptive (Glasser, Kaplan, Herman, Wolpe, Wolpin, Moreno, Perls); and 5) Theory-Oriented (Byrne, Bach, McGregor, Kilert, Haley, Blake and Mouton).

With this rationale it is evident that the research potential for investigating counseling and consultation theory is substantial. To illustrate the parallel of value measurement with the five different counseling and consultation approaches we offer the following comparison.

Value Level	Counseling Approach
Intrinsic - Personal	Acceptant
	Catalytic
Extrinsic - Social	Confrontational
	Prescriptive
Systemic - Organizational	Theory - Orientated

In a very thorough manner, Hartman described applications of I, E, S, on a broad plane. The following chart[14] illustrates his thinking:

APPLICATION TO	INTRINSIC VALUE	EXTRINSIC VALUE	SYSTEMIC VALUE
Individual Persons	Ethics	Psychology	Physiology, Jurisprudence of "Person"
Groups of Persons	Political Science, Social Ethics	Sociology	Law of Persons and Institutions
Individual Things	Aesthetics	Economics	Technology
Groups of Things	Science of Civilization	Ecology	Industrial Technology, Civil Engineering, Games, Law of Property, Ritual
Concepts	Metaphysics	Epistemology	Logic
Words	Poetry, Literary Criticism	Rhetoric, Semantic, Linguistic Analysis	Grammar, Theory of Communication

Value Testing and Research

Much research has been completed in the value field which is based on theories that are both philosophical and/or scientific. With competing theories and tests, i.e., the Study of Values; Rokeach Value Survey; Kohlberg Moral Maturity Stages; Lafferty Life Styles Inventory; Hall-Tonna Inventory of Values; along with many other value, interest and personality tests it is not surprising that value testing and axiological research is on the rise.

More specifically, this writer and many others have conducted research with the Hartman Value Profile instruments. These studies have been reported on at the Annual Conferences of the R. S. Hartman Institute for Formal and Applied Axiology at the University of Tennessee in Knoxville. Hartman's papers are also at the University in a special collection at the James Hoskins Library. Bibliography and reference lists will be found at the end of the present article and at the end of this book. Information about the R. S. Hartman Institute for Formal and Applied Axiology may be obtained by writing to the Institute at 816 McClung Tower, University of Tennessee, Knoxville, TN 37996-0480.

Doctoral dissertations can be obtained from University Microfilms, North Zeeb Road, Ann Arbor, Michigan (see References). Information about the purchase of the HVP tests along with research findings, can be obtained from the publisher, Research Concepts, a Division of Test Maker, Inc., 1368 Airport Road, Muskegon, Michigan 49444. The Research Concepts studies are based on the following populations: elementary gifted students; high school Honor Society members; school dropouts - pushouts; adult community college students; a count jail population; senior citizens, teachers;

administrators; and school psychologists. These studies for the most part demonstrate construct validity which involves a battery of value tests for comparison and correlations purposes. Business applications and consultation with the HVP and other measures are available from the associated firms of Value Measurement Technologies and Human Synergistics which can be contacted through Research Concepts in Muskegon.

In working with people and in gaining experience with the HVP Axiogram and Axiograph, Robert Hartman found that development of certain selected value capacities were very evident. Much of his insight and understanding was an outcome of his work in a consultant capacity with leaders and mangers in business and industry. Accordingly he developed a procedure whereby these selected value capacities could be illustrated. The title, "General Evaluation Report - Axioscope," describes an instrument which may be used in several different ways to help a person develop and improve value awareness. A manual and special scoring forms will soon be available for the Application of the "General Evaluation Report - Axioscope." This instrument, (prepared by Richard Clarke and the author, and currently in press) will have an important impact for training and human resource development.

Concluding Remarks and Discussion

Value science is still very much a pioneering effort. Value experts, i.e., "Axiologists," or practitioners of axiological science, are not yet to be found in the yellow pages of the phone book. This does not mean that people are not making value decisions, they are just as they always have been and always will be, for to be human is to value. However, value capacity in individuals differs from the most sane sensible, and humane level to the most insane, fiendish, and inhumane level that one can imagine. Value preference, value judgment and value decision making in both positive and negative frames all are related to capacity and knowledge. Hartman (1967) illustrates the rationality of value by pointing out that

> I can value a thing only if I know its name and its properties. That this is true is confirmed by the fact that when we want to value something precisely, we call in an expert. The difference between him and us is that he knows more about the thing than we do. Thus knowledge and valuation go hand in hand.

Because knowledge about value has not been treated in an orderly way expert valuation about value is not recognized as being apparent and possible. Consequently we are short on value scientists and each person has to serve as his or her own value philosopher without a rational standard against which to compare his or her expertise, wisdom, and achievement. If we liken value science to behavioral science and health science, we can establish a perspective and an expectation of what can come to be. Health knowledge has developed so that individuals can learn much about their own health and can act in a rational manner on the basis of scientific facts and principles. Also, specialized health knowledge and assistance can be obtained from a large number of health consultants and experts. Behavioral knowledge, though lacking the scientific range and depth of the health sciences, nevertheless is developing in a meaningful way. Thus it is possible for individuals to learn much about their own behavior and the behavior of others on a logical basis. Just as in the case of the health field, a variety of specialists can be consulted. It is our expectation that as the value sciences develop, they will parallel the health and behavioral sciences. Knowledge about value will be open to learning; and just as individuals learn about health and behavior, they will also be able to learn about value. Such knowledge will enable people to be more human and moral in their valuations. As for the value specialist in your future, Hartman points out that he (or she) will be

> neither a saint nor a fiend specializing in value exercises; he has no commitment to a particular way of life of which value exercises are a part; he values like anybody else. And it may well be that, when the science of valuation is as fully developed as is the science of medicine (health science), the axiologist, if there is something wrong with his valuing, will need to consult a colleague.[15]

NOTES

1. Robert S. Hartman, The Structure of Value: Foundations of Scientific Axiology. Carbondale: Southern Illinois University Press, 1967, p. 68.

2. Robert S. Hartman, "Axiology as a Science," Journal of Human Relations. Wilberforce, Ohio: Central State University, 1973, p. 32.

3. From Hartman, The Structure of Value, Figure 14, Secondary Value Combinations, pp. 272-73, with revisions by Austin, 1990.

4. Hartman, "Axiology as a Science", pp. 35-39.

5. Robert S. Hartman, The Hartman Value Profile (HVP): Manual of Interpretation. Muskegon, MI: Research Concepts, 1973, pp. 37-38.

6. Hartman, The Structure of Value, p. 127.

7. Ibid., pp. 293-295.

8. Ibid., pp. 297-299.

9. Statements in this section are mainly from Hartman, The Structure of Value, pp. 293-302, and Hartman, The Hartman Value Profile (HVP): Manual of Interpretation, pp. 26-34.

10. Robert S. Hartman, The Hartman Value Profile (HVP): Manual of Interpretation, p. 26.

11. Statement in this section are mainly from Hartman, The Hartman Value Profile (HVP): Manual of Interpretation, pp. 26, 34, 41-42, 61-62.

12. Statements in this section are mainly from Hartman, The Hartman Value Profile (HVP): Manual of Interpretation, pp. 41-42, 61-62. Studies cited are available from the Hartman Papers, Special Collections, The James Hoskins Library, University of Tennessee, Knoxville.

13. Statements in this section are mainly from Hartman, The Hartman Value Profile (HVP): Manual of Interpretation, pp. 42-43.

14. Hartman, The Structure of Value, p. 311.

15. Ibid, p. 7.

REFERENCES

Acquaviva, Gary, "Evaluation Analysis (SEA) Value Questionaire," 1982, Selective Evaluators Associates, Inc., P. O. Box 771, Morristown, TN 37814.

Adair, Norman and Austin, John J., "The Interpersonal Check List - IBM Form," 1966, Research Concepts, Muskegon, Michigan.

Allport, G. W., Vernon, P. E., and Lindzey, G., Manual for Study of Values: A Scale for Measuring the Dominant Interests of Personality," 1970, Houghton Mifflin, Boston.

Austin, John J. and Lafferty, J., and Clayton, "Ready or Not? The School Readiness Checklist," 1963, Rev. 1988, Research Concepts, 1368 Airport, Muskegon, MI 49444.

Austin, John J., Educational Evaluation: A Handbook for the Educational Evaluation form, 1964, Research Concepts, Muskegon, MI, 49444.

Austin, John J., "School Psychology As A Value Science?," 1972, The School Psychology Digest, Vol. 1, No. 1, National Association of School Psychologists, Washington, D.C.

Austin, John J., and Van Arkel, Clyde, Muskegon County Jail Rehabilitation Program: An Evaluation, 1973, Muskegon Publish Schools, Muskegon, MI.

Austin, John J., "The Hartman Value Profile (HVP): A Review of Applied Research and Future Applications," 1975, Interdisciplinary Value Conference Proceedings, American Society for Value Inquiry, Florida State University.

Austin, John J., "The Behavioral Check List," 1975, Research Concepts, Muskegon, MI.

Austin, John J., and Garwood, Barbara A., "The Relationship of the Hartman Value Profile (HVP), Rokeach Value Survey (RVS), Allport-Vernon-Lindzey Study of Values (AVL) and Kohlberg's Theory of Moral Development (KMD)," 1976, National Association of School Psychologists Convention, Cincinnati, OH.

Austin, John J., "Values That Promote Learning," 1985, R. S. Hartman Institute for Formal and Applied Axiology Annual conference, University of Tennessee, Knoxville, TN.

Austin, Joyce E., Social Learning, 1981, Grand Valley State College, Allendale, MI.

Baez, Victor, The Valuing Process and Social Work Practice; A Correlational Study, 1986, University of Denver.

Binet, Alfred & Simon, Th., The Development of Intelligence in Children, 1916 Williams & Wilkins Co., Baltimore, MD.

Blake, Robert & Mouton, Jane, Consultation, 1976 Addison-Wesley, Reading, MA.

Carpenter, Wayne, "Sales Profile I & II," Value Resources Group, Inc., 7400 Dunaway Drive, Nashville, TN 37221.

Carter, Robert, Dimensions of Moral Education, 1985, University of Toronto Press.

Davis, John W., Value and Individuality; An Inquiry Into the Worth of the Human Person, 1959, Doctoral Dissertation, Emory University.

Davis, John W., Value and Valuation: Axiological Essays in Honor of Robert S. Hartman, 1971, University of Tennessee Press, Knoxville.

Ellis, A., & Harper, R.A., A Guide to Rational Living, 1961, Prentice-Hall, Englewood Cliffs, NJ.

Ellis, Albert, "Psychotherapy and the Value of a Human Being," pp. 117-140 in Value and Valuation; Davis, John W., ed., 1971, University of Tennessee Press, Knoxville.

Forrest, Frank G., Management Development Today, 1986, Valuemetrics, Inc., 2828 N. Atlantic Avenue, Dayton Beach, FL 32018.

Fujimoto, Takahashi, Science and Formal Axiology: The Philosophy of Robert S. Hartman, 1964, Tetsugaku-Zassi, Tokyo.

Hajduga, Jolanta (Polish Translator), "Ocena Wartoscjowa Hartmana - The Hartman Value Profile - Polish Research Versions," 1987, Research Concepts, Muskegon, MI.

Hall, Brian P., The Genesis Effect, 1986, Paulist Press, 997 MacArthur Blvd., Mahwah, NJ 07430.

Hall, Brian P., and Tonna, Benjamin, Hall-Tonna Inventory of Values, 1987, Behaviordyne, Inc., 994 San Antonio Rd., Palo Alto, CA 94303-0997.

Hartman, Robert S., Can Field Theory Be Applied to Ethics?, 1946, Doctoral Dissertation, Northwestern University.

Hartman, Robert S. & Cardenas, Mario Trigos, "The Hartman Value Inventory," 1966, Rev. 1973, Research Concepts, Muskegon, MI.

Hartman, Robert S., The Structure of Value: Foundations of Scientific Axiology, 1967, Southern Illinois University Press, Carbondale, IL.

Hartman, Robert S., The Hartman Value Profile (HVP): Manual of Interpretation, 1973, Research Concepts, Muskegon, MI.

Hartman, Robert S. and Cardenas, Mario Trigos, "Inventario De Valores Hartman (H.V.I.), Spanish Version," 1973, available from Research Concepts, Muskegon, MI.

Hartman, Robert S., "Axiology As A Science," 1973, Journal of Human Relations, Central State University, Wilberforce, OH.

Hartman, Robert S., "The Hartman Value Profile - Pictorial Form, rev. ed.," 1973, Research Concepts, Muskegon, MI.

Hino, Tom (French Translator), "Le Profile De Valeur Hartman - The Hartman Value Profile - French Research Versions," 1986, Research Concepts, Muskegon, MI.

Jastak, J. F., "Intelligence Tests and Personality Structure," in J. Zubin & G. Jervis (eds.), Psychopathology Mental Development, 1967, Grune & Stratton, New York, NY.

Katz, Marvin C., The Philosophy of Robert S. Hartman, 1966, Doctoral Dissertation, Southern Illinois University.

Kohlberg, Lawrence, <u>Moral Judgment Interview and Procedures for Scoring Al & Bl</u>, 1973, Moral Education and Research Foundation, Larsen Hall, Harvard University, Cambridge, MA.

Lafferty, J. Clayton, <u>Values that Defeat Learning</u>, 1963 Edison Institute, Dearborn, MI.

Lafferty, J. Clayton, <u>Life Styles Inventory: Self Description</u>, 1970, Human Synergistics, 33819 Plymouth Rd., Plymouth, MI.

Leary, Timothy, <u>Interpersonal Diagnosis of Personality</u>, 1957, Ronald Press, New York, NY.

Levin, Luce, and Lafferty, J. Clayton, "The Measurement of Self Concept in Kindergarten Children," 1967, Research Concepts, Muskegon, MI.

Martin, Edward C., "The Management Instrument," 1989, Evaluation Systems, Inc., 161 Belle Forest Circle, Suite 207, Nashville, TN 37221.

Maslow, A. H., <u>The Farther Reaches of Human Nature</u>, 1971, Viking Press, New York, NY.

Masonis, Edward J., <u>A Preliminary Study of Several Measures of School Psychologists' Background, Achievement and Performance</u>, Broadened Perspectives in School Psychology, NASP, Washington, D.C., 1972.

McClelland, David C., <u>The Achieving Society</u>, 1961, D. Van Nostrand Co., Princeton, NJ.

Mefford, David, "HVP The Hartman Value Profile," 1983, Combined Version HVP & HVPII, Value Measurement Technologies, Inc., 1811 Riverside Drive, Knoxville, TN 37915.

Mefford, David, "The Hartman Value Profile (HVP) Vocational Version," 1972, 1982, Value Measurement Technologies, Knoxville, TN.

Mefford, Vera (German Translator) "Das Hartman Wert Profil - The Hartman Value Profile - German Research Versions," 1972, rev. 1987, Value Measurement Technologies, Knoxville, TN.

Moore, G. E., <u>Principia Ethica</u>, 1903, London.

Murray, H. A., Explorations in Personality, 1938, Oxford University Press, New York, NY.

Rokeach, Milton, The Rokeach Value Survey, 1967, Halgren Tests, 873 Persimmon, Sunnyvale, CA.

Rokeach, Milton, Beliefs, Attitudes and Values, 1968, Jossey-Boss, San Francisco, CA.

Rokeach, Milton, The Nature of Human Values, 1973, Free Press, New York, NY.

Rokeach, Milton, Understanding Human Values Individual and Societal, 1979, Free Press, New York, NY.

Schildt, Jr., Evert, "Pro-Evaluator - Swedish Version & English Version," 1983, Evaluator AB, Box 3534, Centralvagen 28, S-18303 Taby, Sweden.

Schultz, W. C., Firo-A Three Dimensional Theory of Interpersonal Behavior,1958, Holt, Rinehart & Winston, Inc., New York, NY.

Sepeshy, Michael L., Values and the School Dropout, 1978, Michigan State University, East Lansing, MI.

Shostrom, E. L., Man, the Manipulator, 1967, Abingdon Press, Nashville, TN.

Spranger, E., Types of Men, 1928, Halle (Saale) Max Niemeyer Verlag, Germany. (O.P. Books, Xerox University Microfilms, Ann Arbor, MI).

Terman, Lewis, M., Intelligence of School Children, 1919, Houghton Mifflin, Boston, MA.

Terman, Lewis M. and Merrill, Maud A., Stanford-Binet Intelligence Scale, 1960, Houghton Mifflin Co., Boston, MA.

Chapter XIII

PSYCHOLOGY AND VALUE THEORY

Leon Pomeroy and Arthur R. Ellis

Introduction

Progress in most disciplines is advanced when some individual seizes with unusual force an idea! The idea or concept of value is at once the most important and least understood in the field of psychology. In this assertion we are in complete agreement with Milton Rokeach (1975) who devoted most of his professional career to the study of values. Professor Rokeach, a psychologist, belongs to the tradition of pioneers like Allport et. al. (1958), Piaget (1932), Kohlberg (1963), Morris (1956), Smith (1961), and Maslow (1965). All studied values--terminal (ends) values and instrumental (means) values and their developmental aspects. Such an approach was largely academic, having limited clinical relevance; and the authors are writing from a clinical perspective primarily.

It was left to a relatively obscure philosopher by the name of R. S. Hartman, Ph.D. (1967) to seize with unusual force the idea of value in a manner that made a difference for the first time in the history of philosophy and psychology. Hartman's discovery of formal axiology has by now inspired a following in psychology that includes: Krojanker (1971), Roquet (1978), Schildt (1978), Austin (1977, 1983), Ellis (1971, 1978) and Pomeroy (1982a, 1982b, 1982c, 1983a, 1983b, 1983c, 1983d, 1983e, 1984a, 1984b, 1984c, 1985a, 1985b, 1985c, 1985d, 1985e, 1985f, 1985g, 1985h, 1986, 1987, 1989, 1990a, 1990b, 1990c, 1990d, 1990e).

Psychology is a discipline that plays a meaningful role in many fields of human endeavor including mental health and peace making and conflict resolution at a global level. It is a field that has aimed to become a science of human behavior; but it remains a pre-scientific discipline like its sister disciplines of sociology, economics, political science, etc. In our view, it is through the assimilation of and integration with Hartman's formal axiology that psychology will emerge as a science. The basic problem areas in psychology that stand to benefit the most from formal axiology are those areas where efforts sponsored by natural science have failed, the so called soft areas of clinical and personality or humanistic studies. Pomeroy and Davis (1982a) have discussed such a synthesis which they have termed <u>behavioral axiology</u>. This new orientation in psychology is both a valuemetric oriented psychometrics and a valuecentric oriented cognitive behavioral theory and practice for clinical psychology.

Historical attempts at a rigorous study of personal and clinical issues in psychology have drawn largely upon learning theory concepts and practices. This approach missed the uniqueness and individuality of the person and was never fashionable among clinicians treating patients.

Much is at stake in the evolution of psychology as a future science, for it is a field that plays an important role in our civilization. A behavioral axiology with a command of a moral science or value science offers much to the mental health movement and to the larger picture of inter-national relations where a moral logic having the universality of a mathematics will contribute much to cross cultural communication and peace making efforts (Pomeroy, 1985b). A behavioral axiology could go far in filling the gap left by present systems of law and discourse. The need is obvious to all who follow current events and to writers like C. P. Snow (1959) who discusses at length the unhealthy emergence of two intellectual cultures in the face of our preeminent natural science revolution that creates people who can not speak to each other and specialists who can not apply natural science methods to human behavior.

In his writings, Hartman has wisely drawn an historical parallel that speaks volumes--namely that natural philosophies like alchemy and astrology evolved into natural sciences like chemistry and astronomy respectively, while the moral philosophy of the ancients has remained moral philosophy, having failed to evolve into a moral or value science discipline. High tech material culture and low tech moral culture might be seen as a "time bomb" for our civilization, and C. P. Snow (1959) devoted much of his professional life as a writer to an analysis and discussion of this problem.

Albert Speer (1981), commenting as an insider on Hitler's War, has observed the human condition as follows:

> When I look back today, the image of a romantic and also cruel and ruthless world rises before me--romanticism in its unruliness and wildness, not in its pleasant ... Gemutlichkeit. I am reminded of the religious siege of Munster during the time of the Anabaptists. In both eras, I see a blend of romantic notions of salvation, cruelty, religious selfishness taken to bizarre and peculiar extremes, self-sacrifice and brutality, excessive obedience and dilettantism. This blend produced a society that drove a sixteenth-century Westphalian town to the verge of ruin and plunged the twentieth-century world into chaos.

This commentary by Albert Speer is replete with examples of moral distortions and implicates disvaluation in the most serious of human activities that include war, pillage, death and destruction. Clearly a moral compass is a difference that makes a difference!

Jay Newman (1986) writing as a contemporary philosopher in Canada, and concerned about moral questions, has commented at length on the moral chaos of today. He cites the disvaluation of disturbances in commitment as producing fanaticism and hypocrisy and urges us to look at such problems as disturbances in moral reasoning rather than just jumping to classical psychological analysis. His writings have convinced us that moral dynamics (value dynamics) and psychodynamics must both be studied and that they cannot be separated; for, moral problems are pre-clinical disturbances that can evolve into clinical signs and symptoms of the sort psychologists catalogue in their diagnostic manuals, from character disorders to the psychoses.

Given the importance of values to the optimal integration of the human mind, we are also convinced that renewed attention must be given the "mass mind," "collective mind" or "zeitgeist." In this age of planetary consciousness, we might even coin the expression personagaia in this regard, based on the concept of "gaia" designating a "organismic earth" or "living earth" that humankind would better attempt to preserve and not merely exploit. Personagaia would serve to designate the collective mind or mass mind of humans living on the earth. At this stage of human evolution, it is not all that homogeneous; but among the intelligentsia of the earth there exists a personagaia or mass mind whose moral structure and dynamics shape individual mental lives! Thus Newman has encouraged us to look beyond provincial psychodynamics and consider moral dynamics in their own right, and we would add from our experience that we had better add the "mass mind" or personagaia as well; for it is the "mother" of all minds and is implicated in individual integration and mental health.

Hartman's formal axiology and the initial behavioral axiology integration of Pomeroy and Davis (1982) offer a powerful tool to bridge the current gap between the "mass mind" and the moral dynamics and psychodynamics of individual minds. In short the field of psychology stands to benefit from formal axiology in the near future and especially in its humanistic subdisciplines, such as personality and clinical. Indeed, clinicians in search of a science have found a science in the body of Hartman's work!

As for contemporary psychology, it is made up of many subdisciplines including: learning theory, emotion and motivation, sensation and perception, physiological, psychophysics, cognitive science, behavior modification, self theory, personality theory, assorted clinical orientations, cross cultural psychology, psychological anthropology, psychogenetics, psychopharmacology, psycholinguistics, psychonutrition, computer simulation, information theory, signal detection theory, psychology of religions, history of psychology, to list a few. The relevance of formal axiology to these subdisciplines will vary. However, value orientations can change physiological thresholds as shown by the data of psychophysics as well as change the levels of some blood chemistry variables (e.g., cholesterol) as shown by the work of Pomeroy et. al. (1985a, 1983c): thus, even the natural science areas, the "hard" areas of psychology would be expected to exhibit some axiological impact. It goes without saying that the so called "soft" areas of psychology are ripe for advancement through the applications of formal axiology.

An Historical Note

The history of psychology is the story of a struggle to separate from its "mother" discipline of philosophy. In this attempt to become a scientific enterprise, psychology adopted the model of the natural sciences in general and physics in particular. Psychology made extensive studies, much as Hartman did, of the scientific method. Insofar as it was dealing with the material body and brain this model worked; but insofar as it was dealing with the mind and behavior (soft areas), this model failed miserably! B. F. Skinner (1957) at Harvard captured the spirit of post WWII psychology in his operant conditioning laboratory study of pigeons and learning theory. Skinner was famous for his frequently expressed view that concepts like value, mind, emotions, personality, attitude, belief were all "mentalistic" and not worthy of scientific study. How would you expect clinicians to react to this? Well they revolted! In their frustration with such academic psychology and posturing they escaped into fields known as Psychoanalysis, Rogerian, Gestalt, Rational-

Emotive Psychosynthesis and Logotherapies. There emerged two cultures in psychology analogous to the two cultures precipitated by the broader natural science revolution about which C. P. Snow (1959) wrote at length. The political pressures within the psychological community mounted, and the clinical right hand did not know what the scientific left hand was doing! There was no language to bridge the gap between the clinician's world of practical experience with needs and patient care, and the behavioral "scientist's" world of studying mechanisms employing natural science models. These forces nearly split the American Psychological Association during a period when it had an impressive new building in Washington, D. C. from which to lobby government policies. The clinicians were a large percentage of membership in APA and brought in the money, and as a consequence a peace of sorts came about. Other evolutionary forces came into play so that the subdisciplines continued to evolve.

The politics of organizational psychology in this large country with many state, city and private university departments of psychology has given the field a great North American impetus unmatched the world over. This center of psychological thought has captured an international imagination, following and leadership; but the field has not come to any significant unification and integration as a science. The distinction of "hard" and "soft" areas is still hotly debated, giving rise to two conflicting intellectual cultures within the field paralleling the two cultures C. P. Snow writes about as afflicting human thought generally in the wake of the natural science revolution already mentioned. The two cultures within psychology amount to clinical vs. experimental traditions emerging within a pre-scientific discipline. The remedy here, as in the broader world of C. P. Snow's interest, will not be found in plumbing the depths of natural science discoveries, but, rather in the pursuit of a revolutionary new model of human thought--namely the formal axiology of Hartman as integrated with psychology and known after Pomeroy and Davis (1982a), Pomeroy (1985b) and Pomeroy and Bishop (1990a, 1990b) as <u>behavioral axiology</u>. The pursuit of this new orientation in psychology makes a scientific study of the "soft" clinical areas possible. It is hoped that this beginning will inspire future interdisciplinary efforts to further integrate psychology and formal axiology in the years ahead towards the achievement of a scientific psychology of natural science oriented brain studies and axiologically oriented mind studies.

How receptive is psychology to such a synthesis? Is the field ready for the inclusion of moral and value studies on a much deeper and broader scale? We have already noted how the concept of value is at once the single most important concept in psychology and the least understood and studied! This was the view of Milton Rokeach (1975), a psychologist of considerable stature in value studies, and the view held by the authors. From this does it follow that the field has any special receptivity to value studies? Bearing on this question is Pomeroy's (1982) invited paper presented before the Annual Meeting of the American Psychological Association at Anaheim, California entitled: "A Psychologist Looks at Morality." While nearly 18,000 psychologists were attending that meeting, fewer than twenty showed up for this paper. In the discussion period that followed, the view was offered that perhaps it was the word "morality" that turned psychologists off, that this concept seemed so old fashioned; and the clinical relevance of moral reasoning seemed largely to escape them! Even Newman (1986), already cited for his fresh new approach to moral studies, is not at all clear in his thinking about moral dynamic and psychodynamic interactions and the progression of amoral processes into clinically recognizable signs and symptoms. It is not surprising that psychologists fail to appreciate the co-play and counter-play among moral dynamics, psychodynamics and biodynamics in the etiology of psychopathology. This multiplex interface is clearly the new frontier in mental health and demands a behavioral axiology approach and contribution along with more traditional approaches! Perhaps this interface marks the point in the discipline of psychology where formal axiology can offer its greatest contribution, illumination, and clarification. Few authors have written on this subject with any precision to date. Our raising the issue here at this time is likely breaking new ground or at least sounding a much needed corrective emphasis! Perhaps it is time for the 19th century concepts of moral psychology and acrasia to be re-examined in the light of behavioral axiology and the formal axiology foundations given us by the contemporary philosophy of Hartman. Clearly there is a 19th century precedent for such a new orientation in psychology at this time. This is long overdue in our view, and such an effort would do much to clarify the confusion surrounding how disvaluation, amoral reasoning, immoral behavior constitute a <u>preclinical issue</u> for clinical psychologists. We have here the conceptual foundations of a "preventive medicine" or "preventive psychology" in the sense of a health care rather than a sickness care approach to mental health issues!

Relevant Psychological Mechanisms

The Hartman Value Profile (HVP), including Pomeroy's (1982a, 1985a, 1990a, 1990b) interpretation and validation of this valuemetric instrument, is both a product of formal axiology and a test of formal axiology. This valuecentric, valuemetric profile of personality and clinical status is a bridge between Hartman's work in philosophy and our work in psychology. The HVP stands as a beacon illuminating formal axiology and its implications for behavioral studies and clinical therapeutics. This instrument, Hartman's best public relations tool, has drawn psychologists into closer examination of axiology and inspired some to take his work seriously. Most of Pomeroy et. al.'s (1982-1990) conference and published papers have been inspired by the Hartman Value Profile (HVP). These studies in turn have done much to validate the relevance of the HVP and its assumptions to psychological practice. What has emerged is a behavioral axiology which is a valuecentric, cognitive behavior theory, practice and orientation in psychology that challenges the field to take formal axiology seriously. Fortunately, the HVP has proven to be a powerful public relations event that draws the attention of psychologists oriented to belief systems, attitudes, and cognitive processes!

At this point let us review some relevant psychological mechanisms so as to locate a discussion of values in the field of psychology. At the outset let us affirm core cognitive processes known as the General Capacity to Value (GCV) that emerge from Hartman's work in axiology especially. These cognitive dynamics give rise to less than twenty instrumental (means) values and less than twenty terminal (ends) values. There appears to be a cognitive mapping of facts and values in the form of descriptive cognitive processes (DCP) and evaluative cognitive processes (ECP). The convergence of these two processes form belief structures which in turn give rise to attitude structures. A minimum of three attitudes are required to trigger emotion, motivation or behavior; and this is known as a kinetic attitude sum (KAS), of which we will have more to say.

Much as the human eye has a retina that works on the basis of three receptors to process the three primary colors so as to permit a perception of a rainbow of colors, so, too, the core evaluative cognitive processes (CECP) at the level of the GCV have three structural dimensions yielding a rainbow of perceived value richness in the world and in the self. Hartman designated these three dimensions of value as the Intrinsic (I), Extrinsic (E), and Systemic (S) dimensions of the GCV.

The dynamism among the I, E, S dimensions and their co-play and counter-play give rise to terminal and instrumental values that merge with descriptive cognitive processes, maps of facts, to produce beliefs which in turn produce attitudes that mediate final behavior. The final behavior is triggered by three or more attitudes coming together in a kinetic sum and consisting of attitudes towards an object (figure) designated the Ao, plus an attitude towards the context (ground) designated the Ac, and an attitude towards self in the moment designated as As. Thus, a superthreshold summation of $\underline{Ao}$ + $\underline{Ac}$ + $\underline{As}$ = behavioral, emotional, motivational consequence which is the end of a generative chain of events beginning with I, E, S dynamics in the GCV to belief formation to attitude formation, resulting in overt behavior. As previously noted, most value studies in the field of psychology have focused on terminal and instrumental values and their developmental aspects. Other studies have focused on attitudes. The concept of a General Capacity to Value (GCV) is thus a revolutionary new idea coming from Hartman's work and needs to be studied by psychologists. If present validity and reliability studies by Pomeroy and Davis (1982) etc. hold up under replication in the future, and we are confident they will, we will be well on the way to validating the GCV concept for broad psychological use and study. Indeed, much as we have an intellectual quotient (IQ) in psychology today we might expect to produce a moral quotient (MQ) in the future that would bear directly on issues of moral intelligence, moral reasoning, and mental health itself, if moral dynamics and psychodynamics are as closely interconnected with mental health issues as we have argued in this chapter.

The three governing or driving attitudes (Ao, Ac, As) come together in a fashion that a valuecentric cognitive science has yet to explain. Moreover, the Intrinsic, Extrinsic and Systemic dimensions of core valuation (GCV) obey balance theory, and hierarchical theory in what appears to be a naturalistic fashion--naturalistic in the sense that the selection pressures of biosocial and psychosocial evolution place a premium on axial (dimensional) balance and on a hierarchical ordering of $I > E > S$. Moreover, balance theory notes the premium placed on a relatively equality of the absolute value of I, E, S for "self" and "world" valuation. Any marked deviation from relative equality of test values for I, E, S points to "irritation" or conflict for the individual. Thus a balance and hierarchical subordination imperative appears to exist for naturalistic evolutionary reasons, and any deviations signal conflict and clinical signs and symptoms to the trained interpreter of the HVP. The HVP is a very sensitive detector of deviations from balance and hierarchy rules for the GCV intrinsic, extrinsic and systemic cognitive dimensions or the information processing axes! Further comment on the selection pressures of evolution shaping balance theory and hierarchical outcomes will be found in the next chapter in this volume by Pomeroy and Bishop dealing with cross cultural data employing the HVP.

Thus, formal axiology points to the existence of core evaluative cognitive processes capable of being assessed by the Hartman Value Profile (HVP) from which inferences and predictions of behavior and cognitive styles can be made. We have in the HVP a "Quick Test" of personality and clinical status that in skilled hands can lead to an action diagnosis readily translated into psychotherapy interventions, as well as a bridge between Hartman's formal axiology in the field of philosophy and the clinical concerns of psychologists who are in quite another discipline. In the future, it is hoped that parallel forms (PF) and specialized semantic forms (SSF) of the HVP will be studied in order to explore more deeply concepts like anger, anxiety, depression, self esteem, and Shapiro's (1965) "neurotic styles" such as the paranoid, the hysterical, the impulsive, the passive, the "weak character," as well as Shapiro's (1981) obsessive-compulsive, rigid character, sadistic, masochistic, and rigid personalities. We also need to know more about a growing clinical problem of dissociative personality disorders as discussed elsewhere by Pomeroy (1984a) and Pomeroy and Cirillo, (1985c). Application of the HVP, parallel forms, and targeted special forms (TSF) of the HVP are expected to add considerably to our understanding of these phenomena of "splitting" and "switching" of poorly integrated personalities. Our axiological assisted explorations of personality and clinical status have just begun, and much more work needs to be done to reach the status of a substantive behavioral axiology! This is a challenge to the future of a valuecentric cognitive behavior psychology, to valuemetric oriented psychometrics, as well as to valuecentric gestalt, psychoanalytic, logotherapy, rational-emotive therapy approaches. Indeed, the richness of axiology lies in its potential for productive use in any of the subdisciplines of psychology.

Further Considerations of Axiology and Psychology

The concept of "axiology" is defined in Webster's Dictionary as the branch of philosophy dealing with the nature and type of values--as in morals, aesthetics and religion. Formal axiology was conceived by R. S. Hartman, Ph.D., who stood on the "head and shoulders" of many philosophers including G. E. Moore, Edmund Husserl and the ancients. "Axiology" as value theory has been formally studied since Plato, and the terminological distinction of "formal axiology" is attributed to the German philosopher Edmund Husserl in 1903. Husserl, like others including Plato, Kant and Descartes had sought in vain to develop a value or moral science discipline or a formal logic of valuation or moral reasoning. Hartman's approach has succeeded where the others failed largely because of his knowledge of the history and philosophy of science and the more recent contributions of Moore and Russell. Hartman's system of formal axiology is a value system which is "consistent, universally applicable, and historically continuous" (Hartman, 1963; pp. 58-59). Formal Axiology applies mathematical set theory to property sets which make up all entities discriminated by human attentional processes (e.g., the Orienting Reflex of the Reticular Activating System of the brain stem and other attentional or focusing mechanisms). Discriminated properties are employed in all evaluative and descriptive cognitive maps or classifications.

The "value" of an entity is defined by Hartman as residing in the fulfillment of its concept or definition and in the perception of its concept fulfillment: i.e., the degree of correspondence between the properties of a thing (entity) and the properties which its concept defines for it. Therefore, the more of the concept's properties possessed by a given entity or thing, the more valuable it is, and the more it is said to possess the "good." What passes for the current "science" of psychology, as it now stands, is defined by the application of extrinsic (E) value concepts to persons. It has become obvious that the science of psychology cannot be defined by the extrinsic (E) dimension of valuation alone: human beings are not merely extrinsic things or "machines," and indeed they encompass nondenumerable and infinite numbers of properties. The order of complexity of a human being far exceeds anything subsumed under the heading of the extrinsic level of valuation. Psychology, as a science, must be approached in multidimensional value terms that include the extrinsic, systemic, and intrinsic orders of valuation to capture the richness of human properties possessed by persons. Extrinsic definition of human beings alone amounts to disvaluation of persons, treating them more as things or material objects and ignoring their uniqueness and individuality as well as spirituality. This can only be captured by an integrated and complex I, E, S valuation of the person.

Formal axiology offers the field of psychology a means of looking at how individuals structure their identities and lives in respect to the fundamental dimensions of value operating at the GCV level of cognitive processing. It offers psychology revolutionary new lenses with which to view the person and problems in living. The I-Lens, the E-Lens, and the S-Lens of axiology can provide psychology with fresh new perspectives that more deeply penetrate the humanistic and mental side of life ("soft" psychological areas) than do any of the existing conceptual approaches or test instruments. The optical metaphor is an ancient one that appears in the Bible and in early Greek literature and is an apt reference to how we struggle to see truths, to see or understand what makes us tick, so to speak! These dimensional lenses (I, E, S) of the General Capacity to Value (GCV) are powerful dimensions of the HVP having enormous clinical value and relevance.

Patterns of self or world valuation are immediately evident from the test result with the HVP, and patterns of balance and hierarchical distortion also communicate much information about an individual's life style, mind sets, and problems in living. This information assists in counseling the individual towards getting the good things in life for the person as judged by the person. Among psychology's expressed goals is that of helping the individual "unlock his or her potential." Formal axiology or behavioral axiology presents to us a structural analysis of one's capacity to value and the pattern of one's habitual evaluative habits in such a manner that one can gain a deeper self knowledge and understanding. Since knowledge is power, especially when it comes alive within us, and since the inscription "Know Thyself" has been inscribed on Greek Temples since ancient times and echoed in Biblical writings since, we can only assume that information provided axiologically about the individual will enrich his or her prospects for growth in the manner alluded to. We all may be said to possess a <u>moral compass</u>, and the better we see it and know it the better our chances for fulfillment; and axiologically based feedback can only enrich these possibilities. It is often remarked that mental health consists of: 1. Not being stuck anywhere; and 2. Being on friendly terms with our crazies (self defeating behavior.) Here it is easy to envision formal axiology as helping a person meet these criteria of mental health in the spirit of "knowledge is power." If we use the score card of pro-self vs. pro-social vs. anti-self vs. anti-social behavior in characterizing a human response, it also goes without saying that formal axiology is a source of personal information that can be expected to enhance the possibilities for pro-self and pro-social behavior by the same logic!

It is hoped that a systematic and integrated extrinsic, systemic and intrinsic study of individuals will overcome the limitations imposed by the historical accident of using natural science models instead of moral science models, e.g., the brain as computer, the sensory organs as electronic signal detection devices, emotions as chemistry, sexuality as hormones. Such natural science reductionism distorts our perception of the person. Indeed, the notion that "for every twisted thought there is a twisted molecule" is born of a psychology dominated by natural science influences. Originally psychoanalytic theory was dominated by the reductionism of hydraulic metaphors. Thus we see the possibilities for a revolution in psychology by simply changing its metaphors of physical science to metaphors of moral or value science!

In conclusion, formal axiology offers a clarifying dimensional analysis or structural analysis of thought, of valuation, of feeling, of behavior, of mental life so as to clarify our thinking about the basic realms of human existence: 1) the systemic realm giving us our sense of order, opinion, rules, regulations, the theoretical, the ideal; and 2) the intrinsic realm giving us a sense of the uniqueness of the individual and of the personal and spiritual; and 3) the extrinsic realm giving us a sense of the practical, social and material world around us. The cultivation of an expanded consciousness in and of these valuational dimensions can enrich the experiences of all of us regarding self and the world. This can contribute to more optimal and efficient adaptation and survival and the experience of a joy in living!

Apropos moral dynamics influencing psychodynamics, already cited in this chapter, we have examples in disturbed commitment. For example, hypocrisy and fanaticism are disturbances in moral dynamics generally and specifically in commitment processes. Greater attention to commitment can be expected to remedy the distortion and minimize the psychodynamic distortions that come to the attention of the psychotherapist at a cost to society. Hartman points out another example of disvaluation. Where the systemic dimension is greatly overvalued, the result is an individual like Adolph Eichman of Hitler's Germany. Eichman saw himself as a "transportation specialist;" and the fact that he transported thousands to their deaths was quite incidental to him and wholly oblivious to his conscience (Hartman, 1973, pp. 68-69). Eichman was also very <u>fanatical</u> as a result and so exhibited disturbances in commitment, as well as a violation of the hierarchical imperative: I > E > S! While we have not seen his HVP test results, it can only be assumed that the imperative of balance among the subdimensions of the GCV was violated as well. Thus we have a structured language to aid us in thinking about behavior that is at <u>the subclinical, moral stage of personal "disintegration."</u> Given time, even Eichman's interpersonal behavior would have suffered, and his immediate family would painfully feel it. Thus is envisioned the progression from moral dynamics to clinically disturbed psychodynamics in the case of Adolph Eichman!

It is not uncommon for clinicians to report mentally disturbed individuals as viewing and treating other persons as "things" and as thinking nothing at all of hurting such "things"! A psychopath or a malignant narcissist may approach this level of functioning at times. A schizophrenic may also exhibit this behavior. More and more, the inner cities are reporting this behavior in association with substance abuse. This is not a drug-effect, but, rather a person-effect, or rather a person-values effect! The drug is bringing out what is already there in the way of values, principles, beliefs! The inner city mass mind (subpersonagaia?) shapes values; and one of the consequences of this life style for the under classes is disvaluation of the person, and human life is cheapened in a way that shocks us all--an example of primary axial distortion! Such distortions at the axial level of valuation, at the core level, produce tragic consequences often mediated by unconscious processes without reality function checks and balances, effectively dissociating the amoral perception and allowing it to take on a "life of its own," so to speak! Such split, dissociated amoral perceptions are all the more dangerous in dissociated, low self esteem, fragmented, poorly integrated personalities of the sort that inhabit the inner cities and under classes. Obviously, moral dynamics should not be separated from psychodynamics; yet contemporary psychology and psychiatry do just that. One can modulate the other, and reciprocal amplification or inhibition can occur, changing the probability of violence and antisocial behavior towards self or others in any given moment. Perhaps it could be argued here that <u>moral dynamics</u> are a legitimate civic and public concern; whereas, psychodynamics are more a private, individual (doctor-patient) remedial concern. If so, public policies should be concerned about personagaia dynamics or the zeitgeist and should strive to cultivate improved "moral climates" more favorable to the mental health of communities and individuals. Ideology and issues of public and personal philosophical responsibility are raised here when the cultivation of a healthy "moral climate" is debated. Hence, the future debate will involve controversy and possibly the surrender of some individualism (See Pomeroy and Bishop, this volume) and freedom in accordance with the greatest good for the greatest number principle.

More socially acceptable versions of such axial distortions may be seen in "intrinsification" behavior where a proud owner of an automobile may speak of it as a "she" and relate in strangely human ways that personalize the object. Thus I, E, S distortions can be playful and internalized to varying degrees and exhibit varying degrees of social acceptability. There is a plasticity around the naturalistic hierarchical and balance principles that is exploited by the individual in personal survival strategies and ego investments. The plasticity of axial distortions adds to the complexity of our studies of the dimensional dynamics of the GCV. Presumably the level of consciousness of the individual varies in such "intrinsifications" (car owner) or pathological axial distortions (Eichman) such that the result can vary from "good fun" to "human tragedy." Thus we have cited examples of "intrinsification" "extrinsification" and "systemification" reflecting the idiosyncratic moral dynamic and psychodynamic behavior of individuals. This plastic tendency of axial distortions invites future studies. Here we see the opportunity for a rich interplay between axiologists and psychologists in the future study of human behavior. We are now at the frontier of a vast new adventure in human thought; and at stake is the development of psychology, along with other social sciences, as strong, authentic sciences.

Commentary on Research and Validation Studies

Most research relating to formal axiology has employed the Hartman Value Profile (HVP). Details regarding its use are contained in the Manual of Interpretation (Hartman, 1973). Use of the HVP was initiated in Mexico in the early 1960s, and introduction into the United States took place about 1966. Versions of the HVP have been produced in English, Spanish, German, Swedish, Hebrew, Japanese and Indonesian. Pomeroy is currently gathering Japanese data and translating the HVP into Russian. Rigorous development of translated versions requires back translations, and this control measure has not always been followed. Pomeroy and Bishop (1990d,e) offer cross cultural data involving a comparison of Mexico, Republic of Indonesia and the U.S.A. in the following chapter included in the present volume.

The Department of Mental Hygiene, Social Security Administration of Mexico has used the HVP, Spanish version, extensively; and these data have been used in validation studies for the Spanish test (Hartman, May 16, 1970).

Lohman (1968) found significant correlations between the Allport-Vernon-Lindzey Study of Values (AVL) but space does not permit a full presentation here.

Elliott (1969) performed a factor analytic study of the HVP which confirmed orthogonal separation of Parts I and II of the test as was intended by Hartman. She showed that Parts I and II are assessing different dimensions of valuation, "world" and "self" respectively, and that the test does what Hartman says it does. Pomeroy (1983b) performed a factor analytic study confirming Elliott's findings of orthogonality of Parts I and II of the HVP confirming Hartman's success in constructing an instrument that would assess world valuation and self valuation separately. Pomeroy (1983b) also found two additional dimensions characterized by DIM%-1 loading on Factor III and DIM%-2 loading on Factor IV, suggesting that the DIM% scores provide additional, independent measures from the other subscales. The percent of variance captured on Factors III and IV is small however, and more work needs to be done to interpret these findings. In general DIM% scores fail to load on most criterion scales from the MMPI, CMI, CAQ, PBI etc. The CAQ did show a tendency for the DIM% subscale to correlate with tough poise (TP) or what we might characterize as the "thick skin" defense style. Axiologists note this dimension as relating to "abuse of reason," "creativity," "lack of faith," "failure to face reality"; however, Pomeroy and Davis (1982) and other studies by Pomeroy have failed to show a significant pattern of criterion correlations that could define this dimension of the HVP with any precision. Its usefulness is guarded and limited at the present time; although, Hartman warns that a high DIM% invalidates the test--see the <u>Manual of Interpretation</u>! The overall impression is one of clean factor structures of the sort confirming Hartman's attempt to construct an instrument that reflects basically two dimensions of valuation: world and self objects; i.e., the test does what it is designed to do.

Krojanker (1971) used the HVP in psychotherapy with N = 300 cases. He compared the results of the HVP to those obtained from administration of the MMPI on the same cases. He found the HVP to be consistently useful as an adjunctive procedure in psychological testing for diagnostic purposes. He found the HVP to be even more beneficial as an evaluation of progress in psychotherapy when given periodically during the course of treatment--repeated measures or longitudinal application. Pomeroy (1982) has confirmed these findings in clinical practice. Repeated measures often reflect advance in some areas and regression in others in a see-saw fashion. Areas of resistance in therapy are identifiable, and areas of meaningful progress can also be spotted. For example, advances in extrinsic valuation may be bought initially at a price of lost intrinsic sensitivity or vice versa. The HVP profile can direct interventions and the timing of interventions by the clinical psychologist to achieve therapeutic goals, and it can be used to set such goals.

Pomeroy and Davis (1982a) carried the validation of the HVP even further in their study employing the MMPI, Cattell's CAQ, a Personal Belief Inventory (PBI), and an Index of Autolethality (AL). This study remains one of the most systematic and thorough validity studies of the HVP and a paper summarizing its findings was presented at the 1982 Annual Meeting of the Southeastern Psychological Association held at New Orleans, as well as published in the prestigious Proceedings of the Second International Conference on the Cattell 16PF by the Institute of Personality and Aptitude Testing at Champaign, Illinois, long known as one of the more prestigious centers for psychometric studies in the world then and now. The findings established once and for all the clinical relevance and validity of the HVP. The subscales measuring depression (AI%) correlated with the criterion depression scales at highly significant levels statistically ($p < .001$). The subscales measuring anxiety (INT%) correlated with the criterion anxiety scales at highly significant levels statistically ($p < .0001$). In general the pattern of significance was so great that the HVP had no trouble discriminating patients from students and even distinguished student profiles from doctor profiles included in the study. The HVP exhibited an exquisite sensitivity to valuational styles associated with these populations of students, patients, doctors, as well as correlating with criterion measures on the MMPI, CAQ, PBI and AL tests. Subsequent studies by Pomeroy et. al. (1985a, 1983b, 1985f) have established biomedical validation of the HVP; i.e., the INT% index of stress and anxiety correlated positively and significantly with cholesterol levels.

Ellis (1971) in a small scale pilot study at the Atlanta Employment, Evaluation and Service Center, a rehabilitation facility serving the physically, psychologically and socially handicapped, found an unusually high percentage of atychal cases (35%). "Atychal" refers to an inability to deal with the world effectively: the score pattern on the HVP shows substantially greater value sensitivity to the self than the world. In brief, such an individual exhibits greater sensitivity to self than the world; and this may be associated with withdrawal into self as a secondary defense strategy in the absence of other more mature defenses or options. Carried to a sufficient degree of moral dynamics, we would have a progression to the psychodynamic state of narcissistic character disorder.

Ellis (1978) also employed the HVP to measure positive changes in a group of alcoholics in treatment. Significant changes were found reflected in HVP scores between admission and treatment termination reflecting improved functioning. Also on the topic of alcoholism, Pomeroy (Unpublished Data) has looked for HVP subtest correlations with the alcoholism scale, the McAndrews Scale, of the MMPI. No significant correlations were found. DIM% was the one subscale that <u>approached</u> statistical significance (at the $p < .05$ level) as a negative association or correlation; i.e., as DIM% scores decrease, the risk of alcoholic problems increase. We have previously commented on how DIM % is a variable that fails to load on most criterion clinical scales other than Cattell's Tough Poise (TP) index, which does not correlate significantly with DIM%.

Austin and Van Arkel (1973) conducted a study of $N = 148$ inmates of the Muskegon County Jail. These subjects were classified by offense into three groups: 1) victimless crimes, 2) crimes against property, 3) crimes against persons. The HVP results revealed a continuum of value capacity within the group charged, with victimless crimes exhibiting the better general capacity to value on average than those charged with crimes against persons. A relationship was also found between "atychal" tendencies as measured by the HVP and learning achievement: subjects with the lowest learning achievement scores on the Adult Basic Learning Examination (ABLE) and the highest percentage of school dropouts were those individuals having the "atychal" profile on the HVP. A relationship which the investigators found interesting, though not significant, was evident between the HVP and the Interpersonal Checklist (ICL): an above average HVP "world" score profile tended to correlate with the ICL components of managerial-autocratic and responsible-hypernormal. Below average capacity to value the "world" with sensitivity and clarity was associated with rebellious-distrustful, self effacing, masochistic elements of the ICL. Similarly, above average HVP "self" valuation scores related to competitive-narcissistic, aggressive-sadistic behaviors; and below average "self" valuation scores tended to be associated with the ICL components of docile-dependent, cooperative-over-conventional behavior.

Austin and Garwood (1977), in an involved exploratory study, established relationships between the Rokeach Value Survey (RVS) of terminal and instrumental values and the HVP. They provided tentative axiological classifications of the RVS. They also correlated many factors between The HVP, RVS, Allport-Vernon-Lindzey Study of Values and the Kohlberg Theory of Moral Development. The study was a comparison among these instruments and an attempt to relate them to the GCV dimensions of intrinsic, extrinsic and systemic valuation provided by the HVP.

Salvador Roquet, MD, a psychiatrist, in Mexico City has administered the HVP to N = 2000 patients and subjects during a ten year period of practice. He has used the HVP to measure treatment progress, much as Krojanker and Pomeroy have done, and has shown that it is very suitable for this sort of longitudinal monitoring of patients under treatment. From his studies Roquet has developed a theory of treatment he calls psychosynthesis based on axiology or axiological psychosynthesis.

Schildt, E, M.D. (1978) has been working in Sweden with a modified version of the Hartman Value Profile (HVP) which he calls the Hartman-Schildt Value Profile (HSVP), based on the same axiological assumptions discovered by Hartman. At a meeting with Pomeroy (1985d) and others at the Annual Meeting of the Eastern Psychological Association held in Boston, Massachusetts, he communicated the great importance he attributed to the relationship among the I, E, S dimensions of the HVP. He advised Pomeroy at the time to spend as much time as possible working out the meaning of these dimensional configurations, as the I, E, S patterns carried much meaning in his view. Schildt was attempting at the time a further validation and refinement of his work with the HVP scales which his associates in Sweden now carry forward following his untimely death.

McDonald et. al. (1987) performed construct validity studies on the ranks of the Hartman Value Profile (HVP) items for Part I (World) and Part II (Self). Construct validity has much to do with whether the test does what it is supposed to do. We have already referred to factor analytic studies by Elliott (1969) and Pomeroy (1983b) that provided construct validity for the HVP. Here McDonald et. al. (1987) found that the sample of N = 6,354 subjects ranked the test items significantly in accordance with the axiological model at the 99.9% confidence level. Pomeroy and Bishop (1990b) have obtained RHO values that reflect a mean population correlation with the axiological "norm" ranging as follows: Part I (World): 1) Mexico = 0.74; 2) U. S. A. = 0.84; 3) Republic of Indonesia = 0.82. For Part II (Self): 1) Mexico = 0.72; 2) U. S. A. = 0.80; 3) Republic of Indonesia = 0.74. These are significant mean population correlations with the axiological "norm" or "standard" cross-culturally. However, it can be noted that U. S. A. data correlates most highly with the axiological ranking standard with RHO-1 = 0.84 and RHO-2 = 0.80. By comparison Mexico and Indonesia drop to 0.74, 0.72 and 0.82, 0.74 respectively. Overall the association of population mean rank ordering of test items is higher for "world" than "self and achieves a remarkably high level of correlation for behavioral data. These data argue for the construct validity of the HVP on the basis of cross-cultural findings. For the McDonald et. al. (1987), data the Spearman Rank Order Correlation for these nonparametric data results in a Part I correlation of 0.96 and a Part

II correlation of 0.95. These data were taken from a more homogeneous population than the cross-cultural data; they involved a much larger sample of N = 6,354 subjects, and hence the higher correlation achieved. In any event, both studies permit us to conclude the test is doing what Hartman claims it should do; hence, we have added to its construct validity with both the factor analytic study outcomes and the rank order correlation (RHO and Spearman Rank Order Correlation) studies.

Bystam (1978) reported on a reliability study employing Schildt's version of the HVP: the test, re-test reliability data proved to be better when the same test was used rather than parallel forms. The primary scales (I, E, S) were generally highly reliable while the ratio scales (e.g., INT%, DIM%) were less reliable.

Finally, Pomeroy et. al. (1982-1990) have presented a series of studies bearing directly on the reliability and validity of the Hartman Value Profile (HVP) and indirectly upon the assumptions underlying Hartman's formal axiology. These data, obtained by a psychologist, make it difficult for other psychologists to ignore Hartman's pioneering work in formal axiology and its relevance to psychology. The HVP amounts to a "Quick Test" of personality and clinical status and is a revolutionary new psychometrics, unorthodox in its test construction methodology. These data cover topics such as morality (Pomeroy, 1983a), factor analysis (Pomeroy, 1983b), biomedical correlations that showed a dramatically significant association with cholesterol (Pomeroy, 1983c, Pomeroy et. al, 1984b), use of the HVP with stuttering patients where no significant psychopathology was found with stuttering behavior (Pomeroy and Schwartz, 1983d), alternative scoring procedures adopting the method of Frank Forrest, Ph.D. (Pomeroy and Forrest, 1983e), the use of the HVP in the testing of Vietnam Veterans with PTSD and dissociative personality disorders (Pomeroy, 1984a; Pomeroy and Cirillo, 1985c), psychoaxiology vs. bioaxiology as new concepts in psychyology (Pomeroy, 1985e; Pomeroy 1985f), invited three day seminars on behavioral axiology given to the faculty of the University of Indonesia at Jakarta (Pomeroy, 1985h; Pomeroy, 1990c), validation studies reported to the Hartman Institute Conferences (Pomeroy 1986a; Pomeroy, 1987; Pomeroy, 1989), behavioral axiology findings reported to the World Congress on Mental Health Counseling (Pomeroy, 1990a), behavioral axiology findings shared with the 22nd International Congress of Applied Psychology at Kyoto, Japan (Pomeroy, 1990b), and cross-cultural findings reported to the Kyoto, Japan Conference and the Hartman Institute Conference (Pomeroy, 1990c; Pomeroy, 1989).

In conclusion, the research findings in support of formal axiology and in support of the construct and concurrent validity of the Hartman Value

Profile (HVP) are impressive and argue for the clinical and psychological relevance of Hartman's valuemetrics and value science assumptions as embodied in formal axiology. Clearly, the community of psychologists is obliged to take formal axiology seriously and add to the current list of studies exploring the implications for a behavioral science that is valuecentric. We stand at the knife edge of research in behavioral axiology, and much work needs to be done. There is clearly room for contributions from all sources and orientations in mental health, and fortunately the HVP is a perfect public relations tool. It does the job of psychometrics in such a successful manner as to invite further consideration of formal axiology and Hartman's pathfinding assumptions generally!

REFERENCES

Allport, Gordon, et. al., <u>A Selected Bibliography on Values, Ethics and Esthetics in the Behavioral Sciences and Philosophy</u>, 1920-1958, New York, The Free Press, 1960.

Austin, J. J., and Garwood, B. D., "The Relationship of the Hartman Value Profile (HVP), Rokeach Value Survey (RVS), Allport et. al. Study of Values (AVL), and Kohlberg Theory of Moral Development."

Austin, J. J., and Van Arkel, C., "Muskegon County Jail Rehabilitation Program: An Overvaluation." Muskegon, Michigan Public Schools, 1973.

Bystam, E., "A Review of a Report on the Validity of the HVP." Paper presented at the Annual Meeting of the Hartman Institute, May 26, 1978.

Elliott, B. C., <u>Factor and Cluster Analyses of the Hartman Value Inventory: Homogeneity and Factorial Invariance for Normative and Ipsative Scales</u>. Doctoral Dissertation, University of Tennessee, Knoxville, 1969.

Ellis, A. R., "Hartman Value Profile (HVP) Pilot Study at the Atlanta Employment, Evaluation and Service Center." Unpublished manuscript, September, 1971.

Ellis, A. R., "Value Profiles of Two Groups of Alcoholics." Paper presented at the Annual Meeting of the Hartman Institute, May 25, 1978.

Hartman, R. S., "Memorandum for National Institute of Mental Health," May 16, 1970.

Hartman, R. S., <u>The Hartman Value Profile (HVP) Manual of Interpretation</u>, Research Concepts, Muskegon, Michigan, 1973.

Hartman, R. S., <u>The Structure of Value: Foundations of Scientific Axiology</u>, Southern Illinois University Press, Carbondale, 1967. (Spanish Version, 1959).

Kluckhohn, et. al., <u>Variations in Value Orientations</u>, Evanston, Illinois, Row, Peterson, 1961.

Kohlberg, L., "The Development of Children's Orientation Toward a Moral Order," Vita Humana, 1963, 6: 11-33.

Krojanker, R., "Psychological and Axiological Testing," Paper presented at the Annual Meeting of the Association of Humanistic Psychology, Washington, D. C., Sept. 9, 1971.

Lohman, J. S., The Professor's Influence on the Students' Capacity to Value, Boston University, 1968.

Maslow, A. H., "Self Actualizing People: A Study of Psychological Health," Personality Symposia No. 1, 1950.

McDonald, et. al., "Construct Validity-Ranks, Hartman Value Profile -Part I (Report 5), and Part II (Report 6)." The Institute for the Study of Human Values, Brentwood, Tennessee, 1987.

Morris, C. W., Varieties of Human Value, University of Chicago Press, Chicago, 1956.

Newman, Jay, Fanatics and Hypocrites, Prometheus Books, Buffalo, N.Y., 1986.

Pomeroy, Leon, and Davis, John, "Introduction to Behavioral Axiology: Validity Study of Hartman's Valuemetrics and Value Science Assumptions." (Paper given before the Annual Meeting of the Southeastern Psychological Association, New Orleans, 1982) Published in the Proceedings of the Second International Conference on the Cattell 16PF by The Institute for Personality and Aptitude Testing, Champaign, Illinois, 1982a.

Pomeroy, Leon, "A Psychologist Looks At Morality," Invited Paper Given before the Annual Meeting of the American Psychological Association, Anaheim, California, 1983a.

Pomeroy, Leon, "Factor Analysis Of The Hartman Value Profile (HVP)," Paper given at the First International Conference on Formal Axiology, Mexico, D.F., October, 1983b.

Pomeroy, Leon, and Bishop, R., "Biomedical Correlations With The Hartman Value Profile," Paper given at the First International Conference on Formal Axiology, Mexico, D.F., October, 1983c.

Pomeroy, Leon, and Schwartz, M., "Results Of A Study Of Stuttering Patients Employing The Hartman Value Profile (HVP)," Paper given at the First International Conference on Formal Axiology, Mexico, D.F., October, 1983d.

Pomeroy, Leon, and Forrest, Frank, "An Alternative Scoring Procedure For The Hartman Value Profile (HVP)," Paper presented at the First International Conference on Formal Axiology, Mexico, D.F., October, 1983e.

Pomeroy, Leon, "A Look At Combat Induced Dissociative Behavior," Paper given before the First International Conference on Multiple Personality and Dissociative States, Rush Medical Center, Chicago, October, 1984a.

Pomeroy, Leon, Fox, E., Bishop, R, Davis, J., "A Third Replication of HVP-Biomedical Correlations," Paper given at the Annual Conference of the Hartman Institute, Knoxville, TN., May, 1984b.

Pomeroy, Leon, and Cirillo, Jean, "Some Clinical Impressions Of Dissociative Behavior: A Look At The Splitting Defense," Paper given before the Second International Conference on Multiple Personality and Dissociative States, Rush Medical Center, Chicago, Ill. October, 1985c.

Pomeroy, Leon; Fox, E., Bishop, R., and Davis, J., "A New Tool For Health Psychology And Behavioral Medicine," <u>VA Practitioner</u>, July 1985a.

Pomeroy, Leon, "Beyond Terrorism And War: An Introduction To Behavioral Axiology," <u>Journal of the Organization for the Study of Group Tensions</u>, 1985b.

Pomeroy, Leon, "An Introduction To Behavioral Axiology: A New Orientation In Psychology," Paper given before the Annual Meeting of the Eastern Psychological Association, Boston, March, 1985d.

Pomeroy, Leon, "Psychoaxiology," Paper given at the Annual Conference of the Hartman Institute, Knoxville, May, 1985e.

Pomeroy, Leon, "Bioaxiology," Paper given at the Annual Conference of the Hartman Institute, Knoxville, May, 1985f.

Pomeroy, Leon, "Seminar On Behavioral Axiology," South Oaks Hospital, Long Island, New York, November, 1985g.

Pomeroy, Leon, "Seminar On Behavioral Axiology," Three Day Seminar, Faculty, University of Indonesia at Jakarta, December, 1985h.

Pomeroy, Leon and Bishop, R., "Further Validation Studies Of Hartman's Valuemetrics," Paper given at the Annual Conference of the Hartman Institute, Knoxville, May, 1986.

Pomeroy, Leon, and Bishop, R., "Results Of Further Validation Efforts With The Hartman Value Profile (HVP)," Paper given at the Annual Conference of the Hartman Institute, Knoxville, May, 1987.

Pomeroy, Leon and Bishop, R., "Cross Cultural Studies Employing The Hartman Value Profile (HVP)," Paper given at the Annual Conference of the Hartman Institute, Knoxville, September, 1989.

Pomeroy, Leon, and Bishop, R., "A Valuecentric Approach to Clinical Assessment for Cognitive Behavior Oriented Clinicians," Paper given before the World Congress on Mental Health Counseling, Keystone, Colorado, June 14-16, 1990a.

Pomeroy, Leon and Bishop, R., "Introduction To Behavioral Axiology: Part II: Validation Of Hartman's Valuemetrics And Value Science Assumptions, (Cross Cultural Data)" Invited Paper Given Before the 22nd International Congress of Applied Psychology, Kyoto, Japan, July 22-27, 1990b.

Pomeroy, Leon, "Introduction To Behavioral Axiology And Valuecentric Cognitive Behavior Psychology," Second Invited Seminar Given Before the Faculty of Psychology, University of Indonesia at Jakarta, August, 1990c.

Pomeroy, Leon, and Bishop, R., "Cross Cultural, Cross National Study Of Values Update," Paper given at the Annual Conference of the Hartman Institute, Knoxville, October 25-27, 1990e.

Rokeach, Milton, <u>The Open And Closed Mind: Investigations Into The Nature Of Belief Systems And Personality Systems</u>, Basic Books, New York, 1990. Also, <u>The Study Of Values</u>, Published, 1975.

Roquet, S., "Clinical Axiology," Paper Presented At The Annual Meeting of the Hartman Institute, Knoxville, May 26, 1978.

Schildt, E., A "Modification And Extension Of The HVP Test." Paper presented at the Annual Meeting of the Hartman Institute, May 26, 1978.

Shapiro, David, <u>Neurotic Styles</u>, Basic Books, Inc., New York, N. Y., 1965.

Shapiro, David, <u>Autonomy and Rigid Character</u>, Basic Books, Inc., New York, N. Y., 1981.

Skinner, B. F., <u>Verbal Behavior</u>, New York, Appleton, 1957.

Smith, M. D., "Mental Health Reconsidered: A Special Case Of The Problem Of Values In Psychology," <u>American Psychologist,</u> 16: 299-306.

Snow, C. P., <u>The Two Cultures And The Scientific Revolution</u>, New York, Cambridge University Press, 1959.

Speer, A., <u>Infiltration: How Heinrich Himmler Schemed To Build An SS Industrial Empire</u>, McMillan, New York, 1981.

Chapter XIV

BEHAVIORAL AXIOLOGY: CROSS CULTURAL STUDY OF VALUES

Leon Pomeroy and Richard Bishop

Introduction

Psychological Anthropologists interested in such things have speculated for years on the relative impact of culture on personal values. Some have argued for considerable cultural specificity or unique influences; whereas, others have argued for cross cultural homogeneity or uniformity in the face of the psychosocial and biosocial selection pressures of evolution. It will be our hypothesis in this study that such evolutionary selection pressures on human development confers substantial cultural similarities across cultures in the context of being human and dealing with a social and earth environment.

As cited in another chapter in the present volume, Pomeroy and Ellis have argued that traditional value studies in psychology have been academically limited largely to the examination of terminal (ends) and instrumental (means) values and their developmental histories. In the present investigation, a behavioral axiology approach will be taken to the cross cultural examination of values for the first time in history. Indeed, this approach, which draws upon formal axiology, may well be the introduction of this discipline to psychological anthropology for the first time.

Behavioral axiology is a compound phrase designating a valuecentric, cognitive behavior theory and practice based upon the formal axiology of Hartman (1967). It involves the application of the Hartman Value Profile (HVP) as a valuemetric psychometrics. The HVP provides a basis for the measurement of value structures and dynamics at the deep core of evaluative cognitive processes known as the General Capacity to Value (GCV). The gyroscopic set-points at this level of the "moral compass" consist of three habitual evaluative dimensions known as the Intrinsic (I), Extrinsic (E) and Systemic (S). They may well constitute the cognitive equivalent of "invisible hand" dynamics! These dimensions of valuation obey naturalistic constraints of a balance imperative and a hierarchical imperative. The co-play and counter-play of these axial dimensions of valuation generate beliefs and ultimately attitudes. Three attitudes are required to trigger behavior, emotion or motivation and they are attitude towards the subject or attentional object (Ao), attitude toward the context or background in the moment (Ac) and attitude towards self in the moment (As). The attitudinal sum triggering behavior is the Kinetic Attitude Sum (KAS). Thus this cross-cultural study of valuational habits is aimed at the general capacity to value (GCV) cognitive level or core level of evaluative cognitive processing and the gyroscopic axial dimensions of the GCV value compass, the I, E, S, dimensions which are programmed by natural selection to work towards balance in absolute sensitivity and towards a hierarchical imperative where the order of dimensional importance is: $I > E > S$.

Behavioral Axiology is psychology that draws upon Hartman's formal axiology. It focuses on the axial dynamisms of the three dimensions of value (I, E, S). With the HVP we can measure the absolute sensitivity of each dimension, the relationships among the dimensions, the order of importance given the dimensions and the level of approximation of the individual's valuational habits to the axiological standard derived from formal axiology. We refer to I, E, S as gyroscopic set points because their interaction shapes beliefs and attitudes cognitively "down steam," thus calibrating the "moral compass"! While we are hypothesizing that in a comparison of students in Mexico, Republic of Indonesia and the U. S. A. the similarities will outweigh the differences, we are also asking: Which cultural sample reveals the greatest, or deepest value conflicts? Where there is substantial axial (I, E, S) imbalance as to absolute sensitivity, or where there is axial violation of the hierarchical imperative ($I > E > S$) we can expect moral conflict, value conflict, emotional conflict and clinical signs and symptoms as shown by Pomeroy and Davis (1982) and Pomeroy et. al. (1985). While the integrated personality is an ideal, the prior integration at the GCV level of valuation is a necessary, thought not sufficient, condition for personality integration to take place.

The behavioral axiology approach to cross cultural studies or psychological anthropology is a new approach to comprehending cultural differences.

All cultures require individuality and variation of personality structures to survive. Such variability is the raw material of evolution: a variation gets thrown up to be acted upon by the environment, and selection pressures favor this or that variation. In our statistical study of the axiological value structures in three cultures, we are averaging across individuals and "washing" out variability to strike a mean or central tendency measure. Thus, our methodology ignores individual differences in search for a cultural average so we can compare the cultural averages obtained in this report to examine overall trends.

Experimental Methods

The Hartman Value Profile (HVP) was translated into Spanish and Indonesian; no back translations were carried out. The HVPs were administered to approximately N=200 students in Mexico, Indonesia and the U. S. A.[1] The Mexican students were the youngest, of High School Age. The other students were drawn from the college level. The task was to rank order two lists of eighteen items appearing in Part I and Part II of the Hartman Value Profile (HVP). The reader is referred to the "Manual of Interpretation" for further information regarding this instrument. (Hartman, 1973)

Results

RHO is a nonparametric measure of association or correlation. It specifically measures the closeness of fit between the subjects rank ordering of test items to the axiological order given the same items. If we average all subjects in Mexico, Indonesia and the U.S.A. we will have an average RHO or average degree of fit of that cultural sample with the axiological "norm" or standard. Figure 1 summarizes these data:

Figure 1.

	Culture:		
	U.S.A.	MEXICO:	INDONESIA:
RHO-1	+0.83	+0.74	+0.82

---

[1] ACKNOWLEDGMENT: The cooperation of Professor Engelina Bonang, University of Indonesia at Jakarta and Professor Alfonso Lozano in Mexico made possible the acquisition of these date, which is greatly appreciated.

RHO-2   +0.80   +0.71   +0.73

Part I of the HVP measures "world" valuation, i.e., personal, practical situations, social situations, and authority. The comparison between U. S. A. and Indonesia on RHO-1 shows comparable levels of sensitivity to the world in terms of habitual evaluative habits at the GCV level of analysis. This would confirm our hypothesis that the selection pressures of psychosocial and biosocial evolution on human beings shape comparable value habits at the level of core evaluative cognitive maps. The Mexican students are High School and not College level students, and the RHO-2 = +0.74 may reflect this. The higher the correlation the more mature and adjusted the individual. The U. S. A. sample data shows greater balance between RHO-1 and RHO-2 of the test, which is desirable. The Indonesians are less sensitive to "self" than "world" with values of +0.73 and +0.82 respectively. Here is an instance of <u>imbalance</u> that would be expected to produce emotional and behavioral consequences. Thus the RHO data present a mixed picture when it comes to interpreting our hypothesis. The fact that all RHO correlations were positive also contributes to the construct validity of the HVP. Let us now turn to other aspects of the axiological testing.

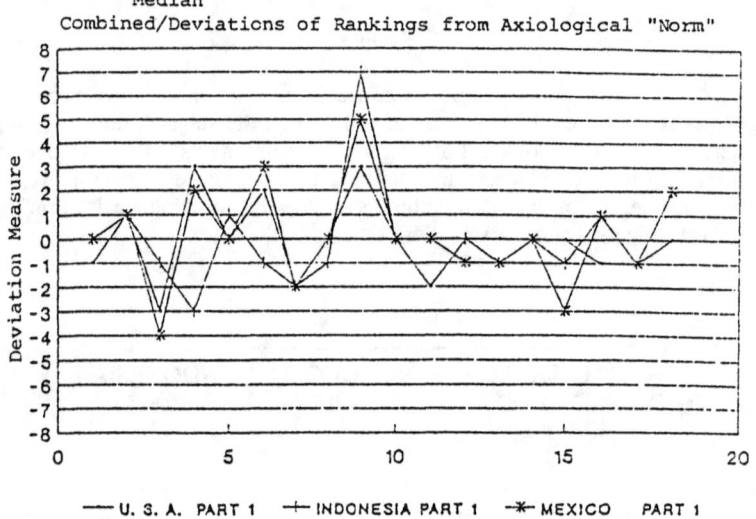

Figure 2a.

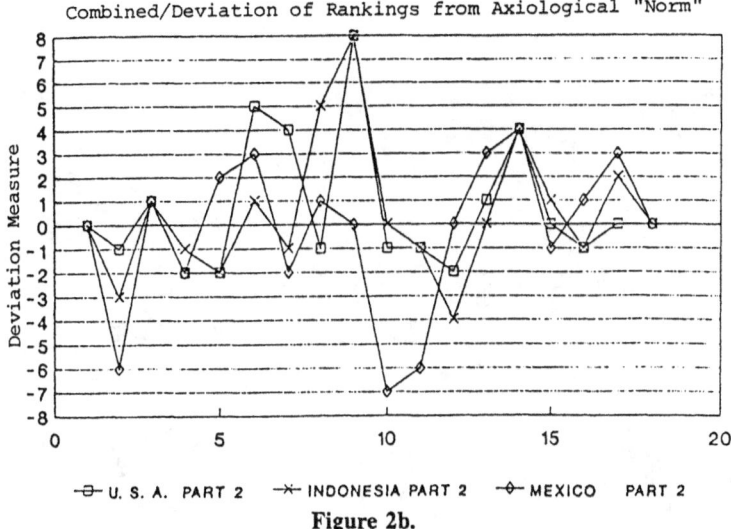

Figure 2b.

Figure 2 is a line graph depicting the average deviations of the rank orderings for each of the populations (Mexico, Indonesia, U.S.A.) from the axiological rank order. The test items are represented along the x-axis of the graph and number eighteen. The y-axis records the average rank deviation from axiological ranking for each of the eighteen test items for each of the population samples: Mexico, Indonesia, U. S. A. Thus population mean ranking data is being compared--the population mean rank vs. the axiological standard derived from Hartman's formal axiology. Figure 2A shows superimposed distributions for Part I of the HVP, and Figure 2B presents the superimposed distributions for Part II of the HVP. By superimposed distributions is meant a comparison of all three cultural mean ranking distributions in one graph. From Figure 2A we see similarity of ranking data for the "World" valuation for the three cultures under comparison. Figure 2B shows some similarity; but there is a tendency to break away from the greater uniformity of Figure 2A. These data reflect "Self" valuation patterns.

In general, these data partially confirm our hypothesis that, on average, there appears to be more cross-cultural similarity than dissimilarity, for habitual evaluative habits aimed at the "world"; but, this pattern breaks down when valuation of "the self" is considered: here there is much more differentiation cross-culturally perhaps reflecting different levels of self organization as a function of cultural pressures: e.g., the greater importance of family in Indonesia.

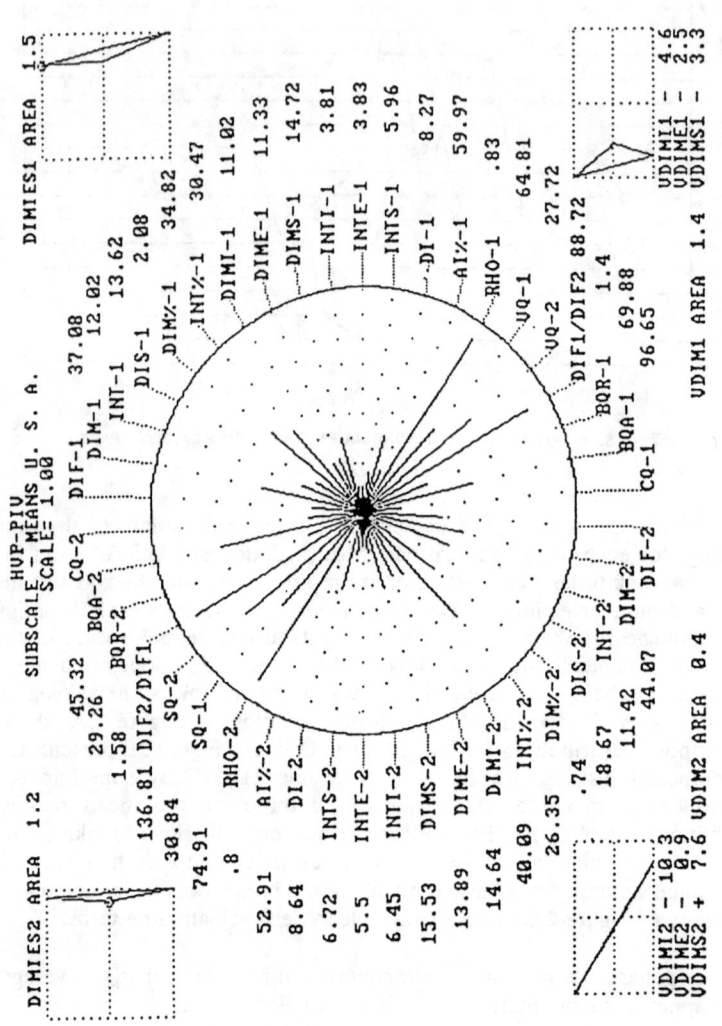

Figure 3A.

Psychology and Value Theory

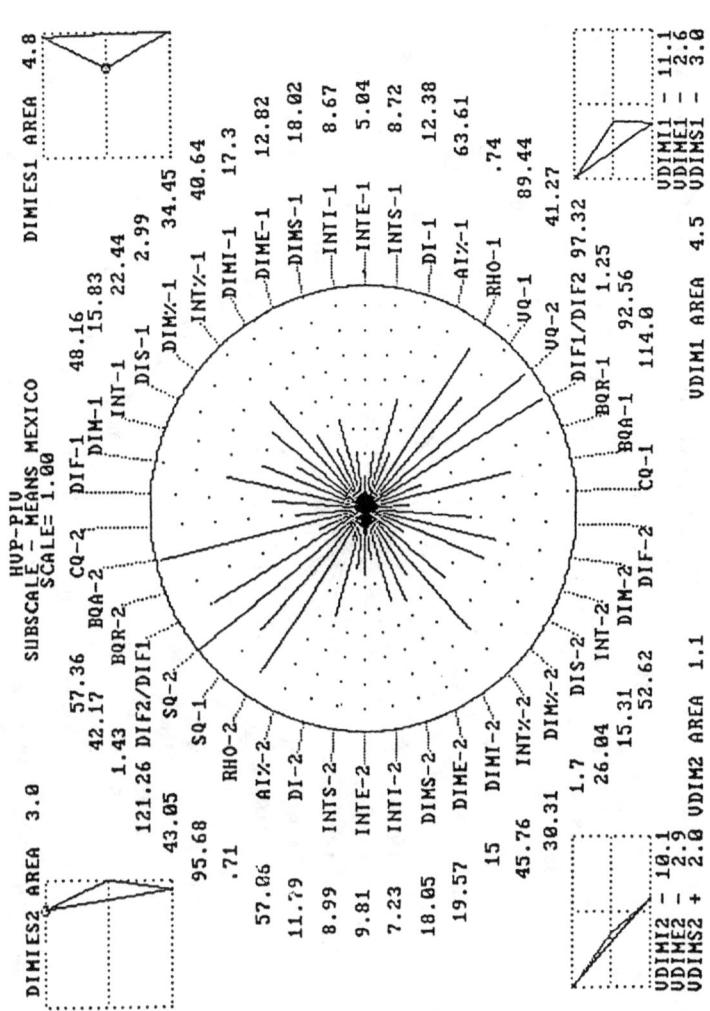

Figure 3B.

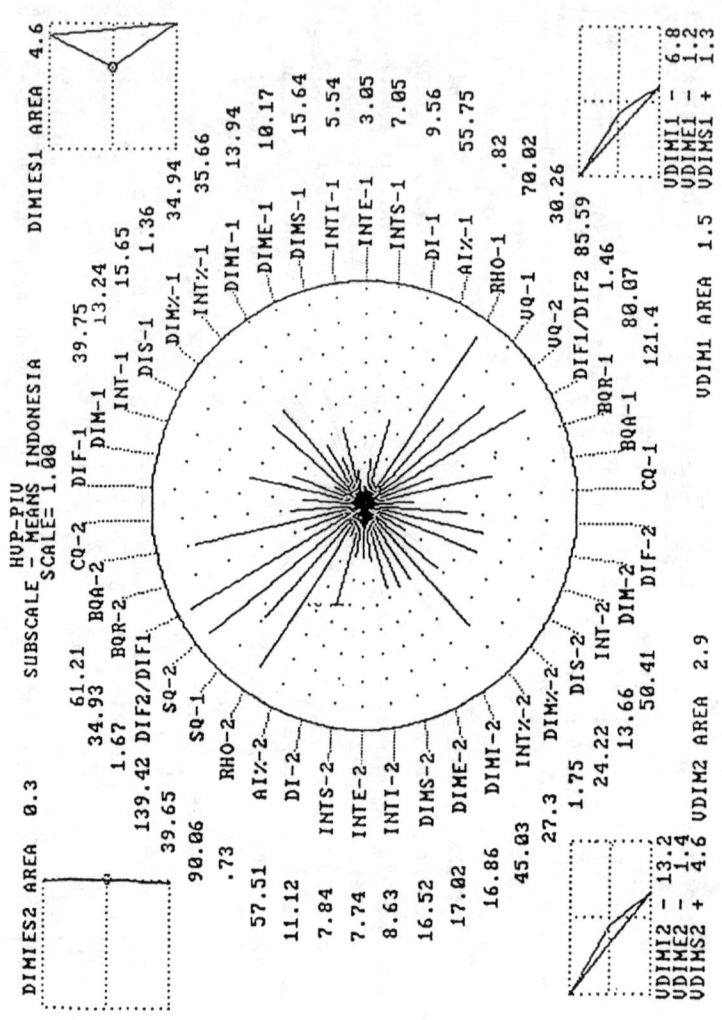

Figure 3C.

Figures 3A, 3B, and 3C are <u>Value Circles</u> used to depict the subscale distributions of the Hartman Value Profile (HVP). The absolute magnitude of each scale is recorded as a circumferential value, and the radiating spokes of the circle are vectors recording the magnitude of each subscale. The lower the number (absolute value) the better; high numbers point to value conflicts that get translated into behavioral problems. Note that the VDIM-1 scores are negative in all three populations with the exception of the Indonesians, who reflect a positive VDIMS-1 value of + 1.3. This is a unique, positive orientation to authority in the world not shared by the American or Mexican students.

For the VDIM-2 scores on the left of Figure 3 (Value Circles) we see a consistent pattern of two negatives and one positive in the lineup. All three student populations are positively oriented to their own "inner authority" (VDIMS2) and negatively oriented to "self" (VDIMI2) and their role in the work world (VDIME2). If we are correct in interpreting VDIMI as an partial index of self esteem, then the order of self esteem is from 14.64 (-4.6) (U. S. A); to 15.0 (-10.1) (Mexico) to 16.86 (-13.2) (Indonesia) respectively. Thus, Indonesia exhibits the lowest level of self esteem (Highest absolute DIMI-2; Most negative VDIMI-2 scores). Clearly these data both support and contradict our hypothesis of cross cultural value homogeneity at the GCV level of analysis. The value circle patterns tend to confirm our hypothesis on visual inspection. However, on closer inspection we see differences that make a difference. Yet, the obtained range of VDIMI2 scores (attitude toward self) is not great, i.e., 10.1 to 13.2. The associated DIMI2 scores exhibit a narrow range as well, i.e., 14.64, 15.0 and 16.86 for U. S. A., Mexico, Indonesia respectively!

Figure 4 summarizes some of the more clinically meaningful findings in this application of formal axiology to a cross cultural study of values: these parameters are derived from the HVP subscales seen in the value circles already presented.

Figure 4:

CLINICAL INDEX:	U. S. A.	MEXICO	INDONESIA
DEPRESSION;	52.91	57.06	57.51
ANXIETY:	40.09	45.76	45.03
SELF ATTITUDE	-10.30	-10.10	-13.20
SELF CONFLICT	29.26	42.17	34.93
DEPENDENCY	13.89	19.57	17.02
FAITH LEVEL	26.35	30.31	27.30
CONCENTRATION-S	8.64	11.79	11.12
CONCENTRATION-W	8.27	12.38	9.56
TRUST-OTHERS	11.02	17.30	13.94
MANIPULATIVE	11.33	12.82	10.17
AUTHORITY PROB	14.72 (-3.3)	18.02 (-3.0)	15.64 (+1.3)
SENSITIVITY-W	37.08	48.16	39.75
SENSITIVITY-S	44.07	52.62	50.41
CONTENTMENT	1.40	1.25	1.46
STUBBORN/RIGID	+7.60	+2.00	+4.6

These scales are derived from AI%-2, VDIMI2, BQA2, DIME2, DIM%-2, DI-2, DI-1, DIME-1, DIMS-1 (VDIMS-1), DIF-1, DIF-2, BQR-1 and VDIMS-2 respectively. See **Value Circles (C)**.

From Figure 4 data we see a pattern of convergence of values across the cultures sampled (e.g., VDIMI2, DIMI2 scores). The differences that exist, in most instances, are not dramatic; and therefore we regard our hypothesis as confirmed. There are some differences that make for interesting study, e.g., the U. S. A. student sample exhibits the highest level of personality stubbornness and rigidity with a calculated value (VDIMS-2) of +7.60 vs. +2.0 and +4.6 for the Mexico and Indonesian samples respectively. Another remarkable difference is the more positive orientation of Indonesians to authority. This is consistent with Pomeroy's impression on his trips to Indonesia, and it is consistent with the high value Indonesians place on family solidarity. The "value vision" of family may have compromised their "self vision"; for the latter score is the worst. The U. S. A. and Mexico averages are (14.64; -10.3), and (15.0; -10.1) respectively against a value of (16.86; -13.2) for the Indonesian average. These are indices of self vision, self awareness and self-sensitivity, self acceptance where the lower the first score and the more positive the second the better. On the other hand Indonesians have the highest score for social sensitivity and awareness of (10.17; -1.2) against the averages of (11.33; -2.5) and (12.82; -2.6) for the U. S. A., and Mexico respectively. We interpret this to mean that Indonesians cultivate higher levels of social consciousness and family than individualism and the self. In this respect we offer Slater's (1970) opinion. In his powerful book, The Pursuit of Loneliness, he suggests that "nothing will change (in this country) until individualism is assigned a subordinate place in the American value system--for individualism lies at the core of the old culture, and a prepotent individualism is not a viable foundation for society in a nuclear age." (Taken from Bock, (1988).) In the Mexican and U. S. A. data, we see the emphasis on individualism when compared with the Indonesian data, with its emphasis on family and social values!

Thus, on average, it appears to us that at this level of axiological study of values the similarities speak louder than the differences. However, the differences are interesting and invite further study.

When we inspect data reflecting on how much the students agree among themselves in this cultural comparison, we encounter the highest level of agreement (within culture, population homogeneity) among the U.S.A. students in their "world view" scores of Part I of the HVP. This stands out dramatically. Mexican and Indonesian students do not come close. For Part II scores, self valuation, the interstudent consensus level is highest among the younger Mexican sample, with the U. S. A. and Indonesia more comparable, and exhibiting greater interstudent differences.

Conclusions

Employing a formal axiological approach as reflected in the Hartman Value Profile (HVP), student data was obtained from Mexico, U. S. A., and Indonesia. The hypothesis that evolutionary selection pressures would tend to result in a convergence of values at the level of the General Capacity to Value (GCV) has met with mixed results. On the one hand, these data show a remarkable and surprising cross-cultural homogeneity; but, on the other hand, there are differences that invite further study and analysis!

So far as our review of the literature indicates, these data constitute the first systematic cross-cultural or cross-national study of values employing Hartman's formal axiology or valuemetrics as embodied in the Hartman Value Profile (HVP). These data have the added advantage of drawing upon three populations for comparison, where often cultural comparison studies have limited themselves to two population comparisons.

Our hypothesis of the relative homogeneity of values in response to biosocial and psychosocial selection pressures inherent in the evolutionary process has mixed support from these data. Clearly, there are differences that make a difference among patterns of striking similarities! Inasmuch as this approach aims at the deep cognitive evaluative structures (GCV) as against the attitudinal structures of valuation, these findings are not surprising. These data in turn affirm the value of axiological testing of deep value structures and dynamics and indirectly add to the construct validity of the HVP (recalling that the RHO correlations are all positive (+) lends further construct validity to the Hartman Value Profile (HVP)), and the validity of the methodology as a measure of meaningful personality and behavioral dimensions. Regarding the question of which culture exhibits the greatest level of value conflict, we look at the BQA2 subscale of the HVP or index which Pomeroy and Davis (1982) have shown as having high correlations with indices of psychopathology. The BQA2 range is 29.29 (U. S. A.), 42.17 (Mexico), and 34.93 (Indonesia). The lower the index the better, and thus the American students have the least and the Mexican students the highest level of value conflict. The younger age of the Mexican students may account for this finding.

Much more work needs to be done to interpret fully these findings, and this study is regarded as a pilot study of the feasibility of using formal axiological as a methodology for psychological anthropology. We feel that the results are encouraging and we hope that we have contributed to the birth of a new discipline of axiological anthropology.

It is our hope to extend this study to include Japan and Russia in the near future and to devote more time to back translations as an added control measure over the translation process, which is a weakness of the present study.

REFERENCES

Bock, Philip K., Rethinking Psychological Anthropology, W. H. Freeman and Company, New York, New York, 1988.

Hartman, R.S., The Hartman Value Profile (HVP) Manual of Interpretation, Muskegon, Michigan, Research Concepts, 1973.

Pomeroy, Leon and Davis, John, "Introduction to Behavioral Axiology: Part I: Validity Study of Hartman's Valuemetrics and Value Science Assumptions." Published in the Proceedings of the Institute of Personality and Aptitude Testing, Champaign, Illinois, 1982.

Pomeroy, Leon; Fox, E., Bishop, R., and Davis, J., "A New Tool for Health Psychology and Behavioral Medicine," VA Practitioner, July, 1985.

Pomeroy, Leon, and Bishop, R., "Introduction to Behavioral Axiology: Part II: Validation of Hartman's Valuemetrics and Value Science Assumptions as a New Orientation in Psychology (Cross Cultural Data). Paper given at the 22nd International Congress of Applied Psychology, July 22-27, 1990, Kyoto, Japan.

Slater, Philip L., The Pursuit of Loneliness, Beacon Press, Boston, Massachusetts, 1970.

Chapter XV

SELF KNOWLEDGE AND SELF DEVELOPMENT

David Mefford

Anyone investigating the roots of our western culture soon comes across the essence of Greek wisdom inscribed on the temple at Delphi, "Know Thyself." Seriously considering what this may mean for one's life has always been of great value to guide and nurture the growth of each person's potential and as a sign-post for the understanding of our collective humanity. In this chapter, we will be discussing what we can learn about the self using concepts from a new theory of value, formal axiology. Axiology comes from the Greek word "axios" meaning "worthwhileness" or "valuable." German and Austrian psychologists and philosophers began to use the word, "axiology" to designate "value theory" about 120 years ago.

Guiding our discussion is a version of formal axiology developed by Robert S. Hartman in his pioneer work, The Structure of Value (hereafter SV). The basic concepts of Hartman's scientific axiology can be particularly useful for expanding and deepening our knowledge of the self. The theory is also useful for defining specific methods and techniques for developing the potentials within the self. The topic of the human self has been discussed in many different ways, but the self considered as a "valuing subject" is one of the most interesting and productive.

It is very difficult to define exactly what we mean by "self." We may achieve some clarity about the nature of the self by describing what it does. The self identifies the activity of referring-to-others outside itself with its own referring source, with its immediate, existential ownness. The self is the reflexivity of consciousness, making possible the statement, "I am I."

There are several ways the self achieves a stable identity with its ownness through its referring activity. The self refers to otherness in three separate, often combined, ways: with thinking, with physical actions, and with emotional sensitivities. We can ascribe a sense of self to each of these basic perspectives connecting the self with otherness, with objects of experience. Developmental psychologists believe that the value content of these thoughts, physical behaviors, and emotional feelings which prove successful as a means of coping in childhood, form the foundation of the personality. The success of individuals in stabilizing the surrounding environment happens through adopting certain values that help them stabilize a sense of "fitting-in," and these adopted values form the core of their sense of self. The understanding of personality involves knowledge of the self in many dimensions, including thinking, having, doing, feeling, etc. Hartman's formal axiology provides a foundational structure for formalizing this multi-dimensional structure of the personality and reveals new possibilities for further development of our potential as human beings.

The values of the self are multi-dimensional. This multi-dimensionality of value is one of the central ideas in Hartman's formal axiology. Hartman's starting point for a formal value science is an axiom of value, which is a fundamental definition, an essential expression which can generate a systematic framework for all specific values and valuation instances. This axiom expresses that all values are degrees of concept fulfillment. A concept is said to have three parts: a name, a meaning, and an application. Concept fulfillment is a one-to-one correspondence between the predicates in the meaning part of the concept and the actual properties of the given referent to which it is applied.

The multi-dimensionality emerges when we notice that there are different kinds of concepts for expressing the meaning of a given experience. Hartman identifies three basic kinds of concepts: 1) those which name ideas or constructs of the mind, 2) those which name classes of things, actions, or objects of perception, and 3) those which name unique individuals, the whole of some object or person.

The different kinds of concepts are selectively applied in order to value something given to thought or experience. The application always has a result, and that is a value. There are three kinds or dimensions of value depending on which kind of concept is operative: 1) systemic value, the result of applying a finite and definite idea or constructed concept, 2) extrinsic value, the result of applying a class or perceptual concept, and 3) intrinsic value, the result of applying a singular or holistic concept.

For details of the theory of formal axiology, the reader is referred to the first half of this book. For the sake of clarity we need to stress one very important theoretical point, namely, that the three value dimensions are interlocked and dependent on one another. The thing valued always remains the same in its self-identity, and the three value dimensions represent fundamentally different perspectives one can take toward the given object. For example, we can regard a person from any one of the above three value perspectives: 1) systemically, as "homo sapiens," a minimum set of distinguishing properties acting as the definition, 2) extrinsically, as a "good ball-player," a set of particular, comparative properties, and 3) intrinsically, as "the one I love," a total set of properties referring to a unique individual, who is irreplaceable and incomparable. The actual person always remains the same, regardless of the value perspective taken.

An application of axiological categories to the self focuses first on the structure of the self, synthesized from all the different observations of self-related presence. The structure of the self is basically awareness energy reflected back to a source <u>within</u> its own self. One of the first thinkers in the rationalist tradition to discuss a universal, formal structure of an "inner self" was Edmund Husserl. Husserl believed there must be a sub-structure of consciousness which he called the "primordial." The primordial is the built-in capacity of consciousness to do what it does, both to combine and to separate mental and physical aspects of reality. This primordial sense of self, according to Husserl, is what allows us to form a "whole picture" of the world and of ourselves within it. For this discussion, the primordial sense of self corresponds to the capacity for and source of <u>intrinsic</u> valuation.

In terms of Hartman's formal axiology, the self can be valued in either the systemic, the extrinsic, or the intrinsic value dimensions. Many people's self-identities are constituted by emphasizing value content in only one or two of these value dimensions, and they are thus restricted in their valuation of themselves as whole persons. Each value dimension, as identifying a specific sense of self, has its own potential to discern self values; and, in the opinion of this writer, the most value in life can only be realized by opening up the combined value potential of <u>all</u> three value dimensions applied to the self. Let us examine this multi-dimensional view of self valuation in more detail.

Axiological Self-Knowledge

We know from the common sense point of view that a human being, a self, has value reality in at least three dimensions: mind, body, and heart (emotions). These three aspects have been discussed since the time of Jesus.

Jesus used these three dimensions in his expression of the "greatest commandment," one version of which is, "love the Lord with all your heart, mind, and strength." We observe that if the self relates to the world or to its own self at all, it must do so in at least one of these three different ways: thinking, doing, or feeling. We are using the word, "feeling," here to indicate not only the emotions but also a pure quality of conscious awareness. When the Self constitutes a world, or when it constitutes its ownness in immediate self-reflection, it must do so in one or more of these value awareness modes.

The total Self, in terms of axiological value theory, can be understood as a unity of the three value capacities for discerning or constituting value. The total value potential of the Self consists of the unity of the systemic capacity, the extrinsic capacity, and the intrinsic capacity. These capacities can be considered centers of valuation around and through which a sense of self develops. This writer finds it helpful to distinguish these different senses of self as follows. The sense of self formed around the activity of systemic valuation is the knowledge-based, intellectual ego. The sense of self that forms around the activity of extrinsic valuation is the doing/having-based, social ego. The sense of self which forms around the activity of intrinsic valuation is the wholistic-based, primordial or inner self. We next examine these senses of Self, taking one sense of self or one value dimension at a time, to provide a clear foundation for our new approach to understanding the self as a unified, multi-dimensional whole.

Systemic Self Valuation: The Intellectual Ego

The systemic value of a thing is the bare schematic or definition of the thing. The systemic valuation of the self is the schematic, cognitive perspective on the self. The values which emerge within the cognitive perspective are a reduction of everything in experience to thoughts and beliefs. To illustrate this form of self valuation, a person centered in systemic valuation would say, "I think or believe so and so, and those thoughts and beliefs constitute my own value as a person."

The systemic value of the self may refer to the concept of self that a person has already formed in life, or, in general, to a person's thinking about self in reflecting on his or her experience. The systemic value part of the self is how a person is defined as a mental construct. This already formed, mentally-constructed sense of self is what we mean by the "intellectual ego." It is a concept of self-reference formed by the set of self values which are finite, definite and fixed as necessary to have a sense of self at all.

It is very common for people to identify themselves and others according to the knowledge they possess. The "intellectual ego" is an identity with one's self that is formed as objects of knowledge are reflected back to a center in the knower. The intellectual sense of self is an ego, an I-am-I structure, based on a value content of definite knowledge. The intellectual ego says, "I am I, because I possess definite knowledge." This knowledge constitutes the essence of "I."

Extrinsic Self Valuation: The Social Ego

The extrinsic value perspective on the self, which we have named the "social ego," consists of all sensory experience and activity. The social ego is a broad value container for intersubjective values and includes the fixed values of the intellectual ego, although it has a separate identity structure and a separate center. The social self is an ego with a center of identity in physical and social situations. The social self includes possessions like houses and cars and also possessions of knowledge. The social self reflects the having of these social things back to itself as the haver. The social self also is centered in social activity, in the doing or performing of certain social roles. The social self is an ego identity based on doing and having. Appearance is very important to the social sense of self. How one looks to others, one's grooming and dressing habits, is an integral part of the social ego.

The social self can be valued according to each axiological value dimension. Systemically, the social ego is one's self-image and knowledge of activity potential governed by ethical rules for behavior, dos and don'ts as well as oughts and ought-nots. Extrinsically, the social ego is the set of social and work roles that distinguish people according to their function in society. Intrinsically, the social ego is valued from the perspective of interpersonal relationships.

Our extrinsic valuation of the self involves the ability to value self through activities, through what we actually do and can do. Extrinsic self valuation involves our career or life's work. The choice of a profession or work in life becomes the focal point of a large number of other values. Most of our time is given to our work, and the social ego includes this and all our other activities as well.

We become involved in walking, running, dancing, and other activities because our bodies are constructed in ways which make these activities possible. Those who run particularly well in comparison to others may take up running as a profession. For the majority, running is at most a hobby or part of our chosen exercise program. What we know about the world and about ourselves defines the range of activity we can choose. This is a good reason to learn as much as possible about our world, because it will open up a wider range of value choices for active and productive social involvement.

Whatever we decide to do with our available time in turn gives us value as persons. If we are not in harmony with one or more activities in which we are involved, then we should change the activities according to what we know or feel to be better, or experiment until we feel a full sense fulfillment within ourselves. Experimentation in the social dimension will have the same effect as the experimentation in the intellectual dimension. We can become more aware of our inner capacity for doing, having tried out many different kinds of activities. Through reflecting on this accumulated experience, we become more aware of our bodies and our physical energy. We can then better choose involvements that increase our energy and vitality and avoid those which drain our energy.

When we temporarily withdraw from all activity, doing nothing, reflecting on our experience, we can become more aware of our inner capacity for action. The awareness of our inner capacity to act tends to increase our confidence about the actual range of our action possibilities. This awareness of the inner capacity to act is a part of our primordial self, and when we fully identify with this inner capacity for action, then we feel more in harmony with our inner selves. It seems that an enduring sense of peace and harmony can only be achieved with the cooperation of the inner self. The awareness that this harmony is anchored on the inside tends to create harmony on the outside with virtually any social circumstance that we may encounter. Since the intrinsic source of this inner harmony, the primordial self, is the foundation of self knowledge and self development; and because it is more difficult to describe discursively, we will go into it in much more detail.

Intrinsic Self Valuation: The Primordial Self

The third sense of self is the <u>primordial</u>, which is the foundation and the container for both the intellectual and the social egos. The primordial self is the identity with consciousness as the source of awareness for all experience. It is the necessary foundation for any particular individualized experience. This is the intrinsic value foundation of the self, formed as consciousness is reflected back to itself in the <u>immediate</u> awareness of its own subjectivity. The primordial self is not an ego structure, rather it is the foundation and source of all ego forms. The primordial self is not an "I am I"; it is simply an "I am." It is the self not only as an identity with the subject-who-values, but it is also the self dimension which forms a unity with its own ego values, the intellectual and social senses of self. The primordial self is the self-identity which realizes that it is much more than the intellectual or social ego. This "I am much more than" is the threshold to the intrinsic dimension of the self. This intrinsic dimension can be distinguished by many labels: the original self, the inner self, the primordial self, and the infinite self, among others.

The primordial self is an identity formed with one's inner source of conscious energy, with conscious awareness as pure subjectivity. It is not an identity of self in relation to given objects, whether these objects are knowledge elements, situations or other people. The primordial self forms the fundamental unity of self valuation which accounts for the capacity to be aware of one's own wholeness. Both the intellectual ego and the social ego are incomplete in the sense of being non-continuous. The primordial self contributes the unifying structure which makes possible the self as a continuum, a self-structure of unified wholeness. It is the only sense of self which remains constant through the continuum of time, unifying the present with both the past and the future. The primordial self acts as an observer for the intellectual and the social selves. It is the watcher of the egos. The primordial self has as its objects of awareness the many different subject-object relations of the intellectual and the social egos. It realizes itself as the power which makes possible all the ego subject-object relations. The primordial self is not a super-ego, but rather the substratum of all ego formations.

The primordial self may also be further valued, according to each of the axiological value dimensions. Cognitively, the primordial self is the thinking capacity, the pure ability to know self and others as unique totalities. In the history of one's exercise of the thinking capacity, that which is forgotten forms the content of the subconscious. Extrinsically, in the dynamic sense, the primordial self is the capacity to choose and to act. This is centered in the body with all its abilities for activity and movement (one's state of health). Intrinsically valued, the primordial self is the loving of our innermost center, the capacity for empathy and compassion, the ability to feel-with others and to feel the at-oneness with one's own being. The fulfillment of the intrinsic value potential of the intrinsic, primordial self entails the opening up or the blossoming of our thinking and acting capacities.

Most productive work on the reality of the intrinsic self has been done by mystics, the founders of the world's great religions. In discussing the intrinsic value of the self, Robert Hartman followed this mystical tradition. Throughout his writings, Hartman discussed the intrinsic value of the self in terms of an actual infinity. To become aware of the infinite richness of the intrinsic self, the language of finite logic and definition is left behind. The primordial self does not speak the usual symbol, word and concept language of the mind. The routine activity of mind separates and segments, while the intrinsic sense of self is always acting to integrate and expand awareness. The language of the primordial or inner self, according to Edmund Husserl, is not an "apodictic" but an "apophantic" language, expressing aspects of the original unity and oneness exhibited in the <u>evidence</u> of whole experience. According to Hartman, the language of intrinsic value is metaphorical (<u>SV</u>, p. 113). Applied to the inner self, metaphor must be used to convey meaning about the sources of intrinsic valuation--for example, radiance and light. It is not ideas or concepts of personhood that are illuminated, but personhood itself. In India the name for philosophy is "darshan," which means insight, vision, or "seeing." This is no accident. In India the emphasis is not on the logical mind, but rather on the "seeing" capacities of conscious awareness. This intrinsic kind of seeing is done with the light of the inner, primordial self.

Other expressions of the primordial self are "listening to your inner voice" and "playing the music within." Gaining in self value through expanding conscious awareness with the aid of these intrinsic metaphors develops each person's sense of uniqueness. This sense of being unique is the realization or crystallization of our <u>ownness</u> of self as the very source of all social and intellectual ego values.

Intrinsic, metaphorical expressions of the value of the inner self call upon us to look beneath and beyond the social involvements in which we are engaged. What we find when we look deeply within is the <u>source</u> of all our values, and the capacity for a continuum of consciousness which is able to tie all specific values together into <u>one single whole</u>. To clearly understand this point, we must go beyond Hartman's formal structure of value to an integration or unity of the three separate dimensions of value. Hartman indicated this himself in the story of the botanist who uses his technical knowledge to dissect a rose, but not when he picks the rose to present to his fiancee (<u>SV</u>, pp. 5-6). The rose can be dissected with scientific precision and each part may be methodically labeled, but the most essential values are missing: the life and beauty of the rose. It is the same with ourselves. We can use formal axiology to separate and label all the parts of the self, but to capture <u>all</u> the value potential of the self, we must integrate all the parts into a whole, if we are to realize our full potential.

This axiological integrated whole can become the ideal for human self development. How we can understand this ideal and apply it to our own lives for realizing more value is a very productive and interesting topic, which we will discuss next.

Self Development

We are all born as seeds, having built-in capacities to discern value and to create new values. What we are as human beings depends on how these value capacities have been filled, and what we may become is a question of how these value capacities could be or ought to be filled. The question is how one values the values constituting one's own self identity. We need greater quality of valuation rather than greater quantity of things; we want to live the good life rather than the "goods" life. Perhaps we can gain control of our own destiny if we carefully consider how to develop the value potential of our own selves.

When we define an ideal of value realization for the human self, we can use it as a norm for measuring differences in people. We can also use it as the basis for a disciplined program for self development. That ideal is the balanced integration of all three axiological dimensions. We can discover the structure of the personality through examining how persons value the content in the three dimensions of the self discussed above. How persons value their own capacities to value reveals the structure of how the personality is crystallized. The axiological ideal is attained when persons value each self value capacity, integrated with equal and balanced emphasis, as a complete whole, forming a harmonious unity between self and world. Since the axiological dimensions are held separate in Hartman's formal foundations, the nature of this integrated ideal and how it can be attained must be explained.

When the three different value dimensions of the self are fully integrated with respect to each other, they can be considered equal. We can obtain this equivalency with exponentation operations, as Robert S. Hartman did, where each value dimension is valued intrinsically. This can be formalized as $S^I=E^I=I^I$, or $(S=E=I)^I$ (SV, p 275). Thus, the power set (the set of all subsets) of the three value dimensions of the self, can be formalized as, P • (S, E, I). We can then deduce the possible value forms of the human personality, using the operators "=" for equality and ">" for inequality to indicate the relationship of the three value dimensions of the set. Each of the following power set forms can be understood as human self types, and each can be interpreted as a stage in the value development of the self. The relationship of equality or inequality reveals the structure of emphasis among the dimensions of self valuation, and all the emphasis patterns together can be used effectively as a value typology of persons. The deduction yields thirteen forms. These thirteen self value forms, types of self identity, start with the ideal, then decrease in order according to the value richness expressed. The descriptive names are taken from The Hartman Value Profile: Professional Manual of Interpretation, 1986, by this author.

Axiological Form **Descriptive Name**

1. (I=E=S)   "self-transcending"
2. ((I=E) > S)   "role-authentic"
3. ((I=S) > E)   "morally-authentic"
4. (I > (E=S))   "self-authentic"
5. ((E=S) > I)   "achievement-motivated"
6. (E > (I=S))   "role-motivated"
7. (S > (I=E))   "duty-motivated"
8. (I > E > S)   "potential-anchored"
9. (I > S > E)   "potential-bound"
10. (E > I > S)   "role-anchored"
11. (E > S > I)   "role-bound"
12. (S > I > E)   "ought-anchored"
13. (S > E > I)   "ought-bound"

This deduction gives us the universal forms which may be understood as the axiological grounding of all self-identity possibilities, and consequently these forms define the range of potential within which a subject crystallizes a specific concept of self identity. For better understanding let us take two of the above as an example.

The Type 2 form is called "role-authentic" because people who value themselves in this way define themselves according to their present professional or work role, identifying with this role intrinsically. This type has a weaker, more flexible self image (S) which is malleable according to the demands of the primary social role. The Type 13 form is named "ought-bound" because people who value themselves in this way live up to a self image or self concept adopted from others, which is not their own. The fact that the self concept is not their own motivates them to make it their own; and, consequently, they continually strive to live-up-to this adopted self image

These axiological forms of self valuation identify all the different ways people can form a <u>cognitive unity</u> with the value content and capacities of their own reality. Formal axiology also provides a means for differentiating the degrees of <u>emotional involvement</u> with that cognitive unity. These involvements are obtained by using axiological "valences," (see <u>SV</u> p. 228) and are characterized as either positive (+), negative(-), or balanced (o). The axiological deduction of all emotional involvement value forms follow in ascending order ending with the ideal. These are also taken from this author in the above mentioned manual of interpretation.

Axiological Valence	Temperament Name
1. (I-,E-,S-)	"Depressive"
2. (I-,E-,S+)	"Obsessive"
3. (I-,E-,So)	"Passive"
4. (I-,E+,S-)	"Impressionable"
5. (I-,E+,S+)	"Compulsive"
6. (I-,E+,So)	"Industrious"
7. (I-,Eo,S-)	"Reluctant"
8. (I-,Eo,S+)	"Assertive"
9. (I-,Eo,So)	"Introspective"
10. (I+,E-,S-)	"Martyr"
11. (I+,E-,S+)	"Dedicated"
12. (I+,E-,So)	"Indulgent"
13. (I+,E+,S-)	"Narcissist"
14. (I+,Eo,S-)	"Hyper-sensitive"
15. (Io,E-,S-)	"Avoider"
16. (Io,E-,S+)	"Expressive"
17. (Io,E-,So)	"Dependent"
18. (Io,E+,S-)	"Discriminating"
19. (Io,Eo,S-)	"Flexible"
20. (Io,Eo,So)	"Open"

For clarity about what these temperaments mean, let us again take a couple of examples. Temperament 1 is named "depressive" to characterize a person whose self concept does not provide any foundation for self esteem. A person of this temperament may feel a tremendous sense of guilt and worthlessness, which has become the only means available to make sense out of his or her desperate situation. In extreme cases of depressive psychosis, the person's self concept becomes both necessary for survival and at the same time is trivialized in value. The person's range of possibility becomes reduced to near zero, and every relation to the world seems necessary and mandatory, but these relations have lost all positive value in the person's self condemnation. Temperament 20 is named "open" to characterize a person who has attained an objective and open-ended balance in all axiological dimensions. People of this temperament are open to their actual becoming, indicating that they are realistically aware of the wealth of their own value potential. "Open" personalities are consciously aware of their full involvement in the process of actualizing their value potential. The objective openness of this temperament indicates that these persons are ready to add value to their cognitive value type (from one of the thirteen types above) which will enable them to move further toward self transcendence.

For a complete typology of persons, the cognitive types must be put together with the temperaments. To characterize a person's valuation of his or her own self, we would combine these from the weakest form of value realization, the "ought-bound/depressive" to the axiological ideal, the "self-transcending/open." The complete axiological system of self valuation has thirteen types and twenty temperaments, which provides a typology of 260 distinct forms of self valuation.

The Road to Self-Fulfillment

We have shown in the above discussion that formal axiology can be a very effective framework for analyzing and understanding the human self. Now, we want to investigate how the integrated system of formal axiology can be used as a framework for self fulfillment. We have seen that the values of life are multi-dimensional, and these dimensions always coexist, even if we are not aware of one or more of them. Once we become aware of the interconnectedness of the value dimensions through the system of formal axiology, we can work toward filling-in each of the dimensions with more value.

To develop the self, to attain real fulfillment, beauty, peace and harmony, we need to first step into a different dimension, the dimension of the within-one's-self. The characteristic value surrounding that first step into the within, is a deep feeling of gratitude--gratitude not that we can think, do and achieve, but a deep feeling of gratitude for the simple fact that we are, that we exist, whatever the conditions of that existence. In order to become aware of the richness of self value potential, we should go into this feeling of gratitude very deeply. Existence has given us so much. We should be joyful and very grateful for these tremendous potentials for realizing value. Being grateful opens up the intrinsic value potential of our innermost selves. This means being open to loving ourselves. In this attitude we can celebrate the wonderful gift of life, embracing the changes necessary for fulfilling our potential with open arms.

Love is the essence of the harmonious integration we are seeking, and an axiological program for self fulfillment must be based on this fundamental intrinsic value. Robert S. Hartman addressed this topic in his lectures on Advanced Management held for the General Electric Company in 1960. In these lectures he provided a summary of what religious thinkers and moral philosophers have written on the topic, "how to love yourself," divided into four phases. Each of the four phases are characterized by a definite pattern of emphasis among the value dimensions:

Phase one: knowing the self (emphasizes self-knowledge)
Phase two: choosing the self (emphasizes self-acceptance)
Phase three: creating the self (emphasizes awareness of self-potential)
Phase four: sharing the self (emphasizes interpersonal harmony)

We can use the thirteen integrated value emphasis patterns, shown above, to formalize Hartman's summary. This would provide three stages for each of Hartman's phases, marked by a shift in the value emphasis pattern. We can take the axiological forms of self identity in reverse order, starting with the form that contains the least value and ending with the ideal of full, multi-dimensional self integration. The result can serve as a map of value enrichment to develop the value potential of our own selves.

To attain self fulfillment, we can follow a progression through each value pattern toward the ideal of self-fulfillment and integration. The purpose of following this progression in order is to provide stability in the process of expanding our conscious awareness to include and fulfill our whole Being. The set of all thirteen universal value patterns form the map of the road to self value fulfillment. These patterns are listed below, in ascending value order, with common language names themeatizing the stages of personal value development.

Knowing Your Self
1. $S > E > I$ The Ego "Lie" and Your True Self
2. $S > I > E$ Finding Your Own Voice
3. $E > S > I$ Exploring Your Potential

Choosing Your Self
4. $E > I > S$ Choosing Your Special Pathway in Life
5. $I > S > E$ Awakening to the Silent Beauty Within
6. $I > E > S$ Celebrating the Miracle of You

Creating Your Self
7. $S > (E = I)$ Your Destiny in Your Own Hands
8. $E > (S = I)$ Doing, Achieving and Having
9. $(S = E) > I$ Health and Prosperity

Sharing Your Self
10. I > (S = E)   Loving and Caring
11. (I = S) > E   Ethical Values for a New Age
12. (I = E) > S   Conflict Resolution

Ideal:
13. (I = E = S)   Balanced Self Value Integration

For more details about this program, see <u>Values For Living: Becoming the River</u>, a book on self development by this author. The value formulae are pure logic patterns and have no content as such. Value themes from life are assigned to each pattern, however the scope of application for each universal axiological pattern is potentially much broader.

A journey of a thousand miles begins with a single step. If we want to develop the value capacities of our own selves to the fullest, then we are ready to take that first bold step. We refer to this as a "bold" step because it means stepping away from the comfort zone of the ego. But there is no need to be afraid. Down the road of this journey to self fulfillment the only people we will meet are our own true selves. Once we <u>love</u> ourselves and become aware of the tremendous inner potential for developing our value capacities, we will already be well down the road toward self-fulfillment.

BIBLIOGRAPHY

Hartman, Robert S., "The Axiometric Structure of Intrinsic Value," The Journal of Value Inquiry, Vol. 8, 1974, pp. 81-101.

Hartman, Robert S., The Structure of Value. Carbondale: Southern Illinois University Press, 1967.

Husserl, Edmund, Formale und Transzendentale Logik. Second Edition. The Hague: Martinus Nijhoff, 1974.

Mefford, David L., Phenomenology of Man as a Valuing Subject. Doctoral Dissertation in Philosophy, Knoxville, The University of Tennessee, 1989.

Mefford, David L., The Hartman Value Profile: Professional Manual of Interpretation. Knoxville, TN, Value Measurement Technologies, Inc., 1986.

Mefford, David L., Values for Living: Becoming the River. Knoxville, TN, Value Measurement Technologies, Inc., 1990.

Chapter XVI

WHY GOOD PEOPLE DO BAD THINGS

Wayne Carpenter

The contrast between order and system in the natural world and disorder and chaos in the moral world is a constant theme in the writings of Dr. Robert S. Hartman. The achievements of modern science have opened pathways to new knowledge in a myriad of fields and have literally brought the world to our doorstep. The contemporary situation for moral knowledge and improvements, however, is different. Countless examples of chaos and disorder in moral issues verify Hartman's observations. Consider the territorial and political wars which rage throughout the world and even prevent medical and food relief to starving populations, the acts of terrorism and hostage taking which hold the world and its institutions as hostage, the acts of individual power maneuvering and avarice which threaten our financial and political institutions and the acts of individual aggression of neighbor against neighbor.

One example of our inability to maintain moral order and consistency centers around individuals who have well established family ties, who are productive members of society, who are leaders of the business and civic community and yet commit bad (immoral, dishonest and even heinous) actions. The bad actions of these people who have been classified as good people include:

(1) acts of murder committed by teenagers who are excellent students or who have no history of violence;
(2) acts of rape committed by trusted family members;

(3) physical violence committed by family members against one another
(4) sexual molestation of children many times by members of their own families or by scout masters, ministers and friends;
(5) alcohol and drug abuse by high achievers and by business and civic leaders;
(6) acts of theft by long time, productive and trusted employees;
(7) acts of deception by the business community which are utilized to promote products and services;
(8) the greed and avarice of business and political leaders.

A quick glance at the evening newspaper or television newscast will confirm examples of good people doing bad things on a regular basis.

How can we account for this apparent paradox? A simple answer is that those individuals who commit bad actions are not in fact good people. Obviously they were not being good people at the time of their bad actions. The problem, as we have noted, is that in many cases individuals who have a well documented history of dependable, accountable, productive and caring actions do commit bad actions. How do we define the problem, and where do we look for a consistent and reliable answer?

There appears to be no simple answer to these questions. We have well-accepted ideas of what a good person is, and of a good parent, a good and faithful person who does not violate his/her marriage vows, a dependable person who stands by personal beliefs, a good, honest person who has integrity, a good, a reliable and industrious individual who is a productive member of society. The fact that individuals meet the requirements and still commit bad actions demonstrates the risk that we face. How do we explain, measure and control this risk? How can we objectively and reliably
determine, before the occurrence of the bad action, that an individual is susceptible to making a bad decision? What can we do to help individuals understand where and how they are at risk and what they can do to prevent the risk?

In this paper, we will explore a new model for defining, explaining, measuring, and preventing the risk of making bad decisions. In the process, we will provide a rationale for understanding why good people make bad decisions which we will argue to be objective, consistent, testable and reliable. This model is based on the science of axiology as created and formulated by Robert S. Hartman. The focus of this analysis is on measuring the risk of making bad decisions. First, we will examine the methodology behind the analysis to define what we mean by risk. Second we will explore the measuring of the risk of making a bad decision in two particular types of decisions. Next, we will propose a model for explaining why people, even good people, make bad decisions. Finally, we will consider the implications of this model.

Measuring Risks

The key concept in our examination of why good people do bad things is risk. For us, risk measures the susceptibility of an individual to making a bad judgment or decision. Susceptibility is an open concept, a variable, rather than a black and white, closed concept. Measuring the risk for making a bad decision does not mean, therefore, that a person categorically is honest or dishonest, good or bad, moral or immoral. Rather, an individual is determined to be at risk (to be susceptible) in specific situations and under certain conditions. What we are after is the definition and measure of just those conditions and situations which put a person at risk and why in fact that risk exists. The measure of these risk conditions ranges from no or low risk, situational risk indicating that there are definite situations in which a person is susceptible, conditional risk indicating that there are conditions that create a high susceptibility that a person will make a bad decision, and real risk indicating that a person is at risk to make a bad judgment regardless of conditions and circumstances.

There are three parameters to risk which are important for our analysis. First, risk involves the capacity of an individual to make a judgment or decision. In this sense, risk involves the ability to identify problems correctly and accurately, to size up situations, to evaluate alternative courses of action and to make sound and objective decisions. The objective measure of this facet of risk requires an objective and accurate standard for evaluating a person's capacity for problem solving and thinking in general. Second, risk involves the probability of occurrence of either a good or bad judgment. Is a person is a good or bad risk for taking something that does not belong to him or her? This facet of risk requires not only an objective standard but also a methodology for quantitatively defining and assessing risk conditions. Third, risk includes sensitivity to both good and bad influences which affect a person's capacity for thinking and problem solving. Sensitivity to good influences defines inhibitors which can act as a means of preventing bad judgments. Sensitivity to bad influences indicates a breakdown in the problem solving and decision making process. The measure of this aspect of risk requires a methodology for assessing a person's capacity to consistently translate values and beliefs into decisions and actions and for determining the effects of personal biases on the ability to make decisions.

348 *Forms of Value and Valuation: Theory and Applications*

The science of Axiology offers a unique and effective methodology for the measure of risk. Value concepts have traditionally been considered to be intangible, unavailable to quantitative analysis, or have been reduced to behavior which can be statistically analyzed. Neither approach has ever produced a satisfactory resolution of value conflicts, and even the latter methodology cannot produce a consistent and universal methodology for measuring value. Robert S. Hartman broke with tradition through his discovery of a value mathematics which brings order to value concepts in the same way that mathematics brings order to the natural sciences. As a result, Axiology has the same ingredients as the key elements of a natural science:

(1) It provides a quantitative standard of measure, a mathematical means for measuring objects or experiences against a standard, which functions as a measuring rod for making decisions.
(2) It generates new knowledge about the everyday world, a frame of reference which provides a new perspective, a new way of looking at ourselves and our environment.
(3) Axiological knowledge is objective, independent of any one observer, and empirical, describing something which is observable in the world.
(4) Axiology measures and orders its subject matter with a standard which is universally applicable.
(5) Axiology has its own special concepts and language.
(6) Axiology provides tools which can be applied to everyday problems and situations.

The uniqueness of Dr. Hartman's discovery is that value mathematics is inherent in the way we think and value. For Hartman, the key to the measure of value. A thing has value, is good, to the extent that it fulfills the meaning or intension of its concept. He discovered two things about the intension of concepts which are important for our measure of risk:

(1) The intension of concepts is structured, and
(2) The structure of intension can be quantitatively measured.

The structure of value is mirrored in the structure of the intensions of concepts. For Hartman, this structure has three dimensions which correspondingly measure three dimensions of value. The intrinsic value dimension measures uniqueness and authenticity, the infinite and irreplaceable worth of individuals. Its objects of value include individual human beings, reflecting an infinite source of value, metaphors, and potentially any individual thing as it exists in its own uniqueness. The intrinsic value dimension measures identification, seeing the object of valuing in its totality. The extrinsic value dimension defines practical, functional and concrete value, class membership. Its objects of value are things, circumstances, situations and the roles that people play. The extrinsic value dimension measures comparison, whether an object of value is good, better, bad or worse, and focuses on doing and practice. The systemic value dimension measures system, order, consistency and ought. Its objects of systemic value are concepts, ideas, systems and images. The systemic value dimension measures whether the object of value conforms, has structure, is what it ought to be.

Dr. Hartman's three dimensional value structure provides a unique methodology for defining the parameters of concepts of risk. Consider, for example, the concept of "honesty." The intrinsic value dimension involves identification with the uniqueness, the irreplaceable worth and totality of the concept or object of value. This process of identification describes sensitivity to irreplaceable worth. In terms of the concept "honesty", this sensitivity indicates an awareness of the potential for goodness and badness, for honesty and dishonesty. We define this sensitivity as conscience. Conscience refers to how we feel about the potential goodness and badness of a decision. Can we see the decision in its totality, identify the goodness or badness which is inherent in the decision? The extrinsic value dimension defines the functional, practical aspect of honesty. This dimension describes the translation of principle into action, defines comparative goodness or badness, i.e. what the decision is good for or bad for. Is the decision the practical thing to do in the sense that it is an application of the principle of right, or HOW is honesty the practical thing to do? This dimension is practical ethics. The systemic value dimension defines honesty in terms of commitment to a moral code, that is, in terms of a sense of obligation to be honest.

By applying Hartman's three dimensional model to honesty, we have identified three dimensions of honesty:

(1) conscience,
(2) practical ethics,
(3) moral code.

We can make the same application to any concept such as responsibility, accountability, dishonesty or ethics. Hartman's model does more, however, than provide a methodology for definition. He discovered that there is a hierarchy of values composed of the combinations of value dimensions which themselves have different value. Our experience demonstrates that there is a difference in value among the value dimensions. For example, my love and acceptance of my wife is more valuable than my appreciation of what she does for me. Moreover, both of these valuations ARE more valuable than my ideas, images, expectations and fantasies about her. Hartman confirmed what experience tells us by mathematically and logically defining a quantitative difference among the value dimensions. He also discovered that the value dimensions can be combined and that the valuational possibilities of these combinations are not random. Regardless of whether Hartman used symbolic logic, the theory of types, set theory or transfinite set theory to quantify the relative value of the combinations of value, the order of value of the combinations always came out the same.

Hartman's discovery of the regularity in the structure of concepts defines a norm for value. Research has confirmed that the correlation between Hartman's value norm and objective reality is extremely close to a one-to-one correspondence. What we have, then, is an objective standard for measuring the structure and dynamics of a person's ability to make value judgments, to think and value concerning any concept, to mirror our value experience. Referring again to the concept of honesty, what does this norm mean for our study of risk? We can measure how clearly we can think about honesty, that is, our ability to distinguish conscience, practical ethics and moral code. We can detect our sensitivity to the goodness and badness of actions both in ourselves and in others. We can identify and level of acceptance for and commitment to moral code and principles for action, and can also measure our willingness to translate our principles consistently into action.

We have demonstrated how Axiology generates an objective model for measuring risk. Now, we will see that value science also provides a methodology for creating instruments for data collection. These instruments, value principles, are constructed from combinations of the three value dimensions. Value combinations are axiological formulas, for example, the intrinsic valuation of extrinsic value. To build a profile instrument, we translate axiological formulas into words and phrases which mirror the value experience represented by the formula. Intrinsic value reflects identification with the uniqueness of the object of value. Extrinsic value reflects practical, concrete value. The intrinsic valuation of extrinsic value measures identification with the uniqueness and the totality of the concrete object of value. The value capacity represented by the formula measures the ability to see the concrete in its uniqueness and irreplaceability, to see the object of value in its completeness and totality. We translate this valuation as creativity, the ability to see correctly the value of the object without imposing a preset concept or interpretation. Each axiological formula must be translated into its appropriate representation.

The value combinations include the compositions (positive valuations) of value and the transpositions (negative valuations) of value. The following table reflects objectives which can be used to translate axiological formulas into words or phrases.

COMPOSITIONS	TRANSPOSITIONS
Intrinsic Valuation means to identify with, to love and accept, to create, to see the uniqueness, totality and irreplaceability.	Intrinsic Disvaluation means to hate, to despise, to destroy the value totally.
Extrinsic Valuation means to make better, to be good for, practical, functional.	Extrinsic Disvaluation means to detract from, to make dysfunctional, impractical, to decrease the value of.
Systemic Valuation means to make meaningful; to give order, consistency.	Systemic Disvaluation means to make meaningless, to indicate confusion, a lack of order, purpose, and direction.

The Hartman Value Profile (HVP 1 and HVP 2) is the first translation of the value combinations into a profile instrument. The HVP is a proven, reliable instrument for measuring a person's capacity to make value judgments about people, practical situations, systems and order, self esteem, social/role awareness and one's self direction. Theoretically, any concept can be translated into the value combinations and then into a value profile instrument. We are currently using profiles to measure Work Environment, Sales, Management, Customer Service and Excellence (defining, instilling and communicating excellence). Moreover, we have researched other concepts ranging from honesty, dishonesty and pedophilia, to family concepts such as husband, wife, son, daughter and concepts such as work environment, excellence and quality.

We will now shift our attention to the analysis of a specific risk situation: --the risk of being dishonest and stealing--in order to demonstrate the dynamics and power of axiological methodology and build a model for interpreting why good people are susceptible to doing bad things.

Measuring Dishonesty

Our contention is that valuation is a natural, logical activity of the mind and that Axiology provides an objective, quantitative methodology for measuring the structure and function of that activity. In effect, we measure how people think and value. As a result, we can identify the influences on

their thinking which lead people to make the decisions they make. The fascinating aspect of measuring the value process is that each concept we can think of has its own unique structure and function for each person but, at the same time, all concepts for all people have a common structure and regularity. It is this unique aspect of Axiology which opens a new door for defining and measuring risk, specifically for identifying the susceptibility to making bad decisions.

We will now focus on one specific risk problem, dishonesty. This problem is the focal point of research designed to test the usefulness and reliability of Axiology for defining and measuring risk. Although the research on the validity of resulting models is still in progress, what we did accomplish:

(1) provides an interpretive model for defining the risk of making a bad decision,
(2) establishes the validity of the Hartman Value Profile for measuring how people think and value in general, and
(3) lays the foundation for the development of analytical tools and methodology for investigating any concept.

We will examine the general strategy for the research of this risk concept (dishonesty), define the models for interpreting and measuring risk of dishonesty in this situation, examine the results of the research, and consider the implications of these results for our key question: "Why do good people do bad things?"

There are certain key questions which guide our investigation of dishonesty. We know that the Value Profile for World and Self measures a person's general capacity to make value judgments. Is the information generated by the HVP sufficient to detect the risk for making bad decisions in general; and more specifically, will the information detect the risk for being dishonest? What does the HVP tell us about a person's susceptibility to bad influences in the decision environment? We also know that we can construct value profile instruments to measure any risk concept. Will the information generated by these profiles be sufficient for measuring risk? How can the information generated by these profiles be combined with information generated by the HVP to measure risk? Finally, what can the information generated from the HVP and specific risk profiles tell us about measuring risk in general, and what implications does this have for understanding how we think and value?

We will focus on the definition of the key concepts for honesty and on the decision models for interpreting these risk conditions. Honesty is a difficult concept to define clearly and consistently and to measure accurately. Typically, the idea of honesty is constructed as a black-and-white issue: either a person is honest or dishonest. Dishonest actions are used as a negative way of defining honesty by demonstrating what it is not. Circularity may be used to define honesty; for example, an honest person is referred to as a person who has integrity, and a person with integrity is a person who is considered to act with honesty. Honesty may also be defined by terms which themselves lack precision; for example, an honest person may be referred to as genuine, sincere, or honorable. Our day-to-day experience with people who have built reputations for being trustworthy and loyal also creates confusion about honesty when these people are dishonest.

Axiologically, we have already defined honesty in terms of three parameters:

(1) sense of conscience,
(2) practical ethics,
(3) moral code.

An honest person is one who: (1) has a keen sense of conscience generating sensitivity to the potential goodness and badness of his or her decisions and actions, (2) has a deep sense of respect for people, for things, for the need for conformity to rules and order in society or in a company, (3) has developed a strong sense of practical ethics which consistently translates ideas about what is right and wrong into day-to-day decisions and actions, (4) has a strong sense of commitment to inner ideals and principles, that is, has a clear idea of and strong commitment to a personal code of conduct.

The axiological process of analyzing honesty is complicated by a series of potential problems: (1) each of the value judgments which compose an honest action can be subdivided into component valuational elements, (For example, conscience includes both personal and social conscience, that is, sensitivity to the goodness and badness of one's own actions as well as those of others), (2) each person has developed value capacities to different degrees, and (3) the fact that there is a different degree of tolerance for good and bad influences in different decision environments. For example, a person may have a strong sense of personal and social conscience, a deep respect for people, things and society and for the general worth of order and authority but be inconsistent in the practical application of his or her code into action.

Moreover, this same individual may tend to rationalize that dishonesty is an acceptable or practical alternative. This individual can go through life and never face a situation which tests this rationalization, and in so doing, can be seen as an honest person in the community. On the other hand, this same person may come face-to-face with a decision in which the weakness of his or her inconsistent application of a code of conduct leads to a dishonest action.

We utilize axiological analysis to define the parameters of honesty. This analysis expands the concept of conscience to include:

(1) sensitivity to the dishonesty of others,
(2) sensitivity to self dishonesty,
(3) sensitivity to fulfilling one's social obligation to be honest,
(4) sensitivity to fulfilling inner moral code,
(5) sensitivity to one's own potential for badness.
(6) strength of one's obligation and commitment to be honest.

The analysis expands the concept of practical ethics to include:

(1) ability to practically evaluate honesty,
(2) willingness to treat honesty as a good, fulfilling alternative,
(3) willingness to treat honesty as a practical, useful alternative,
(4) willingness to accept dishonesty as a practical, useful alternative,
(5) willingness to rationalize or excuse dishonesty.

Moreover, this axiological expansion of honesty defines moral code to include:

(1) respect for company property,
(2) respect for company principles about what ought to be done,
(3) respect for inner principles of ought,
(4) respect for authority and conformity to order,
(5) respect for one's moral obligation to do the right thing.

To measure this expanded concept of honesty, we need two things:

(1) value profile instruments for measuring honesty, and
(2) a model for interpretation and assessment of the risk of being dishonest.

The Hartman Value Profile anchors the measure of risk by providing the following functions:

(1) identifies risk which occurs because of erroneous or inadequate thinking,
(2) measures the level of respect for people, for things in general as well as for things or property which belong to a company or organization, and for rules and codes of conduct,
(3) identifies inhibitors which can act as risk preventers,
(4) measures the degree of inner security and self confidence which reinforces one's ability to understand temptation and stand firm on one's sense of right,
(5) measures the strength of one's commitment to inner self principles,
(6) identifies the willingness to do things right,
(7) measures the overall level of optimism which generates an expectation for the best.

The early stages of our research disclosed, however, that the Hartman Value Profile overlooked the riskiness of certain individuals. These individuals had very clear thinking and valuing capacities. They were organization people who valued property in general and property which belonged to the company in particular. They had respect for people and for rules and codes. They had a strong sense of confidence in themselves and commitment to what they believed to be right. As far as we know, these individuals had never before committed a dishonest act; yet they were caught being dishonest.

The construction of two honesty profiles provides an added dimension to the information which can be generated by the Hartman Value Profile. One honesty profile measures the concept of honesty in general, and the other profile measures the concept of self honesty. The following chart reviews the I, E, S dimensions of these two profiles:

HONESTY IN THE WORLD	SELF HONESTY
Intrinsic Valuation: The ability to value honesty as a unique, fulfilling experience.	Intrinsic Valuation: The ability to value self honesty as a unique, fulfilling experience.
Extrinsic Valuation: The ability to value honesty as a practical, functional experience.	Extrinsic Valuation: The ability to value self honesty as a practical, functional experience.
Systemic Valuation: The ability to value honesty as an obligation.	Systemic Valuation: The ability to value one's personal obligation to be honest.

Utilizing these profiles, we can further probe the ability of an individual to handle risk situations by assessing:

(1) the willingness to see and accept the practical value of being honest;
(2) the ability to correctly identify the negative effects of dishonesty;
(3) the willingness to consistently remain committed to being honest;
(4) the awareness and attention one gives to honesty in the world and in oneself.

The process of measuring the risk of dishonesty is based on an understanding of the thinking and valuing process. This process defines and clarifies the steps which one goes through to decide what is important, to decide to decide, to translate the decision into action, and to evaluate the consequences of decisions and actions. Working within the boundaries of the expanded concept of honesty, the following model reflects the parameters of the decision process as it relates to honesty. The individual:

(1) knows the difference between right and wrong,
(2) believes that honesty is the right thing to do,
(3) has the ability to make an honest decision.

An analysis of these parameters lays the foundation for understanding why and how a person is susceptible to making a bad decision in general, and provides a model for measuring the risk of making a dishonest decision in particular.

Knowing the Difference Between Right and Wrong

This module measures the ability of an individual to think clearly and objectively about the world, about oneself and about moral issues in general. The emphasis is on the ability to make reliable judgments, to size up issues correctly and to see and understand potential problems. There are three sources of potential risk.

(1) Perceptual biases in the world:
This risk area measures a person's ability to think clearly and objectively about people, about practical situations and problems, and about issues of order, conformity to principles of order and codes in general.

(2) Perceptual biases in the self:
This risk area measures a person's ability to think clearly, objectively and positively about self including one's self esteem, social and role competence and self direction.

(3) Moral clarity:
This risk area measures a person's capacity to identify correctly moral issues in situations (1) concerning the honesty of others, (2) dealing with respect for personal or organizational property, (3) dealing with self honesty, (4) dealing with personal obligation, (5) dealing with social obligation and (6) dealing with the inner principles about what is right or wrong.

When problems occur in these risk areas, some of the potential effects include:

(1) bad decisions which happen out of misunderstanding or ignorance of things which are socially acceptable,
(2) a feeling that the world owes him or her a living, that his or her ideas about right and wrong are the only ones that count,
(3) being misled or manipulated by others into inappropriate or dishonest actions,
(4) difficulty sizing up the potential harm which inappropriate or dishonest actions can cause,
(5) difficulty handling confusing ethical situations or new ideas or problems which force this person outside the boundaries of accepted ideas and practices.

358   *Forms of Value and Valuation: Theory and Applications*

Believes that Honesty is the Right Thing to do:

This module measures the strength of one's commitment to inner principles which decide what is right or wrong, and of one's belief in and reliance on an internal code of conduct. This confidence and commitment to right determines whether a person (1) pays attention to what is right, (2) believes that he or she is and ought to be seen as honest, (3) feels a strong sense of mission and purpose, and (4) has respect for norms and rules whether these are internal or external. This module measures five sources of potential risk:

(1) Commitment to what a person thinks is right:
This risk area involves the strength of one's convictions about personal obligation to do the right thing. This conviction indicates the strength of an individual's belief that he or she ought to obey inner principles of right and wrong.
(2) Confidence that things ought to be done right:
This risk area includes one's belief in the rightness of standards and codes of conduct, both external in terms of social and organizational norms, and in terms of internal norms of conduct. This feeling creates a belief that honesty is the best policy and ought to be the best policy.
(3) Expectations that things be done right:
This risk area involves the attention to doing things right indicating both that the individual knows what is right and wrong and feels an urgency to see to it that things are done right.
(4) Inner belief on one's own honesty:
This risk area includes a person's seeing and accepting that he or she ought to be an honest person.

Two general types of problems can occur in these risk areas. One type is created by excessive attention to norms, rules and codes of conduct, to perfectionistic, dogmatic and rigid thinking, and commitment to what one thinks is right, regardless of circumstances. This rigid adherence to what one believes to be right can lead to rationalization of inappropriate actions, to impulsive and emotional responses and to a stubborn unwillingness to see or accept viewpoints which contradict his or her own. The other type of problem is created if a person has either a combination of uncertainty about his or her personal code of conduct or sense of direction, mission and sense of purpose, and/or has a disregard for rules, norms and what is right. This can lead an individual to:

(1) demand less of oneself than he or she is capable of, creating a susceptibility to inappropriate action,
(2) become confused, hesitant and indecisive in situations where the decisions are complex and confusing,
(3) covertly or overtly get around rules, norms and accepted ways of doing things,
(4) overlook the badness of actions.

Has the Ability to Make an Honest Decision

This module measures a person's ability and willingness to translate principle into action. The focus is on two basic functions, one dealing with problem solving and decision making, and the other dealing with consistency and accountability. The first function concerns a person's ability not only to identify the problem correctly but also the capacity to get things done. The second function deals with a person's capacity to be consistent in his or her ability to make day-to-day ethical decisions. This model measures four sources of potential risk:

(1) Sense of responsibility and accountability:
This risk area involves a person's willingness to pay attention to, be responsible for, and be willing to answer for the consequences of decisions and actions.
(2) Practical ethics:
This risk area consists of a person's willingness to see and accept honesty as a good, practical and meaningful alternative, and/or dishonesty as a good practical and meaningful alternative, and the strength of a person's sense of conscience.
(3) Moral code:
This risk area includes one's ability to respect (1) rules, principles, norms and codes of conduct whether internal or external, (2) property and thing in general, (3) individuals, (4) self honesty, (5) one's social obligation to be honest, and (6) one's personal obligation to be honest.
(4) Ability to make a decision and to get things done:
This risk area involves three things. First, the focus is on ability to solve problems including, (1) intuitive insight about what needs to be done, (2) practical problem solving ability, and (3) the ability to integrate one's thinking into clear concepts, plans and solutions. Second, the focus is on ability to manage stress and anxiety and maintain freedom of action in one's decisions. Third, the focus is on one's ability to maintain a sense of balance in one's thinking and valuing.

The effects of problems generated by the inability to make an honest decision can be especially critical and be specific to the specific risk area. As a result:

(1) when problems arise with responsibility and accountability, the following can occur. These persons tend to:

(a) have a difficult time deciding what their obligations are,
(b) be inconsistent in their thinking and decision making and to have inconsistent attitudes about and responses to the dishonesty of others,
(c) lack a willingness to deal with inappropriate actions of self or others,
(d) shift the blame to anything or anyone other than themselves.

(2) when problems arise with practical ethics, the following can occur. These persons tend to:

(a) demonstrate a willingness to accept and rationalize the practical value of dishonesty,
(b) underestimate their own potential for dishonesty,
(c) be insensitive to the potential harm of dishonesty,
(d) develop an indifference to the inconsistency between belief in their own personal honesty, and the willingness to accept the value of, and practice dishonesty.

(3) when problems arise with moral code, the following can occur. These persons tend to:

(a) be hesitant and timid about standing up for what they believe is right,
(b) develop complacency about taking care of personal property or the property of others, especially company property,
(c) disregard rules and norms for conduct unless they are a benefit to themselves,
(d) trust the wrong people,
(e) take things out of context, blowing up the significance of minor issues and overlooking or discounting the importance of crucial ethical issues.

(4) when problems arise with the ability to make an honest decision, the following can occur. These persons tend to:

(a) have difficulty making a decision and, as a result, are pushed and pulled by circumstances and influences around themselves,
(b) rationalize that what they believe is right, regardless of circumstances,
(c) become susceptible to making bad decisions simply to relieve the pressure of stress and anxiety,
(d) make expedient decisions without thinking about the consequences.

Research on the application of this model to establish its predictive capacity is still under way. We have been able to establish, however, some results and trends with the application of the model. The following observations about measuring the concept of honesty resulted from an examination of individuals who had been caught stealing and terminated from their jobs:

(1) Information derived from the Hartman Value Profile did not consistently identify these individuals as a risk. As a matter of a fact, these people, as a group had a strong sense of respect for company rules and a strong commitment to their own inner principles of
 right and wrong, were proactive individuals who paid attention to the consequences of their actions, were optimists who believed that the best is possible and had a good sense of practical, common sense ability. The HVP information did identify potential problems:

(a) Self Depreciation:
a tendency to not give themselves enough credit, to feel a sense of guilt and inadequacy when they do not live up to their own expectations or the expectations of others. This problem can create a willingness to accept one's own potential for badness potentially generating a self fulfilling hypothesis.
(b) Over Confidence:
a tendency to overestimate their ability to perform, to have a false or specious sense of confidence which can cause them to overlook their own potential for error and to become so concerned about image that potentially a willingness to be insincere and even dishonest can
result, in stressful situations.
(c) Rationalization:
a tendency to attempt stubbornly and dogmatically to insist that their way is right regardless of circumstances can lead them to become locked on a tangent which may involve the\justification of inappropriate or even dishonest actions as necessary to fulfill their commitments, objectives and plans.

By and large in this group, these problems did not occur at a level which would create a real risk but they could create a situational risk.

(2) Information derived from the Hartman Value Profile and The Honesty Profiles showed that the potential situational risk was increased by the following tendencies:

(a) a strong sense of commitment to principle and a belief that people should be honest but this sense of honesty was combined with a lack of sensitivity to the badness of actions in others and in themselves.
(b) a strong belief that there ought to be rules and norms for conduct but they also believed that these rules did not always apply to them, indicating a willingness to accept the breaking of rules and norms for conduct without actually seeing themselves as dishonest.
(c) a tendency to treat honesty as a practical, functional alternative but there was also a willingness to accept their own personal dishonesty as a practical alternative.

At this time, our research has confirmed that these trends exist in dishonest people and not in honest people and that these trends in and of themselves will always lead a person to be dishonest. We have been able to diagnose these trends using the honesty model to help explain, after the fact, why these people became a risk, the type of risk, and the situations which would increase the risk. Moreover, the expanded concept of "honest," the honesty model and the experience with interpretations of people who have been caught being dishonest have served as a basis for creating a new interpretive model for explaining why people make bad decisions. This interpretive model defines the risk problems even in individuals who from the profile information see themselves as honest and believe they ought to be honest. An examination of this model will further illuminate the implications of applying axiology to risk.

Risk Conditions for Dishonesty

The unique and powerful contribution of axiology for measuring how a person thinks and values creates a pathway for understanding how and why "bad" decisions are made even by good people. The risk of making a bad decision is measured by measuring the person's ability to think clearly, correctly and objective, by identifying what a person pays attention to and by assessing the sense of balance in a person's thinking. Risk at all levels (situational, conditional and real risk) is created by fallacies in an individual's thinking and valuing process. For example, a person who does not have a clear sense of self esteem, who has a fuzzy sense of what is morally right, who tends to be an individualist and covertly or overtly gets around authority but who believes in his or her own self honesty and has a strong desire to be seen as an honest person can be at risk in situations which are complex and confusing, where the rules and norms for conduct are not clear, or in situations where practical urgency to do something and be recognized for the action seems more important than maintaining the consistency of principle.

There are three general risk conditions which result from the application of our model and define how and why a person is susceptible to making a bad decision. The first condition defines the risk generated by inadequate thinking. In this risk condition, the person does not know the difference between good and bad and hence chooses bad. The capacity to distinguish clearly what is right, to identify himself or herself as an honest, principled person and/or the ability clearly and consistently to size up situations in the world is not adequately developed. As a result of inadequate thinking, a person at risk will have difficulty knowing what to do and thus becomes susceptible to the bad influences in his or her environment. The second risk condition defines the risk generated by irrational thinking, that is, by fallacious thinking which attempts to rationalize the correctness of decisions regardless of circumstances or acceptance by society in general. This person knows the difference between good and bad but chooses bad anyway and justifies the choice as the only "right" option. The third risk condition defines the risk generated by the person who sees good as bad. This person sees dishonesty not only as a practical alternative but as the right or correct choice. Honesty for this person is impractical and meaningless and as a result he or she feels no obligation to be honest and in some cases no sense of conscience about the destructiveness of his or her dishonest actions.

Amplifying these risk conditions, we can identify and define the parameters of a model for interpreting risk. As we examine this model, the reference to honest or dishonest can be taken also to indicate right and wrong, appropriate or inappropriate, moral or immoral.

We define the instances of the risk conditions as (1) Type A: People Who Choose Wrong Because They Cannot Tell The Difference Between Right and Wrong, (2) Type B: People Who Know The Difference Between Right And Wrong But Choose Wrong Anyway, and (3) Type C: People Who See Wrong As Right.

Type A: PEOPLE WHO CHOOSE WRONG BECAUSE THEY CANNOT TELL THE DIFFERENCE BETWEEN RIGHT AND WRONG

Risk Condition A1: Inability To See And Understand What Is Happening

This person's ability to see and understand what is happening is either fuzzy and somewhat faulty, creating uncertainty about what is seen, or is severely restricted such that this person sees part of the picture but at the same time is absolutely convinced that the part that is seen is the whole picture.

The risk this individual poses for making a wrong or dishonest choice is strictly an indirect result of this unclear thinking and not a direct result of morally defective thinking. This person is not directly at risk for planning dishonest or wrong actions, but because of faulty and potentially irrational thinking, this person can be put at risk in the following:

(1) situations where the difference between right and wrong is not clear cut and obvious;
(2) situations which require a quick decision;
(3) difficult problem decisions involving many elements which are tangled together;
(4) situations where the normal rules about what is right and wrong do not apply.

Risk Condition A2: Inadequate Self Image

This person tends toward self depreciation, generating feelings of guilt and inadequacy when he or she does not measure up. The impact of this self depreciation can lead to inconsistent feelings, sometimes being on top of the world and other times being down in the dumps. There is also a susceptibility to emotional and impulsive actions, reacting to problems and difficult situations rather than thinking through them.

Although this person is not a direct risk for designing and implementing dishonest and/or immoral actions, the effects of the inadequate self image can create a risk potential under certain conditions and situations. These risk conditions can lead to a reactiveness which, in turn, can cause this person to commit actions and make decisions which would not normally be made.

The following are three risk situations which can become a potential threat:

(1) The person already believes and accepts his or her own potential for being bad and inadequate. This acceptance of the potential for badness generates a susceptibility to the following situations:
(a) Because of self depreciation, there is likely to be a strong and compulsive need to be recognized and accepted by others. This need can conflict with the desire and commitment to be honest and may lead this person to overlook the inappropriateness or badness of actions which he or she may deem necessary to win approval from others.
(b) In confusing situations where the guidelines for what is right and wrong are not straight forward or where this person does not have time to think through the consequences of actions, he or she will be at risk. In this case, the acceptance of the potential for badness becomes a self fulfilling hypothesis potentially leading to bad decisions.

(2) This person's emotional inconsistency can lead to rash reactions such that he or she impulsively commits an action in the heat of the moment which he or she would never plan or carry out in ordinary, less stressful circumstances.

(3) This person does not have a good understanding of personal strengths and limitations either overestimating or underestimating his or her ability. As a result, this person is likely to have difficulty determining how much temptation is too much and as a result is susceptible to the bad influences in the environment.

Risk Condition A3: Self Conceit

This person's inflated sense of self importance can generate risk situations where inappropriate decisions and actions are not only possible but are rationally accepted as the right and only course of action.

Three general conditions can generate a risk situation:

(1) a belief that he or she does not get enough credit and attention from others, i.e., feelings of self sacrifice and self pity,

(2) a false sense of overconfidence which leads him or her to be over optimistic about the ability to perform and to underestimate his or her potential for error,

(3) a perfectionistic, idealistic belief in self ideals which pushes this person constantly. This person lives his or her sense of ambition and self ought, rather than his real self. This person is susceptible to feeling that he or she ought to be better than anyone else or that no one else is quite as good as he or she is. This person can overlook the potential for dishonesty since the rigid and dogmatic belief that he or she is right can lead to a refusal to admit guilt or error and to a rationalization of any action necessary to accomplish his or her sense of mission and purpose.

Risk Condition A4: Moralism

This person presents an unusual combination of risk which may be an all too common occurrence. He or she is basically an honest and moral person, has a good sense of conscience, a strong disapproval of dishonesty, a strong belief that he or she ought to be and is honest and an even stronger desire to be seen as honest by others. Moreover, this person has a good capacity for thinking clearly and for problem solving, has good practical common sense, and has a positive self image expecting the best. So! Where is the risk?

Three ingredients blend together to create a potential risk situation. First, this person does not have a clear internal moral code, which makes it difficult for her or him to identify internal principles which decide what is right and wrong conduct. Second, even though he or she does not clearly see inner principles, this person is uncompromisingly committed to one particular principle, set of principles or way of thinking as "the answer" to morality and honesty. Finally, this person has a dogmatic insistence that his or her thinking is right regardless of circumstances.

The combination of these three ingredients becomes a problem when this person becomes a moral reformer imposing his or her sense (or brand) of moralism and honesty on the world regardless of whether the world really needs or accepts his or her views. This imposition of his way of thinking can lead him or her to:

(1) rationalize or justify that whatever has to be done to carry out his or her moral sense of right is itself appropriate and right even though

it may involve actions which are seen as unacceptable, inappropriate and, in some circumstances, even dishonest;

(2) consider his or her way of thinking above all other codes and principles and hence as a superior way of thinking and acting;

(3) overlook his or her own potential for error to the point that this person completely disbelieves that he or she is capable of dishonesty.

Risk Condition A5: Moral Indecisiveness

This person has a good capacity for seeing and understanding what is happening, for clear thinking about problems in the world and for good practical problem solving ability. The uncertainty centers on the principles which guide conduct telling him or her what is right or wrong. This person may have a strong sense of conscience, will probably disapprove of any form of dishonesty and have a strong desire to be seen as honest and moral; however, the capacity for deciding what is right or wrong, what is moral or immoral, what is honest or dishonest is not clearly developed. This uncertainty can lead him or her to react impulsively and rashly to situations pushed and pulled by circumstances.

Risk Condition A6: Moral Dogmatism

This person's profile is best characterized by extremes. He or she is either extremely loyal or not loyal at all, either pushing very hard and demanding all of himself or herself, or not pushing at all. This person is either convinced that people around him or her are right or will be crusading against what he or she sees as unjustifiable actions by others.

This condition of shifting from one extreme to another is generated by a confusion about his or her internal sense of direction. This person's code of conduct is unclear; and, as a result, either his or her actions tend to be pushed and pulled by circumstances, or this person rigidly holds onto personal beliefs regardless of the appropriateness or rightness of doing so.

Risk Condition A7: Inability To Understand and Make Sound Judgements

This person's thinking is faulty, fuzzy and likely to be impulsive and irrational. As a result, he or she tends to:

(1) exaggerate the importance of situations which either may or may not be important;
(2) overlook or depreciate the importance of really crucial issues;
(3) trust the wrong people;
(4) be distrustful of everyone;
(5) take things totally out of context;
(6) be unable to change his or her mind once it is made up;

In short, his thinking capacity is highly restricted resulting either in extremes of skepticism and pessimism or rigid, dogmatic and stubborn thinking.

This person is at risk for making dishonest decisions in the following:

(1) situations which require a quick and accurate response;
(2) situations which require him or her to deal with new ideas or ways of doing things;
(3) situations which require him or her to go against the tide even in situations where the result is a dishonest action;
(4) situations which are controversial and contradictory;
(5) situations which require level headed, consistent thinking.

Risk Condition A8: Moral Inadequacy

This person is totally lacking in the ability to withstand the pressures of situations where he or she is tempted by others to carry out immoral or dishonest actions, where he or she must rely on inner moral principles to guide conduct, where this person must choose for himself or herself what is right or wrong, honest or dishonest. This person suffers from:

(1) extreme self inadequacy, leaving him or her feeling doubts and fears about self worth, feeling totally inadequate and unable to function and pessimistic about the chance to succeed;
(2) extreme emotional inconsistencies where his or her feelings leap from one extreme to another;
(3) uncertainty what his or her principles ought to be, shifting from rigid adherence to rules which are too confining to be functional to the complete depreciation of rules whether internal principles and ideals of social and/or company norms, rules and expectations.

Risk Condition A9: Moral Confusion

This person is lost without a sense of moral order or internal direction. He or she is frozen in a continuous state of indecisiveness, being pushed and pulled by circumstances. He or she has no set of principles, either external or internal, to guide conduct; therefore, this person's conduct is likely to be inadequate. This person has no sense of internal direction nor respect for social norms about what is right or wrong. Moreover, this person is like a ship without a rudder, susceptible to situations where he or she is tempted either by others or his or her own inadequate and improper conduct.

Risk Condition A10: Moral Deception

This individual will actively seek either to:

(1) Force people and situations to conform to his or her ideas or
(2) Overtly or covertly get around any principles and norms other than his or her own.

He or she is unconcerned about any principles of conduct, any norms about honesty or morality other than his or her own, will likely distrust people and the company in general and may show outward disrespect for company property and company rules and regulations. This person may on the surface, conform to social and/or company norms; however, his or her actions will be guided by what he or she feels is in his or her best interest to the total disregard of others.

TYPE B: THIS PERSON KNOWS THE DIFFERENCE BETWEEN RIGHT AND WRONG BUT CHOOSES WRONG ANYWAY

Risk Condition B1: Rationalizer

This individual has the capacity to make moral and honest choices. This person has a strong internal moral code which guides him or her about what is right or wrong, has a sense of conscience about dishonesty both in the world and in the self, and has a depreciation of dishonesty as a potential means of getting things done. He or she is, in fact, unlikely to plan or design an immoral or dishonest action.

There is a potential risk, however, generated by this person's stubborn commitment to what he or she thinks is right regardless of circumstances. As a result of this commitment, this person tends to:

(1) become locked on a tangent focusing only in a partial view of what is happening;
(2) be dogmatic and rigid in his or her thinking;
(3) become excessively idealistic and perfectionistic.

Moreover, this stubborn insistence can lock a person into unreasonable or unfounded justification of his or her way of thinking which can in turn lead him or her to:

(1) overlook his or her own potential for error or for being dishonest;
(2) justify actions which help to accomplish his or her "mission" or ideals even though these actions may not be seen as clear cut, appropriate actions by society;
(3) measure the honesty or integrity of others and the validity of others' code of ethics and norms for honest and ethical behavior against his or her beliefs.

Risk Condition B2: Individualist, Non-Conformist

This person has an interesting and stimulating profile. On the one hand, he or she generates unique ideas, spontaneity and a keen appreciation of freedom of expression; yet, on the other hand, in this person there may be a conflict between a commitment to what he or she thinks is right, moral and just and what the world sees as right and wrong.

The key element of this person's profile is an unconventional way of thinking which can create ideas and problem solving techniques which others may miss because of their more habitual ways of thinking and acting. This brand of non-conformity also sparks a sense of individualism such that this individual does not like to be boxed in by restrictive ideas, relationships or situations (including private, family, company or societal situations) which do not allow the opportunity to speak for himself or herself.

This tendency to get things done covertly or overtly in his or her own way can put this person at odds with society and can generate a potential risk that he or she will:

(1) actively choose to ignore accepted norms and codes about what is right and wrong;
(2) covertly find ways of getting around rules and regulations, norms for behavior;
(3) rationalize that his or her actions, even though they not be seen as acceptable or appropriate, are necessary and practically what is best;
(4) become susceptible to impulsive actions and reactions when he or she is at odds with accepted ways of thinking and acting.

Risk Condition B3: Moralist

This person's risk situation is very similar to "A4 Moralism," but the conditions which generate the risk potential are somewhat different. The moralist is not confused about internal principles. He or she thinks in black and white, turning ideas into causes which demand unswerving faith and uncompromising commitment to and acceptance of his or her norms and canons of conduct.

A rigid belief that the world ought to be ordered and structured according to principles of right, coupled with a dogmatic insistence that his or her way is right, leads this person into situations where, either because his or her thinking does not fit what others think, or others simply reject his or her norms and ideas, this person becomes a risk for:

(1) rationalizing or justifying the correctness, necessity and integrity of judgements and actions regardless of what society may think;
(2) feeling a sense of pride in actions consistent with his or her beliefs even when these actions are not appropriate or acceptable;
(3) becoming less sensitive to the potential for badness simply because he or she sees only goodness, or rationalizes that the badness is necessary.
(4) reducing all norms and rules about right and wrong to his or her way of thinking such that this person feels justified in placing himself or herself beyond all norms which do not fit his or her way of thinking.

Risk Condition B4: Social Reformer

This person's profile is best characterized by two dominant aspects. First, he or she is an individualist who has the ability to spontaneously create novel ideas and who will covertly or overtly get things done in his or her own way. Second, this person sees the world in chaos and disorder and feels a compulsion to "right things" by imposing on the world his or her own sense of order and principles of right and wrong. This combination leads to a tendency to:

(1) be impatient with ideas different from his or her own;
(2) be rigidly dogmatic about his or her own way of thinking;
(3) be susceptible to skeptical and suspicious ideas about the world, potentially leading to a "chip on the shoulder" attitude when things do not work out as expected;
(4) develop feelings of superiority based on the belief that his or her way of thinking is best;
(5) base decisions on a principle of practical expediency which values what works best sometimes instead of "what is best";
(6) practice "technical dishonesty" which operates on a day to day principle of practical expediency as a means of achieving what he or she thinks is right;

Risk Condition B5: Moral Extremist

The risk situation in this case is an exaggeration of the commitment to one particular idea or principle or way of thinking represented in "B3 Moralist." This person has a fanatical sense of the rightness and necessity of his or her way of thinking and acting.

Therefore, this person's ability to see right and wrong and the capacity for thinking and problem solving can lead one to miss the fact that ultimately this person owes obedience to what he or she thinks is right and this faith requires rationalization of whatever is necessary in order to satisfy personal beliefs. This person's thinking can lead to the following risk situations:

(1) This person is susceptible to the illusion that there is no other way of thinking than his or hers and to a compulsive insistence that everyone else must conform to his or her way;
(2) He or she is likely to offer irrational justifications and vigorous defenses of her or his judgements and actions even when they are inappropriate or dishonest;
(3) This person will tend to shift responsibility when caught in an inappropriate or dishonest act to someone or something beyond him or her;

(4) This person is insensitive to the badness of actions and feels that the normal ideas about badness do not apply to him or her because he or she is beyond the law or beyond the range of norms of conduct.

Risk Condition B6: Social Rebel

This person's individualism and non-conformism is exaggerated to the point of rebellious contempt for any sense of order or norms of conduct other than his or her own. As a result, he or she is susceptible to:

(1) skeptical, cynical and possibly pessimistic attitudes toward the world;
(2) feeling no obligation to maintain social norms other than those which meet his or her purposes;
(3) feeling no sense of wrong doing if he or she breaks codes of conduct;
(4) likely showing overt and/or covert disrespect for the rights of others when they conflict with his or her own goals;
(5) rationalizing or justifying any action which furthers his or her way of thinking and thus feels no sense of responsibility for the consequences of the actions and decisions.

TYPE C: PEOPLE WHO SEE WRONG AS RIGHT

Risk Condition C1: Moral Oversight

There are two risk conditions which define the potential risk of this person. First, his or her sense of conscience is weak indicating a lack of sensitivity to and awareness of the potential for badness in self and in others. Second, this person is willing to see and accept as a fact that honesty is not always the most practical alterative and that sometimes being honest is unnecessary and gets in the way of getting things done. As a result of these risk conditions, this person is likely to:

(1) overlook minor instances of dishonesty by others as long as he or she does not have to directly confront the individual committing a dishonest act;
(2) overlook and discount his or her own tendency to commit dishonest actions as a practical necessity;

(3) rationalize or excuse dishonesty as what is needed to get the job done;
(4) feel no strong obligation to be honest even though he or she may feel an obligation to be dishonest.

Risk Condition C2: Moral Misdirection

This person may in fact have the potential to be a "good" person. He or she has a strong sense of conscience which tells when he or she has done wrong and feels an obligation to be seen as honest and hence to not be caught in dishonest actions or situations. He or she has a very good capacity for seeing and understanding what is happening around him and has basically a good decision making and problem solving capacity.

The risk revealed by this person's profile lies in the interconnection of two problem areas. First, he or she is willing to see and accept the fact that honesty may not always be the most practical alternative and that, in some cases, honesty may not be the "best" alternative. Moreover, this person has a distorted sense of moral code which places him or her between two extremes. This person tends to shift from (1) exaggerating the need for a guiding set of principles to (2) rationalizing his or her principles, his or her inner ought, as the only correct way of thinking to acting with little sense of direction or commitment to what is right. Shifting between these two extremes can place this person at risk in:

(1) Situations where there is no clear cut sense of what is right or wrong, opening up the probability that he or she will choose wrong;
(2) Conflicting situations where a practically expedient but dishonest response appears on the surface to be the best or most workable alternative;
(3) Situations which allow him or her to mask his guilt in a righteous belief that he or she is doing what has to be done.

Risk Condition C3: Immoral Justification

This person may have a "good" personality and be a very good problem solver as well as a hard working, self-directed individual. However, he or she has a series of problems which in combination can cause him or her to:

(1) overlook the occurrence of dishonest actions by others;

(2) be insensitive to or unaware of his or her own potential for dishonesty, either exaggerating the ability to act honestly, or underestimating the complexity of a situation;
(3) rationalize any dishonest action on his or her part as a practical expediency.

This person feels strongly that honesty is not always the best policy and hence feels no overriding obligation to always be honest.

Risk Condition C4: Accepts Dishonesty

This person treats dishonesty as a practical, workable alternative; therefore, he or she has no problem accepting dishonesty as a perfectly legitimate response, as a practical response when the situation demands it and as a primary response indicating that it is on many occasions the best response. He or she may have a "good" personality and be a hard worker but feels no obligation to curb dishonest actions or feels no obligation to curb his or her own dishonesty especially in situations where dishonesty is the practically expedient thing to do. Since this person may have a strong desire to be seen as honest by others, he or she will tend to be covert in his dishonesty or versatile and cunning, using problem solving ability to try to hide misconduct.

Risk Condition C5: Rationalizes Dishonesty

This person is placed into a dilemma between what conscience indicates is wrong and what personal beliefs about dishonesty lead him to do. He or she strongly feels that on many occasions, dishonesty is not only the most practical response but that it is necessarily the best response, that is, the response which one ought to make under similar circumstances. However, since his or her conscience is likely to create feelings of guilt, this person is likely to mask dishonesty by telling himself or herself that his or her actions are the only honorable thing to do.

Risk Condition C6: Practices Dishonesty

This person treats dishonesty not only as a practical or workable alternative but also as a necessary option for any and all situations where practical expediency of dishonesty allows him or her to accomplish goals. In other words, this person feels that dishonesty is a legitimate response which one has an obligation to give, especially if success cannot be achieved in any other way.

Risk Condition C7: Moral Insensitivity

This person is not aware of or sensitive to dishonesty either in the world or in the self. Moreover, he or she both disvalues honesty as a workable alternative and sees dishonesty as a fulfilling, workable alternative. He or she feels no obligation to be honest and feel no sense of guilt when dishonesty is used to accomplish his or her purposes. This person will:

(1) accept dishonesty as good;
(2) treat dishonesty as practical;
(3) rationalize or excuse dishonesty as a practically necessary alternative.

This person practices dishonesty more than as a expedient act. He or she sees dishonesty as a normal and accepted way of getting things done. Even so, this person may desire others to see him or her as honest and may use tactics which hide dishonesty until he or she is caught.

Risk Condition C8: Moral Corruption

This person is dishonest and knows it. He or she sees and accepts dishonesty as not only normal and accepted but as a preferred alternative. In other words, he or she is more likely to be dishonest than honest. Moreover, this person is likely to promote dishonesty among others and is capable of using dishonesty to accomplish anything he or she wants. Her or his conscience may, on some occasions, tell that she or he is doing wrong and may temporarily affect her or his ability to be dishonest; however, she or he will likely overcome these pangs of conscience and continue to act in the way that he or she enjoys and prefers, being dishonest.

Risk Condition C9: Moral Disintegration (Failure)

This person is not capable of being honest for any consistent period of time. He or she has no conscience, no respect for right or honest actions, no sense of obligation to be fair or honest. This person has no principles, no moral code to guide in difficult situations and is totally unconcerned by his or her badness or by the dishonesty of others.

This axiological model for interpreting risk provides a groundwork for explaining risk by measuring the bias in one's thinking and values. The measurement of this bias opens new doors not only to the examination of risk concepts but also to the exploration of our ability to think with any concepts. We have a format and a methodology for examining any risk concept in an objective fashion, defining the key elements, building a value profile to mirror the risk concept, generating a model for interpreting the risk conditions, and testing the accuracy and reliability of this model. Moreover, we also have a format for explaining the ability of an individual to think with any concept. This capacity for objectively examining concepts allows us to study the effects of aberrational thinking, to examine the relationship between what one expects to happen and what is perceived as happening, and to measure one's attitudes in an objective rather than a subjective manner.

REFERENCES

Carpenter, Wayne, "Axiological Evaluation of Dishonest Employees," Nashville, TN, Value Resource Group, 1987.

_____, "Introduction to Axiology: The Science of Value." Nashville, TN, Value Resource Group, 1988.

_____, and Charles W. McDonald, "Applying Axiology to Team Building - Introduction," Nashville, TN, Value Resource Group, 1988.

_____, and Charles W. McDonald, et. al., Pre-Employment Program, Construct Validity - RANKS Hartman Value Profile - Part I. Brentwood, TN, The Institute for the Study of Human Values, 1987.

_____, Pre-Employment Program, Construct Validity - RANKS Hartman Value Profile - Part II. Brentwood, TN, The Institute for the Study of Human Values, 1987.

_____, Pre-Employment Program, Construct Validity - RANKS Honesty-One Value Profile. Brentwood, TN, The Institute for the Study of Human Values, 1987.

_____, Pre-Employment Program, Construct Validity - RANKS Honesty-Two Value Profile. Brentwood, TN, The Institute for the Study of Human Values, 1987.

_____, Values and Pedophilia: Construct Validity of Pedophilia 1 Profile RANK Scores. Brentwood, TN, The Institute for the Study of Human Values, 1986.

Chapter XVII

A NEW EDUCATION FOR THE INTEGRAL DEVELOPMENT OF MAN'S PERSONALITY[1]

Alfonso Lozano G.

In many papers, I have affirmed that our personality, the way we are and behave, is determined in a very definite way by education. Education makes us what we are.

Now I would like to ask: What is a human being? To judge by the latest political, social, and even family events, it is clear that although we are not exactly devils incarnate, we are not precisely angels either. In fact, we are nearer the former than the latter; that is, there is more of the bad than of the good in us human beings. This is not because evil is inherent in human nature. We are not born either good or bad. We are all born with potential qualities to develop into complete human beings, into good men and women. However, if we fail to reach the full development of our humanity, it is because of education.

All of us who dedicate ourselves to the study of the science and philosophy of humanity know that unlike animals, human beings need education to ensure moral growth. It follows that whatever a human being becomes depends fully on education.

---

[1] Translated by Jim Valero.

If we accept what I have said, then we must ask ourselves, what is the matter with education? Why has education been unable to produce a society of good men and women? The answer is simple: Formal Axiology, the study of the nature of values and value judgements, allows us to understand the formal and empirical blunders we have incurred with the concept of education. However, those very blunders have been responsible for human-kind's formative education. To illustrate: formally speaking, there is not one treatise on education that adheres to the principles of pure logic; and those which claim to do so have no connection whatsoever with reality. From an empirical point of view, there is not one educational program that contemplates the full growth and development of the supreme qualities of men and women. Even if there were, no one would be able to carry on such a program because those in charge of education, teachers and professors, lack the necessary moral and intellectual background to undertake such a high-reaching enterprise.

It is no wonder then that up to now we are still more devils than angels. The poverty of our moral development results in a deteriorated human being, i.e. a person without morals.

While education remains the same, men and women will also remain the same. Obviously, then the possibilities for a better world will go on being null, and everything said on this point will continue to be nothing but politicians' humbug. A better world, a good world, morally speaking, depends on a completely new education. This new concept of education must have as its main purpose to educate us to reach full development of our potentials as human beings. So far, no educational system has even tried to do so. All have settled for development of some qualities, or rather, skills, that enable us to lead but selfish, limited and mediocre existences. We all know that we have potentials for infinite qualities. Education, nevertheless, has only cared to develop those qualities that allow us to half live. A full human life is a few people's privilege. Education has not taught us to live a full life. Education has rather given us the tools to destroy life in the name of "progress." Education has taught us to create and develop everything but ourselves, and this is driving us to our own destruction.

However, if we succeed in annihilating ourselves and all the planet, it will not ultimately be education's fault because education, just as all other aspects of culture, is our creation.

Why, then, have we failed to create an educational system capable of taking all our potential to the highest degree of development and growth? Probably because we have not known how to do it. However, the history of moral philosophy bears witness to the fact that we have tried. From Socrates to Krishnamurti, all philosophers have dreamed of bringing about complete human beings, fully developed in their highest qualities, in other words, ethically good men and women.

Now, I believe that today we have the potential to create a new sort of education. If we did not do it in the past, it was because nobody knew how to handle axiological principles. But now, thanks to Formal Axiology, we know how to make use of those principles within our system of rational valuation.

For instance, now we realize that education is an axiological term. Thus, it is easy to understand that this term is a predicate of the second order, which states that certain subjects possess certain qualities which classify them as belonging to the more general category of the predicate "educated."

What do we mean when we say that persons have a good education? To say that persons have an education or are educated means that such individuals exhibit certain peculiar qualities in their daily lives. In other words, when we say a person is educated we are trying to say that the person is knowledgeable, refined, discreet, prudent, honest, sincere, and so forth. All such terms describing an individual are summed up in the word "educated."

We understand then, that such a term should be applied to individuals who possess a series of qualities that describe their moral principles, that is, their essence.

I have reached the conclusion that an educated person is one who has developed his or her potential qualities to the utmost by means of education. "Education" comes from *educare*, which is a Latin term signifying "to bring up," "to develop." And what are we to "bring up," to "develop"? Doubtlessly, those qualities that make up and exhibit our moral goodness.

As we can see, the concept of "education" stands in very close relation to the concept of "goodness." And, just as "good" can be used as the predicate of any person who is in full command of all his or her best qualities, so "educated" is the predicate of an individual who has developed all of his or her desirable potentials as a human being.

If what I am stating is true, then education can be derived from Formal Axiology. Because if it is true that, according to Axiology, a thing is good which exhibits all predicates included in its concept, then it is also true that a person is educated who exhibits all characteristics contained within the concept of "education."

Notice the close parallelism between Axiology and Education. Hence, we can follow axiological theory and work out a new concept of education. In other words, Formal Axiology states that a thing that exhibits, or possesses, all of the qualities of its concept is a **good thing**. Moreover, Axiology also says that the larger the number of qualities possessed, the better the thing is. Axio-logical theory tells us that this can be applied on a generic level, and we can stipulate that a person whose total number of qualities have been developed is a truly educated person. Thus, the larger the number of qualities developed, the better educated the person.

As we can see, the concept of education fits exactly the principles of Formal Axiology. Hence, I would like to show how I conceive a new education based on axiological principles.

In his article "Axiological Structure of Personality," Dianoia, 1973, my dear professor Robert S. Hartman presents us with the idea of a kind of personality achieved through development of qualities inherent in the individual. There are three extremely important points in that essay that form part of my idea of the kind of education we need. The first one says that personality is not inherent or innate to man's nature but is of a moral character. The second states that personality is a valuating predicate of the subject "I". And the third says that personality is actually composed of three different "I's", or "selves"--the Systemic Self, the Intrinsic Self, and the Extrinsic Self.

So, if we take this to be true, it becomes evident that a person has three different selves to develop, which is to say that education should be **three-dimensional**, axiologically speaking. In other words, there are three selves within men and women craving for development; and, since personality only develops through education, it follows that we need three different types of education. The first of these would be Systemic Education; the second, Extrinsic Education; and the third, Intrinsic Education.

Systemic Education should be a subsystem composed of mathematics, logic, and the formal features of the natural sciences. Applying this educational subsystem would result in development of our systemic qualities such as love for order, respect and loyalty for social institutions, dedication to work, and a personal commitment to continue improving not only professionally but as human beings as well. Systemic Education, in other words, would create a truly human society, aware of its responsibilities and moral obligations to every single person. Disorderly conduct as well as anarchic, chaotic attitudes so common in our times would be overcome and replaced by disciplined behavior and intelligent attitudes. Ability to solve problems, capacity to plan, impartiality, and emotional restraint would be the empirical outcome of Systemic Education.

Nowadays Systemic Education, as here understood, does not exist. However, it is widely practiced the world over. Its consequences can be perceived in our social, political, and economic environment as a kind of personality that is lacking in love, empathy, and consideration for others. Systemic Education does not develop our intrinsic, spiritual feelings. It merely enhances our intellectual qualities and our social habits so these become more skillful and efficient.

The clearest example of Systemic Education in our times would be military education in the widest sense of the word. In a more restricted sense, other examples would be religious education and family education.

Extrinsic Education would comprehend the empirical features of our physical and social environment. It would include the social sciences, customs and everything relating to our social situation. Applying this subsystem to the development of our personality would result in a greater practical ability to deal with concrete situations in the realm of social interacting. People would be more open in their relationships and would possess the capacity to enrich their extrinsic relations, thus giving birth to an improved social environment. Our erotic and sexual capacities would also be enhanced as to extension and depth.

These days, Extrinsic Education is not appropriately systematized. As is the case of Systemic Education, this kind of education is still widely used at educational centers around the world. The results are also evident in our societies, where people show an obsessive tendency towards gross materialism, with every person worried to death about accumulating material goods. He who is not able to "keep up with the Joneses" and have a fat checking account feels frustrated and diminished in his or her moral value as a human being. People's sense of personal worth seems to be in direct proportion to their income and material possessions. Hence, the conclusion is that Extrinsic Education develops a materialistic personality whose effects can be felt in the lack of true spirituality and realistic self-esteem. It produces people who are selfish, alienated from themselves and others, greedy, vain, and arrogant; in other words, people who are spiritually poor.

Finally, let us consider Intrinsic Education. This would comprehend intrinsic or spiritual sciences, i. e., all those disciplines and courses of study that enhance development of our inner capacities and all our moral potential. Applying this subsystem to our education would elevate us to the highest spiritual and moral heights a person can reach as a human being. Only the development of our intrinsic spiritual capacities can result in the birth of an authentically human person. In fact, these spiritual qualities constitute the true ontological being of man; they constitute the real essence of what we are and that which distinguishes us from all other beings.

But man's inner qualities are never developed in a systematic manner. We have already pointed out that none of our most human qualities are ever developed according to a scientific plan. On the contrary, the exclusive development of systemic and extrinsic qualities is common in our society; and development of our intrinsic qualities remains generally neglected. The sad fact is that personal conduct and social behavior very rarely exhibit intrinsic qualities. It is indeed perplexing that our spiritual qualities, the most legitimately and truly human, are the least developed in our societies. The reason for this is quite simple: no educational plan, from elementary school to the university level, considers the necessity for the ethical development of student's capacities. Every school feels the need to educate people to become employees, workers, and professionals, but it seems that nobody is interested in producing ethically good people. Ethical goodness remains a utopian dream of moral philosophers, and it seems that it will continue to be so until we blow ourselves and our planet to smithereens. Only a new education in the terms expressed here can produce good people, ethically speaking. Any other educational innovation alien to the lineaments of formal axiology will be useless to produce morally good and spiritually sound men and women, i.e. wholly integrated people.

As we can see, when I speak of three kinds of education, I am referring to the three kinds of sciences that should compose the corresponding subsystem in each education set. When I mention Systemic Education, for instance, I do not mean a set of subjects or disciplines that could be grouped under the heading of Systemic Education. The term "education" cannot be composed of a body of knowledge we could name "Education Science." So, the one thing we can do is to gather a set of systemic subjects and group them under the subset called Systemic Education.

Similarly, the other two kinds of education should be composed of other subjects or disciplines that have nothing to do with the concept of education as traditionally understood. There is one thing, however, I am sure of--the integral development of the personality can only be possible through the three educational subsets.

You may be wondering why disciplines other than the science of education should contribute to the development of personality. I can only say that those other disciplines are the ones intrinsically related to our human essence. Hence, it is this intimate relationship which contributes to the development of our truly human potentials. In other words, the science of education cannot offer anything of its own which could lead to the development of our qualities as complete--and I must emphasize **complete**-- human beings. Education means to bring up qualities, but the actual task of enhancing those qualities, of making them grow, can be accomplished only by systemic, extrinsic, and intrinsic disciplines and studies.

I would like to point out that by systemic science or disciplines I mean the formal dimensions of natural science and logic, together with mathematics and axiology, which are capable of developing systemic qualities. By extrinsic sciences or disciplines I mean the empirical dimensions of the physical and social sciences. These, along with culture and tradition, are capable of developing our extrinsic qualities. Finally, I understand by intrinsic sciences or disciplines those which contribute to the development our inner selves-- ethics, for instance. Thus, such disciplines and courses of study should bring about the true unfolding and growth of our intrinsic or spiritual qualities.

Summing up, I should like to say that the idea of a new kind of education implies the necessity of a new way of thinking. In fact, it is precisely our way of thinking and relating to one another that has to be renewed and radically different from the traditional way. Traditional education only concerns itself with transmitting knowledge that is already there and cannot offer anything for the development of our inner selves, since this always depends on existing knowledge. If instead we utilize scientific methods to bring up and improve human qualities, the development of human personality will be logical and orderly; otherwise, it will be chaotic and fragmentary.

Our present educational systems only produce the latter. All of us know, or should know, that our current way of thinking, morally speaking, is very far from rational and scientific.

The task of moral philosophers should be to create the kind of sciences and disciplines that will produce the best kind of human being possible. Natural science has had a lot to do with our development for too long a time. This development so far has always been incomplete and detrimental to our spiritual health insofar as it has only cared to provide us with practical skills and has always neglected the enormous potential for growth and happiness that lie in our higher powers of consciousness.

Chapter XVIII

AXIOLOGY AND EDUCATION

Robert E. Carter

In describing the nature of value experience, Robert S. Hartman identifies three distinctive <u>kinds</u> of value and valuation. In using his schema to illuminate the sorts of valuational decisions that are inevitable in the field of education, guidance of an important and subtle sort results. The educator <u>ought to be</u> sensitive to all three value dimensions, and especially to intrinsic values. The axiologically capable educator will "concentrate on the development of fully rounded persons,"[1] holding the student as being of more value than mere classroom order, or than the comparative academic achievements of the class. Ideally, of course, the system of education will run smoothly, the classroom will be orderly and the students polite, and all will improve magnificently and tend towards academic excellence. Whether or not these hopes are realized, the education of the whole person demands the "setting of the human person into the center of every situation."[2]

The Intrinsic Value of the Person

What is central to Hartman's analysis of intrinsic value is the <u>special status</u> afforded to <u>persons</u>. It is not necessarily the case that only <u>human</u> persons are reflective consciousnesses, but if other species, or remarkable individual members of other species are of intrinsic value, then they must be persons in the sense of being reflexively conscious, or at least must have the <u>potential</u> to be reflexively conscious. This last qualification is important, for it does leave open the possibility that heretofore unactualized proto-persons could become full persons under more favourable conditions. A Jane Goddall might well provide a <u>learning environment</u> which served to actualize the until now dormant potential of primates to communicate with human beings, and to become adequately self-reflective. Hartman's emphasis on persons must be understood to be broad enough to leave open the possibility for any species to achieve this capacity.

Is a human being still of intrinsic value if he or she is no longer capable of self-reflection, due to a blow on the head, or a degenerative disease? Such a "person" might be, in fact, less self-reflective than a dolphin or an ape. "We define a human being, that is a person," Hartman writes, "as that being which has its own definition of itself in itself. A chair does not know it is a chair, but I know that I am I. No matter how people may look on Mars--for all we know they may look like chairs--if they can say 'I' and can reflect upon this, then they are human beings."[3] The capacity to reflect, the power of reflexivity, i.e. to circle back upon your own consciousness by means of consciousness itself, to look at the looker, is the ability to treat yourself as both subject and object, and at one and the same time. Yet, although the power of reflection is real enough, it is an open-ended process which succeeds in grasping itself as object. However, in that very success is failure, for the grasped is grasped by an unknown grasper which forever eludes objectivity:

> The subject, I, thinks the object, Myself or Me. In "I am thinking of myself," or "I think of me" it is myself and me that are being thought. This means that the subject, I, is not thought but does the thinking. We can think of the I that thinks Me only by making it a Me. We then have "I think of Me thinking of Me." Now appears another I. Trying to think it we get "I think of Me thinking of Me thinking of Me," and there appears a third I that cannot be thought of--and so on ad infinitum. By the simple definition of a human being as self-reflective it appears as an infinity. I can never completely reach myself as thinking. ... The human being, axiologically, is an actual infinity. Moreover, he is a non-denumerable infinity; for what is true of I and Me is true of any thought I may have. If I think of this chair, I can think of my thinking this chair, and my thinking [of] thinking this chair, and so on ad infinitum. Each of my thoughts, thus, may be an infinity.[4]

Part of our uncertainty is cleared away in that whatever consciousness is reflective is "human" in the sense of being infinitely rich in resultant properties is limitless, or constitutes an inexhaustible stream of reflective acts. Of course, none of us ever actualizes this power "infinitely." We play at trying to catch the self through three or four receding levels, and then we drop it, and think about something else. Our attention span is short, and while we do think, we never think infinitely!

Living up to the Norm of Conscience

There is a further "rub." If the human being is the only being who has his or her own self-definition <u>within</u>, then someone can only be an <u>actualized</u> instance of intrinsic goodness if he or she has actually <u>fulfilled</u> the required self-definition. In Hartman's words, "The definition of the human being is in himself. Hence, a human being is good when he fulfils his own definition of himself."[5] The subtle shift here is from "value" to "goodness," and whereas intrinsic "goodness" here refers to the ethical application of intrinsic value, at the strictly axiological level it makes no sense to ask whether a human being is good or bad. A human being fulfils the requirement of being who he or she actually is, just by being, and so is axiologically in a class by him or herself. There is nothing else with which to compare. Thus, you can compare yourself to whom you think you ought to be, to whom you were at ten, at twenty, in marriage, etc. There are numerous concepts of self with which to compare who you are now. On the ethical level, one

> ... is morally good if he is as he is. All the words of ethics mean this very same thing, this identification of myself with myself; being sincere, being honest, being genuine, being authentic, being true to myself, having integrity, having self-respect--all these words mean that I am as I am, that I am myself. This seems to be a very simple thing and yet it is most difficult to achieve. For I can define myself in all three ways, systemically, extrinsically, and intrinsically.[6]

Thus, to be ethically good, you must not only <u>be</u>, but you must be the person whom your <u>conscience</u> or highest self-ideal demands that you be. And, of course, few of us achieve this regularly, and some of us rarely, if ever. So, to be <u>ideally</u> who you are, you must live up to your own <u>norm</u> of self, but in order to be <u>human</u>, it is enough to strive to be a morally better person. There can be degrees of moral betterness. But is it enough to be a <u>potentially self-reflective</u> entity, in order to qualify as a being of intrinsic worth? The answer seems to be yes, for Hartman. In his "Four Axiological Proofs of the Infinite Value of Man," Hartman makes clear that an <u>actualized</u> person (I would now simply say, "a better person," or "a more transparent person," or "a more integrated person") is of a higher valuational cardinality, or has more richness of meaning, than one who is not (more) self-actualized. Nevertheless, the unactualized is still of the cardinality of a non-denumerable infinity. Let me quote this important paragraph:

What is the cardinality of the total person? <u>This depends on the state of inner integration or harmonization of the person</u>. The person, according to our four definitions, <u>can never be of a lower cardinality than</u> $\aleph_1$, but he may rise to cardinality $\aleph_2$.

The maximum cardinality of a human person thus is $\aleph_2$, which means the actualization of all the infinite possibilities of one or several of its definitional infinities. Its minimum cardinality is $\aleph_1$, which is the measure of its definitional <u>capacities as a human being, even though not actualized</u>.[7]

It is the potentiality, not the actuality of norm-fulfilment, which <u>minimally</u> defines the human being as infinite, and, therefore, of intrinsic value just as he or she is. Similarly, it seems to be the potentiality of consciousness to reflect, and to do so to infinity, or as I prefer, "inexhaustibly," that minimally defines human consciousness as infinite and intrinsically valuable. <u>Maximally</u>, on the other hand, a human being is good only in so far as he or she fulfils his or her own self-definition (or, in my terms, does so to a significantly greater extent):

> In order to <u>intrinsically</u> fulfil the definition of myself I must neither construct myself nor even abstract from myself but simply BE, namely identify myself with myself. This is the most difficult and most important task of my moral life. It is difficult simply to be, to be natural and not to pretend, nor be proud or ashamed of anything. Sometimes we achieve this by "getting away from it all" on vacation, being alone with ourselves and getting acquainted with ourselves, "putting our souls back into our body" (Paul Weiss).[8]

In the minimal sense, a human being is intrinsically valuable because he or she is a conscious being, capable of reflexive activity. Maximally, a human being is intrinsically valuable, in addition, or in a higher degree, because he or she is able to fulfil or actualize him or herself in accordance with his or her own self-concepts, and so is true to him or herself. One is thereby "genuine," "sincere," "integral," and "authentic." There is an infinite distance between the opaque and the saintly, but an infinity taken from an infinity still leaves, nonetheless, an infinity, albeit an infinity of inexhaustibility and improvement.

The Educating of Persons

The analysis of <u>person</u> is of the utmost importance for the application of Hartman's value theory to education. In broad terms, it follows that however handicapped, or learning disabled, or dumb, or angry, or meddlesome, or troublesome a student is, he or she is still of infinite worth, and still has infinite potential. Of course, to comprehend this, as important an insight as it may be, is not nearly enough to tell you what to do and how to act with respect to a difficult child or adult, but it is enough to tell you how not to act. And that is no small boon. You ought not to interact with another person in such a way as to reduce that person's value to something less than intrinsic value. This does not mean that you cannot imagine circumstances in which it might be necessary to apply the law harshly, for example, or to forcibly confine a person, or even to kill someone who was about to torture thousands of others. It is only to say that you should act against the background recognition of that person's still being of infinite value, and still possessing infinite potential beyond that. Thus, for example,

> Any bureaucratic procedure that sees not humans but instances of a rule, any authoritarian person that tries to impose his will by using the rules of a system, any procedure that imposes conformity is guilty of this evil of transposition of the logical and the axiological. It is the use of a system which gives evil the power to extend its range and, at the same time, to assume the resemblance of good. All great evil is systemic evil.[9]

Not only does systemic valuation see things only in black or white, either as perfect or as simply no good at all, but it also is lower than, and is axiologically unaware of the higher extrinsic and intrinsic dimensions of value. Whereas extrinsic sensitivity includes systemic awareness, and intrinsic sensitivity includes both extrinsic and systemic awareness, systemic awareness is limited to its own sphere. Things valued are thereby reduced, i.e. identified only in terms of the lowest common value denominator, e.g., human beings and chairs are alike in needing to be labelled and kept rigidly in their assigned places. In this case, "there is nothing but a mass of interchangeable, formless elements: chaos numbered and indexed. The culmination of such systemic organization was Nazi Germany."[10] The personhood, the uniqueness, the intrinsic value of each and every individual, is simply unavailable to the systemic mind. The systemic mind reduces persons to so many bodies, or to functions of a machine or the classroom, and assigns him, her or it to a part in the smooth operation of a trouble-free whole or system. The system has clear goals, from which there can be no deviation.

The rigid, inflexible teachers who were unable to interact effectively with their students at a "human" level, are not forgotten by their students, but are remembered for all the wrong reasons. Systemic valuation reduces the parts in the system to a minimum, and blocks out everything else. Intrinsic valuation concentrates on the thing as it is, sensitively grasping its infinite richness in a Gestalt of awareness. The point is made well in one of Hartman's most amusing examples:

> In the natural sciences electrons, spaces, waves, and the like are constructs, but also horses, flowers, and all empirical things encipher as they are elements of zoological, botanical, etc. systems. As such they are referred to by Latin names. Lilac, for example, is botanically "Syringa vulgaris." Syringa vulgaris has the minimum attributes which any lilac must have to belong to the botanical class. But "lilac" has many attributes which Syringa vulgaris does not have, all the fragrance and beauty which the poets--but not the botanists--extol. "Lilac" determines not a logical but an empirical or axiological class. "When lilacs last in the door-yard bloom'd" is full of everyday meaning. "When "Syringa vulgaris last in the door-yard bloom'd" sounds, in comparison, like a joke, and is a joke, for a joke is a transposition of frames of reference. Actually, the transposition means that what the line says is not so or nonsense, and it is; for Syringa vulgaris cannot "bloom." Syringa vulgaris belongs in the botany books and exists only there; and in botany books plants do not "bloom"; they pullulate. "Pullulate" connotes the minimum-and-exact-set of attributes which is to "bloom" as Syringa vulgaris is to lilac -- and homo sapiens is to man, and homo economicus is to man in a certain setting. All these are the minimum sets of attributes within an everyday concept which make that concept a logical rather than an axiological one, and the thing referred to a member of a logical rather than an axiological class. Such a minimum set of attributes is called a Schema. Logical classes consist of schemata.[11]

Systemic valuation allows none of the variety of degrees of valuation found in extrinsic or intrinsic valuation. It allows no diversity, and no deviation, since things and people either conform to the exact and minimum definition of the synthetic concept or they are simply not members of that class. You encounter such attitudes not uncommonly in the classroom and, of course, in ordinary life. "Either you do things my way, or you are no longer welcome." "A good student is one who is neat and tidy." "He'll never get anywhere, for he is only interested in art." But the intrinsic perspective sees beneath or beyond the needs of the system--the minimal needs--even though these needs are still reinforced, or enforced to the higher extrinsic and intrinsic valuational levels. A teacher will recognize that a mark of 26 is considerably better than a mark of 0 and that marked personal achievement is thereby demonstrated, but the comparative or extrinsic result is still a "failure," for it falls below the acceptable standard of achievement which exists outside of the individual student. And the point here is not to criticize that recognition, for, as with systemic valuation, extrinsic valuation is an indispensable part of human judgment and decision making. We need to classify, compare, rank, judge relative merit and defect, and recommend on the basis of external criteria and established (external) standards. The point to remember, however, is that this is but one of three ways of valuing things and people. It is but a third of the whole story, and not the most important third! To value a student-as-person is to respect him or her as a being who must never be treated merely as a means, but always as an end, as both Hartman and Kant demanded. The teacher, while open to all the disappointments and frustration which come with continuous failure, also keeps alive the hope that this day will be different, and that a breakthrough will occur. Like the Zen Master who has brought before him a student who has failed to deal successfully with his koan puzzle on each occasion for a thousand days, it is the Master's duty to engage the student "as though for the first time." The historian will expect another failure, of course, as will the Master at the systemic and extrinsic levels. But the "Intrinsic Master"[12] will see this occasion as an occasion for success, and will be open to the potential which is there, whether or not this is the day for its expression and recognition.

Cooperation, Competition, and Conformity

Educational values are subtlety imposed by means of the learning environment, and it is imperative that educators be axiologically sensitive to overt and covert values which the learning environment assumes and expresses. Thus, the "hidden curriculum" is a phrase which refers to the general atmosphere of the classroom, the attitude towards rules and regulations which provide a workable learning environment, the nature of the sanctions to be applied if children disobey those rules, the rewards of obedience and of academic and creative success, the values of the playground, the attitudes of the coaches in teaching the meaning of physical play and "sportsmanship," and of bus drivers in beginning and ending the schoolday in a less controlled environment than the classroom, etc. The whole environment of the school, and especially the attitudes shown towards and amongst the people who make it up, at whatever level, as well as the quality of the physical environment, its state of repair, its "humanness" in terms of fixed vs. movable desks and chairs, the art and posters on the classroom walls, whether the teacher is always in the position of ultimate authority at the front of the class, whether the grounds are beautiful and encourage imaginative growth and physical delight, or merely functional, etc., is to be assessed in determining the interactional values of those who direct and live within the school milieu.

People may relate to each other in a variety of ways, but all of these ways may be grouped into four, systemically, extrinsically, intrinsically, or transpositionally, i.e., negatively. Systemically, people are not treated as unique, nor even as different, but uniformly as mere elements of a system. The system is imposed on all, and is one to which all members must adhere, making them appear alike, e.g., as citizens of a particular country, or as patients in a hospital. Conformity is the description of how elements in a system interact. Politically, authoritarianism is a frequent application of systemic valuation to human relationships vis-a-vis the state.

Extrinsically, persons are regarded as members of the same class, and are compared as such. They are not assumed to be alike, hence gradational comparison is possible. People are not expected to conform fully, at least extrinsically speaking, but are viewed as instances of the same normative concept, but to greater or lesser extent. They form a collectivity, and rather than being totally defined by the normative concept, as is the case with systemic thinking, they are only functionally related. A functional relationship is a relationship which is a part of the total nature of something or someone, but the someone is more than this function alone indicates. Thus, I may be a student, but I am also a son, and to my younger brother a teacher, and to my little league baseball team I am a first baseman and a slugger. I can be compared in each of these ways, for as a student, I am only a 'B' student, as a son I am less difficult to live with than was my brother, as a slugger I am the best in town, but not the best in the County, etc.

Authoritarian conformity is the least valuationally and conceptually rich form of association, and conformity is easily seen to be less satisfactory, and less human and humane as a form of relational interaction, than is collective interaction amongst persons of various achievements, persuasions, loyalties, intelligence, and good will.

Intrinsic interaction is of higher worth still, however, for it implies empathetic relational interaction between whole persons and whole persons, each fully concentrated on the other such that they form one sympathetically formed unit.[13] "We may call this relationship between persons Community."[14] In a true community persons are not regarded as member of the same class, more or less, or as aspects of a system, but as intrinsically valuable persons, each in a class by him or herself. Together "they produce a new class of which their own classes are intrinsic parts. Here we have the phenomenon of Cooperation."[15]

Systemic relationships are not based on cooperation, or even on competition between its members, but on strict and rigid obedience. After all, you either obey the dictates of the system, perfectly (for there are no other possibilities except to conform perfectly, or not to conform, and, therefore, to cease being a member of the group at all), or you must be "corrected," or expelled as a "hopeless" case. Extrinsic relationships are functional relationships, i.e. together they form a <u>collective</u> in that the class of properties which define the group membership, are "common [to] but not intrinsic to persons."[16] If someone is harmed, the collectivity is left virtually unaffected, and so it is of little or no direct (collective) concern. <u>Competition</u> is the way of interaction at the extrinsic level, for to the extent that one <u>better</u> fulfils the normative concept (intension) which defines the collectivity, "the worse I show up my competitor; therefore, in a collectivity it may help <u>me</u> if I make the other look worse... In competition I regard [the other]...and myself as functions and parts of a supervening concept."[17]

Intrinsic relationships imply total concentration of the persons involved such that they are sympathetically interrelated so as to form a single unit of <u>cooperation</u>. If conformity and obedience are the ruling attitudes and expectations of systemic valuation, and competition and comparative measure are the attitudes and expectations of extrinsic valuation, then good-will, identification, camaraderie, and cooperation by means of which the one cares about lifting the other to higher self-realization and achievement, are the results of intrinsic valuational interaction. The resultant sense of community arises from the parties concerned comprehending that <u>they are participants in the same situation</u> because they together form the situation, the new organic unit or whole, and that "there is no opposition between them since they are both [or all] intrinsically good, being good by being the way they are," together.[18] Rather than being mere functions, they are <u>experiences</u> to and for one another, and actually seek to serve one another. Not merely interacting functionally, and thereby leaving the core of the personalities involved untouched, intrinsic relations occur between personality cores, i.e. from intrinsic infinity to intrinsic infinity, coupled by that sort of mutuality which makes the event unforgettable, worthwhile in itself and for its own sake, a peak experience, a high, a joy, a love-in. As a result, the violation of one with whom I am so interconnected, is also a violation of me. I no longer just observe the fights on the playground at recess, I now feel them as though they were my own, and the righteous indignation is as strong as it would be if someone were to break my arm in a pique of ego, or push my daughter down a flight of concrete stairs, simply because he or she "felt like it."

We identify with close friends, family, and lovers and have made at least some contact with the core of the personalities of our "intimates," at least occasionally and in part. What needs to be done, however, is to build on and to develop this sense of interconnectedness, assisting it to spread beyond the occasional contact with someone with whom we are already close, and to embrace as well those who are smaller, weaker, "weird," or of different racial and cultural background, etc. Perhaps the expansion could--indeed should, given the fears of the times--extend to the natural environment, rendering us empathetically appreciative of and sensitive to animals and birds, flowers and trees, rivers and rocks. How this might be accomplished is less clear, but Hartman does offer some guidance.

Teaching Intrinsic Sensitivity

It is easier to teach people how to behave than it is to teach them to want to excel, and easier to teach them how to excel, than it is to teach them to show loving kindness and genuine understanding towards others, and towards the environment. In fact, most of us already possess considerable <u>systemic</u> skills with which to control and alter one another, and the environment. We have acquired behavioral skills which help us control others, and a system of rewards and punishments can go a considerable distance towards providing an environment in which we can interact with others with predictable success, and with minimal danger and disruption. But neither a tidy home, nor a tidy classroom does a family or an education make! Nor does the honing of the competitive edge create a wholesome person, capable of sensitive and profound concern for the well-being of those around us. A more or less self-actualized person, one whom you wish to be around, who can be counted on to be honest, sincere, and concerned with the well-being of others, able to identify with the successes and tragedies of others, willing to share and to help as need be, must be <u>transparently</u> in tune with him or herself. Such a person must be intrinsically sensitive.

Those who are more rather than less transparent can serve as <u>examples</u> for those who are still opaque and insensitive to intrinsic values. Much teaching is teaching by example, and the degree to which teachers serve as <u>models</u>, or exemplars for those under them cannot be easily overestimated. We learn to love by being loved. By being loved we become lovable, and in turn love. We learn tolerance by living in an environment of tolerance and generosity, and/or by being tolerated ourselves. We can assist others to become more transparent, more sensitive to the intrinsic value realm, by providing constant contact with other transparent consciousnesses, or with the intrinsically worthwhile and "drenched" expressions of transparent consciousnesses in the form of writings, biographies, artistic creations, film achievements, remarkable instances of humane interaction, and so on. To read of Albert Schweitzer's "reverence for life," or his selfless medical help made available to those whom others would not even physically touch, is a major means of educating and sensitizing others. But, as important as teaching by example is, especially for younger children,

> There is another way, too. Before they grasp, they have to grapple. In other words, by exposing them as you do to the trivialities, irrelevancies, and lack of understanding of present day value theory, you make them so mad and frustrated that you force them to something that is more clear. So you use the psychological process of **preparation, frustration, incubation, illumination.** So, first there is preparation--they have to learn in general what is ethics, or what is value. Then, frustration--you just give them modern value theory, and there is nothing more frustrating than that. And when they are thoroughly frustrated, then you let them think a little. And when they have thought a little, then you give them formal value theory, and then they will be appreciative, because they then can compare it with what they have gone through. But if they haven't gone through it, they cannot appreciate it. Some, of course, will just love chaos, and these are the ones who are opaque, and you don't deal with them any more. You forget them.[19]

Hartman was a realist in knowing that the teacher cannot expect to "reach" everyone, and those who are incorrigibly opaque are likely to be treated more systemically than the others. Still, you must continue to hold out hope that they will change, come into their own, undergo a transformation when they find someone who loves them and whom they love when they grow up, i.e. that they will grow into themselves by touching another's core, from their own newly receptive core. The teacher continues to try to find ways to stimulate higher valuational awareness, even though this may prove to be yet another day in the series of disappointments. Still, this could be the day. As a <u>person</u> who teaches and does not merely allow him or herself to be but a professional or a "functioning" teacher, you incessantly reach out to the core of the other from the core in yourself. It is such a wonderful, joyful, fulfilling way to interact that you cannot help but try to share it, for the benefits are as much your own as another's. You are, after all, the other, at least in so far as empathetic identification has occurred, and to the extent to which you have discovered your own capacity for selflessness. Much of teaching, at the intrinsic level, consists in <u>reminding</u> the person being taught that he or she is not just a <u>student</u>, not just a <u>successful</u> or <u>unsuccessful</u> student, but a <u>person</u> who is capable of infinite growth, of infinite happiness, of infinite good-will and good-works, and who is, or could be on the path of infinite self-discovery and self-expression. A person who communicates this to another is a rare find, a living human treasure (as the Japanese designate their living artistic and cultural greats), who goes well beyond the minimum definition and requirements of the professional teacher.

Perhaps it is worth confirming, at this point, that Hartman himself gives the teacher an exemplary place in acquiring and purveying intrinsic value sensitivity:

> The kind of knowledge relevant to <u>intrinsic</u> valuation is exceedingly rare. It is the capacity of complete concentration on a thing or person, the personal involvement of the artist, the inventor, the **teacher**: the capacity of empathy and sympathy. It is the kind of knowledge possessed in the highest degree by the creative genius. It is possible only in a person who is himself fully **integrated** and has all his powers available for outgoing and meeting persons or things. This is not the "outgoing" of the extrovert or the back-slapper, who meets persons extrinsically. It is the projecting of the whole person into others. ... This kind of knowledge is direct, immediate, "intuitional"; it is that of the complete person encompassing the world. It is not a matter of the intellect but of **character**. A strong character with a mediocre intellect is a more creative person than a mediocre character with a strong intellect. True genius is strong character with strong intellect. The world abounds with strong intellects of mediocre character--the professional intellectuals who have to find their security in systems; also, it has many strong characters of mediocre intellect, from business tycoons to politicians--but it lacks the combination of intellect and character--of strong minds that are, at the same time, receptive to value. This sensitivity to value arises out of sensitivity for the value of self, of self-respect. Only where there is self-respect is there respect for the essential, both in men, things, situations, and problems.[20]

Character Education

Our schools emphasize the training of the intellect, but character development is problematic. There are several reasons for this. First, there is considerable disagreement as to exactly what sort of character development ought to be taught. Some simplistically equate excellence of character with the avoidance of masturbation and abstinence from pre-marital sex. Others stress the systemic willingness to obey the rules and to manifest the expected decorum of the classroom and of society. Still others equate character with success within the system, taken broadly to include academic, social and behavioral success at school, or in the workplace, on the playing field, and in peer group popularity. Yet it is obvious that none of these formulations speak the language of intrinsic valuation. Character instruction by means of religious teaching fares no better and carries with it all of the associated problems of involving the churches in the activities of the secular state, of belief versus reasoned evidence, of indoctrination versus education. "Whose church will teach my children how and what it means to self-actualize?" is a question over which many of us would be willing to fight long and hard in order to ensure that character development is not imposed by someone or some organization whose vision of what sound character is we hold in some doubt in the first place.

To be unaware of a value dimension is to be "opaque" rather than "transparent." Therefore, the measure of your capacity to value intrinsically is your degree of opacity, or transparency of self, by means of which you are enabled to empathize or interpenetrate with all that come to you, through your awareness of the nature of your own way of life, character, and fulfilment of chosen projects. If you are intrinsically aware, you are as large as the whole universe: "Man is as large as the whole universe, because he is defined by the range of his consciousness."[21] There is nothing, in principle, which limits the expansion of your capacity to embrace the world--you always have infinite potential, infinite depth, infinite capacity for taking into yourself what it is that you are aware of. This capacity to embrace, to empathize, to love is measured by the degree of transparency achieved. Transparency is the awareness of your own conscious self in terms of its reflective capacity to evaluate itself and to determine itself, thereby allowing it to become free from its own determinations in order to be able to reach out and embrace another in total concentration and caring for that something as it is in itself, and apart from all other considerations. Greatness of character is measured by the extent and by the nature of your concern.

Conclusion

Hartman's system provides a remarkably intense "searchlight" for sorting out otherwise indistinguishable value ingredients and requirements and for systematizing them in a way which allows for correction, production, application and normatively correct education. Your task as value-educator is to keep the image of a human person, as source of infinite potential, in the forefront of your mind, and to steadfastly refuse to reduce anyone to the purely functional, or to treat anyone as a mere means to some end, however noble it may seem at the time:

> If we see the divine image in every man [and woman] and the supreme value in his [her] growth toward divinity, we must abolish all forms of compulsion which obstruct his [her] physical, mental, or spiritual growth. We must declare [an] all-out fight against the crippling effects

of poverty, the straight-jacket of dogma, the insanity of prejudice, the immorality of "sovereign" government. We must abolish these obstacles by the creative method of enlisting the help of all men [and women], the rich and the poor, the dogmatic, the prejudiced, even the politicians.[22]

Functional values must be replaced by human values, and human values are distinctive in that they are intrinsic values. The humanization of the world would consist not in eliminating systemic and extrinsic valuation, but it holding these against the background of the recognition of the infinite worth of human persons, and of their capacity to raise up all values through intrinsic valuation. Then, and only then, will all values be "lined" with the human and the humane, much as a fine suit is recognizable because of the quality of, and the care with which the generally unseen inner lining is sewn to the suit cloth by the tailor, who makes of the outer cloth a "treasure" because of his own workmanship, which is apparent only to the trained observer. The connoisseur, the sensitive appreciator will see through the outer shell as though it were transparent and will rejoice in the achievement. The humanization of the world, at least for the present, requires that people learn to comprehend, and to feel the intrinsic worth and richness of themselves, of others, and of this marvellous cosmos in which we find ourselves. We must become intrinsic masters and teach others to grasp all that is of intrinsic value intrinsically, and without delay. Our cultural and biological world of racial fragmentation and economic exploitation increasingly obscures the vast expanse of potential intrinsic valuation open to us, and of the resultant joy in living.

NOTES

1. Robert S. Hartman, "The Unique Role of the Church in the World to Come, Vital Speeches of the Day, Vol. XVII. no. 4 (December 1, 1950), p. 117.

2. Ibid., p. 116.

3. Robert S. Hartman, "The Value Structure of Creativity," The Journal of Value Inquiry, Vol. VI, no. 4 (Winter 1972), p. 255.

4. Ibid., p. 256.

5. Ibid., p. 256.

6. Ibid., p. 256.

7. Hartman, "Four Proofs of the Infinite Value of Man," Kant-Studien, Vol. 55, no. 4, 1964, p. 436. Italics mine.

8. Hartman, "The Value Structure of Creativity," p. 257.

9. Robert S. Hartman, "The Nature of Valuation," a previously unpublished manuscript, this book, p. 20. A Spanish version of this article was published in Anvario Humanitas (Centro de Estudios Humanisticos, Universidad de Nuevo Leon, Monterrey, Mexico, 1968). A shorter, and in Hartman's opinion, an inferior version of this essay appeared in English as "The Logic of Value," The Review of Metaphysics, Vol. XIV, no. 3 (1961), pp. 389-432. [Editors' note: We have found the latter to be quite a different article from "The Nature of Valuation," which is published on pages 9-35 of this volume.]

10. Ibid.

11. Ibid., p. 24.

12. Robert S. Hartman, and Robert E. Carter, "Dialogue on Intrinsic Value," unpublished manuscript MSS, 1971, p. 81.

13. Hartman, "The Nature of Valuation," this volume, p. 23.

14. Ibid.

15. Ibid.

16. Ibid., p. 24.

17. Ibid.

18. Ibid., p. 23.

19. Hartman, Carter, "Dialogue," p. 133.

20. Hartman, "The Nature of Valuation," this volume, p. 28.

21. Hartman, Carter, "Dialogue," pp. 66-67.

22. Robert S. Hartman, "The Unique Role of the Church in the World to Come," <u>Vital Speeches of the Day</u>, Vol. XVII, no. 4 (December 1, 1950), p. 117.

Chapter XIX

THE THEOLOGICAL IMPLICATIONS OF THE

AXIOLOGICAL FORMULATIONS OF ROBERT S. HARTMAN

C. Stephen Byrum

Maslow was right: our existence as human beings--not merely as **homo sapiens**--is best understood by articulating our lives in terms of needs. If an insight into an individual's most pervasive needs can be gained, who that individual is "as a person" on his most intrinsic level can best be established.

There is that need for survival-level basics, a need for community and the reinforcing dialogue of group existence, and those complex needs of self-expression, creativity, and imagination. Maslow's "self-actualized" human being is highly compatible with Robert S. Hartman's intrinsic valuer, that person who is exercising the capacity to become involved in intrinsic value experiences. Human beings **need** a broad range of "intrinsics," from love to rational explanation. These needs--from love to rational explanation--may finally be subsumed under the general human need which Mircea Eliade called "orientation" or that which allows humans to avoid the experience of "alienation"--alienation from community, from "sense," or from some metaphysical ground of being. For Eliade, this need to avoid alienation and experience orientation is the birth place of both religion and science.

Somewhere along the way of human evolution, a god-concept rises into the midst of human consciousness. It almost obviously does so in response to a variety of needs: an explanation for all that is unexplained--a god of the gaps; a "someone" who can lend strength and protection to more vulnerable and uncertain human life conditions, a "power" that can be judged as being responsible for events well beyond the ability of humans. Humans became aware of cause and effect; and, as the primitive teleological arguments established, it simply "made sense" that there had to be something like a god "up there and out there, beyond and behind the dim unknown." There seemed to be no way to fully explain the events of life without such a factor. This "god of the gaps" has been on the scene of human thought almost from the beginning. The "gaps" were wide at the beginning; there was once room for full pantheons of divinities.[1] As the "gaps" have narrowed in a rational, scientific world, the place of god has become less and less secure.

My daughter is twelve now. Many aspects of our relationship are changing. Gone are the days when she wanted me to accompany her downstairs to retrieve some abandoned stuffed animal that now had become an absolute necessity if she was to go to bed and sleep. "It is dark downstairs," she said. "The dark won't hurt you," came my practiced reply. Her part in our litany continued: "I'm not afraid of the dark, but of what might be in the dark." I always relented, and down the stairs we would go to retrieve the missing animal. Halfway down the stairs, she would grip my hand and hug as closely as she could. But now, the dark is something to play in, to show her courage in handling, to tell other children frightening tales about and laugh at their fear; she doesn't need to hold my hand anymore. (Except when her pet guinea pig dies, and then she seeks me out, holds on as tightly as she can, and wants reassurance that it was not her fault.) I wonder if, in principle, human beings come to the god-concept, grow away from it and discard it, and then find moments of return in a similar fashion.

The evolution of human thinking continues and human beings become more and more introspective. As part of this introspection, doubt appears. Institutions and authority figures disdain this doubt, for once its door is opened their sacrosanct status is jeopardized. What if the "givens" of existence--including divinity--may not have been established on such firm ground after all? Such a possibility could be devastating. Its implications could wreck havoc with the traditional power structures of life--especially the church. The whole force of theology and philosophy--although early on there was little difference in the two--was directed at **proving** that God was not merely a fabrication growing out of human need, a creation of a primitive attempt to "make sense" that simply could not stand the light of a modern, scientific age.

So, across the course of most of the intellectual activity of Western civilization, attention was riveted on proving the existence of God. Thinkers such as Anselm and Aquinas were even granted sainthood, in part, because of their "proofs." The great clear and concise philosopher, Descartes, with all of his emphasis on science and mathematics, could not leave the god-question alone. (I read recently about the work of an English computer expert, also a "confessing Christian," who had used his technical skills to **demonstrate** that the odds of there not being a god were something like one in ten to the 450th power. "Believers" in England were greeting this news enthusiastically. A new substantiation for faith was being offered. It is the "hound of heaven" who now is chased himself. As the old song says: "The beat goes on.")

What I would call the "best" of theology and philosophy being written today has concluded that all attempts to "prove" God's existence--or disprove it--were doomed from the start. Derrida is on target when he talks about "holes" in being that can never totally and absolutely be covered in rational explanation. There simply is no way rationally or demonstrably to deal with the god-concept on the levels of rational proof sought by the old theologians. Like most matters of deep human concern--like Hartman's "intrinsic" or Ockham's "experiences of first intension"--a point is reached in which rationality is exhausted in its attempt to make every idea of human existence clear and concise.

So, what is to be done?

The options seem to be: accept God in blind faith; unilaterally reject the entire notion of divinity; or, forget about the questions, embrace a laissez faire agnosticism, and chase "rainbows" other than those that are theological. If these are the only options, the last one may be the best.

Human need for explanation and articulation can not be slaked this easily. There must be another option. "Articulation" is the key; if the god-concept can not be proven, then at least it can be talked about reasonably. To explicate is all that we can do as human beings; it is, at the same time, the best we can do. Articulation, explication, not proof, must come to delineate the optimal effort of theology in the modern age.

This emphasis on articulation has powerful support from a wide range of important philosophical voices. Whitehead said: "In philosophical writings proof should be at a minimum...Philosophy in any proper sense of the term, cannot be proven. The attempt of any philosophical [or theological] discourse should be to produce self-evidence. The aim of philosophy is sheer discourse."[2] Gabriel Vahanian suggested that there must be a "waiting without idols,"[3] and his "idols" are distinctly the names of gods and the theologies which these names spawn. Michael Novak continues: "We have no suitable language for talking about God. Language borrowed from the object world [the extrinsic world] is systematically [systemically] misleading when applied to God."[4]

Robert S. Hartman moved in these circles. In his writings on the ontological "proof" of Anselm, Hartman was convinced that the most that could be accomplished by theology was **intellectus fidei**. Theology should try to be an intelligible as possible--no problem there--but it could never push beyond faith. "All theological statements are inadequate to their object," he said. "A[n absolutely valid] concept of God is had by God alone."[5] Very clearly an "enlightened" faith would be preferable to a "blind" faith, but in the end "enlightened" and "blind" are value words assigned by people holding certain believes toward themselves--"enlightened"--and against those holding contrary beliefs to their own--"blind." If "enlightened" means "educated," then it must be recalled that for every person who feels more comfortable with an "educated" clergy, for example, there is some other person who believes that education can only have a corrupting influence on religious proclamation.

Hartman believed that Gaunilo, Anselm's adversary, was seeking an extrinsic, material proof which could be validated in sense experience. Gaunilo's argument, for Hartman, was based on the old, Augustinian understanding of the nature of God, **quod est maius omnibus**. This was an "ontic" formulation, which Anselm "noetically" revolutionized. Hartman asserted: "Anselm's is a rule for the **thinking about God**, not for the determination of God; it does not deal with God's existence but exclusively with the thinking of God's existence."[6] In this sense, Anselm fulfills Whitehead's dictum that philosophy should involve itself in discourse and articulation, not demonstrable proof. This "thinking" about God may **imply** existence, but implication--no matter how well reasoned--is not proof. It is **intellectus**, but it is still only capable of being **fidei**.

Hartman was fond of using the categories developed by John Hospers' Meaning and Truth in the Arts.[7] For Hartman, the artist probably knew more of "truth" than the rational scientist or the Cartesian theologian. Hospers distinguished between two types of "truth." His "truth-about" related to extrinsic, demonstrable truths. Beyond this was a "truth-to" that could never capture analytically, but could only point in the direction of. Since God is "too definite" for words or proofs, the best that can be done is to point in the direction of God; any "truth" of the existence of God will forever remain "truth-to" and not "truth-about."

Perhaps it is true of any intense theological pursuit; but Robert Hartman did, in fact, have a tremendous emotional investment in his theological explorations. He was born in Germany in 1910, and was raised in a highly religious atmosphere, receiving his first formal education under both Lutheran and Catholic tutelage. By the age of eight, religion played such a commanding role in his life that he was an acolyte, helped the priest daily, and was preparing for the life of a monk. Although Hartman says in his autobiographical writings[8] that this period of his life was merely a childhood phase, he also readily admits that it had a formative influence on him, and that he was troubled throughout his life with the rigid, self-discipline[9] which he engendered within himself in those "pre-monastery" days.

Also formatively ingrained in Hartman's mind were "ultimate" questions of life and death, war and peace, God and country, which would not have ordinarily interested a young boy. In the atmosphere of Kaiser Germany, which was crazed by a thirst for power and an allegiance to the state that manifested itself in the feeling that it was better to be dead than non-German, an atmosphere which increased in gravity with the death of his uncle in World War I, there was prompted an introspection into the "meaning" of life which would be for most individuals of his age quite premature.

By the time he was seventeen, Hartman's concerns were beginning to crescendo. The presence of some understanding of God in his search for a "key" or "direction" for his life at this time was evidenced as almost a continual refrain in his introspective questioning. There was also a primitive relationship to the axiology he would develop which can be seen in his early autobiographical expressions. Hartman recalls:

> I began to put some pretty tough questions to myself. What is the value of a human life? What is the relation of that life to the state, and to God? What is the relation of life to death? Is my life nothing but a chip? Is God truth, or is the military state truth?[10]

This quote from a teenager's reflection may be quite important. On a rudimentary level, a basic association was occurring between value and God, between the process of exploring value questions and the process of exploring the god-question. In his adult life, Hartman may not have really gotten very far from this basic association.

A quite striking incident occurred in 1932, at a time when Hartman was deeply involved in an active resistance to the rise of Adolph Hitler in Germany. This resistance ultimately led to his having to flee Germany for his life a year later. Hartman had just published an article entitled "The Woman Hitler" which dealt with homosexuality within the Nazi leadership; he was in the beginning stages of another article, "The State and the Political Parties," which was to be delivered in a faculty seminar at the University of Berlin. He describes in his autobiography "seven terrible days of frenzy, frustration, and horror"[11] as he was driven by the overwhelming compulsion of intellectual expression.

> I found myself being driven on and on, getting in deeper as I wrestled, not just with the state and political parties, but also with life and death, war and peace, the One and the Many, and finally God, **because once you start and do not stop you eventually MUST come to the problem of God.** I felt driven to **prove beyond doubt** the beliefs which had piled up in somewhat bewildering fashion throughout my youth.[12]

"Prove beyond doubt" is important here. On some level, Hartman probably meant this in the full, literal sense of the words. In another sense, his expression could simply be that of a young teenager idealizing about a concept that could be expressed with rational verification. Later, as an adult developing a formal axiology, it may be that "proving beyond doubt" was not his goal as a thinker at all.

In the dramatic climate of the frenzied compulsion he had been under for a week, Hartman stood in the hallway outside his father's bedroom in the middle of the night, trembling, wet with perspiration, his eyes staring glassily, and exclaimed: "I am frightened. I have seen God."[13] Here is Hartman's **mysterium tremendum**, after which he collapsed, and had to be hospitalized for six months with a condition diagnosed as a nervous breakdown.

He seemed to be relieved by this diagnosis, for a nervous breakdown was a "definite, palpable thing, a familiar phenomenon."[14] Something had happened, in terms of the outside diagnoses, which could be labelled, codified, explained. He would later confide: "It was my lifelong endeavor to find a rational account for this experience, and I did find it eventually through the precision of formal axiology."[15] (It may also be that this "nervous breakdown" helped him to escape the dangerous notice he was receiving from the Nazis.)

Ultimate intelligibility for Hartman meant science. He wanted to be as scientific about life as Descartes was when he wanted to talk about every aspect of existence with a clarity and conciseness like that found in mathematics. To have this clarity as a goal means that the articulation which rises in this context will be superior to the normal flow of non-introspective, non-self-consciously precise language about God, or about other issues in life in general. To think that clarity and articulation, just because it is termed "scientific," will issue in a tangible demonstration or proof of the metaphysical is to expect too much. I believe that Hartman used the word "science" to separate his attempts at articulation from the general language of theological explanation; I do not think that he conceived his "science" as a new proof of ultimates and unknowns. He did not create a "science" in the normally perceived sense of the word (though the normally perceived sense of that word may have its own inadequacies); he did take a more scientific approach to an arena of concern that has been traditionally treated in the most non-scientific manner imaginable. Hartman's "science" does not prove ineffables; it rather dictates **the type of approach** which is made toward ineffables.

The most significant feature of human existence for Hartman is the human capacity to value. Thus, his basic "science" is axiology, the attempt to talk about valuing in the most rationally scientific and intellectually precise manner possible. The key here is still **to talk about,** the pointing of Hospers' "truth-to." There is no guarantee of goodness in human beings as an outcome, but intelligible dialogue about valuing may be the best ground for making goodness plausible and meaningful that there could be.

As regards theology, the theological application of his value structure is termed "theologic." The two pursuits--axiology and theology--are intimately related. I am convinced that the patterns of living which are at the core of the theologic constitute the most concrete example of what an axiologically ideal person would be like. By this I mean specifically that in the axiology there is the scientific explanation of goodness; in the theologic, there is the concrete example of this goodness as it relates to ethics and morality--the "good." In Hartman's "Value Structure of Creativity," there is the concrete application of axiology as it applies to the "beautiful." For the "beautiful," there is the concrete image of the creative artist using the power of intrinsic valuation with objects. For the "good," there is the concrete image of the person who uses intrinsic valuation in regard to others. In this latter regard, he may expand his image of the moral, intrinsic valuer in terms of Kierkegaard's "Knight of Faith." He also goes to a rather great extent to make Jesus his central paradigm. In some respects, "theologic" to "theology" as Kierkegaard's authentic religion is to what he more derisively termed "religiosity." For want of any better characterizations, Billy Graham or Jerry Falwell may represent "theology," while John A. T. Robinson (or Anselm and Kierkegaard, for Hartman) may represent the "theologic." This is not to say that Robinson, Anselm, or Kierkegaard are "scientists"; but in comparison to most theological approaches, their approach to intelligibility and articulation is different enough in degree that it becomes different in kind and deserves a different name.

An excursion into Hartman's "science" must first start with definitions. "Science" is best understood as **a method for ordering with precision the phenomena of existence.**

> Science in general is neither natural nor moral science. It is simply science. It is **the application of a logical frame of reference to a set of objects.** In others words, science in general is a **method** [i.e., a particular way of talking about or pointing in the direction of], and it has nothing to do with the **CONTENT** of a particular science.[16]

Science has to do with "synthetic concepts" rather than "analytic concepts." Analytic concepts have to do with abstractions from sense experience which are manifested as categories and predicates. Synthetic concepts are constructs of the mind that have to do with axioms and formal relationships. Constructs of the mind ultimately are manifested as language. Again, the basic point is reclaimed that what Hartman is trying to do is simply to establish a track of intelligible articulation. To see him attempting to do more than this is to misunderstand his operating base. If someone gets lost in the Kantian philosophical verbiage, Hartman states his task more anecdotally: his quest for orderly thinking about value was inspired by Adolph Hitler[17]; as Hitler had been able to organize evil, it became his life priority to organize good. "Science" is simply "orderly thinking,"[18] yet order thinking may be among the rarest of commodities, especially in the theological world.

The key to science is the discovery of an "axiom," a **statement** which encompasses a phenomenal field. Thus, Galileo's axiom $M=s/t$ (the formal relationship between the space traversed by a moving body and the time of the traversal) encompasses the phenomenal field of motion. The axiom is a synthetic concept, a construct of the mind, a form of language and articulation. It is a superior way for talking about motion or pointing in the direction of the phenomenon of motion.

With axiology, the phenomenal field is valuing. For Hartman, the axiom which encompasses this field is his definition of "good" as concept fulfillment. Then, Hartman extends the axiom by talking about systemic, extrinsic, and intrinsic levels of fulfillment. In the end, he has not analytically discerned and demonstrably proven "The Good," but he has given a mechanism for talking about goodness. Across fifteen years of teaching ethics and value inquiry using Hartman's approach, all that I can say is that it constitutes a successful mechanism of approach; it does organize in an orderly way the phenomenal field of goodness. Students are given a new language, a new mechanism of approach, and a dialogue is created that they find profoundly meaningful.

Nothing has been proven, but the axiological, orderly thinking seems to add order to at least this significant area of their often chaotic lives.

In turning to the theologic, the desire is still for an axiom. However, at this juncture it seems that the axiom needs to be concretized not so much in synthetic words, but in a person. This is why I emphasized above that I feel that the theologic is not so much "application" of axiology as it is an extension into concreteness of axiology. Axiology defines "The Good," and the theologic follows as a necessary complement which is designed to give a concrete, lived example.

The axiomatic person who concretizes the phenomenal field of goodness and/or godliness is first described in general terms. Hartman talks about a "genius."[19] Genius is the ability to apply infinite personal "power" (for want of a better word) to a situation, the ability of interpenetration and concentration which is the epitome of intrinsic valuation. This is exemplified by the artist (as regards the "beautiful") or by--again for want of a better word--the saint (as regards the "good").

Hartman calls a person who manifests this intrinsic relatedness to life a genius at living; in the highest, theologic sense of the word, this is the "spiritual man." Hartman extends the concept by talking about the Greek concept of **arete**, and explains that to possess "virtue" means that a person is a **virtuoso at living**. Therefore, the virtuoso at living, the genius at living, the person who manifests the power of intrinsic relatedness to life, has fulfilled the essence of human existence. He is, thus, "the **good** man." It is then possible to take a theological phrase, "Man is created in the image of God," and give it theologic meaning: "image of God" is equated with the exercised capacity for intrinsic valuation. The term "God" can also be articulated in terms of the theologic as "the Value of Values."[20]

This virtuosity of living can be subject to enhancement and development. Hartman outlines a program of maturity in becoming a "genius at living," a "good man," by describing "Four Self Rules."

1. Know Thyself--associated with Socrates, and referring to the knowledge of properties that an individual person possesses;

2. Choose Thyself--associated with Kierkegaard, and having to do with existential authentic existence, along with the acceptance and assertion of the "I am the one I am";

3. Create Thyself--associated with the Italian Renaissance philosopher, Pico, and his emphasis on the dignity of human life; and,

4. Give Thyself--associated with Jesus and having to do with loving one's neighbor as oneself. Love here becomes synonymous with the highest level of intrinsic valuation, especially as it is manifested in the mutual inclusivity of intrinsic valuation of self, world, and others.

These four "rules" seem to align themselves into an ascending hierarchy which discloses a predisposition clearly evident in Hartman's thought, the unabashed emphasis on Jesus. In this regard, he is not far removed from the neo-orthodoxy of Barth, the moral teachings of Bonhoeffer, and serves as a historical precursor to the radical theology of Altizer and Hamilton. There is a move of focus from God to Jesus, from theology to ethics. The interface of axiology and the theologic becomes even more self-evident.

Jesus appears in Hartman's thought as one who is attempting to "establish an inner landscape"[21] among human beings which will abridge the chaos of human existence. When this "inner landscape" (a description that is patently metaphorical, rather than realistically scientific) is established, a person is able to ascend the ladder of human potentialities as an intrinsic valuer, and then is understood as this "genius" and "virtuoso" at living.

How does Jesus "establish" this inner landscape? The only possible answer would seem to be by his lived example and his teachings. Jesus becomes, at one and the same time, the paradigm intrinsic valuer and teacher of intrinsic values as it applies to human relationships. As one follows his lifestyle and embraces his teachings, one would thus become a "believer." To be "like Jesus" is infinitely more important than theological beliefs about Jesus. (This is not to say that systemic and extrinsic valuation is not important to the overall living of one's life. To have a balanced development of the capacity for valuing on all three levels is significant. However, I still see intrinsic valuing as a "higher order" valuing and loving as the epitome of the intrinsic valuing level.)

Hartman distinguishes between what he terms the "Man of Faith" and the "Man of Fear." The "Man of Faith" has intrinsic Self-awareness, is secure about his Self, and has the capacity to experience freedom and liberation to be that Self. He is also able to confer the status of Self-hood on others. The "Man of Fear" is out of touch with his own Self, and is defensively insecure in his relation to his own Self and other Selves. These ideas are axiological. Then, Hartman turns to the theologic for a concrete example. He does this by making reference to Jesus' "Parable of the Talents," in which one of the main characters is so insecure and intimidated that he cowers in dismay and hides the money which has been given to him. Perhaps many literary references could have been used to give concreteness to Hartman's axiological concept; that he returns to Jesus time and again as a reference point is of no small consequence.

In general, a "parable" of Jesus is seen as a situation in infinity which is expressed in finite language. A "miracle," such as the transformation of water into wine, becomes an example of the intrinsic "composition" of the material into the spiritual. Conversational narratives, such as that which Jesus had with the woman at the Samaritan well or with Nicodemus, are seen as dialogical juxtapositions of the extrinsic and the intrinsic. Such teachings as "turning the other cheek," or "in being compelled to go one mile, go two," are seen as instances of overcoming the finite with the infinite, overcoming evil with good.

Hartman then extends his discussion to the church.[22] Organized religion is considered to be very positive as far as its **potential** for advancing intrinsic valuation is concerned. The unique role of the church is to "make the teachings of Jesus a living reality so that later generations will as naturally live the moral life as our generation lives the much stranger technological life."[23]

He then tempers this apparently optimistic view of the church with a disappointed realism which sees the church mirroring the lives of the people who make it up and becoming sadly rather dull. This is especially true in regard to the way in which the church has so often been related to the state as a pawn of its political agendas; "Hitler's armies did not lack for chaplains."[24] The state has often replaced the church, becoming a "church proxy, a spiritual proxy, a God proxy."[25] In such a situation, a systemic entity becomes more important than intrinsic life itself. It was the systemic, extrinsic, finite power of the Jewish law and the Roman state which crucified Jesus. When the church becomes married with the state, there is a systemic dis-valuation of an intrinsic value.

It is vitally important to see what Hartman is not doing with the character of Jesus. He is making no proclamations about a Davidic Messiah coming to apocalyptically bring in the Kingdom of God. He is not talking about Jesus in a way that would even be offensive to a Jew or a Moslem. He goes into no theological discussions of Jesus' divine status.

Instead, he posits Jesus as a paradigm who, in the general traditions that Hartman's thought will intersect, is probably the best-known and most viable candidate for paradigm status in terms of what people can recognize and relate to. When his voice turns more to the specialized area of philosophy per se, he talks with equal fluidity about Kierkegaard's "knight of faith."

Therefore, Jesus' status for Hartman does not involve the necessity of including a related baggage train of ideas from the New Testament and the history of Christendom. Instead, Jesus is merely the axiom, the concrete example which epitomizes the phenomenal field. I doubt that Jesus himself would have any problem with the way that Hartman puts his character to use; Jesus had provided his own, parallel bottom line by saying, "I have given you an **example**, now go and do as I have done." (John 13:15)

Perhaps, some other figure from the world religions would have been adequate to serve Hartman's need for a paradigm. He does not breach this issue. Perhaps an ideal image that had no name or real historical reference point would have served his purposes as well. However, given his traditions and the traditions of most of his readers, it probably would have been surprising had he chosen any other paradigm besides Jesus.

Today, I do not believe that Hartman would have any trouble embracing the attitude toward Jesus expressed by William Hamilton:

> [One] is sometimes inclined to suspect that Jesus Christ is best understood as neither the object nor the ground of faith, neither as person, event, or community, but simply as **a place to be, a standpoint**. That place is, of course, alongside the neighbor, being for him. [Or, intrinsically valuing the neighbor.] This may be the meaning of Jesus' true humanity and it may even be the meaning of his divinity, and thus of divinity itself. In any case, now--even when one knows so little about what to believe--one does know where to be.[26]

I don't believe that Hartman would have any trouble substituting Jesus with Bonhoeffer's more abstract conception of "the man for others." Hartman would affirm Bonhoeffer in one of his most critical statements:

> Atonement and redemption, regeneration, the Holy Ghost, the love of our enemies, the cross of resurrection, life in Christ and Christian discipleship--all of these things [i.e., these theological conceptions] have become so problematic and so remote that we hardly dare any more to speak of them...So our traditional language must become powerless and remain silent.[27]

In this "silence" of language, the sheer discourse of philosophy has finally fulfilled itself in Whitehead's "self-evidence." The traditional theological is at least two steps removed from "self-evidence"; Hartman's theologic, one step removed, becomes the bridge to--for want of better words, since now words have run out--the highest fulfillment of the intrinsic. Moral "truth" now is merged with aesthetic "truth" in the intrinsic "awareness" of penultimate "oneness"--language is stretching to its limits here--of Self, others, world, and "God." Now, for want of better words, there is room for the artist, the saint, and--what shall we say?--the mystic.

Having pressed his thinking processes this far, it seems that Hartman simply cannot leave the god-question on some back burner and then live as an intrinsic valuer. Following Anselm, Hartman admits a "passion for discovery" of what he terms the "Known Unknown."[28] This discovery is not, however, on the level of Anselm's pursuit in his **Monologion**, a pursuit of the **omnia**, the material elements, of "**quod est maius omnibus**." The discovery is rather of the "intrinsic," **delectatio**, ecstacy in the face of "self-evidence."

Hartman keys on Anselm's definition of God, "that being than which nothing greater can be conceived." The seminal word is **greater**. In many understandings of God before Anselm, "greater" would have been **maius**: quantitative, material, analytical, extrinsic and systemic greatness. At least, in the more rationalistic and scientifically materialistic world which was coming, some analytic quantity of greatness would be more appealing. In fact, for a thousand years of the most complex Christian theology which preceded Anselm, God had been seen as an infinite, incorporeal, immaterial spirit. This conception may have been meaningful in sacred confessions, but its rational meaningfulness was marginal at best. Anselm was attempting to make some new statement that would bring greater clarity to the vague ideas which the traditions had pursued and extended. His insight is to substitute **melius**: qualitative, synthetic, intrinsic greatness. Hartman can then add one further step of clarification through his axiological model by saying that "God" is thus understood as the intrinsic of intrinsics, the "Value of Values," "that value than which no richer can be conceived."[29] Then, as soon as what might be perceived as an ultimate statement has been made, Hartman realizes that it is not good enough. He corrects himself:

> God is not that than which nothing better can be thought; it is not the value than which no richer can be conceived. Nor is this intrinsic value. Rather, God as the value of values is beyond all numerations or cardinalities of properties...Not even the numbering of the value levels can account for God's nature...This value progression goes on **ad infinitum**, that is, to $\aleph_\triangle$--and only this latter expression approximates symbolically the value than which no richer can be conceived.[30]

At this point, the discussion has reached a critical juncture. There is the need to recognize again that Hartman is making no attempt at proving the material existence of God. It is also important to note that his "science" may have started needlessly reaching beyond itself into an arena that is unnecessary. It would have been enough to stop at the point of transforming the "inner landscape" of human existence in terms of intrinsic valuation. However, it seems to be the character of the human mind to push the edges of complex expression, to move in the ebb and flow of metaphor and rationality, even if such pursuits do threaten to move far afield from the decisive and even simplistic. After all, an axiom is simple--a maximum embraced within a minimum. But the human mind, organizing its own phenomenal field, tends to want to tie in just one more association, make just one more combination of ideas. I continue to wonder if the extremes of Hartman's mathematically scientific formulations are absolutely essential to the main points he was trying to make. If the extreme formulations are given too much notice, it seems to me that attention is drawn away from the center of his contribution.

In the end, Hartman may offer his own disclaimers; he may realize that he had the capacity to make his presentation too involved. He concludes toward the end of his Anselm discussion: "Anselm's is a rule for the **thinking about God.**"[31] With this emphasis, he may be pushing the edges of what Anselm himself thought--that thinking implied existence. Anselm has now become a vehicle for Hartman's own formulation; historically, what he now finds most important in Anselm may not have been exactly what Anselm found to be most important.

> The name of God itself does not presuppose the existence or nature of anything, not even of God. It merely says that if God should be thought then nothing greater than God ought to be thought. Anselm's argument does not deal with God's existence [here Hartman is stretching] but exclusively with the thinking of God's existence.[32]

To me, Hartman's conclusion has the force of saying that he has, indeed, exercised his mental abilities to an extreme degree. The axiological connections can be seen as matching up with every level of theological explication along the way of Christian rationalism. Hartman has been responsible to the traditions, but then it is as if he is saying that the real "meat" of his articulations is back along the way, well before the extreme details of the Anselm explication. He had pushed his model to the edge and it still worked; he could restate the highest moment of theological insight in the terms of his value structure. Now, it makes more sense to retreat to the heart and core, the emphasis on the effect of intrinsic valuation in the real world of day-to-day human endeavor.

Having studied with Robert Hartman for three years and having given significant energy to exploring and teaching the theological implications of his axiology over fifteen more years, I obviously have a profound appreciation for the articulation which his model performs. I like the way that he moves the language of the traditions to a new plateau; it is like there is a hermeneutic efficiency in Hartman's work which is appealing to a more modern audience. I do see Hartman's work, like any intellectual pursuit of human existence, as being limited to a particular place and time. He stands beyond the old, traditional theological attempts to lay claim to the omnia **of God,** either the extrinsic, material existence in terms of rational proof or the near-mystical contemplation of an ultimately non-rational, incorporeal "spirit." He stands alongside the very best intentions of neo-orthodoxy, desiring to find something in the traditions--in this case, Jesus--which can be transformed in a new statement--his axiology and theologic--that will have more concrete application and acceptance by modern man. He precludes, but does not go quite as far, as the radical theologies which begin to appear with Honest to God **and** Radical Theology and the Death of God. If "truth" stands somewhere in the arena of Aristotle's golden mean, Hartman's position between the old traditions and the new, radical theologies may give him a higher credibility than either of the extremes. His statements may become "axiomatic" in the way that they embrace the entire phenomenal field and not simply the edges of it.

I have been looking particularly for more correct expressions which, in my mind, extend Hartman's discussions. Of the most recent statements that I have encountered, I am particularly impressed by two books by Harvard Divinity School professor Gordon Kaufman entitled The Theological Imagination: Constructing the Concept of God and God--The Problem.

I am aware of the work which Rem Edwards has done on the Hartman system. Edwards feels that the more modern theological position that can best do justice to Hartman is the process theology of Whitehead and Charles Hartshorne. In his Reason and Religion, Edwards draws particular attention to Hartshorne's conception of "the doctrine of contributionism" in which all of the value created in the world is ultimately contributed to God. This may be another way of seeing God as the "Value of Values." At this point in my own thinking, I have both an appreciation for process philosophy which I studied in significant detail in my seminary training and a great respect for Edwards' scholarship. He unquestionably raises issues which could be followed with benefit. My own thinking has followed more in the direction of existentialism, the new hermeneutics, and radical theology. I am looking for a greater simplicity, and I am not sure that a parallel explication of process philosophy would serve that end. Kaufman's work seems to serve this end better for me.

The frontpiece of <u>God--the Problem</u> is from Miguel de Unamuno, and perfectly captures the stretching beyond traditional religious metaphysics with which Hartman was grappling. "To believe in God is to long for His existence and, further, it is to act as if He existed; it is to live by this longing and to make it the inner spring of action."

The "Truth" of theology--and in this case of Christian theology--is not nativity, cross, and resurrection. When these "fundamentals" are allowed to slip into the background, that which is "Christian" is then transvalued in a positive manner. The "Truth" is what the character Jesus said, his words and teaching, his life. Beside these teachings and this example of intrinsic living, all that is vested even in the resurrection itself quakes into insignificance by comparison.

Unfortunately, in almost all so-called "Christian" discussions, all "Truth" hinges on the truth of biblical events. Kaufman uses Unamuno to say that true faith involves longing for, acting as if, living by, and making some position/idea the motivating core of personal existence. All of these high, human processes are value processes! Miraculous historical antecedents and rational proofs are of secondary importance. Here is Paul Tillich's "ultimate concern," the New Testament theologian Rudolf Bultmann's "kernel" of the Gospel, and William Hamilton's "standpoint." Here is Hartman's virtuosity of the "genius" at living. Then comes the next step provided by Kaufman when he affirms that:

> the meaning of human existence can be found in the cultural values produced by man's creative genius [or, intrinsic valuation] and the social interaction of which love is the profoundest form [as it is the profoundest form of intrinsic valuation]. Is not talk about God simply a vestige of earlier stages of man's historical development which, however appropriate and necessary in its own time, is no longer relevant or useful in ours?[33] [Note at this point the closeness of what Kaufman is saying to the ideas expressed by Edwards about process thought. There is probably some common ground to be explored at this point.]

The term "God" comes to have deep symbolic meaning, but--like all symbols--its importance is in the function **it pragmatically plays in day-to-day** existence. 7 Kaufman refers to God as "the anchor symbol" the "Value of Values") of a whole new way of life and worldview **the transvalued "inner landscape").** Man created the world of symbols and orients himself within that structure [recall Hartman's emphasis on orderly thinking].[34]

What Kaufman describes at this point is precisely what Hartman accomplishes in his axiology and theologic. Kaufman continues:

> Even though we have not been able to satisfy ourselves as spectators of the world and of man that the interpretation we accept is the final and lasting metaphysical Truth--and I am enough of a skeptic and positivist to believe that finite man will never reach that goal--we have to stake ourselves, our lives, and all that is dear to us on one or another view [set of values], and work from one day to the next in the terms it lays down for us.[35]

> Believing in "God" thus means practically to order all of life and experience in personalistic, purposive, moral terms, and to construe the world and man accordingly; the meaning and significance of human action and ethics are thus enhanced by being grounded on an adequate metaphysical foundation.[36]

This is precisely what Hartman accomplishes. He "orders" life in terms of a model, a value structure, and in terms of a concrete personal paradigm, the virtuoso at living, the Knight of Faith, or Jesus. Hartman "construes the world and man" in terms of this value structure. In doing so, "human action and ethics are enhanced," transvalued. He does not give an absolute metaphysical foundation; that is impossible. He does, however, provide--if, in fact, it is needed--an adequate metaphysical base: his theologic. The base is there; the transvaluation of actions and ethics, the construing of the world and man, are the most exceptional results of his work.

In a short tract entitled "Theology for a Nuclear Age," Kaufman views human existence as having been organized into a "multiplicity of centers."[37] These centers may be personal, group, or national in their organization, and all are involved in some form of self-defense and self-realization. Religion, cultural ideology, and politics are used in differing combinations to reinforce the rights and directions of each center. This method of social organization works out pretty well until one center's needs come in conflict with those of another. If this conflict escalates, the interdependent nature of existence is overlooked and general human existence can be threatened.

A new approach to theology is demanded for the nuclear age. The old approach which saw theology as interpreting the present in terms of traditions handed down from the past will no longer work. A new theology is demanded that is not "received," but rather forward looking, imaginative, creative, and primarily concerned with "the human imagination seeking to provide more adequate orientation for human life."[38] This seems precisely the goal of the theologic.

In this new theologic--rather than "new theology"--the function of the symbol "God" is not to focus attention on some metaphysical being or entity-- whether material **omnia** or incorporeal "spirit"--but to "focus our consciousness and attention on that which humanizes and relativises."[39] To be humanized means to draw primary attention to the maintenance and enhancement of human community and individual human uniqueness; to be relativised means to understand that no one "center" or the ideology which supports it is absolute. Allegiance and loyalty to "centers" is replaced by a "wider loyalty to on-going life."[40]

Kaufman also has a role for Jesus, and it is precisely an extension of what Hartman has said. Jesus is seen as a "paradigmatic exemplification"[41] of attitudes, dispositions, and **values** necessary for the survival of human society.

That which makes a mode of existence "Christian," thus is not some supernatural quality or group of qualities made available only through Jesus Christ; it is, rather, the **valuation** as normative for human life of qualities and potentialities which make for reconciliation and loving community--those potentialities and qualities paradigmatically epitomized in the story of Jesus.[42]

Once this position is understood, it becomes important to get rid of the "ambiguous Christology"[43] which has grown up around the proclamation of Jesus. One side of the proclamation of Jesus, which Kaufman calls the "triumphalistic motif"[44] emphasizes a divine lord type of being who sits at the right hand of God in heaven and drives human history toward his desired end. In this concept, everything which occurs is part of some kind of omnipotent plan which will ultimately issue in the glorification of God and the eternal reward of God's people. The danger in this type of Christology is that it erodes day-to-day responsibility on the part of human beings and encourages them to take less seriously their roles in the insurance of a safe and sane existence.

The other side of the Christology issue sees Jesus as the servant-teacher who is advancing human respect and human dignity on every side. This Jesus encourages peacefulness, forgiveness, and harmony; he is concerned much more with love of enemies than domination. Here is the Christ of the cross, and the cross is as much a scandal and stumbling block to the domineering machinations of modern culture as it was to the culture of Jesus' own time.

Finally, there is the view of Jesus as a non-exclusivistic, paradigmatic exemplification of a set of values which has the potential of transforming human existence. This transformation would be "salvation." But "salvation" can no longer be seen as a "special connectedness" to Jesus or, more precisely, a "special connectedness" to God which can be appropriated through Jesus. Now, for Kaufman, "salvation" consists essentially in "a particular mode and quality of life,"[45] an intrinsic valuation of self, world, and others.

> Salvation should no longer be conceived as a singular process or activity, a unilateral action from on high coming down to earth and working primarily in and through the church. Rather, it comprises all the activities and processes within human affairs which are helping to overcome the violence and disruptions and alienations, the various forms of oppression and exploitation, and all other historical and institutional momentums today which promote personal and social deterioration and disintegration. In short, wherever a spirit of creativity and liberation and healing, of reconciliation and reconstruction, [of intrinsic valuation] is at work in the world, there is to be seen saving activity.[46]

In conclusion, I see the work of Robert S. Hartman to be a comprehensible and reasonable "departure point" for productive, orderly thinking about human existence. In comparison to the continuum of departure points posited in the history of Western thought, his has a great deal of credibility in the sense that it draws the focus of human consideration into life rather than away from it into some vague, metaphysical realm. There must be "departure points," like serves in a tennis match, which put the "ball" of human thinking into play. In this way, the dialogues which lead to more precise articulation--and thus that which is accepted as meaningful--can occur.

Tom Chamberlain, the editor of the outdoor section of <u>The Chattanooga Times</u>, describes how a person should embark upon an outing in the woods, especially that person who has been to the woods time and again but has not found or seen anything of interest:

> Inside, you should wait a moment to let your eyes adjust to the lesser light. It is not hard to see in the forest, but it is important to change your perspective. Life exists up close [recall the idea of "self-

evidence"]. If you are wondering with a purpose, then you may miss a lot while looking for specifics. The best time in the woods are aimless, when surprises can be paused for. Seldom will the forest fail to put on a show for those who learn to watch, and especially for those who learn to listen. Even when you walk, you must move in a series of pauses. At each hesitation, look around and soak up the distinctive landmarks of that particular spot. Look for signs of the things that have occurred in this place.

Remember that the normal inhabitants of this area move in stops and starts. Follow their example. A whitetail can walk right past you in the woods and never be noticed. Move slowly and quietly. There is a lot to see in the forest. You will get more out of it than you put in, a lot more.[47]

Robert S. Hartman created a "pause," an adjustment in the way in which life is perceived. His value structure becomes a new lens, a pragmatically workable lens, a better lens. Within the context of this lens, old ways of theological looking and talking are transformed. He has been "scientific" in his approach, but that approach has not issued in demonstrable proofs. It was never intended to. His new way of talking about God and giving articulation to the religious has great plausibility for modern human beings.

"Religion," according to Stanley Romaine Hopper as he wrote about the German poets Holderlin and Rilke in Carl Michalson's Christianity and the Existentialists, "that is [legitimate and authentic] is a 'direction of the heart'; we are not supposed to be looking at God. Our task is to see things as He sees them; to be looking in the same direction that He is looking."[48] Hartman's value structure provides the parameters for this "new direction of looking."

In the end this "direction of the heart" may not coincide very much with the traditions of Western, systematic theology in its search for proofs. Rather, there may be a meeting with that which is called "liberation theology" that begins--in the Judeo- Christian tradition at least--with the burning bush, finds a high moment in the moral exhortations of the prophets, is epitomized in Jesus, and comes to more modern expression in a line that runs from Francis of Assisi, to Luther, to Rauschenbusch, to Bonhoeffer, to Martin Luther King, Jr., or even to Mother Teresa. Along this route there are instances, such as Gandhi, which rise from other traditions but still embrace the same basic principle.)

Yet, someone might reply: "But Mother Teresa is not a theologian!" And that is precisely the point! At the corner mission in Hell's Kitchen where derelicts find a hot meal (Rauschenbusch), before the procurators of the Third Reich (Bonhoeffer), along the courageous march from Selma to Birmingham (King), and reaching out to the leprous untouchables of Calcutta's crowded streets (Mother Teresa), theology in the common sense of the word is deconstructed. There is an opening--a clearing in the forest (Heidegger) where pauses can occur--and in that opening a theophany occurs in which naming words and theological explications are suddenly far beside the point. There is a stillness in which people, unhampered by the clanging brass of naming words, can hear each other. Theology is replaced by axiology, and axiology is consumed in actions of care; in all this, that which is intrinsic is given the opportunity of being raised to a higher plateau of realization.

NOTES

1. Langdon Gilkey, Naming the Whirlwind: The Renewal of God-Language (Indianapolis, 1969), p. 297. Gilkey believes that there are four areas of ordinary experience in which there is a need to articulate "meaningful ultimacy": 1) when the foundations of being appear as given; 2) when man is threatened by "Fate" and feels absolute helplessness; 3) in the midst of his ambiguity as it appears in the midst of his freedom; and, 4) in his confidence and hope despite his outer and inner threats to security.

2. Ibid., p. 440.

3. Gabriel Vahanian, Wait Without Idols (New York, 1964).

4. Michael Novak, Belief and Unbelief (New York, 1963).

5. Robert S. Hartman, "Prolegomena to a Meta-Anselmian Axiomatic," (The Review of Metaphysics, XIV Fall, 1961), p. 647. Note clearly at this point that Hartman is trying to do more than simply explicate Anselm. He is using Anselm as a base which he is moving beyond in his own thinking. Therefore, to say that Hartman misses some of Anselm's main points is not important. He is taking some of Anselm's main points and building his new structure on them.

6. Ibid., pp. 658-659.

7. John Hospers, Meaning and Truth in the Arts (Chapel Hill, 1949), p. 79.

8. Robert S. Hartman, Freedom to Live: The Bob Hartman Story, (a manuscript prepared for the Nationwide Insurance Corporation Columbus, 1963), p. 10.

9. Ibid., p. 9.

10. Ibid., p. 25.

11. Ibid.

12. Ibid.

13. Ibid., p. 28.

14. Ibid., p. 30.

15. Ibid., p. 139.

16. Ibid., pp. 59-60.

17. Ibid., p. 34.

18. Robert S. Hartman, The Structure of Value (Carbondale, 1967), p. 3.

19. Hartman, The Bob Hartman Story, p. 81.

20. Hartman, The Structure of Value, p. 116. Also see Hartman, "The Value Structure of Creativity," (The Journal of Value Inquiry, VI Winter, 1972), p. 274. Also see The Bob Hartman Story, p. 97 where Hartman says: "God is the supreme value, the value of values. Nothing more valuable is thinkable."

21. Hartman, The Bob Hartman Story, p. 48.

22. Hartman, "The Unique Role of the Church in the World Today," (Vital Speeches of the Day, December, 1950), p. 117.

23. Ibid.

24. Hartman, The Bob Hartman Story, p. 169.

25. Ibid., p. 171.

26. Thomas J. J. Altizer and William Hamilton, Radical Theology and the Death of God (New York, 1966), p. 92.

27. Dietrich Bonhoeffer, Letters and Papers from Prison (New York, 1955), p. 93.

28. Hartman, "Anselm," pp. 638-639.

29. Hartman, "Creativity," p. 273.

30. Ibid., p. 274. There is a symbolization in transfinite mathematics, given by Cantor, which might provide the mathematical symbolization for God which $\aleph_0$ only approximates. The symbol is ת (**tav**, the last letter of the Hebrew alphabet of which **aleph** is the first), which stands for the totality of all alephs i.e., all possible levels of infinity.)

31. Hartman, "Anselm," pp. 658-659.

32. Ibid., p. 675.

33. Gordon Kaufman, God--The Problem (Cambridge, 1979), p. 8.

34. Ibid., 101.

35. Ibid., p. 104.

36. Ibid., p. 106.

37. Gordon Kaufman, Theology for a Nuclear Age (Cambridge, 1983), p. 60.

38. Ibid., p. 20.

39. Ibid., p. 37.

40. Ibid., p. 60.

41. Ibid., 48.

42. Ibid.

43. Ibid., p. 52.

44. Ibid., p. 53.

45. Ibid., p. 58.

46. Ibid., p. 57.

47. Stanley Romaine Hopper, in Carl Michalson Christianity and the Existentialists (New York, 1963).

A BIBLIOGRAPHY OF THE WRITINGS OF ROBERT S. HARTMAN

Dissertation

"Can Field Teld Theory be Applied to Ethics?" Ph.D. Dissertation, Northwestern University, 1946.

Books and Manuals

Author

Profit Sharing Manual. Columbus, Ohio: Council of Profit Sharing Industries, 1948.

Axiologia Formal: La Ciencia de la Valoración. Mexico City: Universidad Nacional Autónoma de México, 1957.

Die Partnerschaft von Kapital und Arbeit: Theorie und Parxis eines neuen Wirtschaftssystems. Opladen-Cologne: Westdeutscher Verlag, 1958.

La Estructura del Valor: Fundamentos de la Axiologia cientifica. Mexico City-Buenos Aires: Fondo de Cultura Económica, 1959.

La Participacion de Utilidades en Mexico. Mexico City: Asesores de Pensiones, 1963.

La Ciencia del Valor. Mexico City: Universidad Nacional Autónoma de México, 1965.

El Conocimiento del Bien: Crítica de la Razón Axiológica. Mexico City-Buenos Aires: Fondo de Cultura Económica, 1965.

El Inventario de Valores Hartman. Mexico City: El Manual Moderno, 1967.

The Structure of Value: Foundations of Scientific Axiology. Carbondale: Southern Illinois University Press, 1967, 1969.

The Hartman Value Inventory. Boston: Miller Associates, 1967; Austin: Axiometrics Incorporated, 1969. Translations in Spanish, German, Swedish, Japanese, and Hebrew.

The Hartman Value Profile. Alcoa, Tenn.: Axiometric Testing Service, 1970.

Manual de Interpretación del Inventario de Valores Hartman. Mexico City: Servicios Psicoaxiológos, 1970.

Research Manual of the Hartman Value Profile. Alcoa, Tenn.: Axiometric Testing Service, 1970.

La Situación Moral: Fundamentos de la Teleología Científica. Mexico City-Buenos Aires: Fondo de Cultura Económica, 1972.

La Estructura del Valor Intrínseco: Introducción Axiológica a la Etica y la Estética. Mexico City-Buenos Aires: Fondo de Cultura Económica, 1972.

Contributor

"Can Field Theory be Applied to Ethics?" Summaries of Doctoral Dissertations. Evanston: Northwestern University Press, 1946, pp. 168-72.

Introduction to Hitler in Our Selves, by Max Picard. Chicago: Henry Regnery, 1947, pp. 13-23.

"Cassirer's Philosophy of Symbolic Forms," The Philosophy of Ernst Cassirer, Library of Living Philosophers, pp. 299-333. Evanston: Northwestern University Press, 1949. German translation, pp. 187-228.

Introduction to Profit Sharing: Democratic Capitalism in American Industry by Kenneth M. Thompson. New York: Harper and Brothers, 1949.

"The Analytic and the Synthetic as Categories of Inquiry," edited by Albert Aevy, Perspectives in Philosophy, pp. 55-78. Columbus: Ohio State University Press, 1953.

"Value Propositions," The Language of Value, edited by Ray Lepley, pp. 197-231, 337-42, 352-74. New York: Columbia University Press, 1957.

"The Science of Value," New Knowledge in Human Values, edited by A. Maslow, pp. 13-37, 233-35. New York: Harper and Brothers, 1958.

"General Theory of Value," Philosophie: Chronique des années 1949-1955, edited by Raymond Klibansky, II, 1-39. Florence: Nuova Italia, 1958.

"The Revolution Against War," Critique of War, edited by Robert Ginsberg, pp. 310-43. Chicago: Henry Regnery, 1970.

"Fundamental Terms of Ethics," Encyclopaedia of Relevant Knowledge (New York).

"Fundamental Terms of Value Theory," Encyclopaedia of Relevant Knowledge (New York).

"Philosophy in the Americas," preface to Paul Kurtz, American Philosophy in the Twentieth Century, Spanish edition. Buenos Aires, Mexico: Fondode Cultura Economica, 1972.

"The Structure of Tertiary Qualities," Man and Value: Essays in Honor of William H. Werkmeister, edited by E. F. Kalin, pp. 126-153. Tallahassee: University Presses of Florida, 1981.

Translator

Strindberg, August. Der Sohn der Magd. Zurich: Büchergilde Gutenberg, 1936. (Swedish into German.)

Hegel, G. W. F. Reason in History: A General Introduction to the Philosophy of History. New York: Liberal Arts Press, 1953. (German into English.)

Coing, Helmut. El Sentido del Derecho. Mexico City: Universidad Nacional Autónoma de México, 1959. (German into Spanish, with José Luis González.)

Aster, Ernst von. La Filosofía del Presente. Mexico City: Universidad Nacional Autónoma de México. 1964. (German into Spanish, with Elsa Frost.)

Stebbing, L. Susan. Introducción Moderna a la Lógica. Mexico City: Universidad Nacional Autónoma de México, 1965. (English into Spanish, with José Luis González.)

Kant, Immanuel. Logic. Indianapolis: Bobbs-Merrill, Liberal Arts Press, 1972. (German into English, with Wolfgang Schwarz.)

Pamphlets

Die amerikanische Produktivität und der Faktor 'Mensch'. Zurich, Switzerland: H. S. Stokar, No. 709, 1951.

Ertragsbeteiligung in U.S.A. Cologne: Deutsches Industrieinstitut, No. 24, Dec. 3, 1951.

Theoretische Grundlagen der Gewinnbeteiligung. Wirtschaftspolitische Gesellschaft von 1947, Nov. 7, 1952.

The Measurement of Value. Crotonville-Ossining, New York: The General Electric Company, Advanced Management Course, Apr. 29, 1959.

Articles

"Prime Number and Cosmical Number," Philosophy of Science, IX, 2 (Apr., 1942), 190-96.

"Profit Sharing: A Moral Reformation," Vital Speeches of the Day, Aug. 15, 1947.

"The Council of Profit Sharing Industries," America, Oct. 11, 1947, pp. 41-43.

"Profit Sharing: Philosophy, Economics, and Technique," Surplus Record, Jan., Mar., 1948, pp. 32-58.

"Profit Sharing: Its Place in the Free Enterprise System," Stores, Apr., 1948.

"The Logic of Profit Sharing," Social Progress (Board of Christian Education, Presbyterian Church, Philadelphia), May, 1948.

"The Moral Situation: A Field Theory of Ethics," Journal of Philosophy, XLV, No. 11 (May 20, 1948), pp. 413-20.

"Is Ethics as a Science Possible?" Tenth International congress of Philosophy (Amsterdam), Aug. 11-18, 1948, I, 485-87.

"Profit Sharing: Democracy's Answer," Journal of Retail Traders' Association of New South Wales (Sydney, N. S. W.), Feb., 1949.

"The Council of Profit Sharing Industries," Industrial and Labor Relations Review (Cornell University), Mar., 1949.

"Employee Capitalists," Trusts and Estates, Mar., 1949.

"The Epistemology of the A Priori," Philosophy and Phenomenological Research, IX, No. 4 (June, 1949), 731-36.

"Vinstdelningens Plats i den Fria Företagsamheten," Arbetarliberalen (Stockholm), Oct., 1949.

"The Task of Value Research," First Report of the Committee for Coperative Research in Values (Wayne State University), 1950.

"Value Analysis of Justice Frankfurter's Gobitis Decision," Second Report of the Committee for Cooperative Research in Values (Wayne State University), 1950.

"The Teaching of Ethics," The Teaching of Philosophy: The Proceedings and Addresses of the Conference on the Teachings of Philosophy (Cleveland), 1950.

"Is a Science of Ethics Possible?" Philosophy of Science, XVII, No. 3 (July, 1950), pp. 238-46.

"Den Goda Viljans Metod," Arbetarliberalen (Stockholm), Oct. 1950.

"Profit Sharing," Research and Technical Report 7 (Industrial Relations Center, University of Minnesota), Nov., 1950.

"The Unique Role of the Church in the World to Come," Vital Speeches of the Day, Dec., 1950, pp. 113-18.

"Value Analysis of Legal Decision," Ohio State Law Journal, XII (1951), 23-35.

"The Secretary of Peace," The Christian Community, Mar., 1951, pp. 6-10.

"A Logical Definition of Value," Journal of Philosophy, XLVIII, No. 13 (June 21, 1951), pp. 413-20.

"Anthropology and Scientific Method," American Anthropologist, LIII, No. 4 (Oct-Dec., 1951), pp. 591-93.

"Gewinnbeteiligung in Amerika," Wirtschaft und Sozialpolitik, Oct. 15, 1951.

"Gewinnbeteiligung in der amerikanischen Wirtschaft," Recht und Arbeit, Nov., 1951, pp. 401-404.

"Grundlagen und Praxis der Ertragsbeteiligung in U. S. A., "Arbeitsgemeinschaft zur Förderung der Partnerschaft in der Wirtschaft, Nov., 1951.

"Vinstandelssystemets Principer och Pratiska Uppbygnad," Svensk Handel, Nov. 31, 1951, pp. 505-508.

"Gewinnbeteiligung der Arbeiter," Das ganze Deutschland, Dec. 15, 1951.

"Research in the Logic of Value," Graduate School Record (Ohio State University), V, No. 4 (1952), 6-8.

"Vinstdelning: Samarbete mellan Arbetstagare och Företagsledning i fria Företag," Arbetarliberalen, Mar., 1952.

"Die menschliche Person als Ausgangspunkt sozialer Erfindungen," Sozialer Fortschritt, Aug., 1952, pp. 181-84.

"Philosophische Grundlagen industrieller Beziehungen," Wirtschafts-politische Blätter, Nov. 1, 1952.

"Theoretische Grundlagen der Gewinnbeteiligung," Mensch und Arbeit, Nov. 15, 1952.

"The Language of Science and the Language of Value," Eleventh International Congress of Philosophy, 1953.

"Group Membership and Class Membership," Philosophy and Phenomenological Research, XIII, No. 3 (Mar., 1953), pp. 353-70.

"The Challenge of Peace," Ohio State University Monthly, July, 1953; also Vital Speeches of the Day, July 15, 1953.

"The Analytic, the Synthetic and the Good: Kant and the Pradoxes of G.E. Moore," Kant-Studien, XLV, No. 4 (1953-54), pp. 67-82; XLVI, No. 1 (1954-55), pp. 3-18.

"La creación de una ética científica," Diánoia: Anuario de Filosofía, II (Universidad Nacional Autónoma de México, 1955), 205-35.

"Niveles del lenguaje valorativo," Diánoia: Anuario de Filosofía, II (Universidad Nacional Autónoma de México, 1956), 254-69.

"Value, Fact and Science," Philosophy of Science, XXV, No. 2 (Apr., 1958), pp. 97-108.

"Value Theory as a Formal System," Kant Studien, 50, No. 3 (1958-59), 287-315.

"El conocimiento del valor: La teoría de los valores a mediados del siglo XX," Diánoia: Anuario de Filosofía, IV (Universidad Nacional Autónoma de México, 1958), pp. 105-41.

"Aspectos éticos de los Satélites," Cuadernos Americanos, No. 100 (1958), pp. 183-200.

"Crítica Axiológica de la ética de Kant," Revista Mexicana de Filosofía, No. 1 (1958), pp. 75-84.

"La diferencia lógica entre la filosofía y la ciencia," Diánoia: Anuario de Filosofía, V (Universidad Nacional Autónoma de México, 1959), pp. 72-95.

"Cuatro pruebas axiológicas del valor infinito del hombre," Examen, No. 9 (Mexico City, Nov.-Dec., 1959), pp. 45-57.

"Axiología y semántica: un ensayo sobre la medición del valor," Diánoia: Anuario de Filosofía, VI (Universidad Nacional Autónoma de México, 1960), 44-77.

"El Humanismo de Samuel Ramos," Revista de Filosofía de la Universidad de la Plata, No. 9 (1960), pp. 71-78.

"Investigación sobre la lógica del valor," Gaceta del Fondo de Cultura Economica, 1960.

"Sputnik's Moral Challenge," Texas Quarterly, III, No. 3 (Autumn, 1960), pp. 9-23.

"The Logic of Description and Valuation," The Review of Metaphysics, XIV, No. 2 (1961), 191-230.

"Valor y Razón," Diánoia: Anuario de Filosofía, VII (Universidad Nacional Autónoma de México, 1961), 79-99.

"Lo analítico y lo sintético como categorías metodológicas," Humanitas: Anuario del Centro de Estudios Humanísticos (Universidad de Nuevo León, Moterrey, Mexico, 1961), pp. 99-128.

"The Logic of Value," The Review of Metaphysics, XIV, No. 3 (1961), pp. 389-432.

"Prolegomena to a Meta-Anselmian Axiomatic," The Review of Metaphysics, XIV, No. 4 (1961), pp. 637-75.

"El conocimiento del Bien en Platón," Diánoia: Anuario de Filosofía, VIII (Universidad Nacional Autónoma de México, 1962), pp. 42-62.

"Capitalismo y Comunismo," Verdad, 1962.

"The Self in Kierkegaard," Jounral of Existential Psychiatry, No. 8 (Spring, 1962), pp. 409-36.

"The Good as a Non-natural Quality and the Good as a Transcendental," The Review of Metaphysics, XVI, No. 1 (Sept., 1962), pp. 149-55.

"Axiology as a Science," Philosophy of Science, XXIX, No. 4 (Oct., 1962), pp. 412-33.

"Does a Corporation Need Spiritual Objectives?" Nationwide World, Oct., 1962.

"La Simbolización del Valor," Diánoia: Anuario de Filosofía, IX (Universidad Nacional Autónoma de México, 1963), 71-101.

"Introduction to Symposium 'Valor in genere y los valores espicificos'," Thirteenth International Congress of Philosophy (Mexico City, 1963), pp. 7-29.

"Value in General and the Specific Values," Symposium, Thirteenth International Congress of Philosophy (Mexico City, 1963), pp. 99-133.

"The Logical Difference Between Philosophy and Science," Philosophy and Phenomenological Research, XXIII, No. 3 (1963), pp. 353-79.

"Razón y razones del Valor: La Axiología de la Escuela de Oxford," Diánoia: Anuario de Filosofía, X (Universidad Nacional Autónoma de México, 1964), 63-92.

"La ilustración y su enfoque científico," Primer Coloquio Mexicano de Historia de la Ciencia, Sociedad Mexicana de Historia de la Ciencia y de la Technología (Mexico City, 1964), pp. 7-24.

"La nación: reliquia feudal," Cuadernos Americanos, No. 3 (1964), pp.33-61.

"Four Axiological Proofs of the Infinite Value of Man," Kant-Studien, LV, No. 4 (1964), pp. 428-38. Reprinted in Marvin C. Katz, Sciences of Man and Social Ethics. Boston: Branden Press, 1969, pp. 29-45.

"The Definition of Good: Moore's Axiomatic of the Science of Good," Proceedings, Aristotelian Society (1964-65), pp. 235-56.

"Nuestra Situación existencial: Pereceremos todos juntos?" Cuadernos Americanos, No. 3 (1965), pp. 63-87.

"La ontogenia del símbolo: Prolegómenos a una filosofía de formas sintomáticas," Diánoia: Anuario de Filosofía, XI (Universidad Nacional Autónoma de México, 1965), pp. 60-78.

"La esencia de Rusia," Cuadernos Americanos, No. 5 (1965), pp. 7-40.

"La axiomática del valor," Diánoia: Anuario de Filosofía, XII (Universidad Nacional Autónoma de México, 1966) pp. 104-31.

"The University and the World," Vital Speeches of the Day, May 1, 1966, pp. 442-47.

"Die Wissenschaft vom Entscheiden," Wissenschaft und Weltbild (Vienna), June, 1966, pp. 81-99.

"Formal Axiology and the Measurement of Value," The Journal of Value Inquiry, I, No. 1 (Spring, 1967), pp. 38-46.

"Sentimento y Valor," Diánoia: Anuario de Filosofía, XIII (Universidad Nacional Autónoma de México, 1967) pp. 248-91.

"La producción del valor: un marco para la Teleologia Cientifica," Diánoia: Anuario de Filosofía, XIV (Universidad Nacional Autónoma de México, 1968) pp. 182-202.

"Singular and Particular," Critica (Jan., 1968), pp. 15-51.

"La naturaleza de la valoración," Humanitas (Universidad de Nuevo León, Monterrey, Mexico, 1968), pp. 45-69.

"Belief and Value," Fourteenth International Congress of Philosophy, Vienna, 1968.

"The Measurement of Value: Set Theory as Value Theory," Fourteenth International Congress of Philosophy, Vienna, 1968.

"Una ciencia moral para la edad atómica," Cuadernos Americanos, No. 5 (1968), pp. 81-103.

"El método científico de análisis y sintésis," Diánoia: Anuario de Filosofía, XV (Universidad Nacional Autónoma de México, 1969), pp. 1-24; XVI (1970), pp. 42-65.

"Axiological Testing and Psychological Testing," Ninth Annual Meeting, Association for Humanistic Psychology, 1971.

"The Hartman (Axiological) Profile Test," Annual Convention, American Society of Psychoanalytic Physicians, 1971.

"El origen de la Axiometría en la República de Platón," Diánoia: Anuario de Filosofía, XVII (Universidad Nacional Autónoma de México, 1971).

"The Value Structure of Creativity," The Journal of Value Inquiry, VI, (Winter 1972), pp. 243-279.

"La naturaleza del valor: Estructura de las cualidades terciarias," Episteme (Universidad Central de Venezuela, Caracas), 1972.

"La situacion como compo etico," Dianoia: Anuario de Filosofía, XVIII, 1972, pp. 103-128.

"Transpersonal Logic in the Gospel," Journal of Transpersonal Psychology, 1972.

"Kant's Science of Metaphysics and the Scientific Method," Kant-Studien, 1972.

"The Value Structure of Justice." In Festschrift for Paul A. Schilpp. LaSalle, Ill.: Open Court Publishing Co., 1972.

"Autoretrato," Autorretratos de Pensadores y Filósofos Latino-Americanos, Sao Paulo, Brazil.

"Axiology as a Science," Journal of Human Relations, XXI, No. 1 (Fall, 1973), pp. 31-53.

"The Axiometric Structure of Intrinsic Value," The Journal of Value Inquiry, VIII, No. 2 (Summer, 1974), pp. 81-101.

A SELECTED BIBLIOGRAPHY OF SECONDARY DISCUSSIONS

Books

Byrum, Stephen, The Value Structure of Theology. Washington, D. C., University Press of America, 1978.

Carter, Robert E., Dimensions of Moral Education. Toronto, University of Toronto Press, 1984, pp. 174-198.

Davis, John W., "A Defense of 'Unique' as an Aesthetic and Value Predicate," in John W. Davis, ed., Value and Valuation: Axiological Studies in Honor of Robert S. Hartman. Knoxville, The University of Tennessee Press, 1972.

_____, "History of the American Society for Value Inquiry, Part I," in Inquiries into Values. Lewiston/Queenston, The Edwin Mellen Press, 1988.

_____, "Human Worth," in E. F. Kaelin, ed., Man and Value: Essays in Honor of William H. Werkmeister, Tallahassee, Florida State University Press, 1981, pp. 154-167.

_____, "Scientific Ethics," in William S. Minor and J. A. Broyer, eds., Creative Interchange. Carbondale, IL, Southern Illinois University Press, 1982, pp. 157-182.

_____, ed., Value and Valuation: Axiological Studies in Honor of Robert S. Hartman. Knoxville, The University of Tennessee Press, 1972.

Ellis, Albert and Harper, Robert A., A New Guide to Rational Living. North Hollywood, CA., Wilshire Book Company, 1975, pp. 98, 204.

Forrest, Frank G., Valuemetrics: the Science of Personal and Professional Ethics. 2828 N. Atlantic Ave., Daytona Beach, FL 32018, Frank G. Forrest.

Fujimoto, Takahashi, Science and Formal Axiology: The Philosophy of Robert S. Hartman. Tokyo: Tetsugaku-Zassi, 1964.

Katz, Marvin, Sciences of Man and Social Ethics. Boston, Branden Press, 1969, Chs. 1 and 4.

Rohatyn, Dennis, The Reluctant Naturalist: A Study of G. E. Moore's Principia Ethica. Washington, University Press of America, 1987.

Simmons, Dale D., Personal Valuing: An Introduction. Chicago, Nelson Hall, 1983, pp. 16-18, 21, 75-79, 91.

Werkmeister, W. H., Historical Spectrum of Value Theories. Lincoln, Nebraska, Johnsen Publishing Co., 1973, Vol. II, Ch. XIV.

Journal Articles in Philosophy

Briones, J. J. Montoya, "Ensayo para un neuvo enfoque en la problematica de la Antropologia," Tlatonai, Octubre, 1961.

_____, Ubicacion de la Etnografia en el cuadro de la investigacion antropologica," Anales, Tomo XVI, 1964.

_____, " Que son los valores?" Comunidad, Vol. 11, No. 6, 1967.

Byrum, Charles Stephen, "A Common Sense Approach to Value Inquiry," The Journal of Value Inquiry, Vol. 18, 1984, pp. 307-318.

_____, "Aristotle's Concept of Individuality," The Journal of Value Inquiry, Vol. 14, Summer 1980, pp. 93-104.

_____, "The Hartman Value Structure: The Possibilities of a Theologic," The Journal of Value Inquiry, Vol. 10, Spring 1976, pp. 18-29.

Carter, Robert E., "Intrinsic Value and the Intrinsic Valuer," Philosophy and Phenomenological Research, Vol. XXXIV, June 1974, pp. 504-514.

Blumenfeld, W., "Die Axiologie R. S. Hartman's," Kant-Studien, Vol. 59, 1968, pp. 454-467.

Brumbaugh, Robert S., "Formal Value Theory: Transfinite Ordinal Numbers and Relatively Trivial Practical Choices," Journal of Human Relations, Vol. 21, 1973.

_____, "Robert Hartman's Formal Axiology: An Extension," The Journal of Value Inquiry, Vol. 11, Winter 1977, pp. 259-263.

Carter, Robert Edgar, "Comparative Value Theory: An Inquiry into the Notion of 'Intrinsic Value' in Contemporary Western and Japanese Philosophy," The Journal of Value Inquiry, Vol. 13, Spring 1979, pp. 33-56.

Curley, William H., "The Axiologically Ideal Man," Kinesis, Vol. 4, 1972, pp. 88-95.

Dacal Alonso, Jose Antonio, "La axiologia cientifica de Robert S. Hartman," Logos, 1978, pp. 37-73.

Davis, John W., "Is Good Only Good?" The Southern Journal of Philosophy, Vol. 11, Spring 1964, pp. 3-7.

_____, "Is Philosophy a Sickness or a Therapy?" Antioch Review, Vol. XXIII, Spring 1963, pp. 5-23. (Translated into Polish as "Filozofia-Choroba Czy Lekarstwo?" Stefan Jasinski, translator, Vol. 11M, Lato 1963, pp. 65-86.)

_____, "Is There a Logic For Ethics," The Southern Journal of Philosophy, Vol. IV, Spring 1966, pp. 1-8.

_____, "Measuring Athletic Goodness: Formal Axiology Applied to Football," Journal of the Philosophy of Sport, Vol. XVII, 1990.

_____, "Must Teachers Love Their Students? The Value Structure of the Teacher-Student Relationship," Teaching-Learning Issues, Winter 1978, Learning Research Center, The University of Tennessee, 16 pp.

_____, "Robert S. Hartman, 1910-1973," Memorial Minutes, Proceedings and Addresses of the American Philosophical Association, Vol. XLVII, 1973-74, pp. 218-219.

———, "What is Axiology?" The American Axiologist, Issue 1, April/May/June, 1985, pp. 1-2.

Edwards, Rem B., "Intrinsic and Extrinsic Value and Valuation," The Journal of Value Inquiry, Vol. 13, 1979, pp. 133-143.

———, "The Value of Man in the Hartman Value System," The Journal of Value Inquiry, Vol. 7, Summer 1973, pp. 141-147.

Gunter, P. Y. A., "Hartman: Three Criticisms," The Journal of Value Inquiry, Vol. 7, Summer 1963, pp. 136-140.

Hierro De Matte, Graciela, "Robert S. Hartman, 1910-1973," Dianoia, Vol. 20, 1974, pp. 191-201.

Maliandi, Ricardo, "La razon aciologica," Cuadernos de Filosofia, Vol. 8, 1968, pp. 343-353.

Mueller, Robert W., "The Axiology of Robert S. Hartman: A Critical Study," The Journal of Value Inquiry, Vol. III, Spring 1969, pp. 19-29.

Plochman, George Kimball, "Robert S. Hartman on the Structure of Creativity: A Critique," The Journal of Value Inquiry, Vol. 7, Summer 1973, pp. 129-135.

Stankovich, Radivoj, "Observationes criticas a la axiologia formal de R. S. Hartman," Logos, Vol. 3, Sept.-Dec. 1975, pp. 115-135.

Welty, Gordon, "Transfinite Cardinality and Hartman's Axiology," The Journal of Value Inquiry, Vol. IV, Winter 1970, pp. 293-301.

Journal Articles in Psychology

Austin, John J., "School Psychology and Racism: A Challenge for America," Broadened Perspectives in School Psychology, NASP, Suite 401, 1140 Connecticut Avenue, N. W., Washington, D. C.

———, "School Psychology as a Value Science," The School Psychology Digest, Vol. 1, No. 1, National Association of School Psychologists, Suite 401, 1130 Connecticut Ave., N. W., Washington, D. C.

Davis, John W., (with Leon R. Pomeroy, senior editor), "A New Tool for Health Psychology and Behavioral Medicine," VA Practitioner, Vol. II, July 1985, pp. 50-61.

_____, (with Leon R. Pomeroy, senior editor), "Introduction to Behavioral Axiology: Part 1, A Concurrent Validity Study of Hartman's Valuemetrics and Value Science Assumptions as a Revolutionary New Basis for Modern Behavioral Science Application," Second International Conference on the Cattell 16 PF Test, Proceedings of the Institute for Personality and Ability Testing, Inc., Champaign, IL, 1982, pp. 117-122.

Pomeory, Leon R., "Beyond Terrorism and War: An Introduction to Behavioral Axiology," Journal of the Organization for the Study of Group Tensions, 1985.

_____, et. al., "Introduction to Behavioral Axiology: Part II: Validation of Hartman's Valuemetrics and Value Science Assumptions as a New Orientation in Psychology," published as an abstract in the 22nd International Congress of Applied Psychology, July 22-27, 1990, Kyoto, Japan.

Summer, Dale, "Purpose-in-Life and the Three Aspects of Valuing," Journal of Clinical Psychology, October 1980, pp. 921-922.

Trigos, Mario Cardenas, "Revista de Psicoanalisis," Psiquiatria y Psicologia, No. 6, Mayo Agosto, 1967.

_____, "El analisis axiologico de los suenos," Revista de Psicoanalisis, Psiquiatria y Psicologia, No. 6, Mayo Agosto, 1967.

Doctoral Dissertations

Baez, Victor, The Valuing Process and Social Work Practice: A Correlational Study. Doctoral dissertation, The University of Denver, 1986.

Byrum, Charles Stephen, Intrinsic Value and Play. Doctoral Dissertation in Philosophy, Knoxville, The University of Tennessee, 1976.

Chance, Cynthia A., A Hartmanian Aesthetic: The Value Structure of Poetry. Doctoral Dissertation in Philosophy, Knoxville, The University of Tennessee, 1978.

Davis, John W., Value and Individuality: An Inquiry into the Worth of the Human Person. Doctoral Dissertation in Philosophy, Emory University, 1959.

Elliot, Billie Cannon, Item Homogeneity and Factoral Invariance for Normative and Ipsative Response to the Hartman Value Inventory. Doctoral Dissertation in Educational Administration and Supervision, Knoxville, The University of Tennessee, 1971.

Hartman, Robert S., Can Field Theory be Applied to Ethics? Doctoral dissertation in Philosophy, Northwestern University, 1946.

Katz, Marvin C., The Philosophy of Robert S. Hartman. Doctoral dissertation in Philosophy, Southern Illinois University, 1966.

Lohman, J. S., The Professor's Influence on the Student's Capacity to Value. Doctoral Dissertation, Boston, Boston University, 1968.

Mefford, David L., Phenomenology of Man as a Valuing Subject. Doctoral Dissertation in Philosophy, Knoxville, The University of Tennessee, 1989.

Moore, Mark A., Can A Theory of Ethical Intuitionism be Defended? Doctoral Dissertation in Philosophy, Knoxville, The University of Tennessee, 1973.

Wilson, Charles H., An Application of R. S. Hartman's Axiology to the Value System of Augustine. Doctoral Dissertation in Philosophy, Knoxville, The University of Tennessee, 1978.

Masters Theses

Acquaviva, Gary J., Reciprocity Between Individuals. Masters Thesis in Philosophy, Knoxville, The University of Tennessee, 1973.

Elliot, Billie Cannon, Factor and Cluster Analysis of The Hartman Value Inventory: A Study of Item Homogeneity and Factorial Invariance for Normative and Ipsative Scales. Masters Thesis in Educational Administration and Supervision, Knoxville, The University of Tennessee, 1969.

Byrum, Charles Stephen, The Development of a Theologic in the Hartman Value Structure. Masters Thesis in Philosophy, Knoxville, The University of Tennessee, 1974.

Ginn, Loyd A., <u>Creative Experience as Value: A Study of Robert S. Hartman's Theory of Creativity</u>, Masters Thesis in Philosophy, Knoxville, The University of Tennessee, 1978.

Kaltreider, Kurt, <u>An Axiological Account of Plato's Theory of Forms</u>. Masters Thesis in Philosophy, Knoxville, The University of Tennessee, 1969.

Pruitt, Raymond M., <u>A Critique of Robert S. Hartman's 'Four Axiological Proofs of the Infinite Value of Man</u>.' Masters Thesis in Philosophy, Knoxville, The University of Tennessee, 1971.

Wilson, Charles H., <u>A Comparison of Martin Buber's and Robert Hartman's Categorizations of Value</u>. Masters Thesis in Philosophy, Knoxville, The University of Tennessee, 1973.

CONTRIBUTORS

JOHN J. AUSTIN received his B.S. Degree from Eastern Michigan University in special education, elementary education and psychology. He was awarded his M.S. degree by the University of Michigan in educational psychology. He was the founder and first President of the Michigan Association of Educator-Psychologists, which became the Michigan Association of School Psychologists and is an honorary life member of both the national and state organizations. He is a life member of the Michigan Education Association. He is also a member of the educational and school psychology divisions of the American Psychological Association.

Austin has been an educator and psychologists for the past thirty four years, serving primarily as a state-approved school psychologist and research director with the City Public Schools of Muskegon, Michigan. He is the author of many publications and research reports. As a professional person and a citizen who has been a lifelong activist, he has served as a Board of Education member with the Muskegon Area Intermediate School District. Currently in independent practice and consultation, he is associated with Research Concepts and the Alfred Benet Society in Muskegon and with the R. S. Hartman Institute of Formal and Applied Axiology which is centered at The University of Tennessee in Knoxville. He is the HVP test editor. In 1990 he was elected Chairman of the Board of Directors of the R. S. Hartman Institute.

RICHARD BISHOP, Ph.D., is Associate Dean of the College of Engineering and Professor of Biomedical Engineering at the University of New Orleans, where he has served on the faculty since 1977. His interest in axiology began while a Master's student at Southern Methodist University. In 1962 he began his doctorate studies at The University of Texas at Austin where he became a member of the Biomedical Engineering Research Group.

In 1966, Leon Pomeroy, joined the group. Bishop and Pomeroy then began collaboration on a research project. Their collaboration has continued now for more than twenty five years and has resulted in a number of scholarly publications which have developed the Hartman Value Profile (HVP) as a more reliable and valid tool for psychologists. Issues of it's efficacy, accuracy, validity, reliability and relevance have been studied.

In 1983, a trip to Mexico reinforced Bishop's observation that extensive study is needed to assure the validity of the HVP in foreign cultural and language applications. A meeting with retired Lt. Colonel Frank Forrest in Florida in 1984 produced some new directions in the study of Hartman valuemetrics.

Bishop and Pomeroy plan to continue their collaborative studies of formal axiology, the HVP, and the frontier of moral reasoning and value science issues, with the goal of furthering the treatment of people with psychological and neurological disorders.

C. STEPHEN BYRUM is Professor of Philosophy and Religion at Chattanooga State Community College in Chattanooga, Tennessee. He has worked primarily as a teacher at Chattanooga State since 1974. During this time, he has also served for three years as Assistant Dean of Arts and Humanities.

Byrum is a native of Athens, Tennessee, and holds the Bachelor of Arts Degree from Tennessee Wesleyan College, the Master of Divinity Degree from Southern Seminary in Louisville, Kentucky, and the Master of Arts and Doctor of Philosophy Degrees from the University of Tennessee, Knoxville. It was during his graduate studies in Knoxville that he studied with Robert S. Hartman. Byrum's Masters Thesis, which was initiated by the suggestion and encouragement of Hartman, was entitled The Value Structure of Theology. It was recently published in a fifth edition. While at UTK, Byrum also studied with John Davis, Rem Edwards, and Rolf-Dieter Hermann.

In addition to his teaching, Byrum has actively been engaged in research and writing. More than 75 of his articles, short stories, and poetry have been published. He is also the author of 17 books. His latest writing efforts have included a four-book series entitled Controversial Biblical Texts: Interpretations for Modern Man. He is presently engaged in a research project which will use the Hartman Value Profile as part of a value-based, student orientation program.

WAYNE CARPENTER is founder of Value Resource Group in Nashville, Tennessee. He is a practicing axiologist dedicated to the development of the ideas and models of Robert S. Hartman. His models have been applied both in business and in personal development strategies.

Carpenter is a native of Talladega, Alabama. He holds a Bachelors Degree from Carson Newman College in Jefferson City, Tennessee and a Masters Degree from the University of Tennessee in Knoxville, Tennessee. During the Vietnam War, he was drafted and made his first application of Hartman's concepts about axiology to the the field of comman decision making. After his stay in the Army, Carpenter did post graduate work at Vanderbilt University in Nashville, Tennessee. He formed a pension and profit sharing business to fund his axiological studies. In 1977, he began the full time development of axiological models and their applications to business. He has development models which have been applied to sales, management, customer service, managing innovation and other business areas. These models have been used, by himself and by consultants who he has trained, for interviewing, assessment, training and development and team building in such companies as GTE, CUNA Mutual Life, and Sara Lee. Carpenter is currently applying a system for measuring excellence at The United States Postal Service.

Carpenter has maintained the same goal from the beginning of his applications of Hartman's concepts: To build a pathway for the application of axiology to everyday problems in personal and business situations such that axiology and Hartman receive the credit and study which both he and the science deserve.

ROBERT E. CARTER was raised on a farm in New England. He received his A.B. degree Magna Cum Laude from Tufts University where he wrote an honors thesis on three Islamic philosopher-mystics. At Harvard University he studied with Paul Tillich, John Wild, James Luther Adams, R. Richard Neibuhr, and George Ernest Wright, amongst others, while earning his M.Div. degree and working as a Unitarian minister. His Ph.D. thesis at the University of Toronto was on the notion of "Intrinsic Value" in the work of G. E. Moore and C. I. Lewis. In connection with that thesis, he lived in Cuernavaca, Mexico for six months to consult with Robert S. Hartman. The consultations included lengthy daily discussions in a cafe, over cappuccino coffee, in the center of Cuernavaca.

Professor Carter has taught at Tufts University, The University of Toronto, Memorial University of Newfoundland, Prince of Wales College in

Prince Edward Island--where he was Chairman of the Philosophy Department, Queen's University, Concordia University in Montreal, and Trent University where he has been for the past eighteen years. He is the author of four books: <u>Dimensions of Moral Education</u>, the University of Toronto Press, and <u>The Nothingness Beyond God: An Introduction to the Philosophy of Nishida Kitaro</u>, New York, Paragon House. Paragon House also published an edited volume titled <u>God, the Self, and Nothingness</u>, and a book of poetry titled <u>Wolf</u> was published by the Edwin Mellen Press. He is the author of more than fifty scholarly articles and reviews. A fourth manuscript, a translation of the study of Japanese ethics by Watsuji Tetsuro, is nearing completion.

JOHN WILLIAM DAVIS received his Ph.D. from Emory University in 1959. Since 1957 he has taught Philosophy at The University of Tennessee where he became a full Professor and department Head in 1966 and Head Emeritus in 1988. As a graduate student at the Ohio State University, during the early fifties, he studied with Hartman. Later, while Hartman was at Tennessee (1968-73), he served as his department head. He is the coauthor of several books, including <u>Value and Valuation: Axiological Studies in Honor of Robert S. Hartman</u>, which he also edited. He has published numerous articles in the areas of his special research interests, value theory, ethics, formal axiology, and American philosophy. He was a co-founder and the first President of the American Society for Value Inquiry. He has served as a member of the Council for the Southern Society for Philosophy and Psychology and as President of the Tennessee Philosophical Association, of which he was also co-founder. From 1977 until his recent retirement, he was Chair of the Board of the Foundation for Philosophy of Creativity. He was a co-founder, the first President and first Chair of the Board of the Robert S. Hartman Institute for Formal and Applied Axiology. He is presently Chair Emeritus of the Institute.

REM B. EDWARDS received his A.B. degree from Emory University in 1956 where he was elected to Phi Beta Kappa. During graduate school he was a Danforth Graduate Fellow. He received a B.D. from Yale University in 1959 and a Ph.D. from Emory in 1962. He taught for four years at Jacksonville, University in Florida and since 1966 has been on the Philosophy faculty at The University of Tennessee. He was a U. T. Chancellor's Research Scholar in 1985 and is a Lindsay Young Professor of Humanities, 1987-1993. He has been a Visiting Professor at Berry College, Rome, GA and at Eastern Illinois University, Charleston, IL. He specializes in Ethical Theory and Medical Ethics, with special interests in Ethics in Mental Health Care, Ethics and Animals, and Formal Axiology. He has published six other books, including <u>Reason and Religion</u>, New York, Harcourt, 1972 and Washington, University Press of America, 1979, <u>Pleasures and Pains: A Theory of Qualitative Hedonism</u>, Ithaca, Cornell University Press, 1979, <u>Psychiatry and</u>

Ethics, Buffalo, Prometheus Books, 1982, and (with Glenn Graber) BioEthics, San Diego, Harcourt, 1988. He has published over forty five articles and reviews, including "Pain Management and the Values of Health Care Providers," Advances in Pain Research and Therapy, Vol. 11 and "Abortion Rights, Why Conservatives are Wrong," National Forum, Fall 1989.

Edwards has been the President of the Tennessee Philosophical Association (1973-4), the Society for Philosophy of Religion (1981-2), and the Southern Society for Philosophy and Psychology (1984-85). He was a Charter Member of the R. S. Hartman Institute, has served on its Board of Directors since 1987, and since 1989 has been its Secretary-Treasurer.

ARTHUR R. ELLIS is a Certified Professional Counselor who has been a clinician since 1971. He holds degrees in psychology and rehabilitation counseling from the University of Tennessee, Knoxville, at which he earned a M.S. degree in 1971. In recent years he has worked as a therapist in the Psychology Service of a Veterans Administration Medical Center. His areas of expertise include quality management in psychiatry and self-image in psychology. He studied axiology under Robert S. Hartman who personally trained him in the use and interpretation of the "Hartman Value Profile" (HVP). Over the years he has administered and interpreted hundreds of HVP's. His research has included explorations of the value patterns of alcoholics. He has written a comparison of Robert Pirsig's concept of "Quality" and Robert Hartman's concept of "Good." He has been active in the R. S. Hartman Institute for Formal and Applied Axiology, serving on the Board of Directors, and holding the positions of Executive Director and President. In 1982, he was chosen as an Outstanding Young Man of America.

FRANK G. FORREST received his B.S. degree from the United States Military Academy, West Point, NY in 1939. He was commissioned as a Second Lieutenant, US Army, in June, 1939 and retired as a Colonel with an aeronautical rating of Senior Army Aviator in March 1964. He served in World War II in Alaska and the Aleutian Islands. In the Korean War he was commander of an infantry company, battalion, and training regiment. On several occasions he was a staff officer in a major Army Headquarters. He was a qualified Army Airplane and helicopter pilot and flew aerial missions during the Korean War.

Upon retirement from the military, Forrest joined Embry-Riddle Aeronautical Institute in April 1964 and retired as Vice President in 1977. In this position he planned and coordinated moving the school from Miami to Daytona Beach, Florida in 1965. Over a thirteen year period, he coordinated the planning and construction of the Embry-Riddle campus and played a major role in the development and transition of the school from an Institute to a University.

Forrest received his M.A. degree from Stetson University in Deland, FL in 1969 and his Ph.D. from International University, San Diego, CA in 1976. His dissertation was titled <u>Human Values Accounting as an Organizational Development Tool</u>. He is the author of <u>Valuemetrics: The Science of Personal and Professional Ethics</u>, Daytona Beach, FL, Valuemetrics Co., 1988. He has been a very active member of the R. S. Hartman Institute and has served the Institute as Secretary-Treasurer.

RITA S. HARTMAN was born in Germany while her father was fighting at the Russian Front. After some financially difficult years, she received the usual schooling of a girl of more or less affluent Jewish parents. Attending a private Licée, i.e. high school, she studied French, German literature (which she particularly liked), history, and math. She reports that she loathed and habitually flunked math to the despair of her parents, teachers, and later Bob, who once told her in desperation: "Don't numbers have a color for you--a beautiful color?" To which she replied: "None whatsoever. They bore me; they mean nothing at all." He gave up. In her own words:

> I learned all the things a well-educated Jewish princess had to learn in order to be able to be presented to her peers and their parents, then get married, have children, run a good home, entertain, and be an asset to her family, husband and community.
>
> I was sent to religious school, learned Hebrew, Jewish history, and to uphold the tradition, as we did in the home of my parent. I still keep the high holidays, enjoying the tradition. Bob was brought up in the Lutheran faith and had little knowledge of our customs.
>
> When Hitler "broke out," my mother immediately instigated our exodus from Germany. My sisters, born in 1919 and 1923, and I were sent to Hamburg where my mother had a sister who had been born in Sonsonate, Salvador. She was not a German citizen, and mother was sure this would protect us. At that time the Nazis were not that well organized. When we returned from Hamburg, where we had a marvelous time with our cousins, Mother had got rid of our villa and had moved everything into an apartment. We went back to school, and all seemed sort of normal. By that time, I was 15 years old, had a boyfriend, and lived--I now think--the normal life of a young girl in love.

But it was to be different. Mother started packing all our furniture, made arrangements to have them shipped to Sweden, and moved us all to a Pension for a few weeks. I remember our leaving for Sweden. My uncles and friends saw us off to Sweden at the train. Mother urged everyone there to leave also. She did not trust that "Parvenue," as she called Hitler. My father, who had an important position, at first did not want to make such a drastic move. Mother said she would move anyway with the three of us; and as he did not want to live without "his women," as he said, he came along. In reality, Mother saved our lives.

We arrived in Sweden, where we had relatives, on my 16th birthday. My grandmother's sister had married to live in Sweden, and her four children were mother's favorite cousins. They, of course, had married and had children more or less our age. To this day, those of us who are still alive are fast friends and stay in touch.

At first we stayed at a Hotel awaiting our furniture. We got a governess who taught us Swedish, the behavior and customs of Sweden, and some history and knowledge of Stockholm, so we could find our way around. We discovered the changing of the royal guards at noon and made our governess take us there every day. This was so new and exciting, and we were thrilled. The guardsmen get to know us and furtively greeted us when they saw us. It was fun.

Mother found an apartment, soon the furniture came, and we moved in. We were enrolled in school, for by that time we had become fluent in Swedish and enjoyed reading and speaking it. The headmistress of the school was an old friend of mother's. Although we had to take an entrance exam, we had no trouble. I finished high school and was enrolled in the Royal Academy of Design and Dressmaking. After one year I got my school report and was ready to take a job. My first job was to make children's clothing. It was piece work, which means one gets paid for the quantity one has done. This I didn't like at all and looked around for another job. I found one in the French Department of the big department store N. K, now a member of Federated Department Stores. That winter, I met Bob.

When I saw him first, I thought to myself: "This is the man I want to get old with." He seemed to think the same. The following August, we were married, eight months after we had met. Our son was born two years later. He too has become an intellectual, as well as our two granddaughters.

Bob saw the war coming, and we came to the United States. After many moves and many different and interesting jobs, we finally settled in Mexico. While Bob was teaching at Wooster College in Ohio, I took courses to be able to help Bob in his work. I have never regretted it. I learned a great deal and also saw that my schooling in Europe had been magnificent. Much of what I learned in Europe was repeated in classes at the College of Wooster. I did not graduate because by that time Bob needed my help in his work. He always said to me: "Why take the Union card? I have one; that's enough."

The thirty eight years I was married to Bob were wonderfully full and gratifying. I was not only a wife, a companion, a mother, and a housewife, but I also became a person in my own right. It was--and still is--a rich and rewarding life. I enjoyed it and hope to keep on doing just that for many years to come.

ROBERT S. HARTMAN was Research Professor of Philosophy at The University of Tennessee and at the National University of Mexico when he died on September 20, 1973. He was buried near his home in Cuernavaca, Mexico. He was born in Berlin on January 27, 1910. He attended the German College of Political Science, the University of Paris, the London School of Economics, and Berlin University, where he received he LL.B. in 1932. For a brief period, he taught at Berlin University and served as an assistant district court judge.

Hartman's rejection of Fascism, which he expressed in speeches and articles, brought him into conflict with the Nazi party and forced him to leave Germany, using a fake passport, in 1932. He legally changed his name (Robert Schirokauer) to the name on his passport, Robert S. (for Schirokauer) Hartman. In 1938, using a Swedish alien's passport, he and his wife, the former Rita Emanuel, and son, Jan, left Europe for Mexico, where they lived until their immigration in 1941 to the United States, where they later became citizens.

Hartman's first teaching position in the United States was at Lake Forest Academy in Illinois. While there, he enrolled at Northwestern University where he received his Ph.D. in 1946. He taught at the College of Wooster in Ohio from 1945-48, and at the Ohio State University from 1948-56. He was a visiting professor at Massachusetts Institute of Technology, 1955-56, and at Yale, 1966. He was Smith Mundt State Department Research Fellow and Exchange Professor at the National University of Mexico, 1956-57. He held more than fifty lectureships in the United States, Canada, Latin America, and Europe. He was a research professor of philosophy at the National

University of Mexico beginning in 1957 and at The University of Tennessee since 1968.

Hartman's formal axiology, as the ordering logic for the value sciences, was developed in many published articles and received its most complete expression in his major work, The Structure of Value: Foundations of Scientific Axiology, 1967. See the preceding Bibliographies for details. In the field of psychology he applied his axiology in "The Hartman Value Profile," a value test widely used in Mexico and by some psychiatrists and psychologists in the United States.

KURT KALTREIDER majored in Philosophy at Gettysburg College. In 1969 and 1977 he received his M. A. and Ph.D. degrees in Philosophy from the University of Tennessee where he was Robert S. Hartman's Graduate Assistant for one year. He has taught Philosophy at the University of North Carolina at Asheville, Mars Hill College, and the University of Tennessee.

His work in the stock market began in 1976 when he developed the axiological stock selection model. He has been a researcher and portfolio manager for Kingley, Boye and Southwood, H. K. Associates, and his own firms, Kaltreider research and its successor, Jefferson Investment Management. His clients include some of the nation's and world's largest banks and several top performing portfolio management firms. He ranks among the best in both his research and portfolio management, being cited by Barrons, Investment Highlights, and Standard & Poore's, among others.

Kaltreider is also active in various human potential and educational organizations, and he devotes much of his time to the study of consciousness and the philosophy of man.

ALFONSO LOZANO was born in Copala, State of Guerro, Mexico. In 1950 he moved to Mexico City to study at the "Escuela Nacional de Maestros," (Teachers' National School), where he graduated as an elementary school teacher. While studying there, he developed a deep interest in moral questions, especially those concerning ethical goodness, and decided to study philosophy and subjects related to the development of our true humanity. In 1961, he entered the School of Philosophy at the National Autonomous University of Mexico (U.N.A.M.), where he met Robert S. Hartman. From then until 1973 he worked under Dr. Hartman's direction, and this invaluable experience opened the doors for him to the realm of values. The knowledge of formal axiology allowed Lozano to reach an understanding of moral goodness and led him to apply his knowledge to the field of education.

Professor Lozano is currently retired after working as a full time teacher at the Teacher's National School for 25 years. There, he taught Ethics and Educational Theory (Philosophy of Education) according to the principles of formal axiology. Nowadays, he is in the final states of writing a book titled The New Education and its Axiological Basis. Lozano has attended the annual conference of the R. S. Hartman Institute five times, always speaking for the necessity of a new kind of education that will completely develop the human personality in an integral and harmonic way.

DAVID MEFFORD is a native Tennessean with over 20 years experience in the theoretical and practical applications of formal axiology. David's career as an axiologist began as a student of Robert S. Hartman, the creator of scientific axiology. As Hartman's first commercial representative for the Hartman Value Profile (HVP) in Europe, David held his first seminar on formal axiology in 1971 for managers of Siemens and Volkswagen at Garmisch-Partenkirchen, an alpine resort in Southern Germany. He continues to conduct seminars and workshops for corporate and professional clients in the U. S. A. and abroad. While in Europe, David attended the University of Paris, France and earned his M.A. in philosophy, psychology, and law at the University of Heidelberg, West Germany. David also holds a Ph.D. in philosophy from the University of Tennessee. His dissertation, Man as a Valuing Subject, achieved a comprehensive typology of persons based on the formal structure of value judgment. This formal axiological personality model consists of 26 cognitive types and 40 emotional temperaments.

Under his direction as president, Value Measurement Technologies, Inc. has successfully developed and marketed innovations in the fields of personality assessment and counseling, business management and sales, and advertising and general communications for numerous clients in North America and in Europe. David is co-founder and board member of the R. S. Hartman Institute and co-director of the Foundation for Axiological Research (FAR) Foundation. David has authored several books and seminar manuals on the applications of value science, available in soft cover. Several newspaper or magazine articles have been published about his work.

VERA MEFFORD is co-owner and Executive Vice-president of Value Measurement Technologies, Inc. She is a professional axiologist working with the Hartman Value Profile (HVP) and several other practical applications of value science. Her work involves consulting with over 100 business clients focusing on individual and group performance improvement. Vera is also co-founder and director of FAR: The Foundation for Axiological Research. Under the auspices of FAR, she directs a research project using the Hartman Value Profile to explore how recovering cancer patients can establish new self-value foundations for a better quality of life. In addition, the cancer research project seeks to define more clearly survivor traits in terms of self-valuation.

Vera Mefford holds a Bachelor's degree from Houghton College (New York) and a Master of Arts from Schiller International University (Heidelberg, Federal Republic of Germany). She also completed three years post-graduate work at the University of Heidelberg and at the University of Tennessee in Archaeology and Cultural Anthropology. She has worked with the Hartman Value Profile in the business context for eleven years and is the translator of the German language version of the six part HVP. She also co-developed a simplified English language version of the HVP for use with younger people in the Job Training Partnership Act (JTPA) programs.

MARK A. MOORE received his Ph.D in Philosophy at the University of Tennessee, Knoxville, in 1973. During his studies, he worked with Robert S. Hartman and wrote his doctoral dissertation on the scientific aspects of Hartman's theory of Formal Axiology. He continued his research while performing his duties as a tenured professor of philosophy at Salisbury State University in Maryland.

Dr. Moore left the University in 1979 to start a consulting and research form dedicated to the application of formal systems to decision making. Working with Harry Suber, Ph.D. in Mathematics, Moore has constructed formal decision models which identify and abstract formal value structures within information streams. These structures are used to optimize decision making and utilize sophisticated computer technology of multidimensional geometry.

Dr. Moore has applied this technology in several important areas. First, it has been used to determine "content relevance" in computer data base search and retrieval; and Moore founded Codeworks Corporation to take advantage of this. Second, he has also applied this technology to the financial markets. Here, formal value structures are used to evaluate trades for their potential profit or loss. To take advantage of this technology, Moore founded and is a partner in TrendLogic Associates, Inc. He is also a General Partner in Millennium Partners.

Dr. Moore is President of the Board of Directors of the R. S. Hartman Institute.

458   *Forms of Value and Valuation: Theory and Applications*

LEON POMEROY, Ph.D., M.A., B.S., B.A., holds advanced degrees in the fields of both psychology and biology from the University of Texas at Austin and the University of Massachusetts at Amherst, respectively. He is a clinical psychologist in private practice in Manhattan and a Staff Psychologist and Director of Behavioral Medicine at the Outpatient Clinic of the Department of Veterans Affairs Medical Center, Brooklyn. He formerly served as an Associate Professor of Psychology at Long Island University, City University of New York, and New York University. During his academic years, he edited the Handbook of General Psychology (Prentice-Hall, 1973), and a multivolume Encyclopedia of Psychiatry, Psychology, Neurology and Psychoanalysis. He also edited five volumes in the series New Dynamics of Preventive Medicine. He has presented twenty six conference papers and has over twenty one publications, while busy with clinical practice and patient care.

Dr. Pomeroy's publications include two that appeared in the prestigious Proceedings of the National Academy of Sciences of the U. S. A. and one in the Journal of Electroencephalography and Clinical Neurophysiology. He is a founding fellow along with Linus Pauling and R. J. Williams of the International Academy of Preventive Medicine (IAPM), and he was the first Ph.D. to be elected its President in 1975. He is also Founding Editor of IAPM Publications and was Editor-in-Chief of the Journal of the International Academy of Preventive Medicine from 1973 to 1985. From 1986 to 1991 he served as Associate Editor of the Journal of Applied Nutrition and Preventive Medicine, reflecting his continued interest in the biopsychology of mental health issues.

Dr. Pomeroy's interests in personal ideologies, comparative belief systems, values, and collective mass mind phenomena were developed while taking a course in the Sociology of Knowledge in Chicago and through his exposure to the writings of Karl Mannheim. These early studies were reinforced while a Post Doctoral Fellow at the Albert Ellis, Ph.D., Institute in New York City. Since 1973 he has spent much research time studying formal axiology and Hartman's valuemetrics from the point of view of its relevance to psychology. He brings a unique scientist-clinician orientation to this study, as the history of conference papers and published papers testifies. He has obtained translations of the HVP into Indonesian and Japanese and is working on a Russian translation. These versions are being employed in cross-cultural studies and further validation efforts with the Hartman Value Profile. He has found axiology to be a stimulating and heuristic discipline, and the excitement of being on the knife edge of this revolutionary new way of thinking in the field of psychology is an involvement he hopes to share with others for the benefit of all.

INDEX

Actuality 16, 43, 94, 268, 390
Actualize 88, 89, 116, 387, 390, 399
Actualized 87, 100, 389, 390, 396, 403
Addition 40, 44, 49, 66, 82, 87, 99, 133, 141-143, 146, 163, 278, 390
Advertising 223, 224, 226, 227
Aesthetic 10, 11, 23, 68, 69, 84, 90, 281, 299, 415
Affective 45, 72, 84, 88, 96, 113, 114
Affectively 47, 50, 107
Aleph 131, 142, 144, 182-188, 425
א 131, 132, 134, 141, 142, 144, 146, 147, 148, 150, 164, 165, 212, 214, 215-219, 228, 329-334, 336-338, 340, 343, 415, 425
Allport, G. 270, 285, 291, 304, 306, 310
Analytic 41, 43, 61, 64, 75-77, 90, 106, 129, 132-136, 143, 174, 222, 304, 307, 308, 410, 415
Animal 43, 82, 85, 87-89, 98, 107, 108, 117, 163, 165, 166, 172, 205, 379, 396, 404
Anselm 404, 406, 409, 415, 416, 424, 425, 426
Application 11, 12, 23, 31, 47, 53, 59, 62, 68-70, 86, 89, 92, 110, 112, 128, 129, 136, 149, 159, 167, 169, 170, 178-181, 193-196, 220, 223, 226, 248, 263, 265, 268, 278, 281, 282, 285, 294, 299, 300, 304, 315, 323, 330, 331, 342, 349, 354, 361, 363, 389, 390, 394, 399, 409, 410, 411, 417

Applied 4, 10, 11, 13, 16, 17, 19, 22, 23, 31-33, 46, 50, 51, 64, 68, 70, 71, 83, 84, 86, 106, 125, 197, 199, 215, 219, 243, 260, 264, 281, 285-287, 308, 314, 327, 330, 331, 336, 348, 381, 393, 406
Aquinas 404
Aristotle 43, 44, 92, 96, 417
Artist 23, 28, 31, 48, 84, 398, 406, 409, 411, 415
Attribute 14-19, 21, 22, 26, 37, 61, 62, 64, 65, 67, 75, 76, 78, 126-128, 132-134, 224, 226, 392
Authentic 67, 112, 116, 150, 168, 254, 303, 338, 389, 390, 409, 411
Authoritarian 20, 24, 52, 391, 394
Authority 70, 218, 222, 318, 323, 324, 354, 363, 393, 404
Autonomy 82, 90, 314
Average 44, 71, 72, 74, 75, 198, 229, 230, 231, 232, 235-238, 267, 306, 317, 319, 324, 325
Axiology 4, 9-13, 18, 31, 37, 53, 59, 64, 67, 68, 70, 79, 82, 83, 86, 87, 89, 105, 106, 114, 125, 169, 170, 193, 194, 197, 199, 201, 202, 204, 205, 211, 212, 215, 223, 227, 229, 234, 236, 237, 243, 245, 247, 249, 253, 260, 262, 264, 265, 267-269, 279, 281, 286, 287, 291, 292, 294-301, 303, 307, 308, 309-316, 319, 323, 325, 327, 329-331, 336, 338, 340, 346, 348, 350, 352, 362, 378-382, 384, 385, 387, 407-412, 417, 419, 423

Axiom 37, 43, 64, 106, 193, 199, 200, 330, 410, 411, 414, 416
Axiomatic 43, 115, 411, 417, 424
Bad 15-18, 22, 32, 61, 63, 64, 66, 69, 71, 72, 74, 90, 99, 110, 117, 118, 128, 135, 139, 169, 175, 176, 179, 193, 203, 205, 233, 245, 246, 248, 252, 258, 262, 266, 267, 345-347, 349, 351, 352, 354, 356, 357, 361-363, 365, 379, 389
Badness 17, 19, 22, 23, 33, 46, 116, 117, 161, 163, 176, 233, 258, 349, 350, 353, 354, 359, 361, 362, 365, 371, 373, 376
Balanced 214, 215, 218, 219, 221, 222, 225, 337, 338, 342, 412
Base 77, 145, 146, 148-151, 155, 157, 162, 163, 181-185, 188, 189, 212, 213, 214, 216, 372, 410, 419, 424
Behavioral axiology 292, 294-297, 299, 300, 308, 309, 311-316, 327
Better 18, 22, 24, 26, 52, 71, 86, 92, 100, 105, 107, 133, 135, 139, 158, 174, 176, 186, 193, 197, 200, 203, 205, 211, 216-218, 230-237, 247, 250, 264, 265-267, 269, 293, 301, 306, 308, 323, 324, 326, 334, 338, 349, 351, 366, 380, 381, 389, 392, 395, 399, 407, 409, 411, 415, 418, 422
Bliss 33, 95, 96
Body 11, 25, 41, 44, 52, 83, 94, 95, 113, 118-120, 139, 140, 226, 294, 331, 335, 384, 390, 410
Brumbaugh, R. S. 87
Business 3, 4, 28, 32, 86, 132, 180, 194, 196, 197, 211-216, 218, 219, 220, 222, 227, 240, 282, 345, 346, 398
Capacities 24, 29, 86, 88, 89, 93, 94, 96, 98, 143, 230, 264, 265, 272, 276, 278, 282, 332, 335-338, 342, 353, 355, 383, 384, 390
Capacity 27, 28, 31, 45, 54, 70, 73, 83, 88, 89-91, 93, 105, 107, 110, 111, 112-114, 116, 134, 136, 173, 194, 195, 214, 254, 255, 264, 265, 266, 268-271, 276, 278, 279, 282, 297, 298, 300, 306, 311, 316, 325, 331, 332, 334, 335-337, 347, 350-352, 357, 359, 361, 363, 366, 367-369, 372, 374, 377, 382, 383, 388, 397-400, 403, 409, 411, 412, 416
Capitalism 195, 199
Cardenas 244, 247, 248, 250, 259, 262, 287

Cardinal 87, 129, 131, 132, 134-136, 141, 143, 169, 174, 175, 181, 182, 184, 185, 187, 188, 191, 192
Cardinality 131-134, 389, 390
Causality 30
Cause 31, 59, 61, 89, 166, 176, 177, 205, 232, 357, 361, 364, 374, 404
Center 3, 18, 39, 87, 88, 90, 94, 95, 97, 101, 105, 113, 173, 295, 305, 310, 312, 332, 333, 335, 345, 367, 383, 387, 416, 419, 420
Character 12, 15, 20, 28, 33, 42, 61, 62, 74, 87, 99, 100, 105, 177, 207, 220, 293, 299, 305, 314, 382, 398, 399, 413, 414, 416, 418
Christ 12, 205, 414, 420, 421
Christian 12, 168, 405, 414-416, 418, 420, 422
Christology 420
Class 1, 14-24, 26, 30, 32, 34, 47, 53, 61, 62-65, 76, 78, 82, 83, 90, 91, 106, 108, 109, 116, 118, 126, 195, 196, 201, 223, 247, 262, 263, 264, 267, 330, 349, 387, 389, 392-395
Cognitive 45, 47, 88, 96, 220, 223, 225, 230, 292, 294, 297-300, 313, 314, 315, 316, 318, 326, 332, 338, 339, 340
Cognitively 45, 46, 50, 316, 335
Collectivity 12, 23, 24, 201, 202, 394, 395
Coma 134
Comatose 93, 94
Combination 27, 28, 45, 49, 50, 71, 85, 112, 125, 129, 136-141, 143, 144, 145-150, 153-162, 165, 167, 168, 169, 178, 179, 181, 182, 184, 185, 187-189, 194, 220, 237, 244, 248, 249, 265, 349, 350, 351, 358, 366, 372, 374, 398, 416, 419
Communism 199
Community 12, 23, 24, 30, 84, 196, 281, 295, 309, 345, 346, 354, 394, 395, 403, 414, 420
Compassion 90, 93, 97, 105, 115, 116, 203, 335
Competition 12, 24, 202, 393-395
Composition 106, 137-140, 146, 148, 149, 151, 155, 160, 161, 178, 186, 187-190, 244, 246-248, 250, 252, 260, 261, 351, 413
Computation 137

Index

Concentrate 23, 29, 31, 65, 84, 208, 387
Concentration 3, 20, 23, 28, 33, 84, 90, 93, 115, 120, 276, 324, 395, 398, 399, 411
Concept 3, 10, 12, 14-19, 21-24, 29-31, 34, 37-45, 47, 49-51, 53, 60, 62-78, 82-85, 87-92, 100, 101, 106, 108, 109, 112, 113, 115, 116, 126-141, 143-146, 149-163, 165, 167, 168, 169, 173, 175, 188, 212, 225, 231, 233-235, 247, 249, 250, 253, 255, 267, 268, 281, 282, 285, 287, 288, 291-296, 298-300, 308, 310, 327, 329, 330, 332, 335, 336, 338, 339, 347-356, 359, 361, 362, 377, 379-382, 384, 389, 390, 392, 394, 395, 403-406, 408, 410, 411, 413, 417, 420
Conceptual 19, 40, 41, 44, 45, 47, 50, 69, 84-86, 89, 106, 111-114, 268, 296, 300
Conceptually 54, 72, 84, 85, 91, 119, 394
Concrete 11, 12, 44, 81, 86, 108, 193, 204, 205, 245, 250, 254, 349, 350, 383, 395, 409, 411, 412, 414, 417, 419
Conformity 20, 24, 52, 79, 89, 201, 353, 354, 357, 370, 391, 393, 394, 395
Conjunctions 136, 146, 156
Conscience 15, 16, 85, 90-92, 99, 204, 302, 349, 350, 353, 354, 359, 363, 366, 367, 369, 373-376, 389
Conscious 45, 47, 54, 84-90, 93-98, 101, 107-112, 120, 176, 261, 332, 335, 336, 341, 387, 390, 399
Consciousness 7, 45, 48, 87, 88, 93-97, 105, 107-113, 115-120, 293, 301, 303, 325, 329, 331, 334, 336, 385, 388, 390, 399, 403, 420
Constitution 16, 54, 81
Construct 18, 19, 21, 31, 33, 38-42, 44, 46, 66, 67, 69, 89, 127-129, 132, 133-136, 143, 150, 167, 168, 180, 262, 270, 282, 304, 307, 308, 311, 318, 326, 330, 332, 352, 378, 390, 392, 410
Construction 42, 125, 133, 196, 204, 224, 226, 270, 308, 355
Continuum 67, 74, 115, 188, 250, 252, 306, 335, 336, 421
Contradiction 39, 49, 50, 118, 138, 139
Cooperation 5, 12, 23, 24, 91, 197, 198, 218, 219, 317, 334, 393, 394, 395
Correspondence 17, 29, 37-39, 62, 71, 129, 130, 270, 299, 330, 350

Counseling 215-219, 270, 279, 280, 300, 308, 313
Creative 28, 30, 31, 37, 98, 99, 178, 205, 219, 226, 248, 250, 393, 398, 400, 409, 418, 420
Creativity 30, 31, 39, 45, 46, 48, 51, 79, 82, 85, 87, 88, 90, 93, 94, 96, 97, 98, 100, 178, 219, 248, 304, 350, 388, 390, 403, 409, 421, 425
Cross cultural 257, 292, 294, 298, 303, 313, 314-316, 323, 327
Customer 15, 23, 212-214, 216, 217, 223, 224-227, 351
Death 1, 48, 91, 96, 98, 100, 101, 119, 139, 140, 165, 176, 205, 208, 293, 307, 383, 407, 408, 417, 425
Definition 10, 13-19, 21, 22, 32, 41, 45, 47, 50, 60, 63, 66, 74, 77, 82, 84, 85, 91, 106, 125-129, 133, 139, 143, 173, 193, 200, 202, 204, 216, 247, 250, 262, 268, 299, 300, 330, 331, 332, 335, 347, 349, 353, 388, 389, 390, 392, 398, 410, 415
Degrees 20, 21, 23, 44, 48, 62, 63, 67, 69, 77, 87, 88, 112, 113, 127, 129, 213, 264, 303, 330, 338, 353, 389, 392
Denumerable 108, 116, 130, 131, 133, 134, 147, 175, 388, 389
Denumerably 64, 67, 68, 175, 182, 185
Descartes, R. 174, 299, 404, 408
Detached 48, 50
Dewey, J. 28, 60, 64, 68, 73, 74, 234
Differentia 66, 74, 77, 78
Dimension 26, 45, 48, 49, 67, 69, 70, 105, 113, 119, 128, 129, 135, 173, 174, 194, 196, 207, 211, 212, 213-219, 221, 223, 224, 226, 244, 247-250, 252, 253, 260, 261, 262, 266, 268, 276, 278, 286, 297, 298, 300-302, 304, 306, 307, 316, 326, 330-337, 339, 340, 348, 349, 350, 355, 384, 385, 387, 391, 399
Diminish 50, 51, 111
Disinterestedness 47
Disvaluation 46, 50, 51, 214, 251, 252, 260, 264, 278, 293, 296, 300, 302, 351
Disvalue 17, 20, 42, 46, 49-51, 66, 77, 117, 118, 128, 138, 175-177, 184, 186-190, 214, 243, 251, 252, 257, 264, 278, 293, 296, 300, 302, 351, 376
Disvalues 46, 50, 51, 214, 251, 252, 264, 278, 293, 296, 300, 302, 351

462 Forms of Value and Valuation: Theory and Applications

Dying 32, 48, 114, 205
Dynamic 21, 45, 84, 85, 88, 219, 220, 293, 294, 296-298, 301-303, 305, 315, 316, 326, 335, 350, 351
Dynamically 45, 47, 50, 267
Economic 2, 11, 12, 16, 26, 33, 41, 44, 64, 68, 83, 193-200, 202, 203, 211, 212, 216, 234, 240, 265, 281, 292, 382, 400
Ecstasy 5, 114
Education 11, 28, 33, 46, 87, 132, 253, 270, 286, 288, 379-385, 387, 390, 396, 398, 399, 406, 407
Efficient Market Theory 232, 240
Eichman 302, 303
Emerson, R. W. 82
Emotion 60, 61, 73, 90, 95, 114, 120, 294, 297, 301, 316, 331
Emotional 47, 48, 60, 61, 72, 85, 96, 114, 116, 140, 220, 222, 225, 227, 253, 264, 265, 279, 297, 316, 318, 330, 338, 358, 364, 365, 368, 382, 406
Empathetic 73, 85, 90, 118, 119, 217, 221, 394, 397
Empathy 28, 87, 93, 94, 96, 97, 115, 116, 117, 254, 269, 335, 382, 398
Enjoyment 85, 93, 94, 98, 100, 114
Enrich 31, 92, 97, 110, 139, 301, 383
Enrichment 47-49, 87, 189, 194, 341
Equal 28, 39, 94, 130, 132, 134, 142, 143, 144, 146, 162, 164, 169, 185, 212, 218, 219, 221, 271, 337, 414
Equivalent 16, 29, 94, 130, 224, 257, 316
Error 50, 177, 187, 214, 361, 366, 367, 370
Eternity 118, 119
Evil 1-3, 20, 22, 23, 33, 46, 52, 94, 96, 116, 117-119, 139, 177, 202, 203, 204, 205, 379, 391, 410, 413
Experience 8-10, 21-23, 37, 38, 41, 64, 65, 66-71, 74, 75, 77, 81, 82, 87, 88, 90, 92, 94-98, 101, 109, 110, 111-113, 115, 117-120, 140, 176, 178, 207, 211, 232, 244, 245, 248, 282, 293, 295, 301, 330, 332-334, 348-350, 353, 355, 356, 362, 387, 395, 403, 405, 406, 408, 410, 412, 419, 424
Expert 70, 76, 168, 194, 220, 231-233, 268, 282, 283, 405
Exponent 145, 146, 148, 150-152, 155, 161, 163, 164, 178, 182, 187, 188, 189
Exponentation 49, 337

Exposition 22, 63, 66, 74, 75, 234, 235
Extension 14, 18, 31-33, 87, 108, 131, 143, 314, 383, 411, 420
Extrinsic education 382, 383
Extrinsic valuation 21-24, 26-28, 34, 64, 67, 72-74, 90, 251, 264, 305, 332, 333, 351, 356, 393, 395, 400, 412
Extrinsic value 14-17, 22, 30, 31, 41, 43, 47, 55, 59, 64-67, 70, 73, 78, 82, 84, 85, 90, 100, 105, 106, 109, 111, 126, 129, 132, 135, 176, 177, 182, 185, 188, 194, 195, 205, 211, 213-216, 246, 247, 250-252, 264, 266, 281, 330, 333, 349, 350
Fair 44, 45, 47, 61, 63, 64, 67, 71, 72, 74, 127, 135, 176, 267, 376
Faith 90, 203, 205, 304, 324, 371, 372, 405, 406, 409, 412, 414, 418, 419
Feeling 8, 45, 48, 61, 90, 95, 99, 107, 113, 114, 115, 171, 253, 258, 301, 330, 332, 340, 357, 358, 364, 365, 366, 368, 371-373, 375, 382, 407
Fetus 93, 98
Fetuses 93, 94
Finite 31, 39-41, 44-46, 50, 51, 66-68, 84, 86, 87, 129-133, 137, 141, 142, 143, 146, 147, 158, 160, 163, 174, 175, 182, 185, 197, 249, 267, 330, 332, 335, 413, 419
Formal 1, 4, 5, 8, 10, 11, 13, 20, 25-27, 37-42, 47-49, 53, 59, 61, 62, 64, 66-70, 79, 82, 83, 87, 89, 105, 106, 113, 114, 125, 171, 172-175, 177, 179-181, 184, 185, 187, 192, 193, 194, 195, 197, 201, 202, 205, 211, 212, 215, 217, 220, 223, 227, 234, 236, 237, 240, 243, 249, 253, 260, 263, 265, 267, 268, 269, 278, 279, 281, 286, 291, 292, 294-301, 303, 308, 309, 311, 312, 315, 316, 319, 323, 325, 326, 329-331, 336-338, 340, 379, 380, 381, 382, 384, 397, 407, 408, 410
Fractions 146, 147, 187, 194, 195
Galileo 26, 42, 43, 59, 410
Genius 12, 28, 29, 37, 251, 252, 259, 260, 398, 411, 412, 418
Gestalt 30, 48, 67, 108, 134, 294, 299, 392
God 7, 13, 29, 34, 43, 53, 54, 85, 90, 95, 116, 130, 134, 178, 248, 403, 404-408, 411-413, 415, 416, 417-422, 424-426

Index

Hartman value profile 45, 85, 191, 220, 223, 228, 243, 246, 250, 254, 259, 261, 264-266, 269, 273, 278, 281, 285, 287, 288, 296, 297, 298, 303, 307, 308, 310, 311-313, 315, 317, 323, 325, 326, 327, 337, 343, 351, 352, 355, 361, 362, 378
Hierarchical 265, 298, 300, 302, 303, 316
Hierarchy 43, 67, 83, 111, 114, 215, 250, 257, 298, 349, 412
Hitler, A. 1, 2, 8, 119, 293, 302, 407, 410, 413
Honesty 82, 90, 177, 217, 253, 349-351, 353-363, 366, 369, 370, 373-376, 378
Husserl, E. 299, 331, 336, 343
HVP 45, 220, 225, 243, 246, 247, 250, 252, 253, 254, 257-261, 264, 265, 266, 269, 273, 278, 281, 282, 285, 287, 288, 296-300, 302-319, 323, 325, 326, 327, 351-353, 361
Ideal 16, 18, 83, 89-91, 108, 165, 174, 180, 212, 214, 215, 219, 221, 223, 224, 226, 301, 316, 336, 337, 338, 340-342, 353, 366, 368, 370, 389, 409, 414
Ideal person 409
Identification 30, 47, 65, 90, 91, 108, 109, 114, 116, 119, 349, 350, 389, 395, 397
Identifying 47, 117, 126, 160, 214, 217, 222, 252, 331, 338, 352, 362
Index 11, 16-18, 21-23, 27, 29, 45, 46, 51, 69-71, 74, 75, 84, 86, 88, 89-91, 93, 94, 98, 99, 105, 131, 132, 212, 213, 216-218, 231, 255, 268, 271, 273, 278, 279, 330, 331, 334, 335, 339, 384, 388
Individual 6, 7, 11, 15, 20, 23, 24, 27, 29, 33, 37, 40, 46, 53, 65, 66, 81, 82-94, 96-101, 106, 115, 117, 171, 172, 175, 177, 180, 193, 196, 198, 201, 204, 211, 218, 219-223, 232, 233, 257, 258, 265, 266, 269, 270, 279, 281, 282, 283, 289, 291, 293, 294, 298, 300-303, 305, 306, 316, 317, 318, 330, 331, 345, 346, 347, 348, 354-356, 358, 359, 361, 362, 364, 369, 370, 373, 374, 377, 381, 382, 387, 391, 392, 403, 407, 411, 420
Indonesia 303, 307, 308, 313, 314, 316, 317, 318, 319, 323-326
Infant 32, 75, 85-89, 93, 98, 203, 245
Infinite 15, 22, 64, 66-68, 83, 85-87, 113, 114, 118, 129-135, 142, 147, 174, 175, 182, 185, 194, 196, 197, 199, 204, 250, 267, 269, 300, 335, 348, 380, 389-392, 397, 399, 400, 411, 413, 415
Integration 196, 219, 221, 266, 276, 278, 292-295, 316, 336, 337, 340, 341, 342, 390
Intension 15, 16, 18, 37, 39, 41, 44, 49, 50, 62, 64, 66-70, 73, 75, 76, 78, 93, 106, 108, 109, 115, 126, 127, 128, 131-136, 138, 143, 144, 146, 212, 233, 266-268, 348, 395, 405
Intrinsic education 382, 383
Intrinsic valuation 17, 22-24, 26, 28, 29, 32, 34, 47, 48, 54, 72-74, 81, 84, 85, 87-89, 91-93, 96, 97, 100, 105-117, 119, 215, 250, 251, 264, 331, 332, 350, 351, 355, 391, 392, 398, 400, 409, 411, 412, 413, 416, 417, 421
Intrinsic value 14-18, 23-25, 28-31, 47, 48, 49, 53-55, 60, 64, 65, 67, 68, 83-85, 87-89, 91-93, 100, 105, 106-113, 115-120, 129, 135, 176, 177, 182, 184, 185, 187, 188, 194, 196, 197, 199, 201, 204, 205, 207, 211-217, 247, 250-252, 262, 264, 265, 266, 281, 330, 331, 334, 335, 336, 340, 343, 348, 349, 350, 387-391, 393, 396, 398, 400, 403, 412, 413, 415
Involvement 23, 28, 32, 37, 45, 47, 48, 50, 53, 54, 67, 73, 84, 85, 89, 93, 96, 108, 113, 114, 116, 222, 264, 334, 338, 339, 398
Jesus 29, 34, 179, 188, 205, 249, 331, 332, 409, 412-414, 417-422
Kant, I. 27, 42, 82, 83, 299, 390, 393
Kantian 88, 410
Kaufman, G. 417-421, 426
Kierkegaard, S. 28, 29, 33, 34, 82, 83, 90, 91, 112, 409, 411, 414
Know Thyself 300, 411
Kohlberg, L. 281, 285, 288, 291, 306, 310, 311
Krojanker, R. 291, 304, 307, 311
Labor 4, 179, 194-199, 212, 214, 249
Language 13, 30, 41, 42, 48, 60, 61, 66, 71, 75, 76, 79, 88, 115, 116, 136, 138, 160, 167, 173-175, 177, 226, 244, 245, 253, 257, 261, 262, 295, 302, 335, 336, 341, 348, 398, 405, 406, 408-410, 413-415, 417, 424

Law 2, 8, 10, 12, 13, 16, 17, 19, 20, 27, 38, 45, 53, 66, 76, 82, 89, 113, 134, 151, 153, 176, 202-204, 207, 214, 221, 232, 233, 281, 292, 373, 391, 413

Logic 3, 8, 10-13, 17, 18, 27, 38, 41-43, 59-62, 67, 68, 70, 73, 76, 89, 108, 113, 115, 125, 128, 136, 139, 141, 167-169, 173, 181, 199, 222, 231, 244, 262, 265, 281, 292, 299, 301, 335, 342, 350, 379, 382, 384, 391

Logical 11, 17-21, 25, 30, 37, 40, 44, 50, 51, 52, 60, 63, 68, 75, 76, 78, 85, 100, 101, 106, 107, 113, 118, 125, 134, 175, 179, 195, 213, 221, 227, 244, 246-249, 266-268, 283, 336, 352, 381, 385, 391, 392, 410

Logotherapy 279, 299

Loss 97-99, 101, 106, 119, 140, 167, 176, 197, 214

Love 5, 19, 22, 23, 25, 31, 52, 65, 66, 82, 85, 87, 88, 90, 91, 93, 94, 96, 98-100, 114, 116, 119, 140, 160, 179, 207, 208, 245, 248, 249, 251, 252, 259, 260, 264, 331, 340, 349, 351, 382, 395, 396, 397, 399, 403, 412, 414, 418, 421

Management 4, 33, 90, 195-197, 199, 211, 212, 215-220, 226, 228, 229, 230, 231, 233, 235, 237, 254, 286, 288, 340, 351

Marriage 8, 19, 34, 65, 66, 74, 76, 137, 151, 168, 270, 346, 389

Maslow, A. 140, 170, 280, 288, 291, 311, 403

Mathematical 10, 11, 26, 47, 50, 68, 87, 126, 128, 129, 134, 136, 144, 145, 146, 158, 165, 168, 171, 173, 175, 179, 182, 184, 197, 249, 251, 252, 259, 260, 268, 270, 279, 299, 348, 425

Mathematics 3, 10, 11, 13, 38, 42, 68, 86, 87, 89, 125, 128, 129, 136, 141, 158, 159, 161, 170, 173, 174, 197, 262, 267, 268, 292, 348, 382, 384, 405, 408, 425

Maximal 54, 84, 85

Maximally 54, 390

Meaning 5, 11, 15, 19, 37, 40, 41, 48, 50, 62, 63, 66, 68, 69, 71, 76, 77, 109, 116, 118, 126-129, 131, 133-135, 137, 138, 140, 143, 151, 152, 167, 168, 194, 204, 220, 244-247, 253, 266, 267, 268, 276, 278, 279, 307, 329, 330, 336, 348, 389, 392, 393, 406, 407, 411, 414, 418, 419, 424

Measure 12, 37, 38, 45, 62, 63, 69, 70, 73, 112, 114, 120, 126-128, 172, 173-175, 189, 199, 212, 217, 220, 223, 247, 255, 264, 265, 266-269, 271, 273, 282, 288, 303-307, 316-318, 326, 346, 347-353, 355-359, 364, 370, 377, 390, 395, 399

Measuring 69, 70, 72, 73, 88-91, 126, 212, 265, 267, 268, 271, 285, 305, 337, 346-348, 350-353, 355, 356, 361, 362, 376

Metaphor 30, 114-116, 118, 179, 249, 250, 300, 301, 336, 348, 416

Metaphorical 30, 86, 91, 336, 412

Mexico 3-5, 105, 198, 303, 304, 307, 311, 312, 316, 317, 319, 323, 324, 325, 326, 391

Mill, J. S. 82, 99, 100

Minimal 51, 54, 74, 83, 390, 392, 396

Minimally 54, 390

Mistake 27, 49, 51, 53, 83, 86, 132, 175, 177, 181, 188, 217, 231

Moore, G. E. 4, 9, 59-62, 65, 68, 79, 86, 92, 96, 106, 126, 234, 288, 299

Moral 10-13, 20, 24, 42, 59-61, 67, 69, 79, 82, 87, 89-92, 101, 119, 126, 134, 193, 194, 196, 198, 199, 201-205, 207, 212, 243, 254, 281, 283, 285, 286, 288, 292, 293-296, 298, 299, 301, 302, 303, 305, 306, 310, 311, 316, 340, 345, 347, 349, 350, 353, 354, 356, 357, 359, 360, 363, 366-370, 372-374, 376, 379, 380-385, 389, 390, 409, 410, 412, 413, 415, 419, 422

Morality 12, 89, 193-195, 199, 202, 296, 308, 311, 366, 369, 409

Mystic 95, 116, 178, 248, 250, 335, 415

Mystical 13, 85, 94-96, 335, 417

Name 2, 14, 19, 22, 41, 64-66, 69, 70, 106, 126-129, 131-136, 150, 168, 184, 205, 215, 220, 221, 225, 226, 233, 257, 264, 282, 291, 330, 336-339, 341, 380, 384, 392, 405, 409, 414, 416

Natural Science 10, 11, 18, 19, 40, 42, 47, 67, 68, 89, 125, 126, 243, 292, 294, 295, 301, 348, 382, 384, 385, 392

Nazi 1-3, 20, 53, 119, 179, 249, 391, 407, 408

Negative 49, 93, 94, 116-118, 148, 151, 161, 176, 178, 179, 181, 184, 187, 222, 224,
Nondenumerable 7, 253, 264, 278, 282, 306, 323, 338, 351, 353, 356
Non-denumerable 108, 116, 388, 389
Nondenumerably 67, 84, 87, 130-132, 134, 142, 175, 188, 300
Nonvalue 39
Norm 11-13, 16, 19, 20, 37, 68, 69, 73, 75, 91, 92, 105, 107, 109, 110, 112, 116, 180, 212, 219, 254, 255, 269, 307, 317, 337, 350, 358, 359, 360, 362, 363, 368, 369, 370, 371, 373, 389, 390
Normative 74, 75, 78, 110-112, 278, 310, 394, 395, 420
Obedience 24, 89, 204, 293, 372, 393, 394, 395
Object 9, 22, 29, 30, 32, 37-41, 44-47, 49-51, 54, 60, 63, 64, 66, 74, 83, 84-86, 88, 89, 91, 94, 95, 107, 108-112, 114-116, 126, 133, 169, 173, 177, 184, 197, 202, 230, 231, 233, 250, 297, 300, 303, 304, 316, 330, 331, 333, 335, 348-350, 388, 406, 409, 410, 414
Objective 48, 60, 72, 73, 92, 112, 126, 129, 171, 172, 212, 217-219, 222, 226, 264-269, 276, 339, 346-348, 350, 352, 362, 377
Objectivity 45, 47, 48, 112, 253, 388
Opaque 112, 113, 115, 117-120, 390, 396, 397, 399
Ordinal 87, 174, 175, 177-182, 185, 186, 187, 188, 190, 191
Ortega 26, 48, 114
Ought 16, 39, 42, 49, 91, 105, 107, 110, 111, 117, 118, 165, 187, 188, 189-191, 194, 205, 212, 223, 243, 250, 255, 265, 333, 337, 349, 354, 358, 362, 366, 368, 371, 374, 375, 387, 389, 391, 398, 416
Pain 38, 48, 82, 91, 96, 97, 99, 140, 165, 245
Paranoia 179, 249
Pedophilia 351, 378
Perfect 18, 20, 34, 39, 49, 53, 66, 75, 106, 135, 139, 208, 278, 309, 391
Perfection 39, 46, 67, 224, 249
Person 1, 3, 6, 8, 11, 15, 16, 18-20, 22, 23, 24-26, 28-32, 34, 38, 40, 46, 47, 48, 50-53, 62, 64-66, 69, 70, 73, 74-76, 79, 82-89, 91-94, 96, 97, 98, 100, 101, 106, 108-111, 113-118, 125, 132, 134, 135, 137, 139, 140, 150, 151, 152, 153, 158-162, 165, 167, 168-172, 176, 179, 180, 194, 196, 201, 203, 204, 207, 211, 220, 222, 223, 231, 245, 249, 250, 252, 254, 255, 259, 260, 261, 262, 264-266, 268, 269, 270, 278, 279, 281, 282, 286, 292, 300-302, 306, 329-332, 334, 336, 337, 339, 340, 346, 347, 350, 351-354, 356-360, 362, 363-376, 380-383, 387, 388-391, 393-400, 403, 406, 409, 411, 412, 414, 421
Personality 15, 24, 31, 85, 119, 140, 178, 248, 254, 270, 278, 281, 285, 287-289, 292, 294, 296, 298, 299, 305, 308, 311, 312, 314, 316, 317, 324, 326, 327, 330, 337, 374, 375, 379, 382, 383, 384, 385, 395
Phenomenological 112, 280
Phenomenology 28, 88, 114, 226, 228, 343
Physical 19, 38, 42, 44, 50, 54, 75, 83, 84, 89, 90, 96, 106, 112, 120, 125, 134, 135, 139, 140, 151, 152, 203, 244, 245, 301, 330, 331, 333, 334, 346, 383, 385, 393, 399
Planning 215, 216, 254, 364
Plato 9, 16, 92, 299
Pleasure 9, 74, 82, 90, 95-99, 245
Pluralistic 81, 82
Poetry 30, 38, 115, 281
Potential 16, 52, 85, 86, 89, 90, 94, 116, 140, 171, 212, 219, 220, 223, 245, 278-280, 299, 300, 329, 330-333, 335-342, 349, 353, 354, 357-362, 364-367, 369-371, 373, 374, 379, 380, 381, 383, 385, 387, 388, 391, 393, 399, 400, 413, 421
Potentially 77, 86, 133, 342, 348, 361, 364, 365, 372, 389
Practical 11, 16, 83, 87-90, 105, 129, 133, 168, 199, 213, 216, 218, 221, 223, 225, 231, 250, 254, 255, 276, 278, 295, 301, 318, 349, 350, 351, 353, 354, 356, 357, 359-363, 366, 367, 372, 373, 374-376, 383, 385
Pragmatic 64, 73, 250
Precision 30, 40, 167, 224, 247, 296, 304, 336, 353, 408, 410
Prejudice 46, 51, 400

Primordial 90, 92, 331, 332, 334-336
Principle 12, 13, 18, 24, 25, 37, 55, 82, 89, 92, 126, 134, 145, 158, 159, 165, 181, 200-204, 212, 213, 231, 253, 283, 302, 303, 349, 350, 353-355, 357-359, 361, 362, 363, 366-369, 371, 372, 374, 376, 379-382, 399, 404, 422
Production 154, 178, 194, 196-198, 202, 211-219, 248, 399
Profit 4, 188, 196, 198, 212-214, 234
Property 60-65, 68, 72, 76-78, 88, 90, 100, 101, 106, 110, 127, 132, 133, 134, 204, 234, 281, 299, 306, 354, 355, 357, 359, 360, 369
Pseudo-system 41-43
Pseudo-systemic 44
Psychoanalytic 299, 301
Psychological 51, 60, 61, 75, 85, 90, 106, 112, 140, 151, 152, 180, 244, 247, 266, 278, 279, 293, 294, 295-298, 300, 304, 305, 307, 309, 311, 313, 315, 316, 326, 327, 397
Psychology 11, 26, 41, 53, 68, 112, 172, 245, 281, 285, 288, 291, 292, 294-303, 308, 311, 312, 314, 315, 316, 327
Racism 46
Racist 91
Random Walk Theory 232, 233, 239
Rational 14, 27, 42, 99, 174, 177, 230, 232, 233, 236, 253, 264, 279, 283, 286, 294, 299, 380, 385, 403, 404-406, 408, 415, 417, 418
Rational-Emotive Therapy 299
Rationality 82, 203, 282, 405, 416
Receptacle 98
Regulation 89, 153, 214, 301, 369, 371, 393
Religion 11, 12, 135, 299, 403, 407, 409, 413, 417, 419, 422
Religious 12, 34, 66, 89, 90, 116, 165, 177, 188, 265, 293, 340, 383, 398, 406, 407, 418, 422
Repeatable 81, 82, 87, 88, 96, 99, 100
Replace 97, 98, 101
Replaceability 92, 93, 97, 98
Replacement 97, 98, 101, 174
Rich 38, 50, 54, 64, 86, 87, 95, 96, 112, 120, 176, 194, 196, 198, 253, 278, 303, 388, 394, 400

Richer 54, 67, 78, 83, 92, 95, 112, 195, 196, 203, 231, 250, 415
Richness 50, 51, 65, 66, 68, 69, 77, 83, 112, 116, 250, 265, 297, 299, 300, 335, 337, 340, 389, 392, 400
Risk 7, 306, 346-353, 355-377
Rokeach, M. 127, 170, 253, 256, 281, 285, 289, 291, 295, 306, 310, 314
Role 11, 13, 15, 26, 76, 90, 133, 134, 195, 215, 219, 221, 270, 278, 292, 323, 333, 338, 349, 351, 357, 387, 400, 407, 413, 420, 425
Roots 11, 126, 129, 163, 164, 188, 329
Roquet, S. 291, 307, 314
Rule 11-13, 20, 25, 30, 52, 89, 107, 143, 144, 145, 150, 151, 153, 155, 161, 163-167, 197, 200, 217, 222, 249, 254, 298, 301, 333, 353, 355, 358-364, 368, 369, 371, 391, 393, 398, 406, 411, 412, 416
S&P 229, 230, 235, 236, 239
Saint 200, 283, 411, 415
Salvation 34, 256, 293, 421
Schema 19, 21, 22, 25, 52, 387, 392
Schildt 191, 257, 289, 291, 307, 308, 314
Science 10-13, 16, 18, 19, 38, 40-44, 47, 51, 59, 67, 68, 70, 73, 79, 80, 86, 89, 100, 106, 114, 125, 126, 127, 128, 169, 170, 172, 173, 174, 178, 181, 187, 193, 195, 196, 197, 206, 207, 240, 243, 247-249, 253, 261-265, 267, 281-283, 285, 286, 287, 292, 294, 295, 298, 299, 300, 301, 303, 309-311, 314, 327, 330, 345, 346, 348, 350, 378, 379, 382-385, 392, 403, 405, 408-410, 416
Score 86, 180, 222, 249, 255, 265-271, 276, 278, 279, 301, 304, 305, 306, 323-325, 378
Scoring 70, 261, 264, 266, 271, 282, 288, 308, 312
Self 9, 15, 23, 25, 28, 31-34, 38, 84, 85, 87, 88-93, 95, 99, 100, 107, 109, 110-116, 118-120, 134, 139, 140, 160, 179, 196, 198, 220, 246, 247, 249, 254-256, 260, 261, 265, 266, 276, 278, 288, 293, 294, 297, 298, 299-302, 304-307, 311, 316, 318, 319, 323-325, 329, 330, 331-342, 351, 352, 354, 355, 356, 357, 359-361, 363, 364, 365, 366, 368, 369, 373, 374, 376, 382, 383, 388-390, 395-399, 403,

Index

405, 407, 408, 411, 412, 414, 415, 419, 421
Self development 255, 329, 334, 336, 337, 342
Self fulfillment 160, 340-342
Self knowledge 300, 329, 334
Sensitivity 28, 42, 45, 70, 105, 107, 117, 118, 243, 266, 268, 271, 305, 306, 316, 318, 324, 325, 347, 349, 350, 353, 354, 362, 373, 391, 396, 398
Set 4, 13, 17, 19, 21, 22, 37, 39-46, 49, 51, 63, 68-75, 77, 78, 86, 91, 92, 101, 106, 115, 125-136, 138, 141, 142, 144, 168-170, 174, 175, 198, 213, 217, 218, 220, 223-226, 230, 231, 240, 255, 266-268, 278, 299, 300, 305, 316, 331-333, 337, 341, 350, 366, 369, 374, 384, 392, 410, 421
Sex 82, 135, 270, 398
Sexism 46
Singular 65-67, 91, 101, 106, 108, 109, 115, 129, 132, 134-136, 150, 167, 232, 250, 330, 421
Singular concept 65-67, 106, 108, 109, 115, 129, 134-136, 150, 167, 250
Skinner, B. F. 294, 314
Society 10, 32, 33, 46, 75, 76, 89, 92, 150, 172, 176, 177, 199, 203, 212, 254, 256, 268, 281, 285, 288, 293, 302, 325, 333, 345, 346, 353, 354, 363, 370, 371, 379, 382, 383, 398, 420
Sovereignty 202-204
Space 18, 21, 26, 27, 29, 30, 39, 43, 60, 64, 71, 73, 75, 88, 105, 112, 113, 114, 118, 119, 172-174, 185, 208, 213, 218, 220, 262, 304, 410
Spontaneous 30, 94, 107
Standard 22, 37, 39, 44, 45, 62, 69, 83, 87, 88, 90, 91, 109, 116, 126, 128, 133, 206, 211, 212, 217, 225, 226, 229, 267, 268, 283, 307, 316, 317, 319, 347, 348, 350, 358, 392, 393
Stevenson, C. 60
Stock 229, 232-240
Subject 12, 25, 26, 29-31, 37, 44, 49, 50, 52, 64, 68, 70, 77, 88, 95, 96, 108, 111, 114, 117, 125, 126, 128, 160, 168, 171, 181, 191, 200, 201, 204, 207, 226, 228, 262, 268, 269, 271, 296, 306, 307, 308, 316, 317, 329, 334, 335, 338, 343, 348, 381, 382, 384, 388, 411
Subjective 29, 61, 92, 112, 128, 171, 266, 377
Subset 71, 127, 130, 133, 134, 138, 240, 267, 337, 384
Symbol 10, 47, 54, 85, 89, 131, 137, 141, 155, 157, 160, 165, 182, 183, 214, 335, 418-420, 425
Synthesis 81, 87, 88, 92, 94, 97-99, 292, 295
System 10, 11, 13, 19-21, 24-29, 32-34, 38, 40-44, 46, 47, 49-53, 66, 68, 69, 73, 82, 83, 86, 105, 106, 110, 113, 114, 125, 126, 128, 131, 136, 137, 140, 141, 158, 159, 162, 167, 168, 169, 174-176, 178-180, 188, 193-196, 198, 199-201, 204, 213, 214, 215-218, 220-226, 233, 234, 236, 243, 248, 251, 252, 255, 260, 261, 266, 268, 270, 278, 280, 288, 292, 297, 299, 314, 325, 340, 345, 349, 351, 380, 385, 387, 391, 392, 394, 395, 396, 398, 399, 417
Systemic education 382-384
Systemic valuation 20, 24, 25, 27, 33, 34, 37, 44-52, 72, 89, 187, 204, 251, 264, 306, 332, 351, 356, 391, 392-395
Systemic value 5, 18, 25, 37-41, 43-45, 47-50, 53-55, 64, 66, 67, 89, 106, 129, 135, 175-177, 182, 185, 187, 188, 195, 201, 204, 205, 211, 213-217, 247, 249, 250-252, 262, 263, 266, 281, 330, 332, 349
Technical 2, 27, 30, 41, 42, 63, 178, 211, 248, 251, 259, 260, 336, 372, 405
Test 5, 6, 85, 144, 180, 240, 243, 244, 246, 247, 248, 250, 252, 253, 257, 258-272, 276, 278-282, 287, 289, 296, 298, 300, 302, 304, 305, 307, 308, 314, 317-319, 352, 354
Theologic 409, 411, 412, 415, 417, 419, 420
Theory 1, 4-10, 37, 54, 55, 60, 67, 68, 79, 82, 86, 87, 97, 110, 111, 125, 126, 128-131, 141, 142, 169, 170, 171, 173-175, 181, 194, 195, 197, 200, 201, 211, 227, 230, 232, 233, 236, 239, 240, 244, 247, 249, 253, 257, 261, 262-264, 266-272, 278, 279, 280, 281, 285, 287, 289, 291, 292, 294, 297-299, 301, 306,

307, 310, 315, 329, 331, 332, 350, 381, 390, 397

Thought 5, 7-11, 18, 21, 22, 27, 29, 34, 37, 38, 40, 43, 53, 67, 68, 83, 85, 86, 88, 92, 97, 105-107, 118, 134, 136, 175, 179, 205, 234, 246, 248, 259, 260, 295, 301, 303, 316, 330, 332, 388, 397, 404, 412, 413, 415, 416, 418, 421

Time 2-4, 6, 7, 9, 10, 12, 18, 20, 21, 26, 27-30, 43, 46, 49, 50, 52, 60, 64, 69, 71, 73-75, 86, 88, 93, 95, 99, 105, 109, 112-115, 118, 119, 129, 133, 139, 158, 174, 188, 189, 194, 198, 201, 202, 204, 205, 207, 213, 218, 219, 225-227, 229, 231, 232-234, 236, 240, 258, 262, 264, 291-293, 296, 302, 304, 307, 315, 326, 331-335, 339, 346, 352, 360, 362, 364, 365, 376, 385, 388, 391, 393, 398, 399, 405, 407, 410, 412, 413, 417, 418, 421, 422

Topology 155, 156

Transfinite 67, 86, 87, 131, 134, 137, 141, 143, 144, 146, 147, 160, 163, 169, 170, 197, 199, 350, 425

Transparency 112, 113, 115, 117, 119, 120, 399

Transparent 107, 112-117, 119, 120, 389, 396, 399, 400

Transposing 160, 163

Transposition 17, 19, 20, 32-34, 46, 49, 50, 52, 137-140, 146, 148, 149, 151, 153, 155, 157, 159, 160, 161-163, 165, 168, 169, 178, 179, 185-188, 190, 191, 244, 246-248, 250, 252, 260, 261, 351, 391, 392

Transpositional 138-140, 145, 226

Type 61, 64, 66, 69, 70, 73, 77, 78, 86, 93, 94, 96, 125, 126, 128-134, 136, 138, 145, 155, 156, 166, 174, 175, 177, 182, 184, 189, 194, 201, 220-223, 255, 279, 289, 299, 337, 338-340, 346, 350, 358, 362, 363, 364, 369, 373, 382, 406, 409, 420

U. S. A. 307, 316, 318, 319, 323-326

Unicept 65, 106

Uniform 25, 47, 52, 179, 201, 248, 251, 252, 259, 260

Unique 16, 22, 24, 26, 30, 65, 67, 81, 83, 84, 85, 87-90, 94, 96, 97, 99, 100, 101, 106, 108, 116, 120, 128, 131, 172, 226, 254, 261, 262, 315, 323, 330, 331, 335, 336, 348, 349, 352, 355, 362, 370, 387, 394, 400, 413, 425

Uniqueness 16, 23, 31, 65, 66, 74, 83, 91, 100, 101, 106, 109, 224, 292, 300, 301, 336, 348-351, 391, 420

Universal 11, 17, 31, 32, 61, 81-88, 92, 93, 94-101, 106, 115, 117, 168, 263, 264, 331, 338, 341, 342, 348

Urmson, J. O. 61, 62, 64, 65

Utilitarian 81, 97, 98

Utilitarianism 98, 99

Validation 268-270, 296, 303-305, 307, 308, 313, 314, 327

Valuation (df) 17, 18, 44-45, 71-72, 84-85, 113-117

Value (df) 13, 14, 37, 62-67, 82-84, 106-107, 126-127, 233, 247, 299, 330, 348, 381, 410

Value index 136, 137, 144, 145, 147, 149, 153, 155, 156, 158-160, 167

Valuemetrics 125, 128, 131, 133, 143, 144, 149, 160, 162, 163, 167, 168, 170, 286, 309, 311, 313, 314, 325, 327

Vidx 138, 145-150, 152-154, 156, 157, 168, 169

Virtue 24, 32, 39, 75, 82, 87, 90, 97, 255, 411

Virtuoso 411, 412, 419

War 1-4, 7, 20, 50, 52, 132, 163, 179, 193, 199, 201, 202, 204, 205, 249, 293, 312, 345, 407, 408

Whitehead, A. N. 44, 47, 81, 96, 405, 406, 414, 417

Work 4-6, 28, 29, 33, 42, 59, 76, 85, 90, 112, 113, 140, 181, 187, 192, 194-198, 200, 213, 215, 216, 217-222, 236, 243, 244, 253, 260, 261, 282, 286, 294, 296-299, 304, 307, 308, 309, 316, 323, 326, 329, 333, 335, 338, 340, 351, 372, 381, 382, 405, 417-421

Worse 18, 22, 24, 26, 118, 169, 193, 197, 205, 230, 231, 233, 250, 264, 265, 269, 271, 349, 395

www.ingramcontent.com/pod-product-compliance
Lightning Source LLC
Chambersburg PA
CBHW052048290426
44111CB00011B/1659